CW01665503

MOHAMMAD GHARIPOUR is an assistant professor at the School of Architecture and Planning at Morgan State University. He obtained his Master's in architecture from the University of Tehran and PhD in architecture and landscape history at Georgia Institute of Technology. As the recipient of the Hamad Bin Khalifa Fellowship in Islamic Art and the Spiro Kostof Fellowship Award from the Society of Architectural Historians, Gharipour has published extensively on architectural history. He is the editor of *Bazaar in the Islamic City* (2012) and the founding editor of the *International Journal of Islamic Architecture*.

'In this book, Mohammad Gharipour does an excellent job of examining the historical, religious, literary and artistic importance of Persian gardens and pavilions. But unlike other explorations of the garden, he focuses on the relationship between architecture and gardens rather than just offering analysis of the gardens themselves. The product of years of dedicated research, it successfully studies and compares three types of documents to uncover the symbolic, metaphorical and historic importance of gardens in the Persian tradition, from the early Zoroastrians to the sixteenth century.'

PROFESSOR ATTILIO PETRUCCIOLI,
Professor of Landscape Architecture, Polytechnic University of Bari

'Mohammad Gharipour develops a line of scholarship in art and architectural history that has largely been ignored by contemporary scholars. Although the Persian garden underlies the basic garden form in the Western world from the third to the seventeenth century CE, the role of the pavilion in these gardens forms a conspicuous absence in the literature. Through detailed examinations of both visual and textual media, this book represents a major contribution to our knowledge in the field of garden art and architecture, linking the development of the *chaharbagh* to its later descendents throughout the Islamic World and beyond.'

DOUGLAS C. ALLEN, ASLA,
Professor of Architecture Emeritus, Georgia Institute of Technology

PERSIAN GARDENS AND PAVILIONS

Reflections in History, Poetry and the Arts

MOHAMMAD GHARIPOUR

SOUDAVAR
MEMORIAL FOUNDATION

I.B.TAURIS
LONDON • NEW YORK • OXFORD • NEW DELHI • SYDNEY

I.B. TAURIS
Bloomsbury Publishing Plc
50 Bedford Square, London, WC1B 3DP, UK
1385 Broadway, New York, NY 10018, USA

BLOOMSBURY, I.B. TAURIS and the I.B. Tauris
logo are trademarks of Bloomsbury Publishing Plc

First published in Great Britain 2013
Distributed in the United States and Canada exclusively
by Palgrave Macmillan, 175 Fifth Avenue, New York NY 10010.

Paperback edition published 2020

This book was published with funding from Roshan
Cultural Heritage Institute and the Barakat Trust.

For legal purposes the Acknowledgements on p.xix constitute
an extension of this copyright page.

Cover design by www.vaguelymemorable.com
Cover image: The duel of physicians in the royal garden, from Khamsa
by Nezami, 1539–43. © The British Library Board, London (Or. 2265, fol. 26v)

A catalogue record for this book is available from the British Library.

A catalog record for this book is available from the Library of Congress.

ISBN: HB: 978-1-7807-6121-3
PB: 978-0-7556-0036-6
ePDF: 978-0-7556-9357-3
eBook: 978-0-8577-3320-7

Typeset by Tetragon, London
Printed and bound in Great Britain

To my parents,
for all their love and support

This book was published with funding from Roshan Cultural Heritage Institute.

This book was published with funding from the Barakat Trust.

ROSHAN CULTURAL HERITAGE INSTITUTE

بركات
BARAKAT

Contents

List of Illustrations xi

Acknowledgements xix

1 *Introduction* 1

2 *The Garden and Pavilion in Near Eastern Pre-Islamic Texts, the Qur'an and Persian Poetry* 11

3 *The Garden and Pavilion in Persian Art* 39

4 *The Garden and Pavilion through the Lens of Travellers and Historians* 103

5 *Conclusion* 147

Matrix 153

Glossary of Terms 159

Poets, Historians and Travellers 165

Notes 179

Bibliography 207

Index 217

List of Illustrations

Figure references that appear in the text are followed by the page number in brackets.

1 A night banquet in a garden. From *Moraqqa' Golshan,* sixteenth century © Golestan Palace Museum, Tehran (no.1663, fol. 46).

2 The feast of Sadeh. From the *Shahnameh* (Book of Kings) of Shah Tahmasp. Soltan Muhammad, Tabriz, 1525 © The Metropolitan Museum of Art, New York, Gift of Arthur A. Houghton Jr (1970.301.2).

3 Tile panel depicting a garden banquet. Isfahan, first quarter of seventeenth century © The Metropolitan Museum of Art, New York, Rogers Fund (1903.03.9c).

4 *(45)* The Gardens of Fidelity (Bagh-e Vafa). From *Vaqi'at-e Baburi,* India, 1590 © The British Library Board, London (Or. 3714, fol. 173v).

5 The Soltan of Syria Malek Saleh, on a throne in his garden, interviewing two dervishes. From *Bustan* (The Orchard) by Sa'di, Bukhara, 1522–23 © The Metropolitan Museum of Art, New York, Frederick C. Hewitt Fund, 1911 (11.134.2).

6 The courtiers of Nushirvan and the enigma of the game of chess. From the *Shahnameh,* Shiraz, 1535 © Berenson Collection, Florence, reproduced by permission of the President and Fellows of Harvard College (fol. 554b).

7 The sick king is treated by the royal doctor and his courtiers. From *Sobhat al-Abrar,* by 'Abdol-Rahman Jami, sixteenth century © Golestan Palace Museum, Tehran (no.2176).

8 Crowded court scene. Eskandar disguised as a legate, with his portrait, before Queen Qaydafa in a palace in a garden. From the *Shahnameh,* Shiraz, 1560 © The British Library Board, London (I.O. ISLAMIC 133, fol. 349v).

9 Yusof and Zulaykha having a feast. From *Panj Ganj* by 'Abdol-Rahman Jami, attributed to Qasem 'Ali, 1521 © Golestan Palace Museum, Tehran.

10 *(49)* The assassination of Khosrow. From the *Khamseh* (Five Poems) by Nezami, 1431 © The State Hermitage Museum, St Petersburg (no. LVR-1000, L.142A).

11 The return of Timur to Samarqand. From the *Zafarnameh,* attributed to Kamal-uddin Behzad, Herat, 1528 © Golestan Palace Museum, Tehran (no.708).

12 An excursion in the garden. From *Panj Ganj* by Jami, attributed to Maqsud, 1521 © Golestan Palace Museum, Tehran.

13 *(51)* Khajeh 'Abdollah Ansari teaching disciples. From *Hayat al-Abrar* by Mir 'Ali Shir Nava'i © Bodleian Library, Oxford (MS. Elliott 287 fol. 24a).

14 The story of a young handsome physician in the city of Marv. From *Bustan* by Sa'di, Herat, 1562–63 © Golestan Palace Museum, Tehran.

15 Khosrow and Shirin listening to stories told by Shirin's maidens. From the *Khamseh* by Nezami, Tabriz, 1539–43 © The British Library Board, London (Or. 2265, fol. 66v).

16 A convivial gathering at the court of Soltan Hoseyn Bayqara in Herat. From *Bustan* by Sa'di, Herat, 1488 © National Library, Cairo (908, fol. Iv-2r).

17 A father advises his son about love. From the *Haft Awrang* (Seven Thrones) by Jami, Mashhad, 1556–65 © The Freer Gallery of Art, Washington DC (FGA 46.12, fol. 52a).

18 The beginning of the feast of 'Id. From the *Divan* by Hafez, attributed to Soltan Muhammad, 1527 © The Freer Gallery of Art, Washington DC (86 recto, no.66).

19 The enthronement of Khosrow. From the *Khamseh* by Nezami, signed by Shah Tahmasp's artists, 1539–43 © The British Library Board, London (Or. 2265, fol. 60v).

20 Courtiers in the garden. From *Farhad va Shirin* by Amir 'Ali Shir Nava'i © Bodleian Library, Oxford (MS. Elliott 317, fol. 21b).

21 *(55)* The shah's wise men approve of Zal's marriage. From the *Shahnameh* of Shah Tahmasp, attributed to 'Abd al-'Aziz, Tabriz, 1525–30 © The Metropolitan Museum of Art, New York, Gift of Arthur A. Houghton Jr (1970.301.13, fol. 86 verso).

22 An ecstatic dance of the dervishes. From the *Divan* by Hafez, 1540–50 © Harvard Art Museums/Arthur M. Sackler Museum, Gift of John Goelet (1958.23, fol. 149).

23 *(56)* Interior reception. From *Bustan* by Sa'di, attributed to Sheykh Zadeh, Bukhara, 1525–35 © The Metropolitan Museum of Art, New York, Louis V. Bell Fund and the Vincent Astor Foundation Gift (1974.294.3).

24 Leyla and Majnun at school. From the *Khamseh* by Nezami, Shiraz, 1560 © Harvard Art Museums/Arthur M. Sackler Museum, Gift of Dr Denman W. Ross (1922.75).

25 The story of the fickle old lover who is knocked off the rooftop of the garden pavilion. From the *Haft Awrang* by Jami, Mashhad, 1556–65 © Freer Gallery of Art, Washington DC (FGA 46.12, fol. 162a).

26 Homay at the castle gate. From *Three Poems* by Khaju Kermani, fourteenth century © The British Library Board, London (Add. 18113, f.18v).

27 Khosrow in front of Shirin's castle. From the *Khamseh* by Nezami, 1431 © The State Hermitage Museum, St Petersburg, (no. LVR-1000, L.112A).

28 Zal and Rudabeh pronounce their marriage vows. From the *Shahnameh*, attributed to ʿAbdol-Rashid Deylami, Isfahan, seventeenth century © Golestan Palace Museum, Tehran.

29 Ardashir meeting Ganjvar Ardavan and Golnaz, the maid. From the *Shahnameh* of Baysonghor, 1429 © Golestan Palace Museum, Tehran.

30 *(60)* Mehrdokht shoots her bow at the ring. From *Hamzenameh*, India, 1564–69 © Collection of Mrs Maria Sarre-Hermann, Ascona (Switzerland).

31 The crazed old Sheykh of Sanʿan. From the *Divan* by Mir ʿAli Shir Nava'i in Chaghatay Turkish © Bibliothèque Nationale, Paris.

32 Shapur brings Farhad before Shirin. From *Khosrow va Shirin by* Nezami, Tabriz, 1406–10 © The Freer Gallery of Art, Washington DC (31.34).

33 Maidens bathing. From the *Khamseh* by Nezami, Herat, 1494–95 © The British Library Board, London (Or. 6810, fol. 190).

34 The so-called Bahram Gur and the Indian Princess, identified here as Turktazi and the Queen of the Faeries, Turktaz. From the *Khamseh* of Shah Tahmasp, attributed to Muhammad Zaman, 1675–76 © British Library Board, London (Ms. Or. 2265, fol. 221b).

35 The Princess of the Blue Pavilion. From the *Khamseh* (Quintet) of Amir Khosrow Dehlavi, India, 1597–98 © The Metropolitan Museum of Art, New York, Gift of Alexander Smith Cochran (1913.228.33).

36 *(64)* Shirin's pavilion. From *Khosrow va Shirin* by Nezami © Keir Collection, London.

37 *(65)* Persian garden carpet. Kurdistan, second half of the eighteenth century © The Metropolitan Museum of Art, New York, The James F. Ballard Collection, Gift of James F. Ballard (1922.100.128).

38 The nightmare of Zahhak. From the *Shahnameh* of Shah Tahmasp, Tabriz, 1525–35 © Museum of Islamic Art, Doha (MS.41–2007).

39 Earthly drunkenness. From the *Divan* by Hafez, attributed to Soltan Muhammad, Tabriz, 1526–27 © Partially owned by Metropolitan Museum of Art, New York and the Arthur Sackler Museum, Harvard University (1988.460.3, fol. 135).

40 *(67)* Majnun coming to the house of Leyla. From the *Divan* by Mir ʿAli Shir Nava'i in

Chaghatay Turkish, attributed to Qasem 'Ali, 1485 © Bodleian Library, Oxford (MS. Elliott 339, fol. 39a).

41 *(68)* Nushirvan with a lady on *iwan*. From *Hayrat al-Abrar* by 'Ali Shir Nava'i, attributed to Qasem 'Ali, 1485 © Bodleian Library, Oxford (MS Elliott.287, fol. 28a).

42 The conversation between the king and the dervish. From *Bustan* by Sa'di, 1553 © Golestan Palace Museum, Tehran.

43 Alexander the Great admires his portrait, ordered by Queen Nushabeh. From the *Khamseh* by Nezami, 1528–29 © Walters Museum of Art, Baltimore (W.607.223B).

44 The games of backgammon and chess. From the *Anthology* of Baysonghor, Herat, 1427 © Berenson Collection, Florence, reproduced by permission of the President and Fellows of Harvard College (fol. 50v).

45 Siyavash captive before Afrasyab. From the *Shahnameh,* Isfahan, 1696 © The Metropolitan Museum of Art, New York, Gift of Alexander Smith Cochran (1913.228.17, fol. 110v).

46 Hand-knotted woollen carpet. Iran, late seventeenth century © Victoria and Albert Museum, London (T.10–1924).

47 Elders pleading with Hormozd. From the *Khamseh* by Nezami, Herat, 1494–95 © British Library, London (Or. 6810, fol. 37v).

48 The 'Aziz and Zulaykha enter the capital of Egypt and the Egyptians come out to greet them. From the *Haft Awrang* by Jami, Mashhad, 1556–65 © Freer Gallery of Art, Washington DC (FGA 46.12, fol. 100b).

49 *(72)* Brass incense burner. Eighth–ninth centuries © The Freer Gallery of Art, Washington DC (F1952.1).

50 Ferdowsi's parable of the ship of Shi'ism. From the *Shahnameh* of Shah Tahmasp, attributed to Mirza 'Ali, Tabriz, 1530–39 © The Metropolitan Museum of Art, New York, Gift of Arthur A. Houghton Jr (1970.301.1, fol. 18 verso).

51 The abduction of the king's favourite maiden. From *Hasht Behesht* by Amir Khosrow Dehlavi, attributed to Mirza 'Ali © The Freer Gallery of Art, Washington DC (F1937.27).

52 Key Khosrow crossing Lake Zarah in pursuit of Afrasyab. From the *Shahnameh,* Herat, 1618–19 © Walters Art Museum, Baltimore (W.602.319a).

53 *(73)* Domed pavilion. From the *Automata* by al-Jazari, Syria © The Freer Gallery of Art, Washington DC (F1930.73).

54 *(75)* Leyla and Majnun at school. From the *Khamseh* by Nezami, Herat, 1494–95 © The British Library Board, The British Library, London (Or. 6810, fol. 106v).

55 *(76)* Celebrations marking the arrival of Timur in Samarqand in 1396. From the *Zafarnameh,* attributed to Kamal-uddin Behzad, Herat, 1529 © Golestan Palace Museum, Tehran.

56 Jamshid and Khorshid on a throne. From *Masnavi-ye Jamshid va Khorshid,* sixteenth century © Golestan Palace Museum, Tehran.

57 Key Khosrow feasts Rustam. From the *Shahnameh,* 1618–19 © Walters Art Gallery, Baltimore (W.602.241A).

58 The conversation between Rustam and Isfandyar. From the *Shahnameh* of Baysonghor © Golestan Palace Museum, Tehran.

59 Khosrow celebrating Nowruz. From the *Shahnameh,* Shiraz, 1560 © The British Library Board, London (I.O. ISLAMIC 133, fol. 519).

60 Shida in the camp of Key Khosrow. From the *Shahnameh,* Shiraz, 1535 © Berenson Collection, Florence, reproduced by permission of the President and Fellows of Harvard College (fol. 296b).

61 Babur receiving Persian, Uzbek and Rajput envoys in a garden at Agra. From the *Baburnameh,* 1589 © The Victoria and Albert Museum, London (I.M. 275–1913).

62 *(79)* Khosrow and Shirin in the palace. From the *Khamseh* by Nezami Ganjavi, 1528–29 © Walters Museum of Art, Baltimore (W.607.93A).

63 *(80)* Zal consults the Magi. From the *Shahnameh* of Shah Tahmasp, attributed to Soltan Muhammad, Tabriz, 1525 © The Metropolitan Museum of Art, New York, Gift of Arthur A. Houghton Jr (1970.301.8, fol. 73 verso).

64 *(81)* Solomon on his throne. From the *Shahnameh,* signed by Mahmud Mozahheb, Shiraz, 1535 © Berenson Collection, Florence, reproduced by permission of the President and Fellows of Harvard College (fol. 1b).

65 *(82)* The princes of the house of Timur. Made by Mir Sayyed 'Ali, India, 1550–55 © The Trustees of the British Museum, London (AN978581001).

66 *(83)* An assembly of sages with the poet Jami. From the Gulbenkian *Baharestan* of Jami, Herat, 1525–30 © Berenson Collection, Florence, reproduced by permission of the President and Fellows of Harvard College.

67 Kuyuk receiving gold, silver, jewels and other gifts from his nobles. From the *Tarikh-e Jahan-Goshay* by 'Ata Malek ibn Muhammad Joveyni, Shiraz, 1438 © The Trustees of the British Museum, London (AN90399001).

68 Zal and Rudabeh celebrating their wedding night. From the *Shahnameh,* Herat or Isfahan, 1602 © Nasser Khalili collection, London (MSS 544, fol. 36r).

69 Siyavash receives a gift from a peace envoy. From the *Shahnameh* of Tahmasp, attributed to Qadimi, sixteenth century © Museum of Contemporary Art, Tehran (171–v).

70 The townsman robs the villager's orchard. From the *Haft Awrang* by Jami, Mashhad, 1556–65 © Freer Gallery of Art, Washington DC (FGA 46.12, fol. 179b).

71 The duel of physicians in the royal garden. From the *Khamseh* by Nezami, 1539–43 © The British Library Board, London (Or. 2265, fol. 26v).

72 Shirin sees Khosrow's portrait. From the *Khamseh* by Nezami, 1539–43 © The British Library Board, London (Or. 2265, fol. 48v).

73 *(87)* School scene. From the *Divan* by Amir Khosrow Dehlavi, 1609 © Walters Art Museum, Baltimore (W.623.259B).

74 *(88)* Prince in a garden courtyard. Tabriz, 1525–30 © The Metropolitan Museum of Art, New York, Rogers Fund (1911.39.1).

75 *(89)* Zal and Rudabeh embracing. From the *Shahnameh,* 1486 © The British Library Board, London (add.18188).

76 Alexander is recognized by Queen Nushabeh. From the *Khamseh* by Nezami, Shiraz, 1549 © Freer Gallery of Art, Washington DC (F1908.280).

77 Solomon and Bilqis sitting together and conversing about Solomon's findings. From the *Haft Awrang* by Jami, Mashhad, 1556–65 © Freer Gallery of Art, Smithsonian Institute, Washington DC (FGA 46.12, fol. 187b).

78 Borzuyeh takes the *Kalileh va Damneh* to Anushirvan. From the *Kalileh va Damneh,* 1429 © Golestan Palace Museum, Tehran (no.2198).

79 Prince Akbar presenting portraits to his father, the emperor Homayun. *Moraqqa' Golshan,* attributed to 'Abdol-Samad Shirin Qalam, Isfahan, seventeenth century © Golestan Palace Museum, Tehran (no.1663).

80 *(92)* The garden of the fairies. Early sixteenth century © The Freer Gallery of Art, Smithsonian Institute, Washington DC (ms.50.2).

81 *(94)* Soltan Hoseyn Mirza in promenade. From *Moraqqa' Golshan,* attributed to Kamal-uddin Behzad, late fifteenth century © Golestan Museum, Tehran (no.1663, fol. 55).

82 Yusof gives a royal banquet in honour of his marriage. From the *Haft Awrang* by Jami, Mashhad, 1556–65 © Freer Gallery of Art, Smithsonian Institute, Washington DC (F1946.12.132a).

83 The court of Ulugh Beg, 1440 © Freer Gallery of Art, Smithsonian Institute, Washington DC (46.26).

84 A lovers' picnic. From the *Divan* by Hafez, attributed to Soltan Muhammad, Tabriz, 1526–27 © Harvard Art Museums/Arthur M. Sackler Museum, Gift of Stuart Cary Welch in honour of Edith Iselin Gilbert Welch (2007.183).

85 A princely banquet in a garden. From the *Shahnameh,* Shiraz, 1444 © Cleveland Museum of Art, Cleveland (45.169 and 56.10).

86 The court of Akbar Shah. From the *History of Akbar Shah,* 1822 © Golestan Palace Museum, Tehran (no.2253).

87 The return of Shapur to Khosrow. From *Khosrow va Shirin* by Nezami, 1539–43 © The British Library Board, The British Library, London (Or. 2265 fol. 576v).

88 Majnun brought in chains by the old woman to Leyla's tent. From the *Khamseh* by Nezami, Tabriz, 1539–43 © The British Library Board, London (Or. 2265, fol. 157v).

89 Prince Ananda, a grandson of Kublai Khan, and his children having a feast. From the *Jami' al-Tavarikh,* 1596 © Golsetan Museum, Tehran.

90 *(97)* Khosrow and Shirin in front of their tents. From *Khosrow va Shirin* by Nezami, Iran, 1431 © Hermitage Museum, St Petersburg (no. LVR-1000, L.126B).

91 The European ambassador brings Ottoman Soltan Morad's son to Timur. From the *Zafarnameh,* attributed to Kamal-uddin Behzad, 1528 © Golestan Palace Museum, Tehran (no.708).

92 *(98)* The king and his young son. From *Guy va Chowgan* by Arefi, Herat, 1523 © Harvard Art Museums/Arthur M. Sackler Museum, Gift of John Goelet, formerly in the collection of Louis J. Cartier (1958.79.11).

93 A nomadic encampment. From *Leyla and Majnun* by Jami, attributed to Mir Sayyed, Tabriz, 1540 © Harvard Art Museums/Arthur M. Sackler Museum, Gift of John Goelet, formerly in the collection of Louis J. Cartier (1958.75).

94 *(99)* Kaveh tears Zahhak's scroll. From the *Shahnameh* of Shah Tahmasp, attributed to Qadimi, sixteenth century © Museum of Contemporary Art, Tehran.

95 Babur supervising the laying out of the Garden of Fidelity (Bagh-e Vafa). From the *Baburnameh,* 1590 © Victoria and Albert Museum, London (IM.276–1913).

96 *(126)* Chaharbagh Street in Isfahan © Nader Ardalan and Laleh Bakhtiar.

97 *(127)* Hasht Behesht and the Bagh-e Bulbul, 1867 © Pascal Coste.

98 A full-colour reconstruction of the garden described in Haravi's *Irshad al-Zira'ah,* including all its prescribed plant species, their colourations and architectural elements in the summer season © Manu Sobti and Mohammad Gharipour.

99 The hues seen by the observer walking through the garden environment. A full-colour reconstruction based on Haravi's *Irshad al-Zira'ah* © Manu Sobti and Mohammad Gharipour.

100 *(130)* The interior of Hasht Behesht in Isfahan, 1867 © Pascal Coste.

Acknowledgements

This book builds on my PhD studies at the Georgia Institute of Technology. It is a product of my eight years of research on Persian gardens and a lifetime of learning. I am greatly indebted to colleagues and friends who gave me their unstinting support in this process. My sincere thanks go to Professor Douglas C. Allen, whose clear-sighted values and enthusiasm made him much more than an academic advisor. His interest in Persian gardens was the great motivating force in my research on garden history. He was always encouraging, gave me a comfortable confidence in myself, and helped me look at this topic from a broader perspective. My easy access to his thoughtful and critical discussions throughout my PhD programme is something I miss very much.

I must also mention my mentor, Dr Ronald Lewcock, whose vast knowledge of Western and non-Western architecture was a rich resource in the early stages of my research. His devotion and his unique precision made a significant contribution to this work. I was also privileged to work with Dr Roxani Margariti. With her high standards and energetic encouragement, she was a source of great inspiration and exceptionally constructive criticism. Her detailed and brilliant comments on the various versions were extremely influential in developing my ideas for this book. It was also a real honour for me to have three notable reviewers of my manuscript: Dr Attilio Petruccioli, Dr Mahyar Arefi and Dr Amy Landau. I also owe special thanks to my dear friend, Dr James Henry Holland, who has been a unique source of motivation and guidance not only in my research projects, but also in my whole academic career.

My sincere thanks go to the outstanding scholars who have been supportive of my research: Dr Bruce Lincoln, who kindly reviewed my writings and provided detailed comments on the section on pre-Islamic gardens; Dr Paul Losensky, whose publications were a great source of inspiration; Dr Ehsan Yarshater, who encouraged me in my studies on Persian architecture; Dr Sheila Canby, whose insights on garden pavilions helped to shape the chapter on pavilions in Persianate art; Dr Faramarz Khojasteh, whose vast knowledge of Persian literature assisted me in unfolding complex layers of poetry and interpreting ancient Persian texts; Dr Sussan Babaie for her help in developing my bibliography; Dr Ladan Akbarnia for advising me on paintings in British collections, and Dr Dede Fairchild Ruggles for generously sharing her images.

I would like to express my special gratitude to Dr Mina Houtan and the Houtan Foundation for their faith in my abilities and for providing generous financial support for this research during my studies. I also wish to acknowledge Dr Sheila Blair, Professor Ken Lambla, Dr Ahmad Karimi-Hakkak, and Dr Mary Anne Akers for their continued support. I would also like to thank Rasna Dhillon, Maria Marsh and Cecile Rault at I.B.Tauris for patiently working with me on the production of this volume, as well as Jodie Robson for her amazing job in copy-editing.

Finally, I must gratefully acknowledge Dr John Beardsley at Dumbarton Oaks for his mentorship and for providing the opportunity to research their documents. The research for this book only became possible with the generous support of Dr Elahe Mir-Djalali Omidyar at Roshan Cultural Heritage Institute and the Iran Heritage Foundation. I also thank the Barakat Trust, especially for providing funding for the publication of colour images. I sincerely thank these organizations for providing financial support for the preparation and the production of this book.

1

Introduction

WHEN hunters first settled the Iranian plateau about six thousand years ago, agriculture became the main stimulus to civilization in the region. In this relatively arid climate, trees, plants and water meant life and activity. With the rise of political and economic stability, gardens not only provided food, but represented spiritual beliefs, the perfection of the universe, abundance, leisure, power and protection. The earliest known gardens in the area, for which there is no remaining archaeological and physical evidence, were constructed in Mesopotamia.[1] The tradition of constructing pleasure gardens and hunting parks was continued by the Achaemenids (550–330 BCE), the first Persian Empire, and continued in the Parthian and Sassanid eras. Later, the invasion of large parts of the Sassanid and Byzantine empires by recently converted Muslim Arabs after the seventh century CE resulted in the diffusion of the concept of the Persian garden in the Middle East. While the tradition of hunting parks declined after the advent of Islam, the design of pleasure gardens, which represented the Qur'anic paradise, was pursued by both the political authorities and the wealthy. During this period, the underground irrigation system of *qanat* allowed the construction of gardens in remote areas despite climatic difficulties.

Persian gardens and courtyards appeared in the form of isolated entities designed for pleasure and recreation. The most famous type of these gardens was the *chaharbagh* (fourfold garden), which probably originated with Cyrus the Great's royal garden at Pasargadae, and gradually spread to distant parts of the world from subcontinental India to North Africa. The Persian garden, despite its diversity in terms of form, plan, function and design elements, was usually based on a square or rectangular plan, designed as an independent retreat (or a micro paradise) with a pleasant environment including shady areas, fountains and water channels, a pavilion, and a wall that separated it from the outside world. The form and function adopted was based on the climate and the needs of the owner, many providing fruit and vegetables for domestic use or for sale. Such lesser-known advantages, however, have been obscured by their primary function as places for recreation, leisure and joy. Historical documents make numerous references to gardens as the backdrop for various political and cultural events, confirming the centrality of gardens in society. The simultaneous use of gardens as places for relaxation, political meetings, parties, ceremonies, encampments and pilgrimage made them dynamic parts of urban design.

A significant methodological decision in this book concerns the definition of a pavilion as any structure located in a garden that is designed for a restorative purpose, regardless of its function and form. 'Garden pavilion' can be used as an umbrella term for more than fifteen words in Persian literature and historical documents[2] which have been used to refer to structures such as kiosks, palaces, houses and places for relaxation in natural settings. The use of this complex vocabulary illustrates the diversity of form, function and cultural significance of pavilions in the Persianate world. Based on the definition used here, examples of pavilions include Timur's tent in Samarqand, Shah 'Abbas's palace in Isfahan, and even Homayun's tomb in Delhi. However, in this book, the term 'pavilion' will not be limited to the common understanding of pavilions as temporary structures or kiosks.

Pavilion structures in Persianate gardens are intersections of three restorative environments: built, natural and social. Historical accounts reveal that most pavilions were used for social gatherings, parties and official meetings. The inhabitants of the structure not only pleased themselves by being part of nature, but also used them as settings for the pleasure of interacting with other people. A pavilion's function and design depends on the relationship between built and natural environments, so that modifications to the layout of the garden would mean that the design and the position of the pavilions would also change.[3] Pavilions not only occupy a significant place in the history of garden design, but also reflect their contemporary architectural traditions. The size of pavilions as semi-closed spaces is based on the overall proportion of solid and space in gardens, which varies in different historic and geographical contexts. Temporary and movable pavilions were transformed over time into fixed and permanent structures in which residents could live. At other times, fixed structures were replaced by temporary ones. Their primary use either as private properties or public places would justify the architectural concepts applied in their design. For example, varying the degrees of transparency and privacy would strengthen or weaken the physical and visual connections inside pavilions, within gardens, and between the two. In order to exalt the owner, possibly a king or caliph, a high terrace or a throne was designed to provide a sense of being above or outside the representative spatial and temporal order. The form depended upon use, and the prevailing cultural view of natural elements. In that sense, the design of pavilions and their placement in gardens is the material translation of cultural, symbolic and social values.

EARLY RESEARCH

The study of Persian gardens and pavilions was part of a broader series of studies initiated by art historians Arthur Pope and Phyllis Ackerman, archaeologist Ernst Herzfeld, and other Western Iranologists and archaeologists who excavated ancient sites in Iran in the early decades of the twentieth century. Pope and Ackerman's chapter on gardens in their book on Persian art and architecture, *A Survey of Persian Art,* was one of the first published works on the topic.[4] Although it was not a comprehensive research study on gardens, it did play a significant role in shaping subsequent studies. In 1962, architectural historian Donald Wilber published the first academic monograph exclusively devoted to Persian gardens.[5] Ironically, his book, *Persian Gardens and Pavilions,* did not discuss pavilions in Persian gardens but instead focused mainly on gardens and the different regions in which they could be found. Additionally, he failed to discuss the origins of Persian gardens or their development in history. However, considering the date of publication, it was an outstanding introduction to Persian gardens and their development after the Timurid Period during the fifteenth century. Later, Islamic art historian Richard Ettinghausen attempted to analyse the typology of Persian gardens, an issue he considered a significant piece of a larger puzzle, which he called Islamic gardens.[6] Ettinghausen's book, *The Islamic Garden,* proposed the concept of Islamic gardens as an analytical category of which Persianate gardens were both a precedent and a subset.

The excavations of the archaeologist David Stronach, first reported in 1978, revealed new facts about the origins of gardens and pavilions in the Persianate world and proved Pope's proposition regarding the Achaemenid origins of Persianate gardens. Based on this report, Stronach subsequently published a paper in which he revealed the layout of a fourfold garden in the Achaemenid palace of Pasargadae in present-day Iran. He also illustrated the strong architectural connection between the buildings and the open space in the palace.[7] In order to explain the function of the garden as the main context for pleasure and recreation, Stronach referred to the Greek writer, Lysander, who described a different Achaemenid garden, most likely an imitation of the Pasargadae garden in design.[8]

Another relevant study by Elizabeth Moynihan, *Paradise as a Garden in Persia and Mughal India*, addressed the development of 'Paradise gardens' in various countries throughout history.[9] The value of this work lies in Moynihan's systematic way of using pre-Islamic literature to clarify the evolution of the garden as a paradise in connection to its material value. Moynihan's main contribution was to apply 'paradise garden' as an umbrella term to narrate a coherent history of gardens in Iran, Mughal India and Timurid Central Asia. She successfully showed that Timurid encampment gardens and Mughal mausoleum gardens had their roots in the concept of paradise developed in pre-Islamic literature in the Near East.

In the late 1980s, geographer and architect James Wescoat proposed a framework for landscape research on Islamic gardens.[10] Wescoat explained that the sharp separation between inner garden and outer landscape has discouraged research on how gardens fit within landscape. He drew a distinction among three types of landscapes: as valued scenery in Qur'anic descriptions, as a functional pattern in Islamic urban settlements, and as a place for social communication. Scenic value, according to Wescoat, originated in the Qur'an, in which vistas and sweeping panoramas are described. The functional pattern of landscape refers to a wider question: how did these gardens fit within the "larger fabric of urban settlement patterns, land use, transportation and economic life?"[11] The social aspect, on the other hand, elucidates how the use of gardens by rulers, viziers, courtiers, servants, harem members and visitors affected their design.

Magdy Tewfik Saad's article, 'Traditional Urban Gardens in Identified Muslim Environments', explored yet another aspect of Persian gardens mentioned but not fully discussed elsewhere: the connection between Persian gardens and cities. Saad's study suggested that, in the eleventh century, gardens established a complex relationship with cities for the first time.[12] According to him, it was then that city boundaries were consolidated and garden-palaces were moved beyond the city walls. These gardens, which were donated to charity as *waqf* (religious endowments), formed a *chaharbagh* pattern and, between the seventeenth and nineteenth centuries, many gardens were placed outside towns. A significant point raised in Saad's paper is how the location of the garden affected or defined its function, an issue that is partially discussed in art historian Bernard O'Kane's study. O'Kane's article on Persian palace design opened debate on how the design of gardens and pavilions is affected by deep cultural traditions.[13] It explored the influence of pastoral nomadism in Iran, the role of the garden as an encampment in Safavid and Timurid historical accounts, and reveals a preference for a nomadic lifestyle among these cultures. Questioning the stable nature of the palace and suggesting a more mobile use, O'Kane referred to Safavid and Timurid historical accounts to demonstrate the choice of gardens for imperial encampments (*ordu*) at various periods. Similarly, art historian Lisa Golombek pursued new topics in her study of the gardens of Timur in 1995.[14] In analysing the meaning of the gardens of Timur, Golombek concluded that the nomadic life of the Timurids caused gardens to shift between residences and encampments.

Using a formal approach, Jonas Benzion Lehrman offered an analysis of gardens in Islamic countries through an architect's lens.[15] With an emphasis on gardens in Islamic Spain, Persia and Mughal India, Lehrman presented a summarized catalogue of gardens in the Islamic world. Nevertheless, he does not illustrate any connection between the aesthetic and other aspects such as function and meaning. Despite its strengths, Lehrman's work represented a common misinterpretation that gives emphasis to the formal aspects of gardens without considering their historic use. In contrast, scholar of architecture Hamid Shirvani offered a mystical reading of the design of Persian gardens.[16] Introducing two different types of gardens, the garden as a container (enclosed field) and the garden as a contained courtyard, Shirvani concluded that Persian gardens occupied both a sacred, visionary, and secular, hedonistic, tradition and differentiated utilitarian gardens from those exclusively designed for pleasure.

Several independent studies explored the development of Islamic gardens and their connection to local traditions. A significant contribution on this topic is *Mughal Gardens: Sources, Places, Representations, and Prospects,* which included twelve papers on the origins, development and cultural and economic aspects of Mughal gardens. One chapter of this book addressed the economic function of gardens, an aspect typically ignored in favour of symbolic elements.[17] By exploring Mughal historical documents, historian Irfan Habib proved that most royal gardens were designed to produce fruits and flowers either for direct use by their wealthy owners or to make money.[18] In another chapter, the architect Mahvash Alemi explored the elements of Safavid gardens such as *talar* (hypostyle halls), trying to make a connection between the Safavid and the Achaemenid gardens. The big question is to what extent a Safavid king such as Shah 'Abbas was aware of the history of the Achaemenids and their architecture, especially knowing that our information on pre-Islamic Persia is indebted to twentieth-century excavations.

Imposing a fundamental shift in this field, two recent valuable contributions are Michel Conan's edited volume, *Middle East Garden Traditions: Unity and Diversity* (2007) and Dede Fairchild Ruggles's *Islamic Gardens and Landscapes* (2008). Several articles in *Middle East Garden Traditions* have shed light on pragmatic aspects of gardens. Yotam Tepper's 'The Rose and the Balsam: The Garden as a Source of Perfume and Medicine' explained the medicinal and cosmetic use of gardens throughout the Dead Sea region during the Roman and Byzantine Empires.[19] The papers in the second section of *Middle East Garden Traditions* deal with the political use of gardens from Marrakesh to India. In 'Princely Safavid Gardens: Stage for Rituals of Imperial Display and Political Legitimacy', Mahvash Alemi showed how the design of Safavid gardens in Persia could be understood with respect to the practices that occurred in them.[20] In *Islamic Gardens and Landscapes,* Ruggles made a significant contribution by not following the conventional chronological timeline and by studying some aspects of Islamic gardens that were not considered in other volumes. She drew attention to widespread religious interpretations of Islamic gardens and how the form and meaning of gardens are often a result of secular needs, and emphasized agriculture and irrigation as two influential factors behind their creation. Ruggles also provided a narrative for mausoleum gardens, attempting to show their progression from "informal settings to formal gardens".[21]

These publications reflect a rising interest in the in-depth study of garden history in a local context, something which had been somewhat sidelined in favour of a broader – and sometimes vaguely defined – 'Islamic garden'. This new trend is paralleled by an attempt to study the complexity of gardens by unfolding their materialistic, economic and agricultural aspects. Most of these studies fail to present a clear image of pavilions, probably as a result of the dearth of archaeological evidence. Neglecting the complexity of pavilions has resulted in ignoring the cultural context behind their development. Some of these studies have referred to miniature paintings and religious writings to show the chronological development of gardens, an approach which has led to analytical inconsistencies, as each medium has its own language, and each language has different restrictions and capacities. Furthermore, many studies fail to recognize the roots of garden design in specific geographical contexts. The role of local cultures is underestimated in favour of a broader, loosely defined Islamic culture, while ideological views and philosophical readings disregard the material aspects and economic benefits of gardens and pavilions as well as the issue of terminology with regard to the geographical boundaries. In view of these problems, I suggest here a framework which has its roots in these earlier studies, but considers the following factors in greater depth: the unification of garden and pavilion; social aspects of gardens and pavilions and the key figures and patrons behind their design and construction; the relationship between urban fabric and gardens and its influence on the typology and design of pavilions; the architectural qualities of pavilions such as order, space, circulation and context, and the mobility and stability of pavilion structure in relation to sociopolitical factors.

REDEFINING THE PAVILION: A DIACHRONIC APPROACH

My original plan was to illustrate the historical development of different types of pavilions in Persianate gardens. This ambitious goal had to be changed since the lack of scholarly research in this field first necessitated a basic understanding of the typology of pavilions. However, the resulting volume does not attempt to classify pavilions based on their historical periods and geographical regions. Instead, my goal is to develop a nuanced set of definitions of the pavilion in the historical context of Persianate gardens and to explore their literary and visual representations, thereby providing a foundation for future studies, which could focus on specific historical periods or typologies. By examining literary and visual documents, I aim to address four major issues in the history of Persianate garden pavilions: definition, use, design and natural relevance. In doing so, I hope to clarify the diversity of definitions for pavilions, including their cultural meanings, semiology and patterns of patronage and ownership, and the cultural behaviour of users. I shall explore whether the pavilion is a permanent or temporary structure, and its function as a setting for restorative, cultural and social activities in a geographical and historical context. Such an analysis of visual and textual documents can help to explain the reasons behind the physical or conceptual features of pavilions, the relationship between the layout of the garden and the pavilion, and the evolution of the structure in literature and art as distinct from the pavilion in reality. My research also covers the ways in which writers and artists viewed pavilions as an isolated or complementary architectural element in a garden.

My inquiry refers to the reflection of garden and pavilion in art and literature and the contextual factors behind this evolution. By exploring different media, a range of metaphysical, social, economic and physical features of gardens and pavilions will be examined here. Since each medium has its own capabilities and limitations, it requires a unique system of criticism and judgement. Consequently, each chapter discusses particular aspects of pavilions and gardens. For instance, visual depictions capture the pavilion's qualities at a specific moment, while historians' notes are able to show modifications through history. Carpet representations abstract the site plan of the garden, while travellers' notes usually provide information on use, design and ownership. In contrast, creative writing, such as poetry and mythology, indicates the metaphysical aspects of gardens and pavilions often neglected in chronicles or travel notes.

Beginning with an analysis of the garden and pavilion in mythological and sacred texts of the Near East, Chapter 2 reconstructs the paradise garden described in the Qur'an to clarify its relation to the pavilion structure. In this section, I analyse the intersections of the Qur'anic gardens and pavilion structures as houses, palaces and raised platforms but, because of the intricate terminology in the Qur'an, it is also necessary to consider the definitions of 'pavilion' itself. The major challenge here is the lack of specific terms, which leaves room for many personal interpretations. The last section of this chapter explores the garden and pavilion in Persian poetry, uncovering its complex layers of meanings and imagination. While some poems refer to historical events or characters, others look deeper for the metaphorical meanings. Persian poetry, though not literally descriptive in most cases, reveals the significance and cultural associations of gardens and pavilions and the relationship between built and natural environments. Most poems, however, are open to interpretation. This high degree of ambiguity and abstraction results both from the use of a wide and often vague terminology, and from the mystical aspects inherent in Persian poetry itself. The works of more than forty Persian poets who lived from the tenth to the eighteenth centuries CE were examined, without prioritizing any of them. Using over twenty key words referring to gardens and pavilions, I searched an electronic database of Persian poetry and discovered over 1800 verses that applied; from this, about 700 verses were selected and analysed based on their cultural significance on a macro-to-micro scale. The outcome of this analysis exposes various approaches in referencing garden and pavilion in Persian poetry.

Chapter 3 explores gardens and pavilions in visual media: painting, sculpture and carpet. Persian miniature painting was developed and flourished because of its potential to depict the royal lifestyle in the court and to illustrate scenes described in Persian literature; this art form serves as a major resource for my study and I discuss the three common forms of the pavilion (building, kiosk and tent) in relation to miniature paintings produced in the Timurid (1370–1507 CE), Safavid (1509–1736 CE) and Mughal (1550–1750 CE) periods. The chapter opens with an introduction to the themes and stylistic developments in Persian painting throughout history and their impact on the typology and form of pavilions. By analysing some 94 paintings, carpets and artefacts (out of a total of nearly one thousand that represented gardens and pavilions), I explore the relationship between the pavilion and garden, and the architectural concepts and features of pavilions. This investigation clarifies the popularity of each type of pavilion (building, kiosk and tent) among artists and the relationship between the formal qualities of the painting and the narrative behind it. Although the cases I discuss here cannot alone elucidate the historical development of pavilions, by comparing them with the texts they illustrate it is possible to clarify the dominant cultural view and use of pavilions. I apply a diachronic framework to expose the fundamental ideas behind the design of pavilions in paintings. This requires an understanding of the context of the paintings, the style of the artist, and the patron's influence on the work. It is also necessary to study the narrative accompanying the painting and its relation to the image, as well as any historical meanings that may attach to paintings which refer to specific historical events or people. Such analysis puts emphasis on the content rather than the style of art to help clarify the cultural synthesis and design concepts of the pavilion.

Chapter 4 concentrates on gardens and pavilions mentioned in historical documents. These gardens, in contrast to the ones described in literature or art, are not imaginary or perceived as a representation of the metaphysical world. The historical basis of pavilions necessitates discussion of their context and users. Identifying four categories of descriptions that provide a complete image of pavilions – objects, people, places and events – I referred to the accounts of local historians, biographers and European travellers who visited the Persianate world between the fifteenth and eighteenth centuries. These documents differ from each other in one important respect: whether they apply an insider's or an outsider's perspective. While travellers, as foreigners, are often more concerned with people and places, native historians and biographers frequently focus on the culture and its involvement in historical events. Travellers' logs are usually more descriptive and informative about the design details of pavilions and their users. In contrast, historians and local travellers are generally less interested in describing places but put considerable effort into recording the historical role of gardens and pavilions in social and political affairs, sometimes with a bias from royal patronage. These two views complement each other and provide a comprehensive picture of Persian gardens and pavilions. As these two types of documents differ in terms of origin, context, patronage and writing style, the use of a diachronic approach enables us to study the pavilion from a wider angle than architectural design alone. This approach can shed light on the cultural view of pavilions and their relationship with cities and gardens in the Persianate world. It can also assist in finding the gaps and mistakes that analysis of one type of document would obscure. Using this method leads to the examination of the pavilion structure as a complex of layers of social interactions, spaces and objects. In order to clarify the impact of issues such as patronage, family and educational background, occupation, levels of cultural familiarity and involvement in society and court, an overview of the historians and travellers whose works are cited in this chapter is provided at the end of the book.

My research confirms that the development of pavilions in Persian architecture does not follow a chronological path; instead, the development aligns with a logical order. This means that the chronological outline applied in most publications on Persian garden history may not necessarily suffice for a study on pavilions. Although the real image of the pavilion must be differentiated from its reflection in painting or literature, this book serves as a foundation for subsequent studies. Such studies might focus on pavilions in specific historical eras, analysing visual and literary images in order to clarify the degrees of idealism versus realism. Reference to archaeological evidence in order to study the evolution of each typology (building, kiosk, tent or throne) could make a significant contribution to this field, perhaps revealing whether the design of buildings in gardens was under the influence of specific styles or local movements during each period. Any further studies on pavilions, especially as royal settings, will require an investigation of cultural behaviour in gardens and its influence in the design of spaces in palaces and kiosks. The geographical categorization of the division of spaces would become possible after comparing plans of garden pavilions as palaces, kiosks and tents designed in various regions of the Persianate world.

2

The Garden and Pavilion in Near Eastern Pre-Islamic Texts, the Qur'an and Persian Poetry

GARDENS appear in early literary fragments from Mesopotamia and Persia. The analysis of narratives, mythologies and instructions in five ancient literary sources of the region – the *Epic of Gilgamesh,* the *Enuma Elish,* the *Code of Hammurabi,* Zoroastrian texts and the *Story of Genesis* – reveals the importance of the garden and its components in this locality. These texts, despite their diversity in terms of chronology, cultural context, character and use, and their different origins in the Mesopotamian, Indo-European and Semitic worlds, show the cultural synthesis of gardens and pavilions in the pre-Islamic age. This ancient Near Eastern literature indicates the deep spiritual value of natural elements such as rivers, plants and flowers, and relates them to the story of creation. A study of the relevant concepts discussed in Mesopotamian texts shapes, albeit vaguely, the image of the garden as it later emerged in Achaemenid Persia, and developed in the Parthian and Sassanid periods. Although silent about the garden and pavilion together, ancient Near Eastern literature and sacred texts highlight the regional concept of the garden, a motif that was further developed after the advent of Islam. What is common to all these texts is the significance of nature, which forms the foundation for the concept of paradise as a garden.[1]

With regard to methodology, any simultaneous analysis of religious texts, mythology and creative writing is bound to meet some obstacles. First of all, the texts discussed in this chapter have different origins and characteristics. While the *Enuma Elish* and the *Epic of Gilgamesh* are categorized as mythology, the *Story of Genesis*, Zoroastrian texts and the Qur'an are considered to be sacred and to have religious value. These texts have different origins: for instance, the *Vendidad* (an early Zoroastrian text) was compiled to answer the major questions of early Zoroastrians by means of a conversation between Ahura Mazda and Zoroaster, whereas the *Code of Hammurabi* serves as a purely legal and administrative document in Babylonian society in the second millennium BCE. In contrast, Persian poetry, which came centuries later, with its metaphoric and indirect tone has complex layers of meanings which vary in terms of degrees of imagination and realism. Most of Farrokhi Sistani's poems have a historical facet, in contrast to those of Hatef Esfahani, which reflect his mystical mindset and Sufi vision. Furthermore, due to the schematic and symbolic nature of the literary genres, we do not expect to reconstruct actual gardens, but to comprehend diverse definitions of nature, garden and pavilion, and their conceptual development in the literature.

Owing to the complexity of the literary documents and the cultural context behind their creation, this chapter will concentrate on the garden and the pavilion in literature, and not on the literary material itself. In order to consider the high degree of interaction among cultures and political dynasties, a cross-cultural and cross-chronological framework will be applied in this analysis. This intercultural approach is based on the fact that different cultures in the Near East have always influenced one another through trade, travel, immigration and war.[2] It allows us to construct the cultural synthesis of the concept of garden and pavilion. It should be emphasized that, throughout, the garden and pavilion will be studied together and the pavilion will not be regarded as an isolated structure, but as one integral to its setting.

MESOPOTAMIAN DOCUMENTS

An investigation of narratives, mythologies and didactic material in the four most important literary sources remaining from Mesopotamia reveals cultural views on the garden and its components. Moreover, a study of the relevant concepts discussed in these ancient texts can lead us to the image of the garden that was later illustrated in Zoroastrian texts. The major Mesopotamian documents, in which natural elements appear as dispersed entities rather than organized gardens, are the *Epic of Gilgamesh*, the *Enuma Elish*, the *Code of Hammurabi* and the *Story of Genesis*.

The Epic of Gilgamesh

The *Epic of Gilgamesh*, a Sumerian text, is one of the few remaining from Mesopotamia (2650–2550 BCE) which makes reference to gardens.[3] This story, originally written on eleven clay tablets in cuneiform script, was based on earlier Sumerian[4] legends of Gilgamesh, the historical King of Uruk.[5] In parts of this story, the palm gardens, which are probably connected to the Ishtar temple,[6] are described as gardens enclosed (presumably) by walls.[7] The missing parts of this epic, unfortunately, do not allow us to reconstruct actual gardens that existed at the time, but we can still find some information about the trees and plants which were the likely components. For example, "Across the face of the mountain the Cedar brought forth luxurious foliage; its shade was good, extremely pleasant. [Where] thorn bushes were matted together, the woods were a thicket...among the Cedars."[8] In another part, we read "cedar,...agate,...of the sea...lapis lazuli, like thorns and briars...carnelian, rubies, haematite,...like...emeralds."[9] It should be mentioned that it is not just the missing fragments that prevent reconstruction of actual gardens, but the schematic and symbolic nature of the literary text. The *Epic of Gilgamesh*, even though it does not directly refer to gardens, shows the cultural significance of natural elements such as trees. This vague image becomes clearer when we look at the *Enuma Elish* and the *Code of Hammurabi.*

The Enuma Elish

While the *Epic of Gilgamesh* reveals some of the elements which could be employed in the design of a garden, another Mesopotamian myth, the *Enuma Elish,* is concerned with a completely different narrative: the story of creation. This text, which is the earliest creation epic, has existed in various versions and dates back to at least 1700 BCE. The majority of scholars believe that it dates back to the Old Babylonian period, the early part of the second millennium BCE. Centred on the existence of mankind for the service of the gods, it is one of the most important sources for understanding the Babylonian worldview. The *Enuma Elish* tells the story of the birth of the gods, who spring from the primordial Apsu and Tiamat, and the choice of Marduk as the champion of the younger gods in the battle against Tiamat.[10] The primary purpose of the *Enuma Elish* was to elevate Marduk, as the chief god of Babylon, above other Mesopotamian gods.[11] Although this story is silent about gardens, we find verses about the sacredness of water. For example, "in the waters gods were created"[12] and "he spoke the word that charmed the waters; it fell upon Apsu, he lay asleep, the sweet waters slept..."[13] Even more interestingly, this myth is quite specific about watering plants: "Asaru cultivates the sown, conducts water by small channels, for seed-time, for shooting green and harvest grain."[14] The *Enuma Elish*'s significance is in intermarrying two concepts of creation and nature and specifically pointing to water as the origin of the gods.

The Code of Hammurabi

In contrast to the *Epic of Gilgamesh* and the *Enuma Elish*, *Hammurabi*'s view on the garden is more materialistic. It demonstrates that gardens, fields and houses were regarded as significant properties in the ancient Babylonian society. Hammurabi was the sixth of eleven kings of the Amorite dynasty which ruled old Babylonia from 1792–1750 BCE. In the second year of his reign, he enacted the law of the land, and the code is one of the earliest documents in history in which the word garden is repeated many times.[15] As a legal text, the code conceptualizes the garden in economic and legal terms and views both gardens and fields as mere resources to earn money and food. Hammurabi establishes a set of regulations for his people to solve the frequent challenges of garden ownership. For example, he says if a man is captured in battle, his fields and garden will be given to another person; if he returns, his field and garden will be returned to him.[16] In several codes, the house and garden are mentioned together:

> If a chieftain or a man leaves his house, garden and field and hires it out, and someone else takes possession of his house, garden and field and uses it for three years: if the first owner returns and claims his house, garden, and field, it shall not be given to him, but he who has taken possession of it and used it shall continue to use it.[17]

This integration of house and garden in Hammurabi's code reveals the existence of houses in agricultural fields and gardens. For instance, if a man deeds to his favourite son a "field, garden, and house" and then dies, when all the brothers divide the estate, they must first respect their father's wishes regarding the paternal property, and only then divide the remainder.[18]

Several regulations about gardening indicate its importance as an official job within this society, and also the gardeners' awareness of the king's policies. For example, if anyone gives over a field for a gardener to plant up as a garden, and he works it for four years, in the fifth year the owner and the gardener can divide it.[19] There are very specific rules for gardeners. One rule states that, if anyone hands over his land to a gardener to work, the gardener must pay to its owner two-thirds of the produce of the garden, but he may keep the other third.[20] There are also regulations regarding the use of gardens in accordance with adjacent properties. In another example, if a gardener fails to plant the arable field that was given over to him as a garden, he must pay the owner the produce of the field for the years that he let it lie fallow, according to the product of neighbouring fields, and then put the field in arable condition before returning it to its owner.[21] Another code states that, if the gardener does not work in the garden and production diminishes, he must pay in proportion to the neighbouring gardens.[22] These detailed codes and rules show the material value of gardens as agricultural fields and fruit gardens, an aspect absent in Mesopotamian mythology.

The Story of Genesis

The oldest evidence of the four-part garden is found in the *Story of Genesis*.[23] The two sections in the Old Testament that refer to the creation story are Genesis 1, which covers the creation week and consists of eight divine commands executed over six days, and Genesis 2, which is the account of Eden. In Genesis 2, the Garden of Eden is described as containing the division of four rivers branching from a single source: "There was a river flowing from Eden to water the garden, and from there it branched into four streams."[24] Adam and Eve were placed in a garden divinely planted in the east of Eden. Here, God made "trees grow up from the ground, every kind of tree pleasing to the eye and good for food; and in the middle of the garden he set the tree of life and the tree of the knowledge of good and evil."[25]

Although the *Story of Genesis* seems to be founded on the Babylonian creation myth (the *Enuma Elish*),[26] it pushes the concept further by equating heaven and the Garden of Eden: "Thus the heavens and the earth and everything in them were completed."[27] At first there was nothing – "when the Lord God made the earth and heavens, there was neither shrub nor plant growing on the earth because the Lord God had sent no rain"[28] – but then it goes on to specify the location of the garden: "The Lord God planted a garden in Eden away to the east, and in it he put the man he had formed."[29] The significance of Eden is that the creation story in Genesis 2 places the original home of mankind in a garden. Much debate surrounds the term 'Eden'.[30] According to the religious scholar, Jean Marie Hiesberger, Eden derives from the Akkadian word *edinu*, a fertile or well-watered plain.[31] The word *edinu* (House of Heaven) might be also related to *E-ana* which is the name given to the temple at Uruk dedicated to the goddess Inana (Ishtar).[32] Moreover, the Genesis text is specific as to the presence of four rivers, and even goes so far as to name them. It states:

> The name of the first is Pison; it is the river which skirts the whole land of Havilah, where gold is found…and the name of the second river is Gihon; this is the one which skirts the whole land of Cush. The name of the third river is Tigris; this is the river which flows east of Asshur. The fourth river is Euphrates.[33]

While two of the rivers, the Tigris (Hiddekel) and Euphrates, are well known, the other two, the Pison and the Gihon, remain the subject of substantial debate.

The Genesis story makes a significant contribution to the development of the concept of garden in the Near East. Here, the conceptual development of gardens is based on the unity of heaven and the garden, the addition of rivers as essential parts of the Garden of Eden, and equating the original home of the human race with their final destination. In other words, in contrast to the Mesopotamian myths, which were concerned with the creation of the world and did not discuss the afterlife, and Zoroastrian pre-Sassanid texts that focused on heaven and hell, and therefore directly on the life after death, the *Story of Genesis* incorporated and unified concepts of heaven and the Garden of Eden. Moreover, it attached the concept of heaven to the image of the garden, which incorporated specific natural elements: water, plants and trees.

ZOROASTRIAN TEXTS

Zoroaster, or Zarathushtra, lived in eastern Iran sometime during the period from the thirteenth century BCE to just before the rise of the Achaemenid Empire under Cyrus II (also called Cyrus the Great) in the mid-sixth century BCE.[34] His religion, Zoroastrianism, remained one of the most influential in the Middle East until the advent of Islam. As the founder of the one of the earliest religions based on revealed scripture, Zoroaster praises trees, plants, flowers and rivers as blessed elements, and strongly encourages people to plant and cultivate. The *Vendidad* is a collection of texts and an ecclesiastical (and not liturgical) manual. It includes twenty-two chapters, which are called *fargards*, containing fragments arranged as discussions between Ahura Mazda and Zoroaster. It begins with a dualistic account of creation and continues with various instructions, through the observance of which evil spirits may be confounded. In the *Vendidad*,[35] Zoroaster asks Ahura Mazda: "Who is the fourth that rejoices the Earth with greatest joy?" and Ahura Mazda answers: "It is he who sows most corn, grass, and fruit, O Spitama Zarathushtra! who waters ground that is dry, or drains ground that is too wet."[36] In several verses, the wind, stars, moon, sun, springs of water, rivers, lands and plants are called holy creatures which are offered by Ahura Mazda to humans: "And to these places, pastures, and dwellings with their springs of water, their rivers, to the lands and to the plants, to this earth and yon heaven, to the holy wind, to the stars, moon, and sun, to the stars…, and to all the holy creatures…"[37]

Zoroaster admires plants for their healing qualities: "And I Ahura Mazda brought down the healing plants that, by many hundreds, by many thousands, by many myriads, grow up all around the one Gaokerena."[38] Water, fire and plants are elements to be worshipped: "And we worship the good and best waters Mazda-made, holy, all the waters Mazda-made and holy, and all the plants which Mazda made, and which are holy."[39] Ahura Mazda desires "for this

Yasna, these Waters and Lands and Plants."[40] Zoroaster praises the land for growing plants:

> This wide earth do I praise, expanded far, the productive, the full bearing, thy mother, holy plant! Yea, I praise the lands where thou dost grow, sweet-scented, swiftly spreading, the good growth of the Lord...[41]

Zoroaster instructs his followers to plant the best trees, the most sweetly scented flowers, and all kinds of fruits.[42] He recommends that humans plant hundreds of plants and trees[43] and water them well: "Whereon grow the seeds of my plants of every kind by hundreds, by thousands, by hundreds of thousands."[44] According to Zoroaster, corpses should be buried in a 'sacred' moment which he describes: "And as soon as the birds begin to fly, the plants to grow, the hidden floods to flow, and the wind to dry up the earth, then the worshippers of Mazda shall lay down the dead, his eyes towards the sun."[45]

Ahura Mazda is worshipped for creating the waters and plants and for making and upholding the stars:

> Thus therefore do we worship Ahura Mazda, who made the Kine (the living creation), and the (embodied) Righteousness (which is incarnate in the clean), and the waters, and the wholesome plants, the stars, and the earth, and all (existing) objects that are good.[46]

Zoroaster praises Ahura Mazda for making the plants grow[47] because that is Mazda's reward to humans: "For him, as a reward, Mazda made the plants grow up."[48] He also makes sacrifices to nature:

> And we sacrifice to all the springs of water, and to the water-streams as well, and to growing plants, and forest-trees, and to the entire land and heaven, and to all the stars, and to the moon and sun, even to all the lights without beginning (to their course).[49]

He recommends perfuming houses with aromatic plants and flowers:

> If they find it easier to remove the house, they shall take away the house, they shall let the dead lie on the spot, and shall perfume the house with Urvasna, or Vohu-gaona, or Vohu-kereti, or Hadha-naepata, or any other sweet-smelling plant.[50]

The *Yasna* is the primary Zoroastrian liturgical collection, the sacred hymns of Zoroaster. Its central portion is the *Gathas*, the oldest and most sacred part of the *Avesta*, believed to have been composed by Zoroaster himself. The *Yasna* is originally the name of a ceremony in which the entire book is recited and appropriate liturgical actions performed. In the *Yasna*, plants and waters are repeatedly praised: "And we worship all waters and all plants, and all good men and all good women. And we worship all these Yazads, heavenly and earthly, who are beneficent and holy."[51] Rivers are considered holy creatures of nature, made by Ahura Mazda, and the river Anahita is a place for purification of both men and women:

> And the (chief) outlet to this one water (Ardvi Sura Anahita) goes apart, dividing to all the seven Karshvars. And this outlet to my river, Ardvi Sura Anahita, bears off its water always in summer and in winter. This river purifies the seed of men, and wombs of women, and women's milk.[52]

According to Zoroaster, people should sacrifice to the springs of water and rivers thus: "We worship You, O Ye Bountiful Immortals! The entire collection of this Yasna, Haptanghaiti (as we sum up all). And we sacrifice to the fountains of the waters, and to the fording of the rivers."[53] Such respect for Anahita reminds us of the story of the goddess of water mentioned in the *Enuma Elish*. In Sumerian mythology, too, Enki as the god of water, wisdom and life was the source of all secret and magical knowledge of life and immortality. He invented civilization for the people, created order in the cosmos and made the grain grow. Enki was often depicted with streams of water emanating from his shoulders.[54] Although Zoroaster believed in a single god, Ahura Mazda, like the Mesopotamians he invited people to worship all aspects of nature and, compared to the earlier Mesopotamian mythologies, Zoroastrian texts are much more specific about the role of nature in the purification of the souls of humankind.

The Concept of Heaven

In Zoroastrianism, the cosmos was basically three-tiered, consisting of earth, atmosphere and heaven.[55] One of the Zoroastrian documents which explains the dream-journey to heaven is *Ardavirafnameh*.[56] This book, which is described as the precedent for Dante's *Divine Comedy* by the literary critic Mary Boyce,[57] is based on a spiritual journey in which Ardaviraf, a Zoroastrian cleric, explains his experience after death: the Chinwad Bridge, hell and heaven. The main purpose behind this narrative is to erase doubt and suspicion regarding the afterlife.[58] Although the date of the book is not known, is generally believed to have originated during the Sassanid age (224–651 CE), when Zoroastrianism experienced a state-sponsored revival. Although this book is more conceptual than descriptive, it describes specific scenes and events in heaven and hell. For instance, on Ardaviraf's journey in heaven, Ardaviraf observes the tank of water on an angel's back:

> Then I saluted, and said thus: "Thy servant, O Adar the angel, it was who, in the world, always put upon thee wood and perfume seven years old, and you exclaim about my green wood!" Then Adar, the angel of the fire of Ohrmazd, said thus: "Come on, that I may show thee the tank of water of the green wood which was put upon me." And he led me on to a place, and showed the blue water of a large tank, and said: "This is the water which that wood exuded, which thou puttedst upon me."[59]

The Sassanid Zoroastrian texts, written in the Pahlavid script[60] and under the influence of Christian thought, integrated the idea of hell and heaven with the concept of the Garden of Eden.[61] The concept of heaven is further developed in a post-Islamic Zoroastrian text, *Dadestan-e Denig* (Religious Decisions).[62] This Pahlavid text was written in the ninth century CE and contains answers given by Dastur Manushchihr Goshnajaman[63] to ninety-two questions raised by his co-religionists.[64] This Zoroastrian cleric talks about comfort and pleasure as two main experiences in heaven: "And through hope for the comfort and pleasure in heaven they should accept willingly, for the neck, much trouble and fear in the practice of virtue in thought, word, and deed."[65] He even differentiates heaven from the supreme heaven:

> And that third night, in the dawn, they go to the place of account on Alburz; the account being rendered they proceed to the bridge, and he who is righteous passes over the bridge on the ascent, and if belonging to the ever-stationary [purgatory] he goes thither where their place is, if along with an excess of good works his habits are correct he goes even unto heaven (*vahishto*), and if along with an excess of good works and correct habits he has chanted the sacred hymns he goes even unto the supreme heaven.[66]

It appears that this is the first time that this division between heaven and supreme heaven occurs in Zoroastrian texts.[67] In the same text, a third stage for heaven is introduced, which is called ever-stationary:

> For the remaining sin it undergoes punishment at the [Chinwad] bridge, and the evil thoughts, evil words, and evil deeds are atoned for; and with the good thoughts, good words, and good deeds of its own commendable and pleasing spirit it steps forward unto the supreme heaven, or to heaven (*vahishto*), or to the ever-stationary [purgatory] of the righteous, there where there is a place for it in righteousness.[68]

In response to the question about the nature of heaven (*vahishto*), Dastur Manushchihr Goshnajaman defines heaven as a place which is "lofty, exalted, and supreme, most brilliant, most fragrant, and most pure". It is filled with beautiful existences, the best and most desirable sacred beings and all comfort, pleasure, joy, happiness and welfare, more and better even than the greatest and most supreme welfare and pleasure in the world. There is no pain, distress or discomfort since it is the perfect space and the boundless world.[69] He explains that the flight into heaven is not material but spiritual:

> The reply is this, that a soul of the righteous steps forth unto heaven through the strength of the spirit of good works, along with the good spirit which is the escort of the soul, into its allotted station and the uppermost which is for its own good works; along with the spiritual good works, without those for the world, and a crown and coronet, a turban-sash and a fourfold fillet-pendant, a decorated robe and suitable equipments, spiritually flying unto heaven (*vahishto*) or to the supreme heaven, there where its place is.[70]

These verses show that the Zoroastrian heaven is not associated with any particular garden because it is imagined as a spiritual territory. However, it also shows that heaven is divided into different stages.

Architectural Elements within Zoroastrian Texts

Regardless of gardens, for our inquiry into pavilions in Zoroastrian texts, we need to research two types of architectural structures that appear in these documents: buildings and movable thrones. Because Zoroastrian texts are largely conceptual, buildings rarely appear. *Aban Yasht,* one of the twenty-one *yashts* (hymns) to angels and ancient heroes, however, gives a clear depiction of a palace:

> Who has a thousand cells and a thousand channels: the extent of each of those cells, of each of those channels, is as much as a man can ride in forty days, riding on a good horse. In each channel there stands a palace, well-founded, shining with a hundred windows, with a thousand columns, well-built, with ten thousand balconies, and mighty.[71]

It further explains:

> In each of those palaces there lies a well-laid, well-scented bed, covered with pillows, and Ardvi Sura Anahita, O Zarathushtra! runs down there from a thousand times the height of a man, and she is possessed of as much Glory as the whole of the waters that run along the earth, and she runs powerfully.[72]

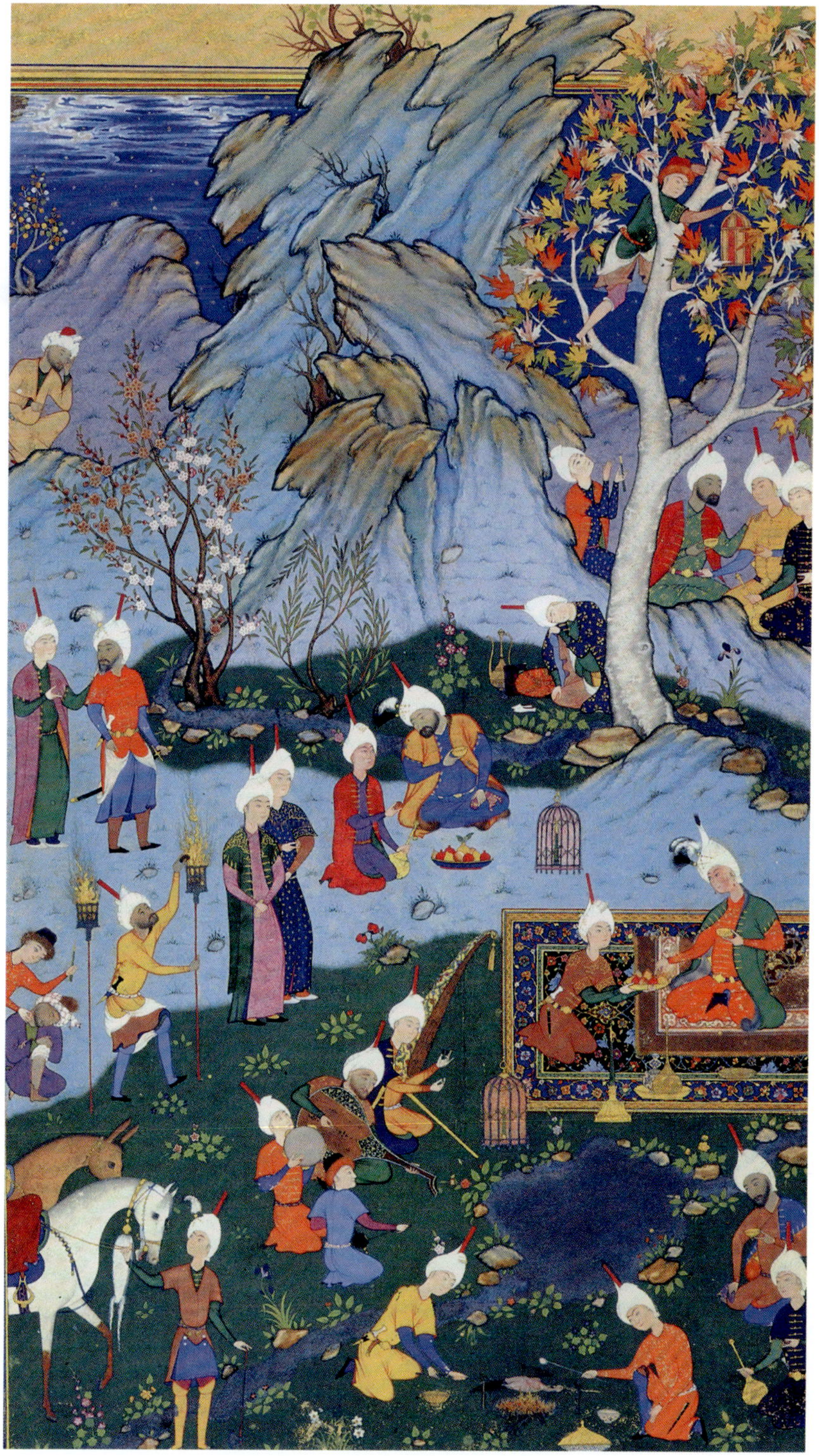

FIGURE 1

A night banquet in a garden. From *Moraqqa' Golshan,* sixteenth century.

FIGURE 2
The feast of Sadeh. From the *Shahnameh* (Book of Kings) of Shah Tahmasp. Soltan Muhammad, Tabriz, 1525.

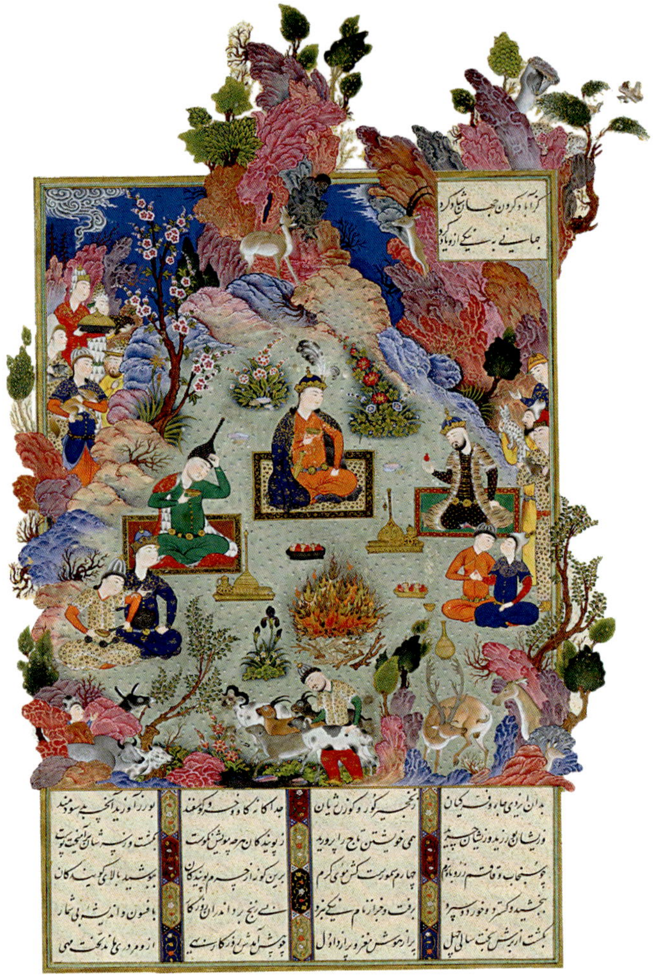

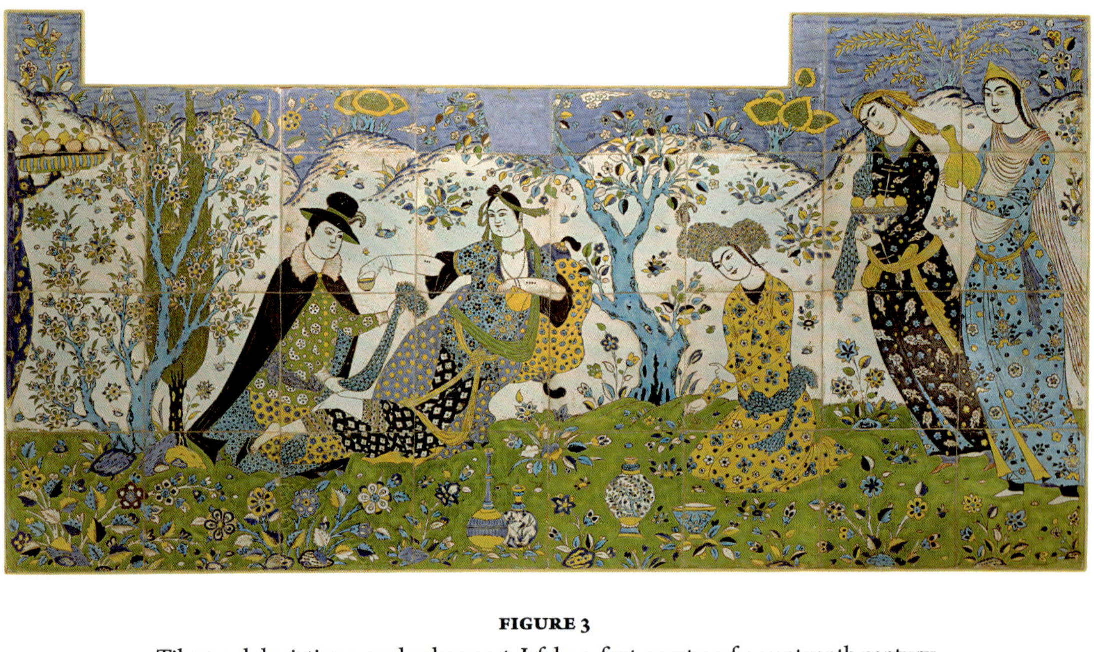

FIGURE 3
Tile panel depicting a garden banquet. Isfahan, first quarter of seventeenth century.

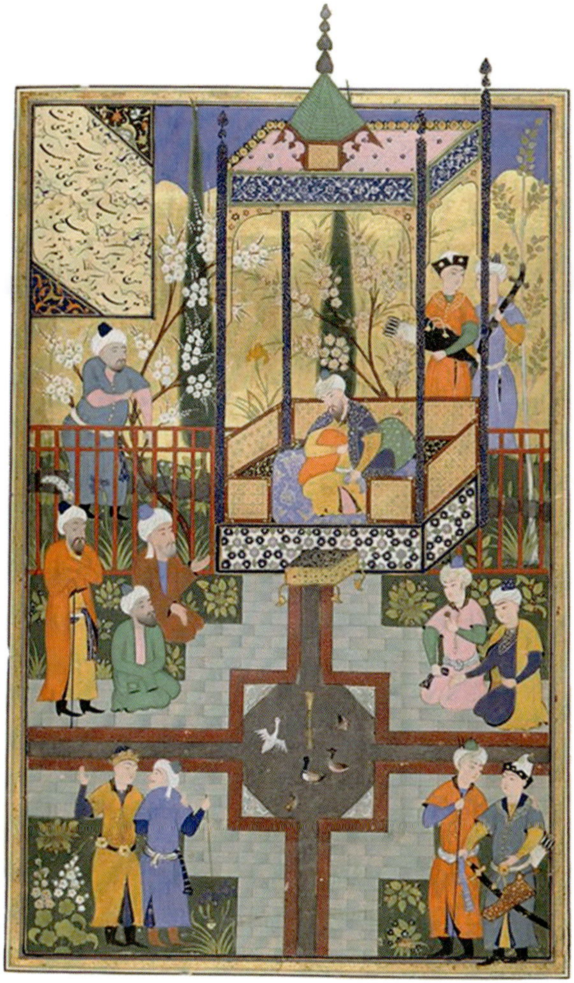

FIGURE 5
The Soltan of Syria Malek Saleh, on a throne in his garden, interviewing two dervishes. From *Bustan* (The Orchard) by Sa'di, Bukhara, 1522–23.

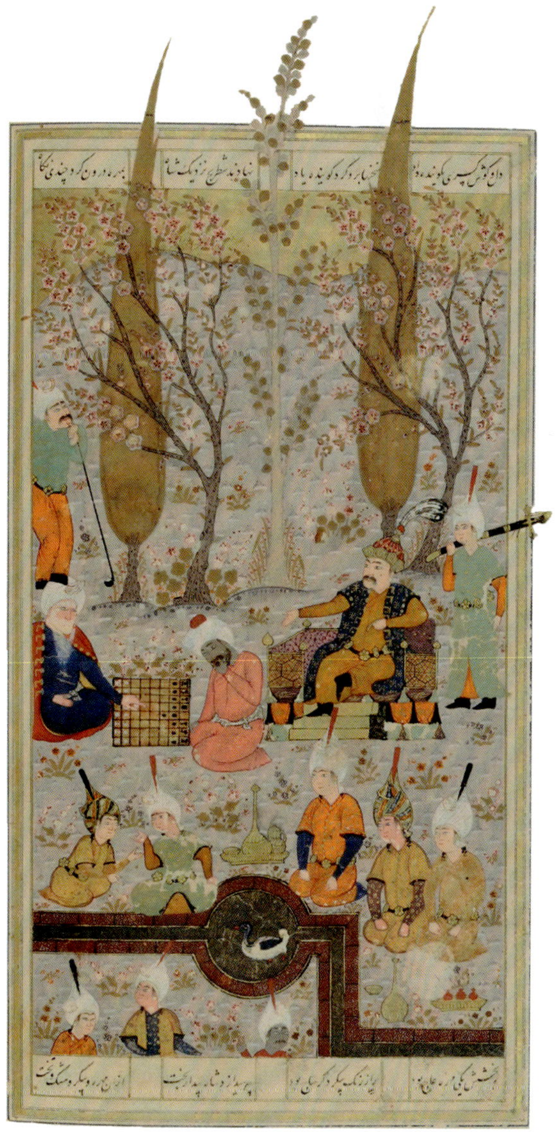

FIGURE 6
The courtiers of Nushirvan and the enigma of the game of chess. From the *Shahnameh*, Shiraz, 1535.

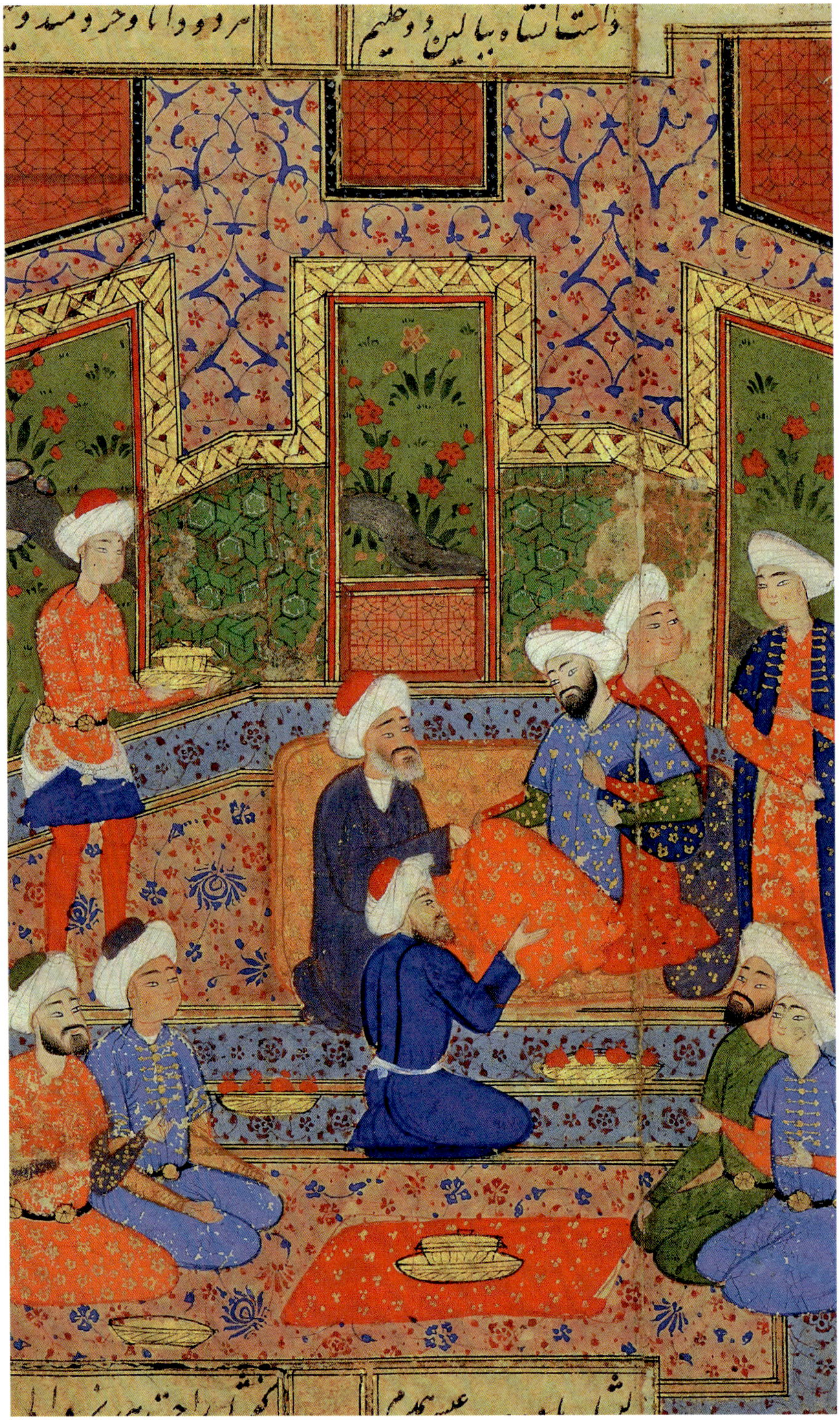

FIGURE 7

The sick king is treated by the royal doctor and his courtiers.
From *Sobhat al-Abrar*, by ʿAbdol Rahman Jami, sixteenth century.

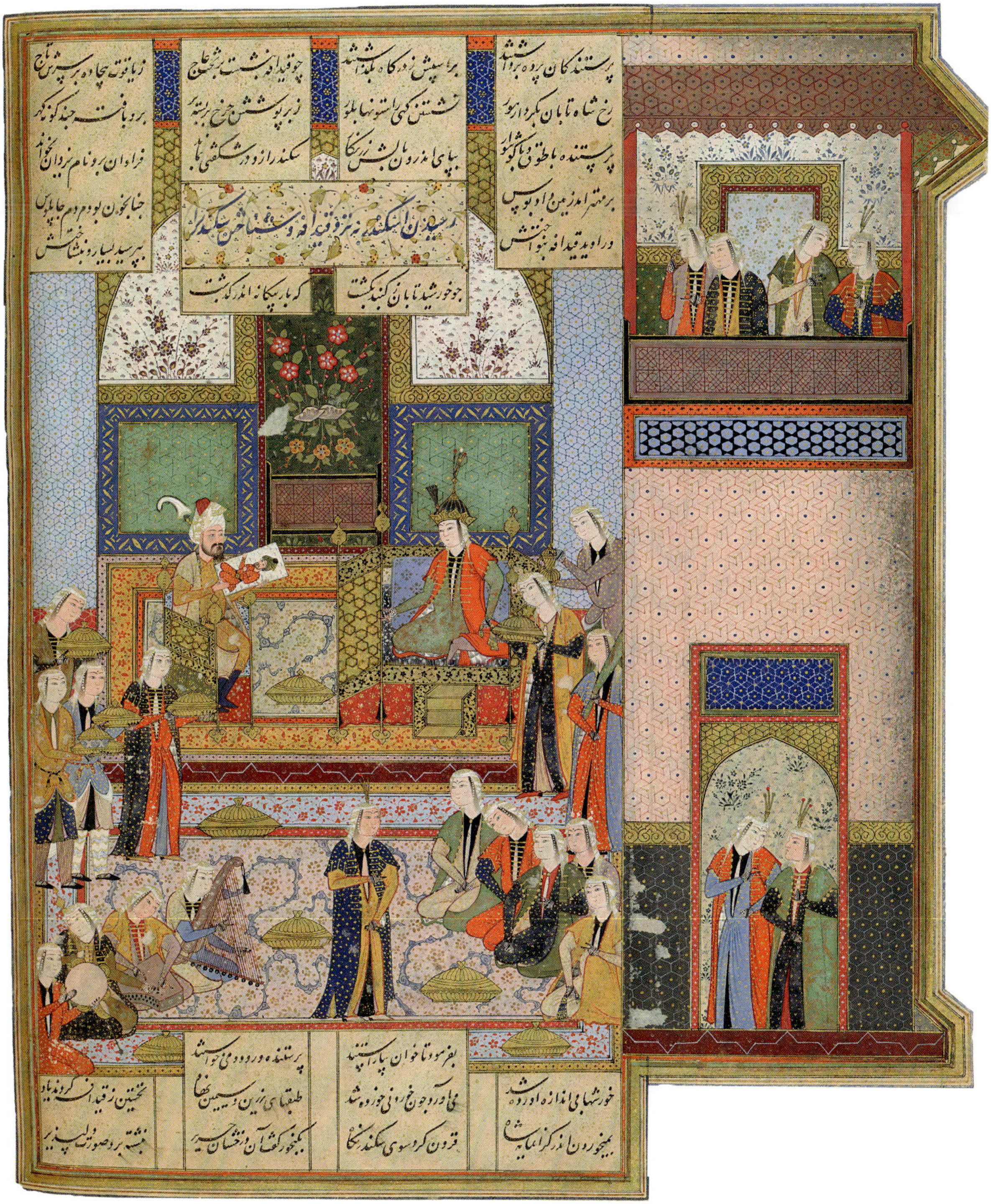

FIGURE 8

Crowded court scene. Eskandar disguised as a legate, with his portrait, before Queen Qaydafa in a palace in a garden. From the *Shahnameh*, Shiraz, 1560.

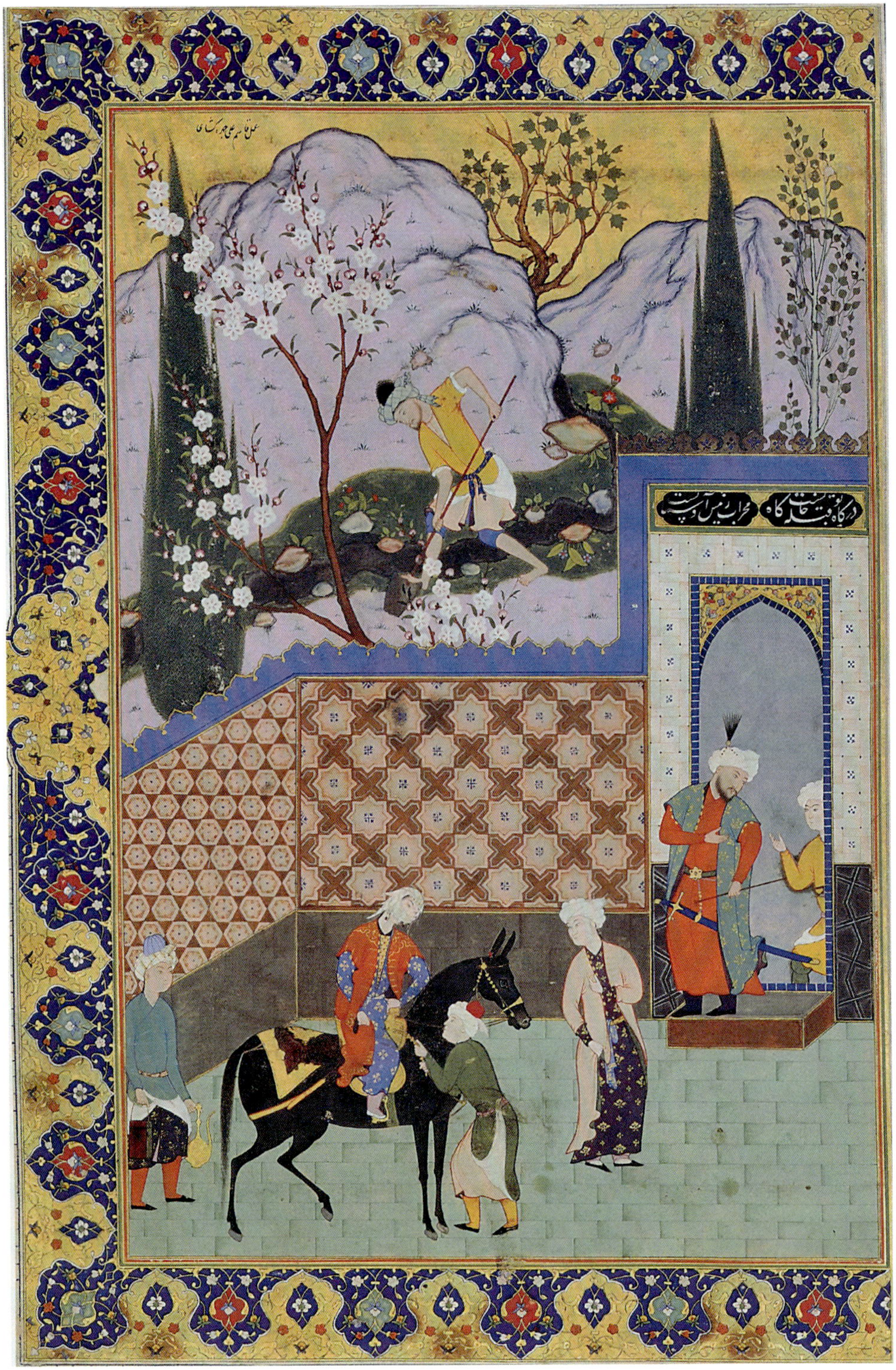

FIGURE 9

Yusof and Zulaykha having a feast. From *Panj Ganj* by ʻAbdol Rahman Jami, attributed to Qasem ʻAli, 1521.

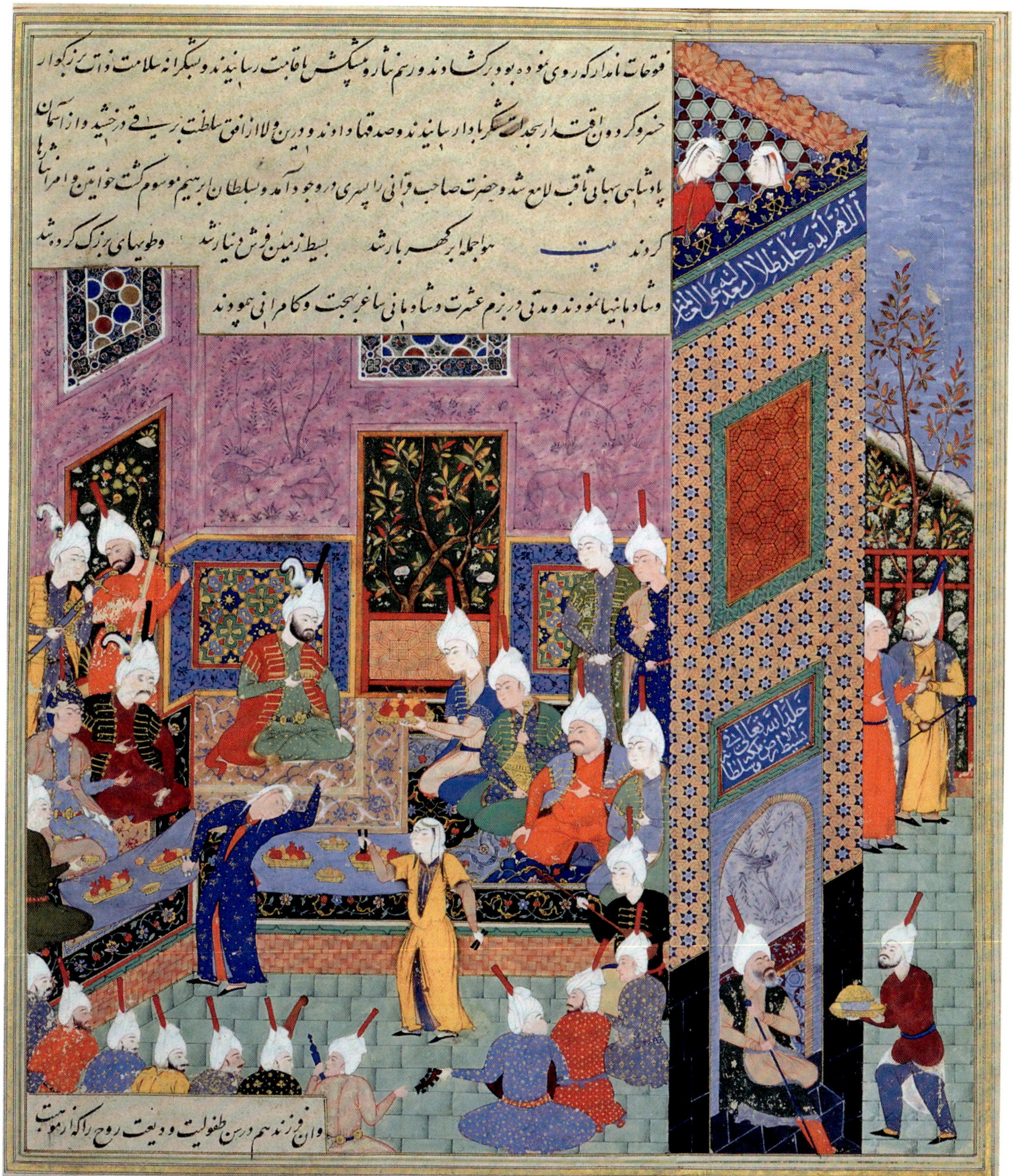

FIGURE 11

The return of Timur to Samarqand. From the *Zafarnameh*, attributed to Kamal-uddin Behzad, Herat, 1528.

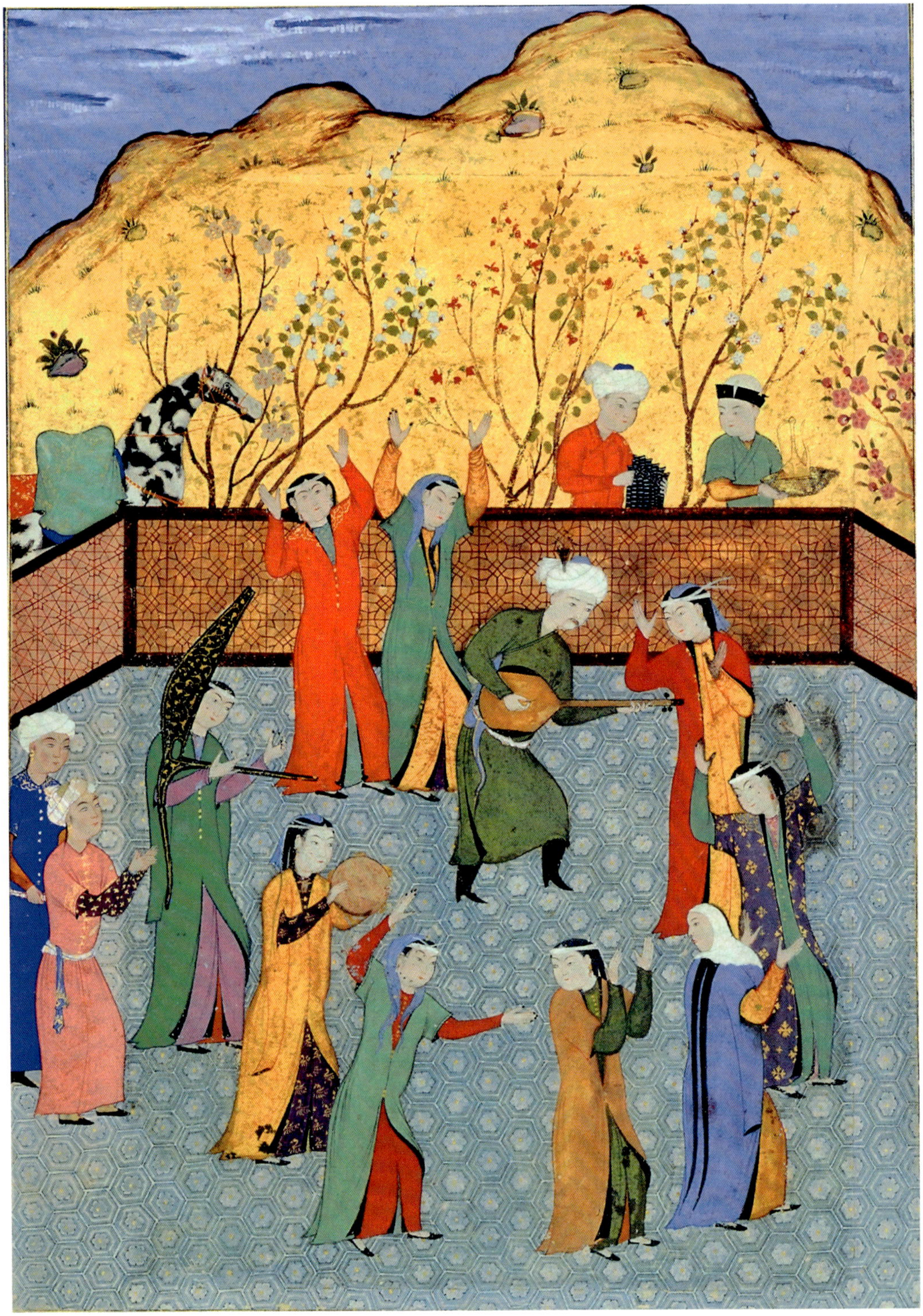

FIGURE 12

An excursion in the garden. From *Panj Ganj* by Jami, attributed to Maqsud, 1521.

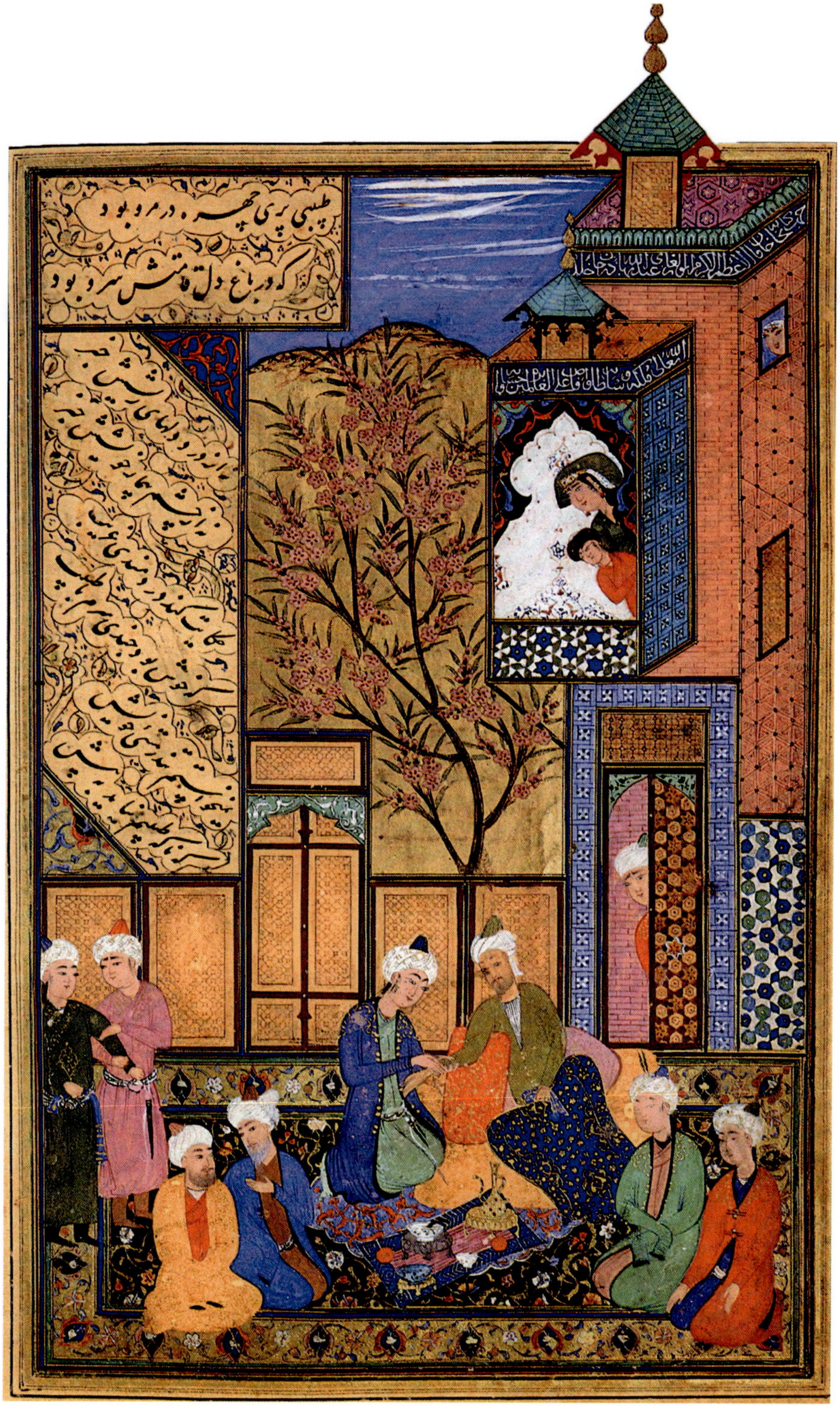

FIGURE 14

The story of a young handsome physician in the city of Marv. From *Bustan* by Sa'di, Herat, 1562–63.

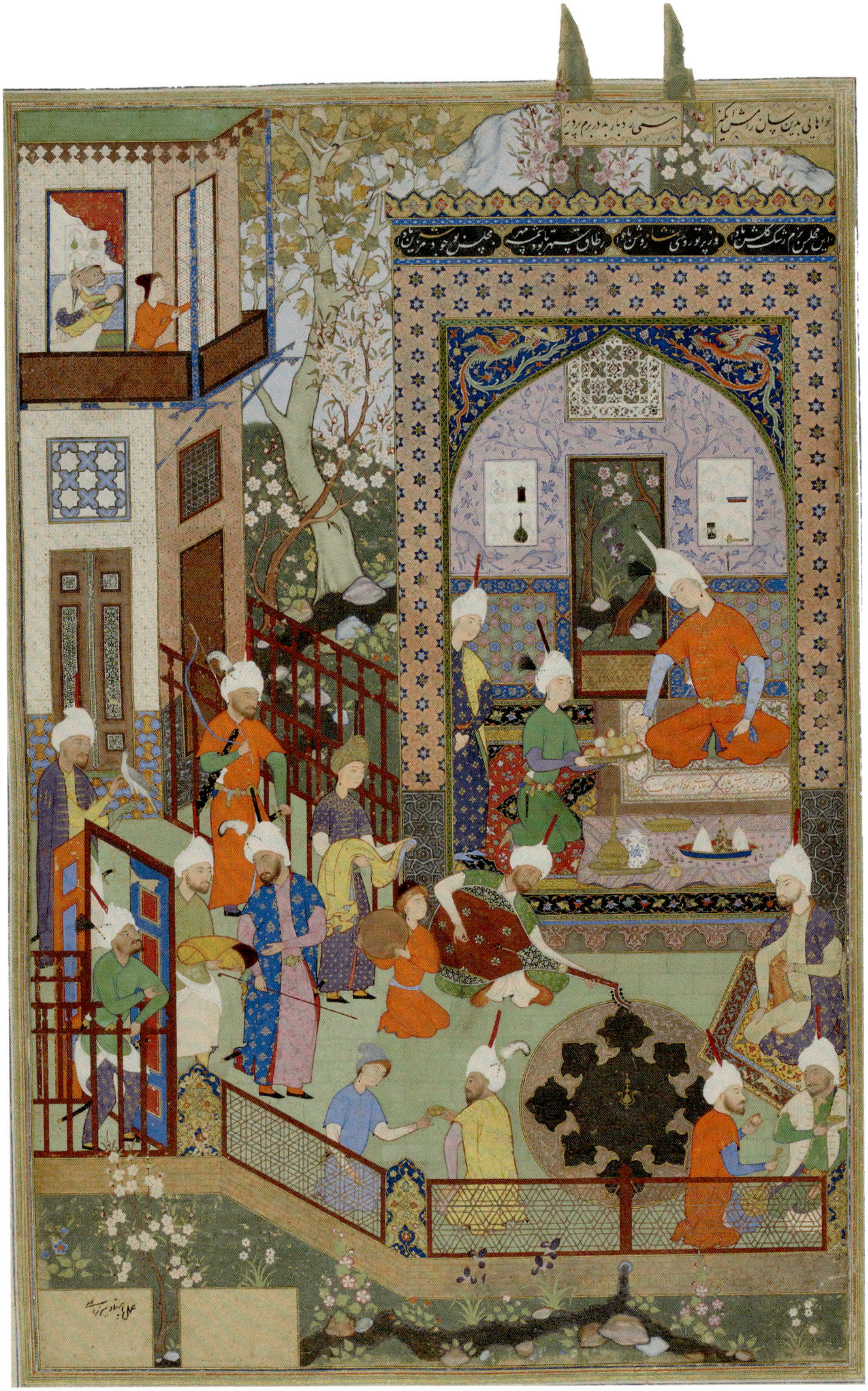

FIGURE 15

Khosrow and Shirin listening to stories told by Shirin's maidens.
From the *Khamseh* by Nezami, Tabriz, 1539–43.

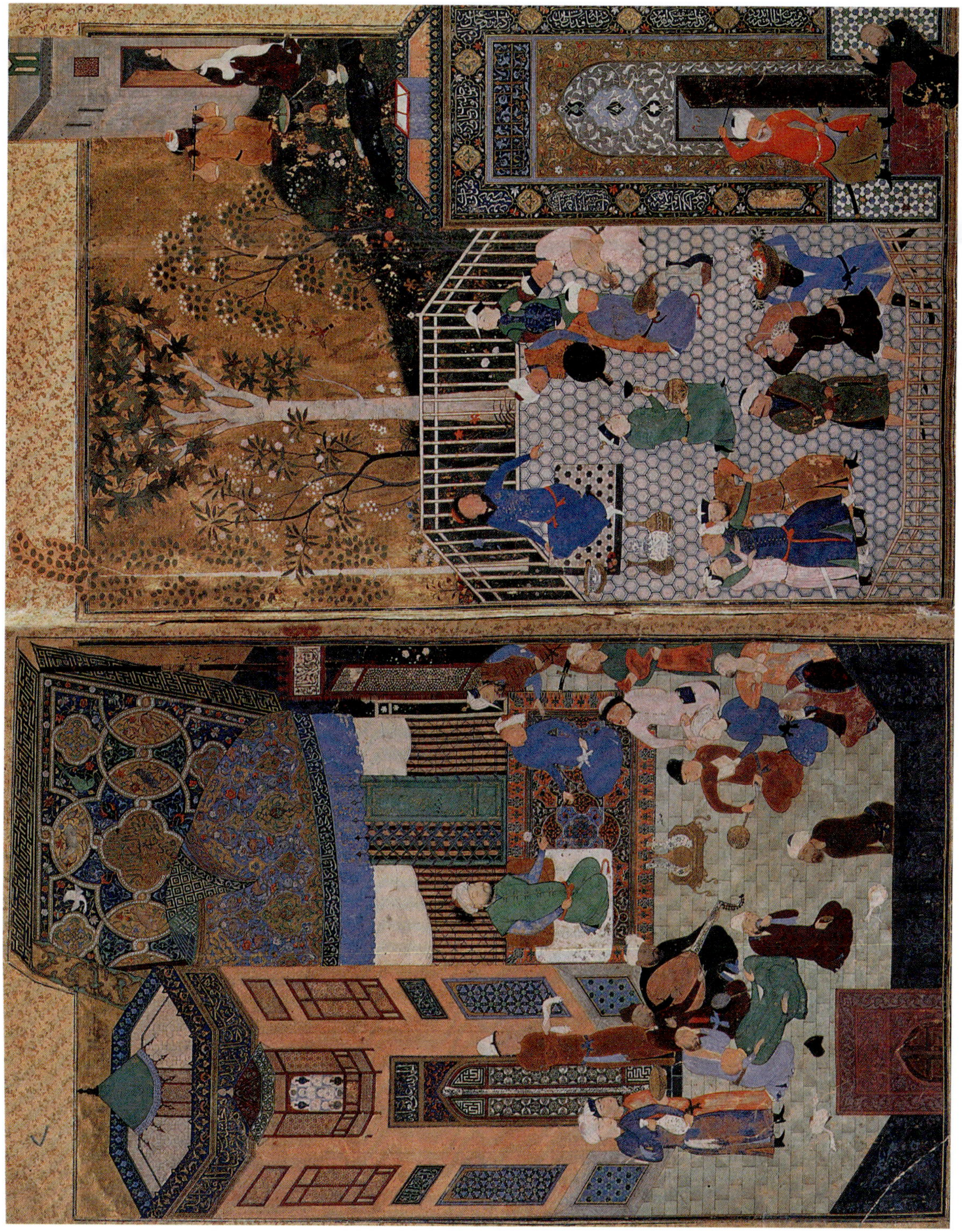

FIGURE 16

A convivial gathering at the court of Soltan Hoseyn Bayqara in Herat. From *Bustan* by Sa'di, Herat, 1488.

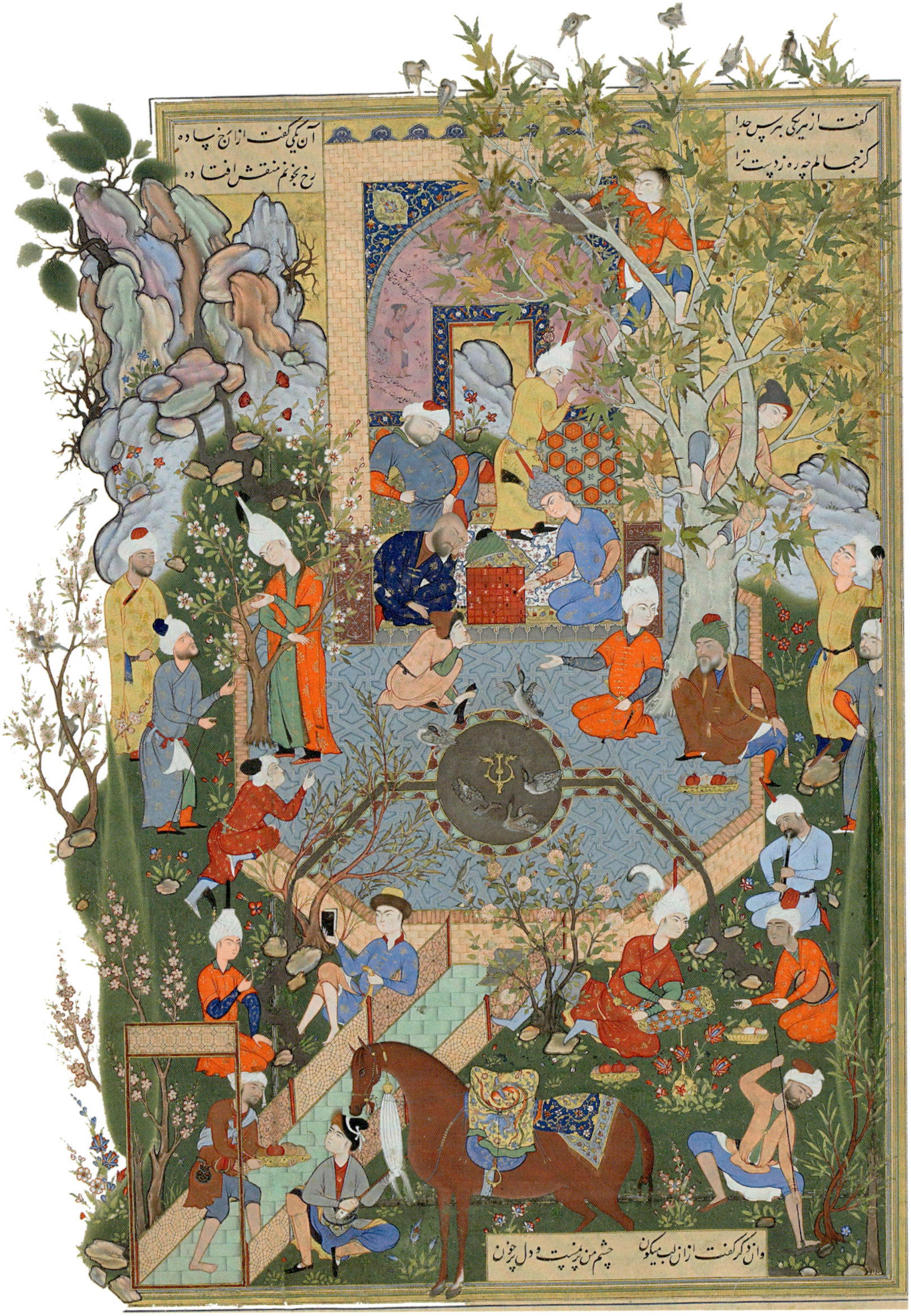

FIGURE 17

A father advises his son about love. From the *Haft Awrang* (Seven Thrones) by Jami, Mashhad, 1556–65.

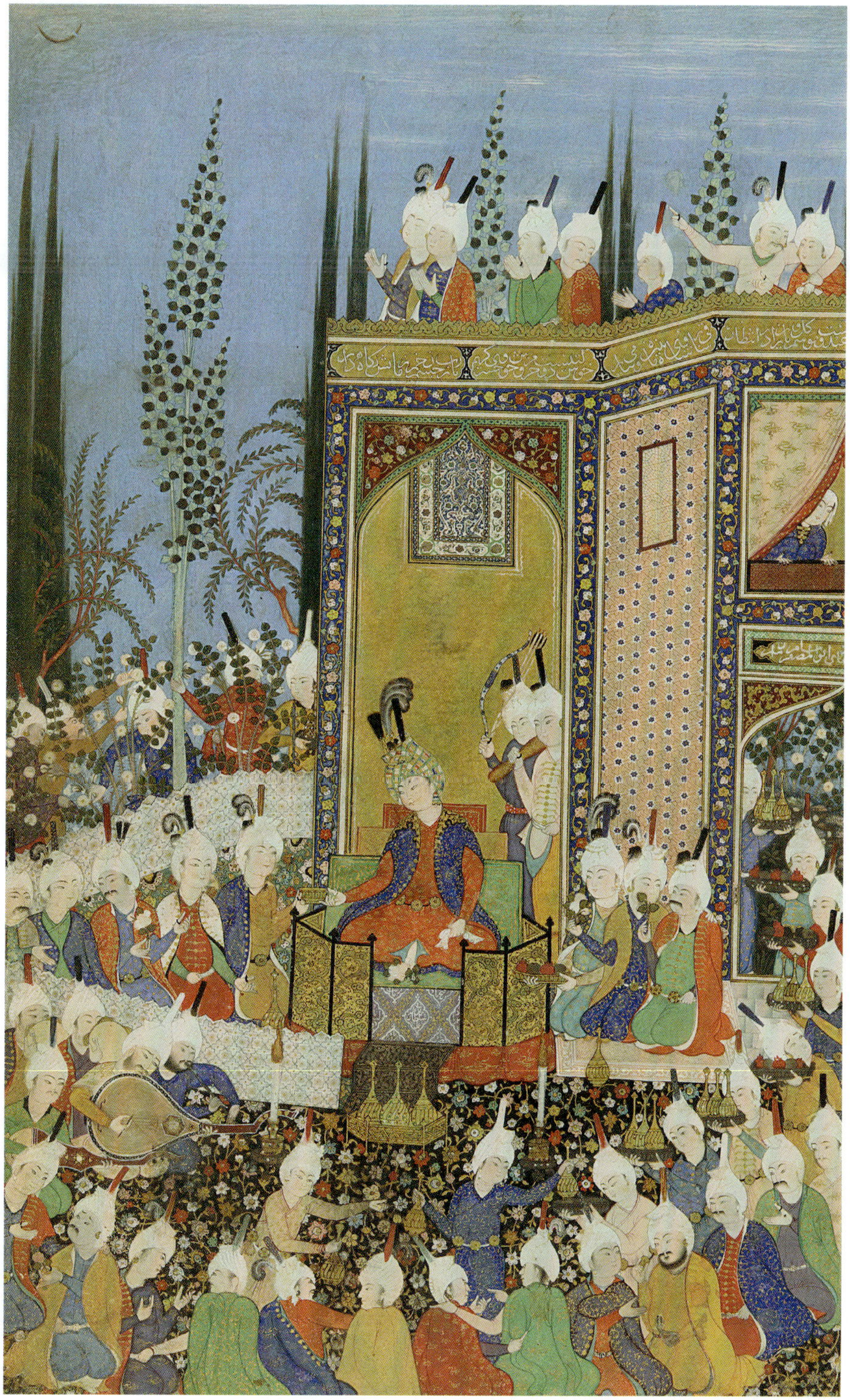

FIGURE 18

The beginning of the feast of ʿId. From the *Divan* by Hafez, attributed to Soltan Muhammad, 1527.

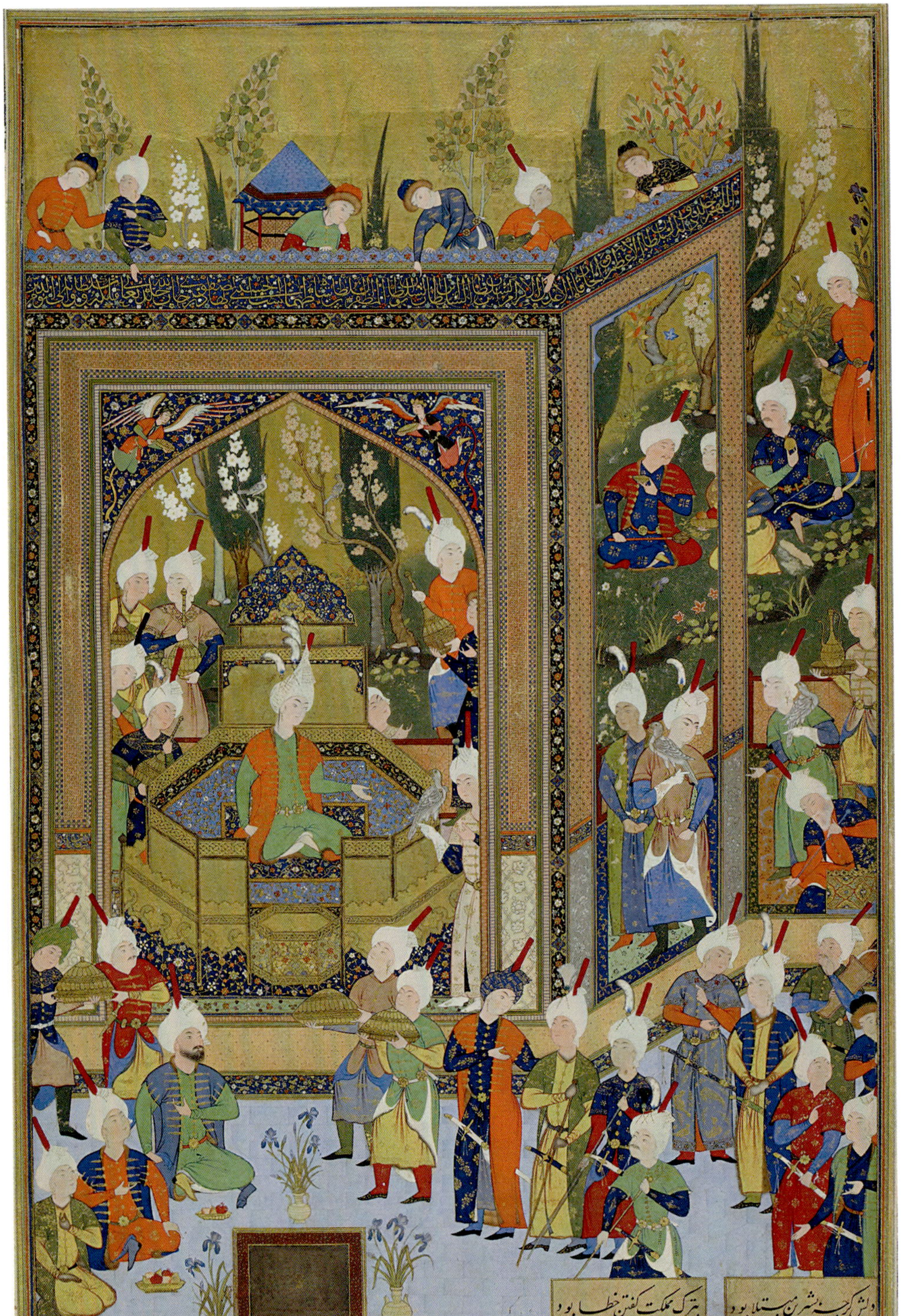

FIGURE 19

The enthronement of Khosrow. From the *Khamseh* by Nezami, signed by Shah Tahmasp's artists, 1539–43.

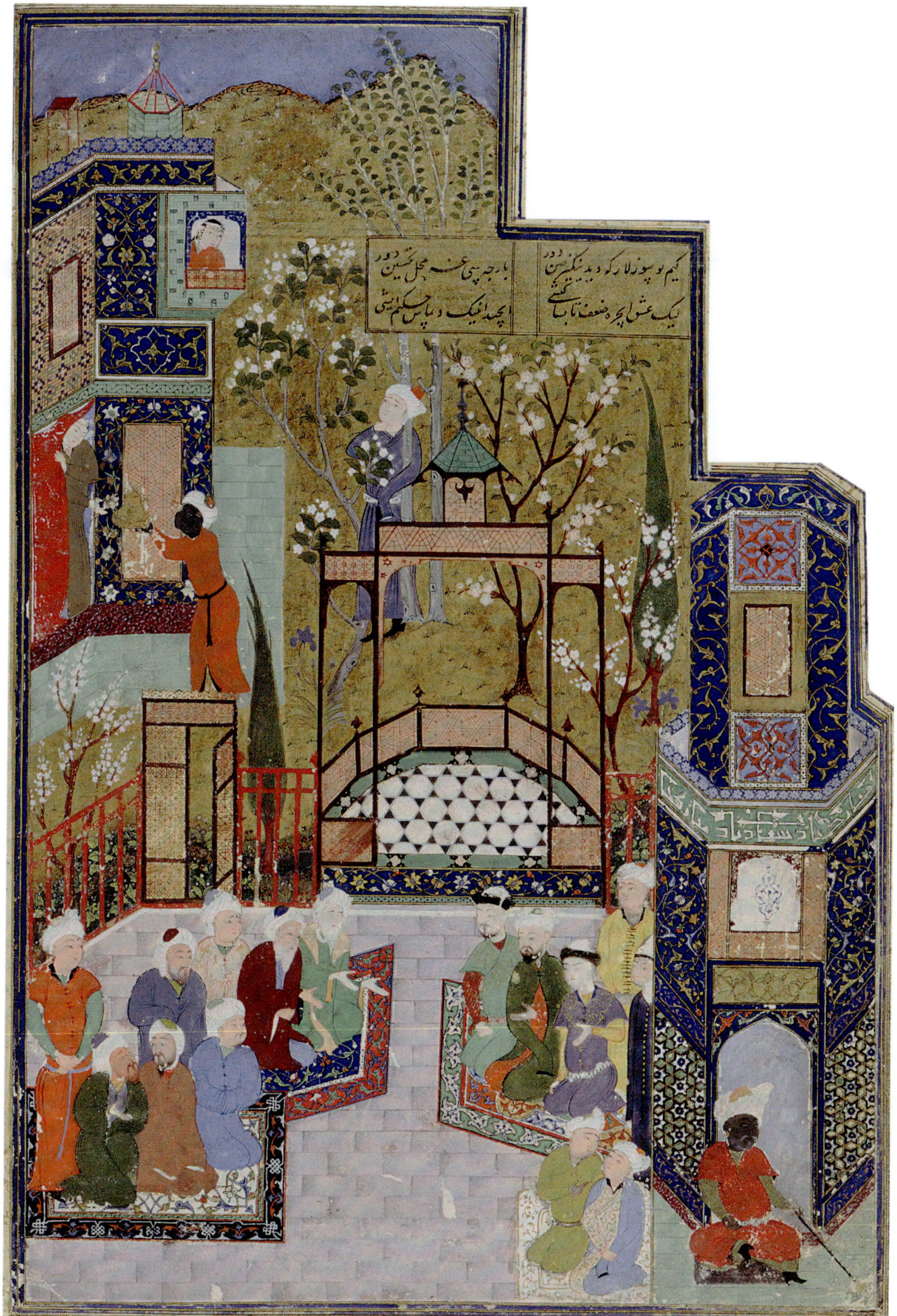

FIGURE 20

Courtiers in the garden. From *Farhad va Shirin* by Amir 'Ali Shir Nava'i.

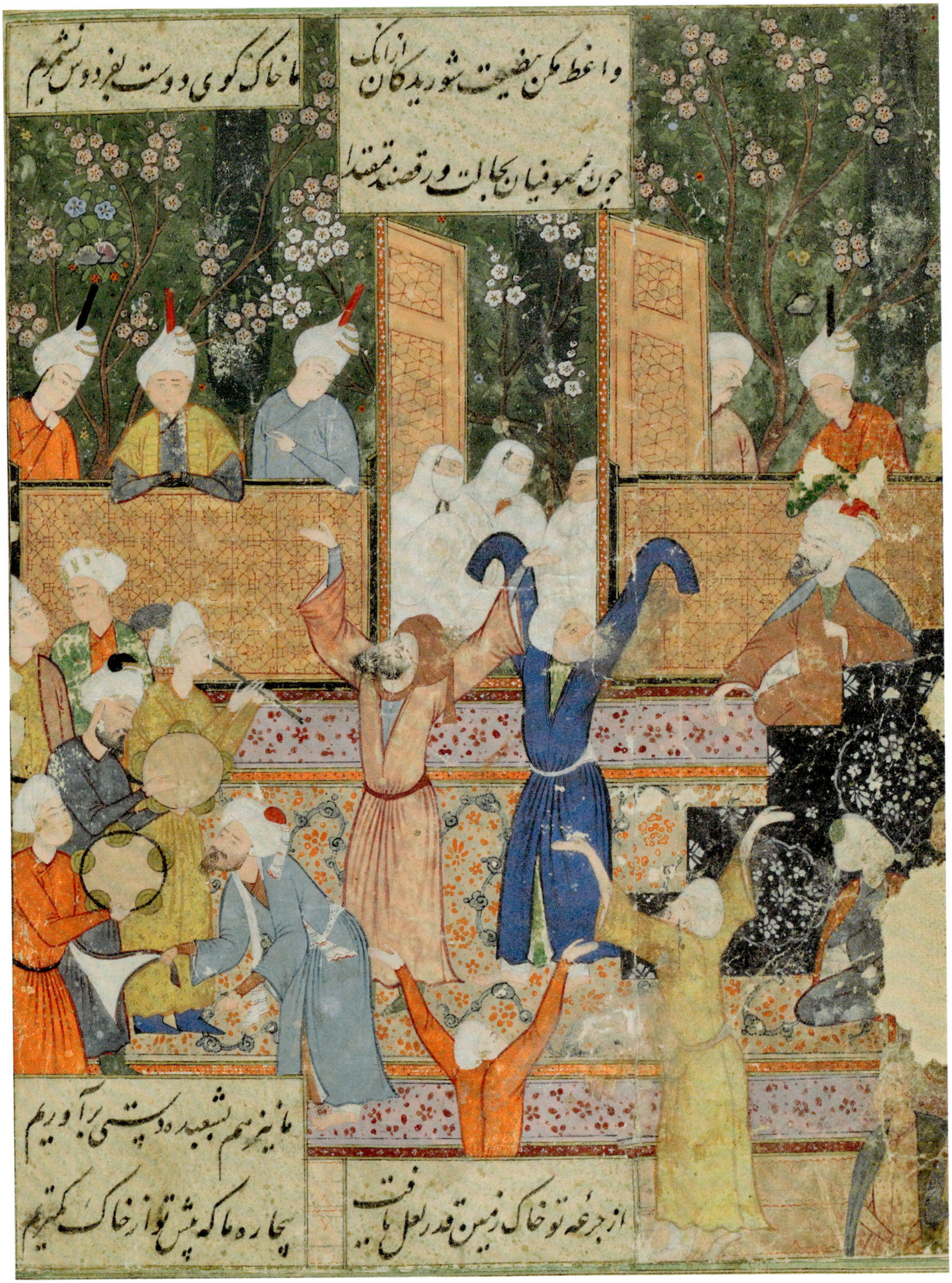

FIGURE 22

An ecstatic dance of the dervishes. From the *Divan* by Hafez, 1540–50.

He even compares a palace to heaven:

> It looks like a palace, that stands built of a heavenly substance, firmly established, with ends that lie afar, shining in its body of ruby over the three-thirds (of the earth); it is like a garment inlaid with stars, made of a heavenly substance, that Mazda puts on, along with Mithra and Rashnu and Spenta-Armaiti, and on no side can the eye perceive the end of it.[73]

In *Ashi Yasht,* Ahura Mazda invites Ashi to a palace which is located between the earth and heaven: "Ahura Mazda answered: 'O fair and wise Ashi, go not back to the heavens, sink not into the earth! Stay here and walk inside the fine kingly palace.'"[74]

Another structure associated with the concept of heaven in Zoroastrian texts is the throne. In contrast to the building, the throne appears constantly in Zoroastrian texts such as *Ardavirafnameh,* in which it is described as a portable plinth for angels:

> Afterwards arose Vohuman, the archangel, from a throne made of gold, and he took hold of my hand; with the words "good thought" and "good word" and "good deed", he brought me into the midst of Ohrmazd and the archangels and other holy ones, and the guardian angels of Zartosht Spitama, Kai-Vishtasp, Jamasp, Isadvastar the son of Zartosht, and other upholders and leaders of the religion, than whom I have never seen any one more brilliant and excellent.[75]

In *Ram Yasht,* a golden-roofed throne in the palace of Kvirinta is described: "Unto him did the three-mouthed Azhi Dahaka offer up a sacrifice in his accursed palace of Kvirinta, on a golden throne, under golden beams and a golden canopy, with bundles of baresma and offerings of full-boiling [milk]."[76] The throne is also described by Ardaviraf in his dream-journey as the place where the souls of the pious, bathed in their ever-increasing radiance, resided.[77] The throne is usually accompanied by golden carpets which symbolize hierarchy.[78] Even the souls of agriculturalists are in thrones located in splendid palaces, before the spirits of water and earth, trees and cattle.[79]

The throne is explained as the first reward given to the righteous in heaven.[80] Ardaviraf describes these thrones as the main setting for souls:

> I also saw many golden thrones, fine carpets and cushions decked with rich cloth, on which are seated the souls of householders and justices, who were heads of village families, and exercised mediation and authority, and made a desolate place prosperous; they also brought many conduits, streams, and fountains for the improvement of tillage and cultivation, and the advantage of creatures. And as they stand before

> those who are the guardian angels of water, and of trees, and also of the pious, in great power and triumph, they offer them blessings and praise, and repeat thanksgivings. And it seemed to me very sublime.[81]

He specifies the users of these thrones: "I also saw the souls of the faithful, the teachers and inquirers, in the greatest gladness on the splendid throne. And it seemed to me sublime."[82] In *Ram Yasht,* a similar throne is illustrated: a structure made of gold, under a golden canopy.[83] In the *Bundahishn* (Primal Creation), which is an account of cosmology, written in the eighth and ninth centuries and reflecting ancient Zoroastrian and even pre-Zoroastrian beliefs,[84] the throne of Ahura Mazda is described: "Above the Sun, he created the Throne of the Beneficent Immortals, which is attached to the Endless Light, the Throne of Ohrmazd. These, too, are the six stations of the six creations, just as the creations of material life are six."[85] The concept of throne, although it seems to be irrelevant to gardens in a Zoroastrian context, becomes very important in religious narratives in the Islamic age. The potential influence of late Zoroastrian texts on Islamic texts is also very probable.

THE QUR'AN

Although silent about the occurrence of garden and pavilion together, ancient Near Eastern literature and sacred texts highlight the concept of the garden in this region, a motif that was further developed after the advent of Islam. What is common to all these texts is the significance of nature, which forms the foundation for the concept of paradise as a garden. The development of the concept of heaven in the Pahlavid texts most probably took place under the rising influence of Christianity in the Sassanid territories. The increasing power of the Christians, especially on the western borders of the Sassanid empire, which were under the control of Sassanid kings and the Magi, encouraged the Zoroastrian clergy to compile and revise their religious documents. This rivalry is reflected in several Zoroastrian texts written in the Sassanid age, as in the fifth book of *Denkard,*[86] in which Adar Frobag, a practitioner of virtue and a guide to the religion, defends Zoroastrianism against Christianity.[87] It is contended by scholars such as Boyce that this rivalry resulted in serious revisions, intended to specify rules and regulations which were missing in early Zoroastrian texts.[88] It should be emphasized that, despite the influence of the Christians, the concept of the Garden of Eden and paradise (as a garden) never merged in Sassanid texts. Moreover, while the Garden of Eden in the *Story of Genesis* referred to the garden from which Adam and Eve were exiled, the heaven described in Zoroastrian fragmentary texts never pointed to the existence of any particular garden or natural landscape even though they were very specific in terms of the spatial and conceptual qualities of heaven. Nor were the garden and natural elements accompanied by a building or structure. However, the concepts of paradise as a garden, heaven and the Garden of Eden were to be developed and unified in the next important religious text in this region, the Qur'an.

The Qur'anic imaginary paradise was clearly built on three major concepts established in pre-Islamic texts: heaven as the final destination, the Garden of Eden as Adam and Eve's home, and the holiness of nature and its components – rivers, trees and plants. But the Qur'an made an important contribution to the development of this imaginary concept: not only did the *ferdows* represent both heaven and the Garden of Eden, but it was promised as a 'reward' to the righteous. This garden was no longer conceptual, but depicted as a real space with very specific design qualities and elements such as shaded areas, running water and evergreen trees. At the same time, the Qur'an was the first sacred and religious document in this region to talk about the existence of buildings and thrones from which people could have a pleasant view to the garden. While the gradual dominance of Muslims in territories from Spain to China disseminated the idea of Persianate gardens, the pre-Islamic gardens in Achaemenid and Sassanid Persia worked as actual examples of this conceptual model (the heavenly garden). The development of the idea of garden as paradise led to a cultural synthesis in which gardens (including pavilions) not only played significant roles as spaces for restoration in the arid climate of the region, but also reflected the celestial heaven. These two factors influenced Persian literature, especially poetry, which usually combined two layers of meaning: real and metaphorical.

The Concept of Enclosure

The Qur'anic words used for paradise are *'illiyun,*[89] *jannat al-khalid,*[90] *ferdows,*[91] and *rawdha.*[92] What is significant here is to note the difference between Eden, as the dwelling place for Adam, and the all-embracing paradise at the end of time. Both these concepts become the same and indistinguishable in the Qur'an.[93] The Qur'anic garden has clear boundaries and main entrances and gates through which selected people enter. Faithful men are told: "Enter ye the Garden ye and your wives in (beauty and) rejoicing."[94] In "gardens of perpetual bliss, they shall enter there as well as the righteous among their fathers, their spouses and their offspring, and angels shall enter unto them from every gate."[95] The gates are opened and closed to control circulation: "And those who feared their Lord will be led to the Garden in crowds, until behold they arrive there; its gates will be opened, and its keepers will say: Peace be upon you! Well have ye done! Enter ye here to dwell therein."[96]

Having gates shows that the garden is enclosed[97] to protect the people inside: "As to the Righteous (they will be) in a position of Security."[98] The boundaries of the paradise are clearly defined by Lote trees: "Near the Lote-tree beyond which none may pass. Near it is the Garden of Abode."[99] The paradise doorkeeper (*ridhwan*) controls the movement of people and their entrance.[100] All this control is provided to ensure that only the faithful make it inside.

Natural Elements

The paradise garden is recognized by its magnificent natural elements. There are lofty trees[101] to create shade, under which people sit on carpets[102] on cushions set in rows.[103] Beneath this garden run rivers:

> For them will be Gardens of Eternity; beneath them rivers will flow; they will be adorned therein with bracelets of gold, and they will wear green garments of fine silk and heavy brocade; they will recline therein on raised thrones. How good the recompense! How beautiful a couch to recline on![104]

The main purpose of these rivers is to create peace in the garden: "But those who believe and work righteousness will be admitted to Gardens beneath which rivers flow to dwell therein for aye with the leave of their Lord; their greeting therein will be: Peace!"[105] These rivers are full of "incorruptible" water, milk and wine that are probably symbols of profusion and peace and calmness:

> (Here is) a Parable of the Garden which the righteous are promised: in it are rivers of water incorruptible; rivers of milk of which the taste never changes; rivers of wine a joy to those who drink; and rivers of honey pure and clear. In it there are for them all kinds of fruits and Grace from their Lord. (Can those in such Bliss) be compared to such as shall dwell forever in the Fire and be given to drink boiling water so that it cuts up their bowels (to pieces).[106]

The Qur'an stresses that there is no sense of weariness in such a garden, thus making the connection between garden and restoration: "There no sense of fatigue shall touch them nor shall they (ever) be asked to leave."[107] The unobstructed views mentioned earlier suggest that the pavilion may be located in the middle of the garden (necessarily the centre) or on a higher level ("in a Garden on high").[108] The Qur'an emphasizes the enormity of the garden: "Be quick in the race for forgiveness from your Lord, and for a Garden whose width is that (of the whole) of the heavens and of the earth, prepared for the righteous."[109] Within this eternal garden,[110] promised to the faithful,[111] no one will be bored or tired. Perhaps that is why its natural components such as fruits, plants, trees and water are in constant change, to make it an exciting place for its inhabitants. Entering such a 'promised garden' and its pavilions would have been an appealing prospect for anyone, especially for people whose life was mostly spent in a harsh climate.

Architectural Elements in the Qur'anic Garden

The Qur'anic paradise is mostly interpreted as a garden, while the few verses of the Qur'an which refer to a pavilion (palace or mansion), indirectly confirm the existence of such a structure. For instance, in the following verse, a palace, rather than a garden, is promised to the righteous: "But it is for those who fear their Lord. That lofty mansions, one above another, have been built; beneath them flow rivers (of delight); (such is) the Promise of Allah. Never doth Allah fail in (His) promise."[112] The operative term here, *ghurfa* (literally meaning chamber, palace and upstairs room), is thus automatically associated with the concept of the garden of paradise. The pavilion or mansion (*sarh* or *qasr*) is located in this garden on a high terrace: "In a Garden on high."[113] The pavilion or palace in the paradise garden (*ferdows* or *rawdha*) is not described in a clear way; however, descriptions of similar buildings in a non-paradisical context in the Qur'an may clarify how the paradisical versions were imagined.

The pavilion in general appears in two different forms, for either temporary or permanent use. The word *sarh*, referring to the permanent structure, is used for towers, as when Pharaoh says: "Make me a tower that I may mount up to Moses' God"[114] or "Build for me a tower that haply so I may reach the cords."[115] The same word is also used to mean palace, which is paved with crystal (*qawarir*):

> She was asked to enter the lofty Palace, but when she saw it, she thought it was a lake of water, and she (tucked up her skirts), uncovering her legs. He said: "This is but a palace paved smooth with slabs of glass." She said: "O my Lord! I have indeed wronged my soul; I do (now) submit (in Islam), with Solomon, to the Lord of the Worlds."[116]

Crystal in this palace, which is used horizontally and not vertically, suggests transparency. That is probably why Mohsin Khan (an interpreter of the Qur'an) has described this palace as one with a glass surface under which water moves. Another word used in the Qur'an is *masane'* (plural), which refers to anything man-made and artificial (in contrast to natural): "And do you get for yourselves palaces (fine buildings) as if you will live therein forever."[117] Two other words which refer to temporary pavilions are *kheymeh* (tent) and *sardaq* (large tent). For example, "Companions (*houris*) cloistered in [cool] pavilions (*al-khiyam*)."[118] The second term, *sardaq* (singular) or *suradiq* (plural), is mostly used to convey a negative meaning; a location in hell where a pavilion is created by fire.[119]

In contrast, the word *beyt,* which literally means house, is used to denote houses in the garden of paradise.[120] In one of the clearest references to a building in the paradise garden, the wife of Pharaoh asks God to build for her "houses in paradise".[121] Another word for pavilions in gardens is *masakin* (literally, habitations):

> Allah has promised to believers, men and women, gardens under which rivers flow to dwell therein and beautiful mansions [*masakina*] in gardens of everlasting bliss. But the greatest bliss in the Good Pleasure of Allah: that is the supreme felicity.[122]

In addition to palaces, other structures such as thrones are widely referred to. The throne is where righteous people can sit and enjoy the garden: "Reclining in the (Garden) on raised thrones they will see there neither the sun's (excessive heat) nor (the moon's) excessive cold."[123] The word throne – *'arika* (singular) or *'ara'ek* (plural) – appears forty times in the Qur'an.

For example, God's throne is described in al-Baqara: "His throne doth extend over the heavens and the earth, and He feeleth no fatigue in guarding and preserving them for He is the Most High, the Supreme (in glory)."[124] His throne is the sign of splendour: "He the Lord of the throne (of Glory) Supreme!"[125] Similarly, in the story of Joseph, his parents are put on a throne which is a symbol of respect: "And he raised his parents high on the throne (of dignity), and they fell down in prostration, (all) before him."[126] Even God is symbolically placed on a throne: "Verily your Lord is Allah, who created the heavens and the earth in six days, and is firmly established on the throne (of authority), regulating and governing all things."[127] The location of God's throne is specified as on the water: "He it is who created the heavens and the earth in six days and his throne was over the waters."[128] The raised throne is also an integral part of paradise, where the righteous can recline and enjoy their time.[129] The faithful are promised to "be in groves of (cool) shade, reclining on thrones."[130] From this place, the inhabitants can have a view of all sides of the garden: "On Thrones (of Dignity) will they command a sight."[131] These verses show that the Qur'anic paradise is conceived as a garden with built areas and mobile objects for its residents.

PERSIAN POETRY

Persian poetry, though not literally descriptive in many cases, reflects the significance of gardens and pavilions and the relationship between the built and natural environments, and to some extent clarifies the cultural associations of gardens and pavilions. Despite its roots in creativity and imagination (but not necessarily observation) and its high degree of complexity of meaning, poetry has the ability to reflect the cultural views of the relationship between the pavilion and garden. At the same time, most poems which mention garden and pavilion in different forms and contexts are open to interpretation. This ambiguity and abstraction is the result of two factors: the use of a wide and somewhat fluid terminology for garden and pavilion, and the mystical aspects of Persian poetry, which make elucidation difficult. Most terms and verses do not carry stable meanings, and consequently cannot necessarily be translated to architectural language.

The three discrete reasons behind the extensive use of the garden in Persian poems are poetry's capacity to describe actual gardens and their natural elements, the garden's unique quality to be compared with tangible beings such as the beloved, and the significance of gardens in cultural affairs.[132] In other words, the garden in poetry plays two simultaneous roles: descriptive and metaphorical. Gardens are not only described in the poetry, but also praised because of their spiritual and metaphysical value. Even portrayals of actual gardens, such as that of Malek Shah, which is described by Mo'ezzi, are quite exaggerated and do not usually have much historical significance.[133]

In this section, I will explore different aspects of gardens and pavilions in relation to their settings and users by analysing the works of Persian poets from the tenth to the eighteenth centuries CE. All the poems discussed here are my own translations, in order to guarantee uniformity while attempting to highlight the literal, and to some extent metaphorical, meaning of the verses, and, at the same time, considering their relationship to the main theme of the whole poem. My main criterion in the translation process was to avoid getting into complex mystical and philosophical readings. My analysis is based on a comprehensive search of the key terms discussed in the next section in the *Dorj Electronic Database of Persian Literature* (2006), which includes 178 books written by 101 Persian poets, rather than in published material. The verses discussed here are selected from over 1,650 verses that somehow address gardens and garden pavilions. It should be emphasized that a thorough study in this field will require a series of in-depth etymological, linguistic and chronological studies, which can uncover various layers of meanings by researching the stylistic trends in literature, the biographies of poets, the patronage behind the poetry, the poetry's audience, and the cultural context in which the poetry was generated, as well as comparing literature with the archaeological and historic evidence.

The transcriptions and transliterations in this chapter and the others follow the *Iranian Studies Journal* scheme.

The Issue of Terminology

The first, and probably the most challenging, step in the analysis of gardens in poetry is to suggest clear and useful definitions for the garden and pavilion. The diversity of terminology is apparent in the vocabulary for gardens and pavilions in Persian literature. The following words are used to name gardens as a whole or planted areas: *bagh*, *golestan*, *bustan*, *golzar*, *golshan* and *chaharbagh*. According to the linguist 'Ali Akbar Dehkhoda (1879–1959), the word *bagh*, which has roots in the Pahlavid language, is usually used to identify an enclosed garden, where there are fruit trees, flowers and vegetables. It has also appeared in modified forms such as *bak* and *bag* in local dialects in northern and central regions of Iran.[134]

The word *bagh* is comparable to the word 'garden' in the English language in terms of its general meaning, and does not impose any specific design or function. This term is also used in poetry to describe the face of the beloved and God's paradise, from which Adam and Eve were exiled. The other four words, *golestan*, *golzar*, *bustan* and *golsha*, not only have similar meanings but also similar structures. All four are combinations of a term and a suffix which means 'place'. Thus, *golestan* is a combination of *gol* (flower) and *stan* (place), *golzar* of *gol* (flower) and *zar* (place), and *bustan* of *bu* (scent) and *stan*. They all refer to a place full of flowers and plants (a flower garden or a flowerbed) and, despite public perception, do not transfer any specific meaning in terms of design, but simply focus on planted areas inside gardens. In other words, these terms do not indicate a garden in which a building is constructed. In rare contexts, they are employed as adjectives for built environments: "I see your *iwan* [which is] filled with flowers." In some contexts, the word *bustan* (or *bostan*) means orchard. In contrast to these terms, *chahar-bagh* and *hasht-bagh*, literally meaning fourfold garden and eightfold garden respectively, clearly impose a certain layout. The *chaharbagh* (*charbagh*) is mostly used to describe the fourfold pattern, which was the major layout for the construction and design of gardens for centuries after the Achaemenids.[135] The *hashtbagh* was used once in a poem by Khaqani Shervani (1100–85) to mean paradise (*behesht*).

The English word pavilion is used here to cover a variety of terms used in Persian literature and historical documents. For example, in Farsi (Persian) the following terms have been used to describe an architectural structure in a natural setting: *kushk*, *'emarat*, *khaneh*, *qasr*, *talar*, *kakh*, *kheymeh*, *sardaq* and *khargah*. Depending on the context, these words refer to the use of the pavilions as kiosks, palaces, houses, or simply as places for relaxation. While some of these terms (*'emarat, khaneh, qasr, moshkuy, sarai, shabestan, taq, iwan* and *kakh*) refer to the pavilion as a permanent structure, the other terms (*kushk, kheymeh, sardaq* and *khargah*) refer to temporary structures in gardens. Their usage in different occasions and places illustrates the variety of cultural views on pavilions and gardens. At the same time, this rich vocabulary does not always reflect actual differences in real structures and could be the result of poetic elaborations.[136] This fact differentiates 'Onsori's poetry, which describes a historic Ghaznavid garden, from Ferdowsi's, in which the garden is more imaginary but still based on his observations, and Rumi's verses (1207–73), in which a garden refers to the mystical paradise. The term *'emarat* is used in Persian literature as both a name and verb. As a verb, it means 'to flourish', 'to be cultivated', and 'to make habitable' and as a noun means a building or building complex which is (usually) brand new.[137] It has been used along with garden (*bagh*) only in two cases in Persian poetry. Adib Farahani writes, "They filled their pockets with gold [money] and bought horse, carriage, garden, and building." Sa'eb Tabrizi (sixteenth–seventeenth centuries) also uses them together: "The universe has made people busy with the material world, they just think on their gardens and buildings."

Among the terms mentioned above, *'emarat* has a more general meaning because it refers to any type of building and is frequently used in historic texts and not in creative writing. The next category of words for pavilion includes *qasr, moshkuy, shabestan* and *talar.* In contrast to *qasr* (palace), the words *moshkuy* (the harem of the royal women), *shabestan* and *talar* (main columned hall in the palace) refer either to specific spaces in a palace or to palaces themselves. All these nouns refer to royal structures built for administrative purposes. As Hafez (1315–90) writes: "The palace was full of plants and flowers and the palace was full of royal furniture." Sa'di (1184–1291) writes: "The garden is built and inside it there is a lofty *iwan* and palace." He also says: "In the middle of the garden, which is full of trees and flowers, there is a palace made of jewels in the garden of paradise." The next category of terms includes *khaneh* and *sarai*, both of which mean house and home. Although these words are also used to name palaces, in most cases they refer to the residential purpose of the building. In the Timurid age, the terms *kakh* and *qasr* were replaced by *sarai*, which became common in Central Asia and Mughal India. Anvari Abivardi (1126–89) writes: "Thereafter, I will be in the corner of a dark house, I have missed [my] garden and [my] house." Naser Khosrow (1004–88) considers his home to be a combination of house and garden: "The garden is yours; the house is yours; my home is yours."

Words which denote pavilions include *kakh* and *kushk. Kushk* is what is known as kiosk in English, and has roots in the Zoroastrian word, *kaozhdaka.* In the Zoroastrian text of *Aban Yasht,* Anahita is described as having a golden crown with 100 stars (*ashta-kaozhdaka*), shaped like the body of a chariot, with pennants/ribbons and a prominent rim.[138] The second term, *kakh,* which nowadays refers to any type of palace, originally meant a huge kiosk. While the word *kushk* is rarely used in poetry along with garden (*bagh*), *kakh* is frequently used in combination with *bagh*. This may be because of the rhythmic harmony between these two words (*bagh* and *kakh*) and the rhythmic difficulty of using *kushk* in poetry. Here are some examples. Anvari Abivardi writes: "I wish the day and night would become longer in such a [beautiful] palace, garden, and sky." The famous Persian poet, Ferdowsi (940–1019), writes: "[He] entered a garden in the corner of which a palace was located." Daqiqi (d. 977) also uses *kushk* in his poetry to refer to a palace: "When will the wind bring the scent of the flowers from the garden to the palace?"

In contrast to the words for pavilions discussed above, all of which refer to permanent structures, *kheymeh, khargah* and *sardaq* refer to tents, which varied in size. In contrast to *kheymeh*, which is quite simple and easy to erect, *khargah* and *sardaq* refer to huge and complex tents, which may even contain smaller tents inside them. Examples of these huge tents, described by Clavijo, are discussed in Chapter 4. In the poetry, on the other hand, pitching tents (*kheymeh*) in gardens is mentioned. For example, Sana'i (eleventh–twelfth centuries) writes: "How long are you going to stay in the mortal garden; Come into the immortal house [of paradise] and erect your tent (*kheymeh*) among flowers." Amir Khosrow Dehlavi (1253–1325) writes: "Now, we should pitch [a] tent in the garden near the water." Mojir-uddin Beylaqani (d. 1190) even compares the space inside and outside tents: "Come out of the tent (*khargah*) because the garden is prettier than a beautiful face." This verse indirectly indicates that the tent is located inside a garden.

Although the words *taq* (arch or entrance) and *iwan* (verandah) refer to components of buildings, in some cases, they mean whole buildings. The *iwan* literally refers to the intermediate space between the garden and the building and the symbolic connection between the garden and pavilion. Ferdowsi, who uses this word widely in his *Shahnameh*, writes, "They went to the garden from the *iwan* [and] celebrated there for three weeks." Sa'di writes, "The garden and flowerbeds are made where a huge palace and an *iwan* are located." It is interesting to see that in this verse, he distinguishes between *bagh* and *bustan*, and between *qasr* and *iwan*. Fakhr-uddin As'ad Gorgani indirectly refers to the existence of buildings in gardens when, in *Vis o Ramin*, he writes: "[Suddenly] the palaces and *iwans* may get ruined, the gardens may become flat (get destroyed)." He also invites his host to play music in the royal palatial garden: "You, as host, start playing music in this royal *iwan* and garden."

Another word that that needs to be mentioned here is *takht*, which is usually used in various contexts and meanings. In some cases, it refers to the fancy packsaddles on animals and pavilions on camels, while in others it is the royal throne in the palace (or the garden) or a couch (a sitting place in the garden). In the majority of poems in which a *takht* in a garden is mentioned, it refers to a throne. For example, Amir Mo'ezzi (1048–1125) writes: "The king is like the sun and his throne is the seventh sky; he is the paradise and his garden is like God's heaven." Ferdowsi writes: "He ordered to bring the royal throne to the royal garden." He also refers to the placements of thrones in the garden: "The garden was so full of trees that they couldn't locate the king's throne there." In general, the use of such complex and diverse terminology by poets has to do with the widespread use of gardens in social affairs as well as their cultural value. Moreover, their widespread use in Persian poetry and prose reflect their importance in the daily lives of people.

THE CHARACTERISTICS OF GARDENS AND PAVILIONS

Gardens as Properties

The majority of contemporary studies on gardens in Persian literature emphasize the metaphorical, spiritual, symbolic, or even religious aspects of Persian gardens.[139] While there is no doubt of the symbolic use of gardens in poetry as a sign of freshness and beauty, a comprehensive review of Persian poetry confirms a dominant materialistic view of gardens and pavilions. This notion is supported by several poems which refer to gardens and pavilions as the properties of kings or other people. Established terms such as *qasr-e shahi* (royal palace) and *bagh-e shahi* (royal garden), which are frequently repeated in the poetry, are witness to this claim. Moreover, using these terms reveals the poets' tendency to highlight the social class of the owners of gardens and pavilions. In several verses, the garden is considered the symbol of the material world, in contrast to the eternal world after death (paradise). This suggests that, in poetry, the perception of the garden as a symbol of paradise or the Garden of Eden is quite inconsistent.

The same worldly vision is applied in describing the pavilions and palaces inside gardens. For example, according to Ferdowsi, the freshly decorated *iwan* (*khoram iwan*) is the symbol of wealth and happiness. Molla Hoseyn Feyz Kashani (1597–1675) talks about the value of gardens as properties: "In [life] the thieves are always lying in ambush [to grab your] wife, children, property, house, store and garden." Naser Khosrow complains about mortality of life and one's belongings: "Why do you put yourself to so much in trouble [in your life], because you won't own your garden and house [forever], never, never!" In another verse, Adib al-Mamalek Hamedani (968–1007) extols the abundance of furniture and ornamentations in the pavilion. Such materialistic vision may also refer to the economic value of these gardens as resources for fruit and flowers. In that sense, the view used in writing these verses is comparable to that of the *Code of Hammurabi*, in which gardens are considered major properties.

Gardens and Cities

The relationship between the garden and pavilion and the city is emphasized in some poems. Two types of gardens are mentioned in Persian poetry: those outside and those inside the cities. Anvari Abivardi speaks about his stay in a garden which was apparently located outside the city: "[Since] I was in the garden for [several] years, [I] did not see the city." Similarly, Nezami Ganjavi (1141–1209) writes: "The wind came with a light in its hands; [It also] brought the gardener from the garden to the city," or "Nezami came to the garden from the city; decorate the garden [in his honour]." The garden inside cities is also explained in poetry, especially in Ferdowsi's *Shahnameh*. He writes, "If you pass by, you will see a city full of flower fields, gardens, palaces, and buildings." Seyda-ye Nasafi writes about a garden in Bukhara: "There is a garden in the city of Bukhara; [which is very] famous in the city." Likewise, Jami (1414–92) writes: "If you come to the city, I will prepare the garden and the house for you." The location of the garden could be related to two factors: the agricultural and the social use of gardens. However, generally speaking, its whereabouts are not very clear. Unfortunately, the analysis of poems does not clarify the relationship between the use of gardens (as places for pleasure or agriculture) and their location inside or outside the city.

The social life inside gardens and pavilions, on the other hand, is mentioned frequently in the poetry. In several verses, we read about music ceremonies and drinking parties. Ferdowsi repeatedly writes about royal celebrations and parties in the garden: "He ordered [them] to prepare food and wine and decorate the building in the garden." Gorgani (eleventh century) also writes: "Now [you] host a party in the royal garden and pavilion." The social function is emphasized, especially when pavilions take the form of palaces and accept administrative purposes. We can see notions of this concept in Ferdowsi's poetry, for instance when he writes about the presence of the king in the garden: "When the king of the world comes to the garden; let me enter to see the hidden world [interior of the pavilion]." He also mentions doing administrative work in the garden and pavilion: "He went to the pavilion and wrote the letter; [then] he went to the garden and planted a tree."

In literature, gardens are also considered symbols of victory, luck, the power of the government, and even freedom within the country. For example, Adib al-Mamalek Farahani writes: "He has a very tall cypress tree in the garden of victory." Similarly, Khaqan Shervani writes: "Phoenix reached the garden of luck and Soleyman sat on the throne of greatness." According to some poets, a good garden is the symbol of a developed city; for instance, Ferdowsi writes: "When he saw the thriving city, he reached Siavash's garden and pavilion." Rumi's verse is another example: "We don't want this building and garden, nor these good wives and peace and safety [any more]." Farrokhi Sistani (960–1037), too, compares cities to gardens and palaces: "The cities of Baghdad and Basreh are [like] your palace; the fields of Amol and Sari are [like] your garden (they all belong to you)." In Rumi's *Masnavi,* the garden is considered the symbol of freedom and even is contrasted (compared) with prison: "Every house without light is [in fact] a prison, not a garden." These examples implicitly demonstrate that gardens and pavilions are representations of the wealth, prosperity, beauty and social class of their owners and residents.

The Psychological Benefits of Gardens

One aspect which might have an impact on the design and placement of the pavilion is the psychological benefit of gardens as areas for relaxation, meditation and restoration. These benefits are related to three major activities which can happen in the garden and the pavilion: walking, beholding and sleeping. The similar terminology used to describe sightseeing (*tamasha*) and walking (*gardesh*) makes it difficult to differentiate between these experiences in the poetry. For example, Sa'eb Tabrizi (1601–76) writes: "The point of roaming in the garden is to get upset; in fact our [real] pleasant garden is inside the house." He also writes: "It would be fine if you don't come out of the mirror house because you have [such] a pleasant garden in your face." As is clear, Sa'eb Tabrizi attempts to offer an indirect comparison between the house and garden. This kind of conceit is typical of the style (so-called *Hindi*) used by Sa'eb, and his contemporaries in the Mughal court, who initiated a complex new form in Persian poetry.[140] Hazin Lahiji (1692–1766) talks about watching natural transformations: "There have been springs; now watch the autumn in the garden." In another example, Farrokhi Sistani writes: "The country (*molk*) is like a garden full of flowers and blossoms; you come to the garden joyfully to sightsee." Nezami writes: "The man went to the garden each week to view it."

As we have seen, the garden is even compared to the face of the beloved. Seyda-ye Nasafi writes, "Let me see your face; the fruit garden won't lose anything by being watched [by others]." However, Jami explains that being in the garden without the beloved is not enough: "I went to the garden to find calmness; missing you in my heart made me [more] sad." Similarly, Forughi Bastami (1798–1857) says: "The spring came and I am [still] bored because the garden without you is the place of boredom." Sheykh Kamal Khojandi (fifteenth century) also writes: "Without watching your face, my eyes are worthless; going to the garden to sightsee is useless." Muhammad Asiri Lahiji talks about his desire to walk in the garden because he is weary of staying indoors: "In the house of separation, I have become lonesome; my desire is to roam in the garden of your presence." While the view from the pavilion is not clearly brought up in the poetry, the use of the garden and pavilion as places for relaxation and sleeping is stated in several verses. For example, Fakhr-uddin As'ad Gorgani writes: "He brought me to the garden from the palace and laid me there", while Qavami Razi (twelfth century) says: "I enjoy my [presence] in the pavilion of the garden with the wine and the beloved, like a smiling flower and strutting cypress." In another poem, he even uses a sexual reference in describing the presence of beautiful ladies in the garden as the representation of delight and entertainment: "The cypresses in the garden and flowers in the grass are like beautiful ladies on an *iwan*."

The restorative use of garden and building is also related to social activities within them, such as music concerts and drinking parties. Ferdowsi writes: "From the *iwan*, they went to the garden; they played music there for three weeks." Nezami writes: "He has a party in the house and garden." And Attar Nishapuri (1145/46–1221) enthuses: "Prepare the party in the garden and make this house a paradise full of music." According to Dehlavi, the pavilion (*sarai*) is located under the shadow of trees: "The land never saw the sunshine through the branches of trees; look at the house which is under the shadow of the garden." He completes this image in another verse: "There is the shadow of clouds in the garden and water is under that shadow, my beloved and I sleeping under this shadow." People use both garden and pavilion to sleep in. However, Seyda-ye Nasafi complains about the noise, which does not allow him to rest: "In the garden I cannot sleep, because repeatedly I hear the noise of the gardener's walking feet." Sa'eb Tabrizi is even more unhappy: "The nightingales in the garden cannot rest and sleep because of my moaning." However, Naziri Nishapuri (1560–1612) points to the significance of relaxation in the garden: "[In such conditions] how can we stay in the secluded corner of the garden?"

The residential use of gardens is emphasized in several poems. Nezami Ganjavi calls his garden the home: "My garden is yours; my house is yours; my home is yours!" He is opening his home (including garden and house) to a friend (the beloved). He equates the garden with the house: both together make up the home. Residential use of the garden becomes possible not only by erecting buildings, but also by pitching tents in the garden. Mojir-uddin Beylaqani talks about one of these tents: "Come out of the tent to the garden because it is more beautiful than the face of the beloved." Amir Khosrow Dehlavi writes: "Now we should pitch a tent in the garden near the creek", while Rumi suggests: "Today the idols (beautiful ladies) will pitch tents in the garden; we will go there to watch them!" Salman Savoji (fifteenth century) says: "The king immediately left the *golestan* (flower-planted area) and went to the tent." Sana'i Ghaznavi compares mortal and immortal gardens as places to live in: "How long do you stay in the mortal garden because of your stupidity? Come to the immortal house (place) and pitch a tent in flowers." What is significant about this poem is that the term *sarai* (house) automatically means "garden and house" together. Ferdowsi even compares a tent to paradise: "[They] decorated the tent like the garden in spring; it is like paradise in colour and ornamentation." Khaju Kermani (1280–1352) writes: "Whoever sees you coming out of the garden will ask why she pitched [her] tent outside paradise (why she is leaving the garden)."

The Pavilion in the Garden

The pavilion as a residence or building is widely praised in Persian prose and poetry, where it is even described as a gem (*negin*). For example, Amir Mo'izzi writes: "Under such moonlight, the garden is honoured to have such a building." Farrokhi Sistani believes that building a house can refresh the whole garden: "Today my friend told me to erect a house because the garden is [now] dark, lifeless, yellow (faded), and empty of visitors." Attar compares the pavilion and paradise: "There is a palace in front of the garden which is made of silver and gold." Similarly, Khaqan Shervani writes: "If you haven't seen the paradise, take a look at the king's garden and his palace." Hatef Esfahani (eighteenth century) compares an ideal city to the paradise garden in terms of beauty: "This city is one piece of the paradise palace (*qasr-e jenan*) and the paradise garden (*bagh-e jennat*)."

In most poems, the building and garden are separated from each other; for example, Ferdowsi writes: "They went to the garden from the building; they [celebrated and] played music there for three weeks." 'Obeyd Zakani (d.1370) writes: "Look after wine and go to plain fields; since the flower is planted in the garden, [you] cannot go to the house." This separation is clearer in Salman Savoji's poetry: "Leave the house and go to the garden." Daqiqi writes: "Sometimes, the wind brings the scent of flowers from the garden to the palace." Manuchehri Damghani (eleventh century) urges: "How long are you going to stay in the palace? Come to the garden because the spring has arrived!" Farrokhi Sistani, similarly, writes: "This is a pleasant garden and a pleasant house; congratulations to the king for [having] such a garden and palace!" Anvari Abivardi says simply: "He granted me many gardens and palaces." All these examples show that, for these poets, the garden is considered to be separated (but not isolated) from the building. In sum, the term garden (*bagh*) never means "garden and pavilion" together.

The connection between the garden and pavilion could be questioned in a different way: which is built first, the garden or the pavilion? Jami answers this: "It is better to make the building of justice in the garden of government using religion and wisdom." Likewise, Qatran Tabrizi (1009–72) writes: "Following your command, I made a new palace in my ancestors' garden." In contrast, Naser Khosrow writes: "I make a palace with my poem and [then] make garden and *iwan* with its verses." Here, for Khosrow, the palace is compared to the outline of the poem, which contains the *iwan* and garden: in other words the palace (*qasr*) automatically means *iwan* and garden (*bagh*) together. The building usually shows the same qualities as the garden; put differently, it is directly influenced by the garden. For instance, Ferdowsi writes: "Following the garden, the *iwan* brought spring inside", while in another poem, he says: "Like the garden, the pavilion was filled with spring." Fakhr-uddin As'ad Gorgani talks about the same influence in a different way: "The garden has the colour of the spring, the *iwan* is paradise." In some verses the building and garden are contrasted as representations of solid and void; for example, Va'ez Qazvini writes: "Sometimes [I] think of the palace and pavilion; sometimes [I] talk about the gardens and *bustans*."

Sometimes, the pavilion is described as a palace in the middle of the garden. Salman Savoji writes: "In the middle of the garden of trees, there is a palace like a jewel in paradise", and "[He] saw a great palace in the centre of the garden." Attar, too, talks about the connection between the building and garden: "There is a garden in front of the palace which is [even] better than paradise." This location in the middle of the garden may refer to the high degree of protection, privacy and invisibility it afforded for the residents. In a few examples, however, the structure is located at the corner (*gusheh*) of the garden, which may also indicate its separation from the planted area. For instance, Ferdowsi says, "[He] entered a garden in the corner of which a palace was located."

A perfect garden pavilion should be huge in height. Ferdowsi states: "[The city] was full of gardens and pavilions, which were as high as the sky." Sa'di writes: "[He] has built gardens and very tall pavilions and palaces inside them." The *iwan* is usually a transparent area that has a view of the garden. The pavilion, usually located on a higher level, has a platform in front of it, which allows views of the garden. In some cases, the royal platform could be placed on the *iwan*. Perhaps that is why Ferdowsi writes: "He ordered [the servants] to bring the royal throne to the garden." Attar writes: "In front of the garden, there is an arch (palace) as tall as the sky; there is a throne on the verandah." Va'ez Qazvini writes: "The [mystic] poverty is like a high *iwan;* if you visit it, you will become the king and see the whole garden of the world." The pathway in the garden is important because it is how people can enter the planted area from the built environment or vice versa. Rumi states: "We have a pathway from the house to the garden; we are neighbours of cypress and jasmine flowers." This pavilion is usually decorated, full of furniture, and ready for public and social events. For example, Adib al-Mamalek Hamedani remarks: "The garden was full of flowers, cypresses and box trees; the palace was full of royal furniture." At the same time, the garden could be filled with couches (*takht*) and carpets to accommodate social events. Rudaki Samarqandi (859–941) describes the garden being prepared for a ceremony: "The other day, the king ordered [the servants] to decorate the garden and placed the couches and spread the carpets." Sana'i, similarly, writes: "The garden is full of sofas and the meadow is full of carpets." In this garden, according to Jami, one can "recline on the couch and eat fruits." These poems indicate the social aspects of gardens and pavilions as well as their symbolic value as reflections of royal power and wealth.

CONCLUSION

The study of literature from the pre-Islamic age to the eighteenth century clearly shows the evolution of the concept of garden and pavilion as cultural and religious themes, as well as the main contexts for social life. The pre-Islamic texts gradually formed the concept of paradise as a garden. While, in the *Epic of Gilgamesh*, the emphasis is put on the elements of nature and their beauty, the *Enuma Elish* discusses the story of creation and the significance of the god of water, Enki. Gardens play a different role in the *Code of Hammurabi*, which treats them as mere properties, not spaces for enjoyment of the beauty of nature. The *Story of Genesis* develops these ideas, offering a more comprehensive view of nature, which is fully integrated with the concepts of the Garden of Eden and heaven. Furthermore, it provides a specific (albeit vague) layout in which four rivers define the Garden of Eden.

The reflection of the concept of heaven in Zoroastrian texts compiled in the Sassanid age (after the *Story of Genesis*) shows the widespread influence of these beliefs in the region. While, in the *Story of Genesis*, the Garden of Eden referred to the garden from which Adam and Eve were exiled, the heaven described in Zoroastrian fragmentary texts did not refer to any particular garden, even though they were very specific in terms of the spatial and conceptual qualities of heaven. Although these early Zoroastrian texts were written in a slightly different cultural context, they carry the same basic concepts as the early Mesopotamian texts, but develop them more fully. These texts stress the symbolic effect of rivers on the earth and the sacred role of plants, flowers, trees and water as elements to be worshipped and purified. In addition, the *Story of Genesis* and Sassanid Zoroastrian texts, for the first time, integrate the concept of heaven (*vahishto*) with the story of creation, which had already appeared in the *Enuma Elish*. While these texts do not directly discuss the pavilion structure in gardens, they clearly reflect the development of the prevailing cultural view on gardens in the region.

All the pre-Islamic literature, despite its diversity, has one feature in common, namely, the lack of reference to any building or any other structure in the garden. The Qur'an, however, not only integrated the concepts of paradise as a garden and, specifically, the Garden of Eden, it offered a very clear description for the paradise garden (*ferdows*) as the reward to the righteous, and also discussed pavilions (buildings and thrones) as specific places from which people could have a pleasant view of the garden. The development of the idea of the garden and pavilion as paradise resulted in its cultural synthesis in Persian literature, especially poetry. By developing a detailed, specific and rich vocabulary, the poetry extensively used the concepts of garden and pavilion both literally and metaphorically. This rich vocabulary not only defines gardens and pavilions and specifies their uses, but also draws a clear boundary between them. Furthermore, even though the garden and the pavilion are praised for their spiritual value, their reflection in the poetry reveals, at the same time, their symbolic value in terms of temporal wealth and power. The language used in mythological, religious and creative writing highlights the cultural association of gardens and pavilions and their development through history, but does not draw a clear picture of the pavilion in relation to the garden nor define it clearly.

3

The Garden and Pavilion in Persian Art

GARDENS and pavilions, as significant cultural elements, are reflected in Persian miniature painting, sculpture and carpet. The few surviving examples of kiosk sculptures and the wide range of garden carpets are witness to this claim. In contrast to sculpture – which, because of religious restrictions, was not highly developed – Persian miniature painting flourished widely, mainly because it was ideally suited to depicting the lifestyle of the royal court and illustrating scenes from Persian prose and poetry, such as Ferdowsi's *Shahnameh* and Sa'di's *Bustan* and *Golestan*. The development of miniature painting was also the outcome of widespread royal patronage, which began in the Ilkhanid era and proliferated in the Timurid and Safavid periods. This special passion for painting – whether of religious or secular subjects – among kings and khans and their families was based on a dominant cultural trend and on their fascination with Persian literature. It also reflected the capacity of painting to show off the grandeur of the court and the ostentation of the royal lifestyle. In other words, painting was used as a tool not only to enliven imaginary figures and to tell stories in visual form, but also to combine them with real characters, lives and events. The reflection of reality in painting, however, depended on the artists' personal interests, the patrons' aesthetic expectations, contemporary stylistic movements, and the cultural context behind the paintings' creation.

This chapter contributes to the study of Persian gardens and three common forms of the pavilions found in them – building, kiosk and tent – through a detailed analysis of miniature paintings, the majority of which were produced in the Ilkhanid (1256–1335 CE), Timurid (1370–1507 CE), Safavid (1502–1736 CE) and Mughal (1526–1858 CE) periods. While the examples discussed here are not intended to elucidate the historical development of the pavilion, comparing the images with the texts they illustrate serves to clarify the concept of the pavilion, the relationship between the garden and the built environment, and the use of the garden and pavilion in the Persianate world. Although most of these paintings may not have stemmed directly from the artists' daily observations, matching the material discussed here with descriptions of gardens and pavilions made by historians and travellers could well reveal hitherto hidden aspects of the subject. It is important to note that the features applied to pavilions in paintings characteristic of particular periods and places should not be generalized to other periods and places. This reflects the cultural diversity of the region, especially between the fourteenth and eighteenth centuries.

An in-depth study of depictions of Persian gardens and pavilions in miniature art requires an understanding of the historical and cultural context of the paintings, the style of the artist, the influence of the client on the work, the narrative accompanying the painting, and the degree of realism applied to a given piece. I will concentrate on examining these factors while avoiding more conventional discussions of 'style' as opposed to 'content'. It is not my goal in this chapter to provide a chronological narrative of the evolution of the pavilion in Persian gardens, but rather to clarify the design concepts utilized and the nature of the cultural synthesis underlying their appearance in art. I draw heavily on Lehrman's model for the study of Islamic garden architecture, which treats the elements of order, space, form, texture, pattern, light and movement as major design concepts.[1] However, before analysing the iconography of the pavilion and garden in Persian art, it is necessary to offer a brief outline of the development of Persian painting.

PERSIAN PAINTING: THEMES AND CHRONOLOGY

The garden became institutionalized in Persian painting from the fifteenth century onwards. One of the preeminent historians of Islamic art, Oleg Grabar, categorizes Persian miniature painting according to seven themes: history, religion, animals, epic, lyric romanticism, realism and ornament.[2] Although these thematic categories are somewhat fluid and overlap each other, they help to classify Persian paintings and to give a clearer understanding of their context. The depiction of history begins with the manuscripts of the *Jami' al-Tavarikh* (Great Chronicles) composed under the direction of Rashid-uddin (1247–1318), the grand vizier in the Ilkhanid court. It was later encouraged by emperors who were interested in representations of themselves and their courts. Several illustrated books, such as the *Majmu' al-Tavarikh* and the *Zafarnameh*, were produced to capture significant events of history.[3] Despite the mystical aspects of Persian culture, religion as a theme appears infrequently in Persian painting, although it seems that the ascension of the Prophet Muhammad was an interesting topic for painters, perhaps because it enabled them to use their imagination in depicting a religious scene while enjoying freedom of interpretation. In addition to the *Me'rajnameh*, which was wholly dedicated to religion, sections of other books such as the *Shahnameh* dealt with religious themes.[4] The appearance of animals in painting is the outcome of the artists' fascination with the hypothetical conversations among animals narrated in the *Kalileh va Damneh* – the animals symbolizing humans and their interactions, and the complications and delicacies of human relations.[5] Among these categories (history, religion and animals), only the paintings dealing with history provide a setting for gardens. There is also only limited use of the garden as a theme or background in the Ilkhanid paintings, mainly because they are more concerned with the historical significance of gardens and less with their aesthetic aspects or with landscape settings.

The garden is also extensively reflected as a background in illustrated epics, which form the biggest category of the miniature paintings. The epic existed in two forms: oral – in collective memory – and written collections. The most significant epic in the development of Persian book painting was the *Shahnameh* (Book of Kings), its different versions providing significant sources of inspiration for artists. The *Shahnameh* was written by Abul Qasem Ferdowsi between 975 and 1025, and was especially significant in attempting to highlight glorious moments of Persian history and culture after centuries of Arab and Turkish dominance.[6] Copying, rewriting and illustrating the *Shahnameh* was strongly encouraged, more than five centuries after the death of Ferdowsi, by Shah Isma'il, the founder of the Safavid dynasty, and his successors, as an influential device to unify Iranians against their Ottoman and Uzbek neighbours. Lyric representation in miniature painting began in the eleventh century, with the support of the court. Parallel to the development of Persian poetry it was used as a tool to adopt and support some of the stories, to give life to their characters, and to enrich their settings through visual language. Several books by famous poets – especially Nezami (1141–1209), Attar (1142–1220) and Hafez (fourteenth century) – were illustrated, over time, by miniaturists.[7]

Paintings in the next category, naturalism or realism (not to be confused with the Western use of such terms), are usually based on observations of daily life and on representations of human figures, objects and spaces, while still being based on Persian literature, especially on works which seem more realistic and less fictional, such as the prose and poetry in *Bustan* (The Orchard) and *Golestan* (The Rose Garden) by Sa'di (1210–1291/1292). Common perception notwithstanding, Persian painting is not merely figurative or necessarily based on narratives, but in many cases has a purely ornamental role. This form of painting, appearing on the surfaces of clothing, walls and objects, aims simply to adorn them and thus make them more valuable.[8] Even though gardens and pavilions appear in all these categories of painting, the large number depicted in the epic and in lyric romanticism proves that, here, a stronger context is provided for their study.

The earliest paintings in the region were produced just before the Arab invasion in Soghdian Central Asia (seventh and eighth centuries CE) in Panjikants, Afrasyab, Balalykh Tepe, Varahsha and Ajina Tepe.[9] They mostly depict religious themes in places of worship, palaces and private houses, and are usually figurative, excluding landscape or garden scenes. The Ilkhanid period can be seen as the age when Persian painting proper emerges. The dynasty was founded by Hulagu, the son of Genghiz Khan. The invasion of Baghdad in the west and good political relations with China in the east enabled Hulagu and his successors, such as Ghazan Khan, to have access to an extensive artistic heritage and tradition, and exposure to a variety of tastes. Moreover, employing Persian viziers such as Rashid-uddin, who were patrons of Persian art and literature, made Persian culture more accessible to the Ilkhanid court.[10] Political strength resulted in the accumulation of wealth, which gradually fostered a culture of royal patronage of art, and especially of painting.

The most significant illustrated manuscripts generated in the Ilkhanid period are the *Manafi al-Hayawan* (The Benefits of Animals), the *Asar al-Baqiyah* (Remains of the Past), the *Jami' al-Tavarikh* and the *Shahnameh*.[11] These manuscripts, although produced in the same political period, show a wide variation in terms of colour, composition and size of elements in the frame. Furthermore, the political relations between the Ilkhanids and the Chinese are reflected in the paintings, where the figures and landscape clearly show Chinese influence.[12] For instance, rocks, monumental trees and large hills are certainly components which do not belong in Persianate gardens. The fall of the Ilkhanids (1335–36) led to the emergence of several local dynasties in different regions of Iran, such as the Jalayerids (from the late 1330s up to the early 1500s), and this complicates the categorization of the manuscripts produced by artists in these areas: widespread patronage involved diverse cultural tastes and interests. Famous works generated in this period are several versions of the *Shahnameh*, the *Kalileh va Damneh*, the *Divan* (collection of poems) by Khaju Kermani, the *Garshaspnameh* (Tale of Garshasp), the *Bahmannameh* (Tale of Bahman), the *Munis al-Ahrar* (Free Men's Companion) and the *Ketab-e Samak-e Ayyar* (Tale of a Mischievous Fish).[13]

The invasion of Persia (Iran) by Tamerlane in about 1390 was accompanied by widespread destruction and massacre. However, Timur's successors showed an interest in art and architecture and shaped a strong tradition of patronage, which led to the establishment of workshops for artists (*ketab-khaneh*) and to the formation of guilds (*senf*) in large cities such as Tabriz, Shiraz and Herat.[14] Achievements of these institutions can be seen in history manuscripts such as the *Jami' al-Tavarikh* (Great Chronicles) by Rashid-uddin, the *Zafarnameh* (Book of Victory), the *Me'rajnameh* (Book of the Ascension of the Prophet

Muhammad), the poems of Khaju, and the *Shahnameh*.[15] The death of Shahrokh (Timur's grandson) in 1447 led to the division of the political realm into two parts: western Iran and Iraq with Tabriz as the cultural capital, and the east with Herat as the capital. The painting associated with Herat was dominated by the patronage of Mir 'Ali Shir Nava'i, Qasem 'Ali, Aqa Mirak and Behzad. It was the glorious age of Persian painting, when significant manuscripts such as the *Zafarnameh*, the *Mantiq al-Teyr* (Language of the Birds), *Bustan*, and the *Khamseh* by Nezami were produced.[16] These paintings create an established relationship between the pavilion structure and garden; however the Chinese landscape still remained the consistent background in the majority of them.

The Safavid dynasty was founded by Shah Isma'il (1487–1524), who attempted to revive Iranian/Persian glory by unifying the fragmented empire after the decline of the Timurids. The widespread royal interest in reviving an Iranian identity brought about a special passion for Persian art, architecture and literature. The illustrated manuscripts were tools to amplify the beauty of Persian literature while developing a universal intercultural language. Behzad (1450–1535)[17] who had already began painting in the Timurid court in Herat, joined Shah Isma'il's court and influenced, inspired and taught many younger painters, who produced thousands of illustrated folios such as the *Shahnameh* by Ferdowsi, the *Divan* by Hafez, the *Khamseh* (Quintet) by Nezami, and the *Haft Awrang* (Seven Thrones) by Jami.[18]

It was the first time that artists and painters had found an independence from the court and princely ateliers, and their paintings acquired economic value and were treated as commercial objects. At the same time, the wars between the Safavids and Ottomans resulted in the exchange of many Persian artists, masons and architects, who had much influence on Ottoman art and architecture. In terms of pavilion and garden, Safavid painting continued the Timurid traditions without demonstrating any specific chronological evolution. Since the second century of the Safavid Empire, most of the artists had emigrated to India where the Mughal court provided great patronage for Persian art and literature. This trend resulted in the development of the Mughal style of painting, which is comparable to late Safavid painting in its use of three-dimensionality. Around this time, Sunni Central Asia, including the Uzbeks, gradually separated from the Shi'ite realm and continued to paint based on the Behzadian style.[19]

THE GARDEN IN PERSIAN PAINTING

Most miniature paintings showing gardens or parts thereof are comprehensive enough to suggest some general information on the garden layout. The garden in miniature painting is illustrated in three forms: as the main setting (in the form of a garden or natural landscape), in close relation to a building, and in the background (out of focus). This classification is very significant in the study of pavilions because it prevents generalizations and misinterpretations. Before studying the pavilion and its depiction in Persian painting, a clear understanding of its setting, the garden, is needed. The close relationship between the pavilion and garden in most paintings indicates their interdependence and their influence on each other.

The garden in painting works as the intersection of natural, built and social environments. In order to explain the social functions and cultural associations of the garden, it should be ascertained whether the painting refers to a specific story, an epic, a spiritual or mystical poem, direct observation by the artist, or simply idealized scenery to satisfy the artist's patron, probably the king or emperor.[20] In addition to the contextual factors, technical and stylistic aspects such as the use of colour, line, composition and symmetry or asymmetry play a significant role in determining the geometric or natural layout of the garden and its connection to other elements such as the pavilion and figures in the painting.[21] Parallel to the stylistic factors are the elements that the artist uses to define architecture or landscape design, such as water channels, pools, flowerbeds, planted and paved areas and pathways. In sum, the appearance of garden or pavilion layouts in art is not only the result of the faithful depiction of architectural elements but also of the artist's overall approach in terms of arranging and designing scenes, buildings, structures, nature, human figures and objects.

There are two general types of garden layout illustrations in Persian painting: the naturalistic and the geometric. In the naturalistic garden (natural landscape), which frequently appears as the main setting for narratives, elements such as rocks, ponds, water channels, trees and flowers are arranged in a natural fashion rather than a geometric pattern, although where the captured landscape has an organic and natural design, it could be part of a larger garden with a geometric pattern. The natural setting is visible in numerous paintings such as two sixteenth-century paintings, one depicting a night banquet in a garden (Figure 1), and another depicting the king and his courtiers based on a story from the *Shahnameh* (Figure 2). Some elements such as rocks have nothing to do with real Persian gardens. The composition and form of the rocks in these paintings, which resemble Oriental drawings, shows a strong Chinese influence, which initially occurred during the Ilkhanid age. The 'natural garden' model also appears in other forms of art such as tiles, and several from the Safavid age use it as the main setting for drinking parties and friendly meetings (Figure 3). Making these tiles seems to be part of a larger attempt to bring natural art (in contrast to abstract art) to the interior of secular buildings.

In contrast, in the 'geometric' or formal garden, the natural components of the garden such as water channels, trees, flowerbeds, pools or planted areas and pathways are laid out in a geometrical fashion,[22] and components of landscape design are aligned, parallel or perpendicular. An example of the latter model (formal garden) is the *chaharbagh* pattern depicted in an illustration of Babur's garden in Kabul, the Bagh-e Vafa, from the 1590 edition of the *Baburnameh* (Figure 4).[23] According to this work, Babur gave very specific instructions

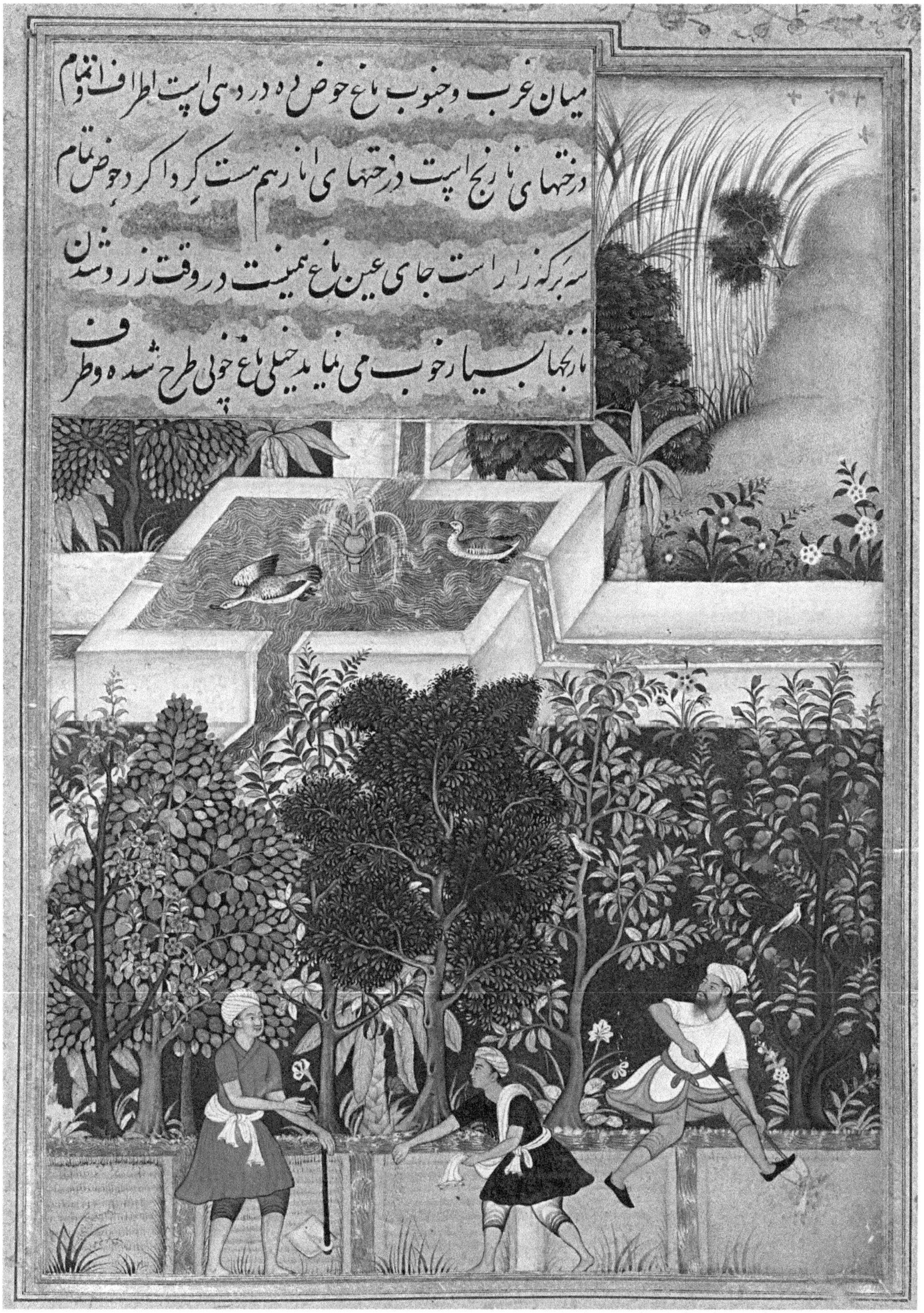

FIGURE 4

The Gardens of Fidelity (Bagh-e Vafa). From *Vaqi'at-e Baburi*, India, 1590.

regarding the design and construction of his royal garden, its orientation and irrigation. The *chaharbagh* also appears in other illustrated versions of the work. Another instance of the *chaharbagh* appears in a painting from *Bustan* by Sa'di, which illustrates the Soltan of Syria, Malek Salih, on a throne in his garden, interviewing two dervishes whom he met the evening before in a mosque (Figure 5).[24] In this painting, different layers of story are depicted: during the interview, the Patriarch Abraham entertains a fire-worshipper at a meal, while a stupid man saws off the limb of a tree on which he is sitting, to the amazement of onlookers.

The elements of these two kinds of garden are combined in an unrealistic way in some paintings. For instance, a painting from the *Shahnameh* depicts a designed water channel in a natural setting (Figure 6). This painting shows the introduction of chess to Persia. The envoy of the Hindu Ray of India brought the game with him when he came to pay tribute to the Shah Nushirvan. The envoy challenged the Shah by saying that he would only affirm the Shah's sovereignty if he could work out how to play the game and beat him in a match within a week. The Shah agreed and asked the most astute sages in his court to examine the game. At the last minute, the wisest of his wise men, Buzarjumehr, discovered the rules and beat the Ray envoy at his own game. After that Buzarjumehr invented the game of backgammon and sent it to the Ray with the same challenge, but he could not figure it out. In this spring-like painting, the violet hills are located above lively pairs of trees. The old man plays with the Indian in the middle, while courtiers take up the lower part of the scene, sitting with a picnic by a stream which flows into a pool.[25] The geometric form of the fountain and channel does not seem realistic at all: the fountain appears to be more of a formal element to frame the painting and also to combine natural and formal gardens in an imaginary manner. The composition emphasizes the water channel as the main focal element. This painting, as well as many others that depict natural settings, reflects the nomadic life style of rulers in the region. They show various activities such as royal feasts and parties, cultural ceremonies, political negotiations and leisure pastimes.

The development of the garden in terms of its form, and its origins in Persian and Chinese garden design traditions, is a matter for further research. Here, however, the focus is on the layout of the garden in relation to the architectural elements. The pavilion in Persian miniature painting appears in three different forms varying in scale: building, kiosk and tent.[26] What is common among these typologies is the separation between the 'built' and 'natural' environments so that, in most paintings, there is a clear boundary between the pavilion, the garden (with its natural components) and human figures as individuals or groups. The separation of areas in the garden and the addition of a pavilion structure as the focal point of the painting enables the artist to define and emphasize a specific zone within the garden which is higher in terms of social hierarchy. This focal point is further defined by innovative use of colour, form and composition.

BUILDINGS IN GARDENS

In Persian miniature painting, the building is depicted in three forms: as a pure volume, which is surrounded by the garden, as a background for the garden, and as foreground. A look at the garden in paintings based on narrative poetry indicates that the first type of building usually functions as a private house within the garden, while the other types work as public space for administrative affairs, social meetings and ceremonies. The first emphasizes the building as pure volume and solid element, while the others emphasize either the interior space or the *iwan*, the intermediate and semi-open space between the building and garden. The relationship between the building and garden also depends on the viewpoint of the painter and his position inside the room or in the garden. In some cases – such as in the paintings of Soltan Muhammad (active 1505–50) – the exterior walls of the building have been removed, so that the artist may illustrate the private affairs and events inside the building. This phenomenon demonstrates one way in which the artist's choice of viewpoint might change the contents within the frame. In this chapter we will consider the various types of relationships between building and garden in Persian painting: garden as a vague background, garden as the main focus, building and garden separated, and garden and building merged.

The presence of the garden as a consistent image reveals its cultural significance as the main setting for daily life, social events and administrative affairs. In Persian painting, most gardens can be divided into two sections: the planted and the built areas. The planted area, which is in most cases a naturalistic setting without any geometric order, acts as a backdrop for the main subject of the painting, that is, the building and paved area with pool, carpets and other furnishings. This concept (garden as a background) features in the majority of paintings, especially in the works of Behzad and his students, even in scenes illustrating the interior of a palace or house. Central courtyards or interiors depicted in paintings usually belong to houses, or occasionally to palaces and courts. Going inside the building enables the artist to observe intimate affairs that do not normally happen in the garden or on the *iwan*. In other words, these paintings usually illustrate secret aspects of people's lives such as love, sex, or even murder. For example, a painting based on *Sobhat al-Abrar* by 'Abdol-Rahman Jami[27] shows the sick king being treated and cured by the royal doctor and his courtiers (Figure 7). Through the window is a view of the garden behind the pavilion.[28] An image from the *Shahnameh* (1560) shows Eskandar disguised as a legate, with a portrait of himself, before Queen Qaydafa in a palace in a garden (Figure 8). Although the left side of the image depicts the interior, the right side shows the balcony and the door. The exterior is, however, illustrated in a way to suggest that the people in these areas have a view of the interior. In contrast to paintings that concentrate on the interior of the garden or garden pavilion, others show the building from outside while putting the garden in the background. These usually depict stories related to public or external relations or that have to do with the city. For instance, in a painting based on 'Abdol-Rahman Jami's *Panj Ganj*, by Qasem 'Ali (1521), the entrance to the garden where Yusof welcomes Zulaykha for a feast is emphasized (Figure 9).

In all these cases, windows or doors frame the garden or the planted courtyard behind the building. Using the image of the garden, which is usually symbolized by one or two trees with blossoms or flowers, the artist is able to bring the outdoor garden to the inside of the building, creating a lighter, more transparent, interior. Enlarging and increasing the number of windows enhances the connection between outside and inside, and floral patterns on windows became a common device, although it is possible that these patterns do not refer to the garden as such but rather work as formal and decorative elements representing natural aspects in the interior of the buildings. In other words, although the narrative poem does not necessarily refer to a garden or natural setting, artists attempt to diversify the interior space, which usually lacks vegetation, by adding a window through which trees and flowers are visible. In the story of the assassination of Khosrow the artist of the Hermitage edition of the *Khamseh* (1431) by Nezami depicts the interior of the building – the bedroom – with views to the garden outside as if the palace is located in the middle of the garden (Figure 10). The lack of walls makes the bedroom look like an *iwan* connected to the central courtyard, but we can assume that it is just a visual modification of the interior space to depict private affairs.[29] The inside of the building with a vague view of the garden is repeated in several other paintings from the same *Khamseh* since all the stories occur in a room with a window to a garden.[30] The same view of the interior is used by Kamal-uddin Behzad (1528) to illustrate the festivities for the return of Timur to Samarqand, where Timur, the central figure, watches women dancing (Figure 11). Behind him a view of the garden can be seen through the two windows, indicating that this palace is set in a garden.[31] In none of these cases do the poems make references to gardens. This indicates that the artist is using the garden view as a formal element in the painting. Different visual interpretations of the same narratives from the *Khamseh* depict the exterior of the pavilion rather than the interior. It is evident that the poetry leaves scope for the imagination of the artist, who need not be limited to its literal contents.

While in many illustrations the garden is treated only as a vague background and secondary element, in some paintings it becomes the focal point and the centre of attention. This is usually a reference to the narrative (prose or poetry), which mentions the garden as the main setting, but occasionally it is an addition by the artist, one which enables him to offer a wide range of spaces in terms of openness, form and colour, as well as landscape elements such as pools, trees and plants. The fact that many artists, including Behzad, Aqa Mirak and Soltan Muhammad, worked in royal courts and most probably observed encampments in gardens, suggests that some of these scenes may refer to the artists' direct observations.

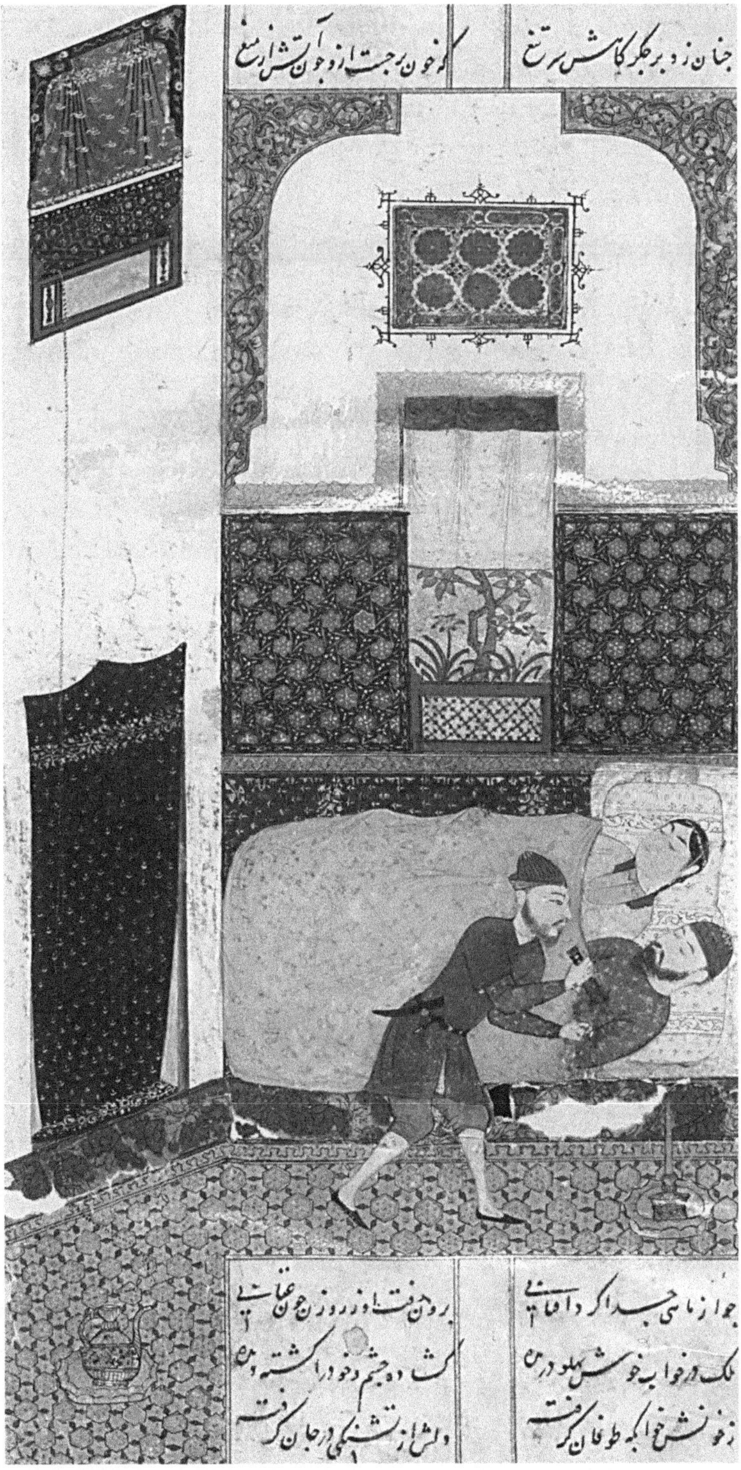

FIGURE 10

The assassination of Khosrow. From the *Khamseh* (Five Poems) by Nezami, 1431.

For example, a painting by Maqsud (1521) from *Panj Ganj* shows an excursion in a garden (Figure 12). Here, the railings separate the built and natural areas. The built area is occupied mostly by women and musicians, while the servants are placed in the natural area, which may denote a lower spatial hierarchy. The garden in such paintings acts as the main place for gatherings, meetings, drinking parties, royal concerts, religious discussions, or even for communal prayers.

In all these cases, the pavilion is treated as a secondary element in the frame, or as a compositional tool that defines the garden, usually with sharp edges to separate it visually from the garden or courtyard. For example, a fifteenth-century painting by Qasem 'Ali from Mir 'Ali Shir Nava'i's *Hayat al-Abrar* (1495) depicts Khajeh 'Abdollah Ansari preaching and teaching disciples (Figure 13) in a courtyard that could be part of a mosque, *madrasa*, or even a private residence. In order to focus on the preaching scene, the artist uses geometry to place the master, Khajeh 'Abdollah, at the focal point and seats the students in a semicircle around him, to make plain the hierarchy of the figures.[32] Using the garden as a place for discussions and meetings is visible in another illustration (1562–63) based on Sa'di's *Bustan*, which depicts the story of a young physician in the city of Marv (Figure 14).[33] The only tree in this painting divides the frame into two equal parts and works as a tool to identify the centre of the narrative, the physician who is curing his patient.

The garden can also be physically separated from the building or the paved area next to it with a railing or a light, transparent barrier which still enables the visitor to view the garden from the pavilion. Is this barrier a consistent component in garden design, or a stylistic element applied in miniature painting? The lack of archaeological evidence for such railings, and their absence in travellers' notes, confirms their formal role in paintings:[34] the fence or railing is there to clarify the 'built' zone of the garden, which includes the pavilion and paved area, and to differentiate it from the planted area. In other words, the fence or the railing defines the boundary of the building area, which functionally belongs to the pavilion. Moreover, except in few cases, it also defines the boundary for social interactions, parties and ceremonies. For example, a painting from the *Khamseh* (1539–43) shows Khosrow and Shirin listening to stories told by Shirin's maidens. Here, the railing and fence separate the planted and paved areas (Figure 15).

In several illustrations, there is a sharp edge, which separates the building from its context and pushes the garden to the background, although the equal emphasis on the building and courtyard could make these two parts equally important. In a painting associated with a manuscript of Sa'di's *Bustan* (1488), depicting the friendly gathering at the court of Soltan Hoseyn Bayqara in Herat, the hexagonal pavilion and adjacent paved area appear completely separate from the garden (Figure 16). Although the level

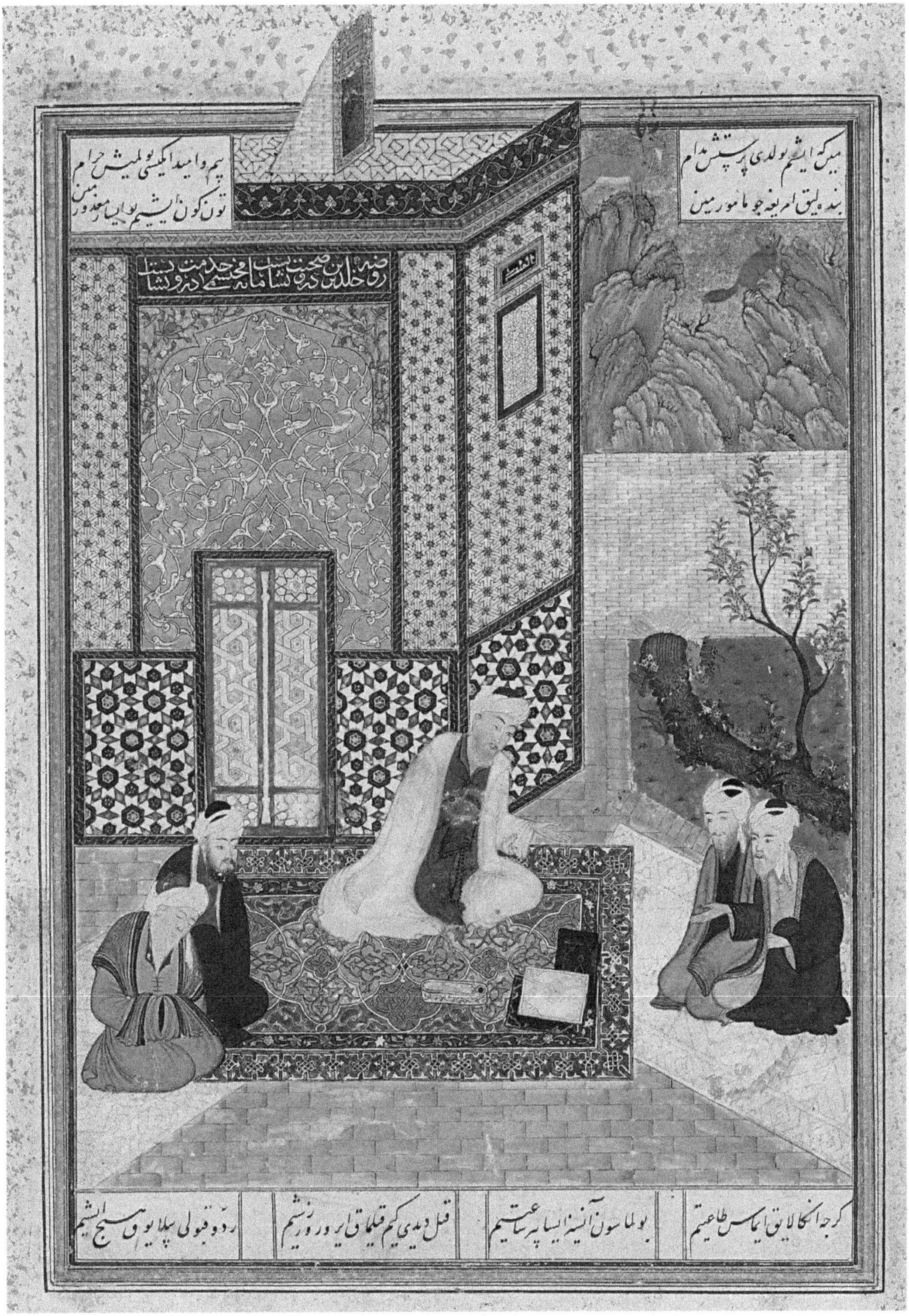

FIGURE 13

Khajeh ʻAbdollah Ansari teaching disciples. From *Hayat al-Abrar* by Mir ʻAli Shir Navaʼi.

of visual connection to the planted area is limited, the open door reveals the presence of the garden behind the built area.[35]

In contrast, some paintings show no clear visual boundary between the building (solid) and the garden (void). Such interdependence of garden and pavilion in painting occurs not only as the result of adding an intermediate space (*iwan*) which acts as a connector between the open and closed spaces, but also through the figures scattered between building and garden. Several elements may be used to forge this connection, including thrones or kiosks; occasionally, even minor details, such as dishes of fruit or wine glasses placed in the lower level while the king is sitting on the *iwan,* create a visual link between garden and pavilion, or define an invisible sense of movement and motion between the *iwan* and the paved area next to it.

The unification of outdoor and indoor spaces can be seen in a painting from Soltan Ibrahim Mirza's *Haft Awrang* (1556–65),[36] in which a father and son are playing chess. Here, the *iwan* and the paved area, including the pool, work as visual links between building and garden (Figure 17). The pathway in mid-frame, which is defined by a railing, leads to an octagonal foundation in the paved area. In addition, the distribution of figures in both the paved and planted areas creates an invisible connection between the building and garden.[37] The *iwan* containing the throne is usually two or three steps above ground level. Seated in this elevated position, the king may enjoy observing his courtiers, guests, musicians and even ambassadors, while being entertained by servants inside or outside. In a painting by Soltan Muhammad from the *Divan* by Hafez, depicting the beginning of the feast of 'Id at the end of the month Ramadan, the prince's throne works as a visual connector between building and garden (Figure 18).[38] While the focus is on the people attending the feast, the portrayal of moon-watchers on the roof and the gardeners working in the background garden helps to define different layers of story, as if the gardening never stops (this is a scene common to many paintings). The low railing and fence, highlighted in white, are weak enough to maintain the unity of the garden. Moreover, the merging of the rows of seated figures on the ground and those standing on the roof stitch together the building and garden.

The 'connecting' role for the throne in the pavilion may be seen in another painting, probably by Shah Tahmasp's artists (1539–43), depicting the enthronement of Khosrow. Here, the pavilion, including its portico, is unrealistically transparent, with the garden clearly visible through it (Figure 19).[39] It appears that all spaces are used to praise the main patron for this painting, Shah Tahmasp. The inscription on right of the throne means "May he be prosperous", and on the left and over the portico "May he be happy". Inscribed over the pavilion is "O Lord protect the sovereignty of the mighty Soltan, the just Khaqan, the most just and most noble Soltan, the son of a Soltan, the victorious Soltan Shah Tahmasp al-Husaini al-Safavi Bahadur Khan, may Allah perpetuate his kingship and his sovereignty for ever." This painting, like many others in which the focus is on the garden, is framed with borders decorated with designs in gold of birds, animals, mythical beasts, trees and plants, as if the garden is extended out of the main frame. Similarly, in a painting attributed to Sheykh Zadeh Mahmud Mozahheb (under Behzad's supervision) from *Farhad va Shirin* by Mir 'Ali Shir Nava'i (1495), the kiosk creates a connection between two palaces and defines a semi-open area between the two buildings (Figure 20).[40] The courtiers sitting in the pavilion garden create an invisible vertical movement, which leads to the door and connects the planted and paved areas. The artist enhances the depth by putting the entrance in the foreground, leaving the courtyard and the garden as the middle-ground, and the servants' house in the background.

THE FUNCTION OF THE BUILDING

Serving somewhat like captions, the text accompanying miniature paintings generally reveals that the buildings associated with gardens are either houses as private domains or palaces as semi-public domains. Unlike public administrative or ceremonial spaces, the private residence in miniature painting tends to have less ornamentation and decoration; it also usually lacks the *iwan*, and the physical and visual connection between the inside and outside is established through a limited number of doors and windows or a balcony. The private residence is commonly depicted as a solid volume fully isolated from its setting, while the palace is usually interconnected with the garden around it. Whether an inside or outside view is chosen for a private residence depends on the story behind the painting. The outside view, which appears rarely, generally refers to social events in which the residents are involved, while the inside view usually illustrates private affairs, events and stories. These buildings usually belong to high-ranking people or royal families.

The majority of paintings disclose the administrative and social function of the garden and the pavilion (palace) inside it. This is shown by depicting parties, royal feasts, enthronement ceremonies, religious and administrative meetings, dance parties and drinking ceremonies.[41] For example, numerous paintings based on stories from the *Shahnameh* or *Khamseh* illustrate feasts in royal gardens. That such social events took place in Persianate gardens is confirmed by historians including Eskandar Monshi, the secretary of Shah 'Abbas, who talks about the Sa'adat Abad Garden in Qazvin as the main setting for administrative and royal meetings, encampments, and even the reception of foreign ambassadors.[42] Another kind of social activity appears in an early Safavid painting (1525–30) from the *Shahnameh* of Shah Tahmasp, in which the Shah's wise men approve of Zal's marriage (Figure 21). Welch believes that the setting and costumes, which show groups of courtiers using stylized gestures, sitting, standing, watching, working in the garden, or just talking, are idealized rather than being true-to-life depictions of contemporary life.[43] This last painting demonstrates one of the major features of Persian miniature painting, namely, the presence of people as both individuals and social groups. Such paintings are valuable not just because they depict beautiful or naturalistic scenes or gardens, but because they show activities and events associated with gardens, and the people involved in them. This unique quality makes the painting an appropriate context for 'layers' of stories. These overlapping tiers of interactions and activities require structures and spaces to provide appropriate settings in which to depict the actors.

Gardens are frequently used as the main settings for motion, movement, interaction and exchange in the court, as well as religious meetings and gatherings among spiritual masters and their students. The majority of paintings based on religious/mystical narratives use the exterior of the pavilion or the garden as the main setting. The lack of *iwan* and enclosure in these cases may help the artist to highlight the garden and the events inside it.[44] For example, a painting from the *Divan* by Hafez depicts an ecstatic dancing ceremony (*sama'*) by some dervishes, which is taking place in a garden (Figure 22). Another instance from *Bustan* by Sheykh Zadeh shows a meeting on an *iwan* that is probably part of a *madrasa* (Figure 23). Using gold for the background of the main tree helps the artist emphasize the *iwan*, and consequently, the meeting that is happening there. Another artist (1560), in an illustration from the *Khamseh* by Nezami, which depicts Leyla and Majnun at school (Figure 24), chooses a different strategy by opening up the interior of the *madrasa* rather than the typical emphasis on the *iwan*. The interior, which occupies two-thirds of the frame, is visually separated from the garden. A closer look at this painting reveals an interesting innovation: the wall separating the interior from the garden behind has the same floral ornamentation as the background. In other words, the outside world is brought inside by using the same abstract monochrome decoration.

All these instances confirm that the garden background is more a matter of formality than a reflection of reality. However, paintings depicting religious ceremonies are less common, probably because of lack of patronage. We can infer that the kings who were usually the artists' main clients were more interested in showing off court activities than in highlighting the role of famous religious leaders (*sufis*), who were sometimes in conflict or rivalry with the administration.

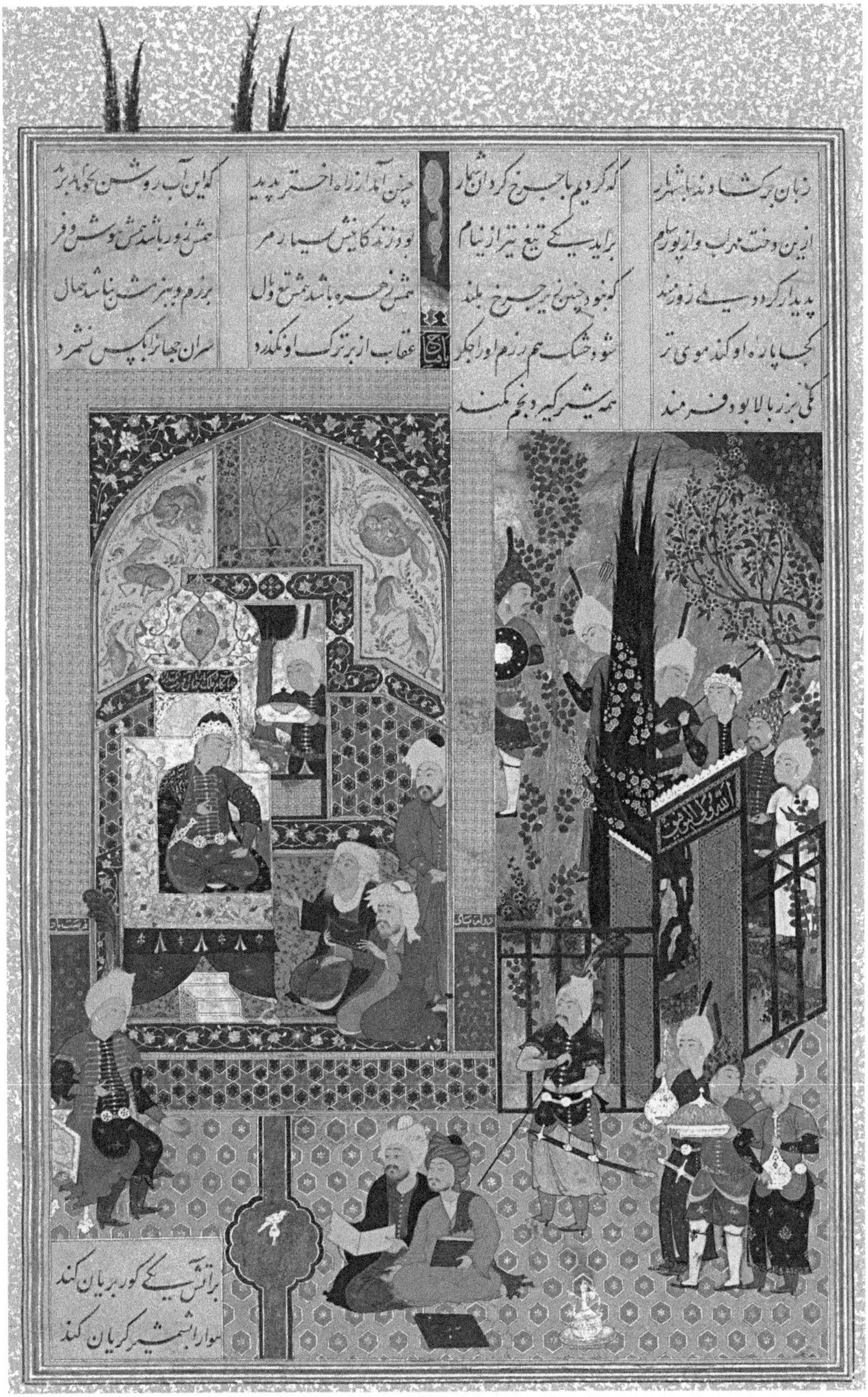

FIGURE 21

The shah's wise men approve of Zal's marriage. From the *Shahnameh* of Shah Tahmasp, attributed to ʿAbd al-ʿAziz, Tabriz, 1525–30.

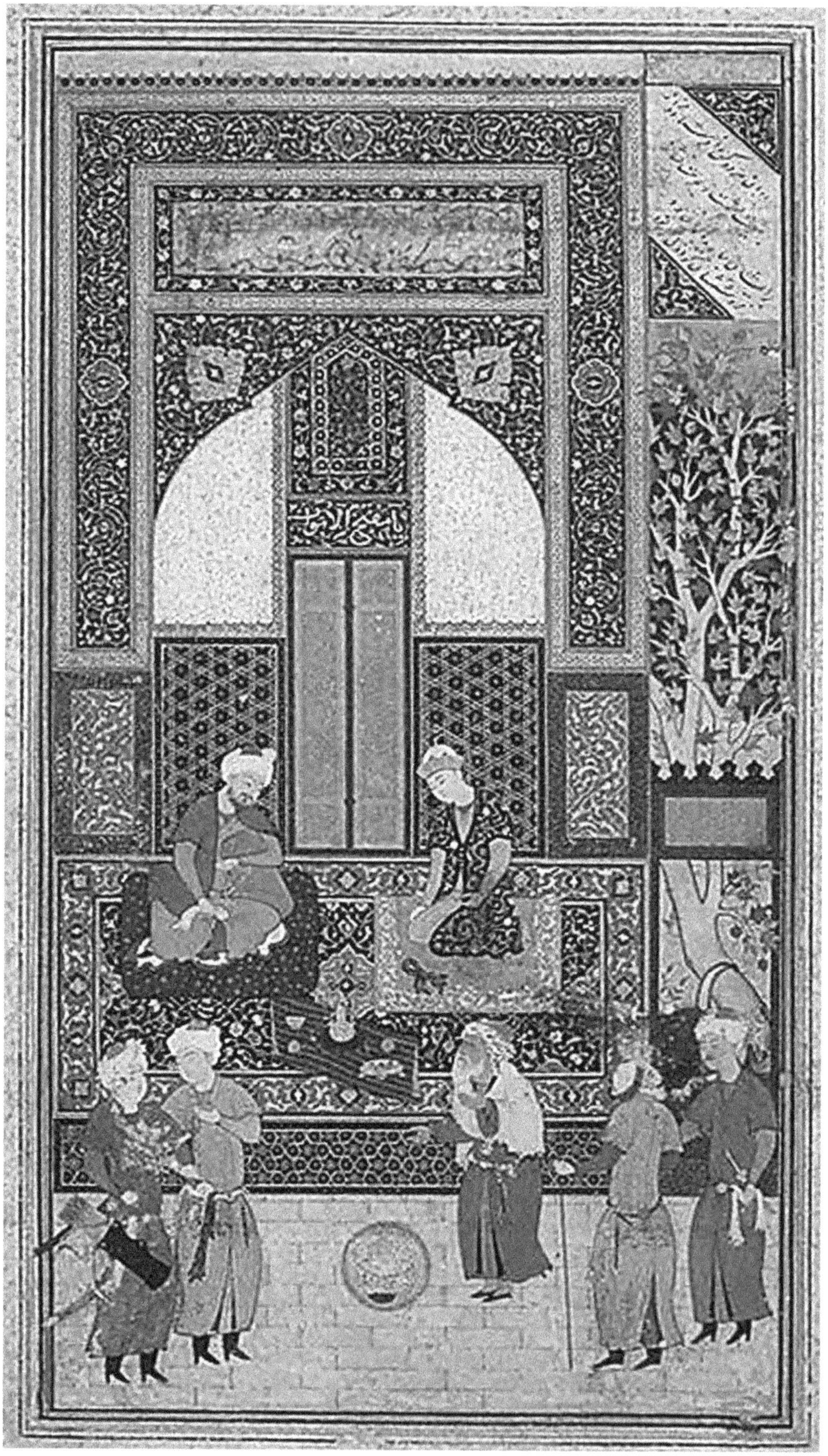

FIGURE 23

Interior reception. From *Bustan* by Sa'di, attributed to Sheykh Zadeh, Bukhara, 1525–35.

THE SPATIAL QUALITIES OF THE BUILDING

The View of the Garden

Depending on the narrative, many miniature paintings portray figures who are looking at the garden from the interior space or looking at the building from an outside area (garden). The concept of the view between the building and garden is tied to the existence of three architectural elements: the *iwan,* balcony and roof, which act as spaces from which people can have a panoramic view of the whole garden. The main formal distinction between *iwan,* balcony and roof is that the *iwan* is usually the focal point while the balcony or roof is normally secondary and somewhat hidden. This difference bespeaks the function of these spaces: the *iwan* is mostly used by the king and courtiers of high rank to watch the garden and the social activities inside it, whereas the balcony is usually used by the ladies of the harem and eunuchs; the roof, meanwhile, is most often the domain of male or female spectators or even angels.

Balconies are usually placed where they can offer a panoramic view of the garden while remaining invisible to the eyes of the strangers. Similarly, the roof functions as a secondary setting from which men or women watch the main event. Sometimes, however, it serves as a vital setting for the story. For instance, in the story of the fickle old lover from the *Haft Awrang* (Figure 25), it plays a vital role in both narrative and painting since the main figure is knocked off the pavilion roof.[45] As is evident, the artist uses all the available spaces – entrance, roof, balcony, window, courtyard and garden – to narrate each part of the story and to create tension. In some illustrations the roof becomes the symbolic location for angels and metaphysical personages. It is common to see people on the ground looking at the roof and balcony and even talking to people standing there. A painting by Junayd (1396) shows the conversation between two famous lovers in Persian poetry. Homayun, outside the garden, is talking to Homay, who is on the balcony of her palace, which is surrounded by the garden (Figure 26).[46]

Scenes which include one or more persons in front of a building appear repeatedly in paintings after the fourteenth century, often to depict conversations between lovers, such as Khosrow and Shirin, Zal and Rudabeh, and Homay and Homayun. One might ask why artists preferred to use this configuration rather than placing both figures (lover and beloved) in the same setting. Well, it was a way to separate the male and female figures, especially in the case of love conversations, and to protect the privacy of the woman and her maids. Moreover, placing the beloved on the roof, balcony, or at the window defined a courtly hierarchy in which the woman was the more dominant, the one with the power to accept or reject the other's proposal. A similar scene can be found in a painting from the *Khamseh* (1431) depicting the conversation between Khosrow and Shirin (Figure 27). Although, in most of these paintings, the house is fully separated from its urban context, this isolation almost disappears in a seventeenth-century painting of Zal and Rudabeh from the *Shahnameh*, illustrated by 'Abdol-Rashid Deylami (Figure 28). Here, the paved area works as a spatial or visual moderator/connector between the garden and the building. This visual connection reflects Ferdowsi's story, in which other characters besides Zal and Rudabeh are involved, unlike the story of Khosrow and Shirin which focuses on the conversation between two individuals. Despite the occasional significance of roof and balcony, the *iwan* still remains the highest-ranking space in the hierarchy of building representation.

Privacy and Gender Segregation

The varying degrees of connection between the inside and outside of the pavilion, and even within the garden, affect the extent to which privacy is possible in the Persian garden and pavilion. Three types of connection are established between the garden and pavilion: physical, visual and symbolic. The changing level of physical connection between areas in the garden and between the garden and building is a tool for the artist to define both hierarchy and privacy. For example, the king's throne is the least accessible to other people, whereas the paved area next to the pavilion is quite accessible to both courtiers and servants. Visual (and formal) connection is forged through the use of colour, decorative patterns and vertical and horizontal composition. Artists also use landscape elements such as a fence, pool and trees to define the visual connection in the garden. For example, we have already seen that, in Soltan Muhammad's painting from the *Divan* by Hafez, the fence between the planted area and paved areas visually and physically separates workers in the garden from the members of the court, making the paved area a more private space (Figure 18).

The visual connection between these areas is controlled by walls and fences in order to enhance the privacy of the king and the women of his harem. In some cases, such as the stories of Khosrow and Shirin and Homay and Homayun, the women are looking down from the balcony or the roof or the second floor while remaining mostly invisible to the people in the garden. Sometimes this connection is more symbolic and less evident. For instance, in the story of the fickle old lover from the *Haft Awrang* (Figure 25), the scene of the fallen lover symbolically connects each element as if the artist has tried to create continuity between the roof and ground, where the story is actually happening. Why should issues of privacy be emphasized thus in painting? As a cultural issue, privacy stems from the interrelated social phenomena of the requirement for segregation of men and women and the exceptional status of the royal family in Persian society. In a painting from the *Shahnameh* of Baysonghor (1429), Ardashir meets Ganjvar Ardavan and Golnaz, her maid (Figure 29). Here, the courtyard is separated from the planted area of the garden by a wall, making it a private space, a perfect setting for an intimate conversation.

The phenomenon of the garden as a gender-specific zone continues in some Mughal paintings, in which it serves as a female-only space. Despite fundamental differences from Persian painting (especially in depicting spaces and figures), Mughal painting reflects the concepts of gender specificity and segregation. In the story of Mehrdokht and the royal women from the *Hamzenameh* (1564–69), the building is occupied only by women, while the gardeners stay in the garden. The sole woman in the garden, the maid, is walking towards the building, marking it as female space. The artist carefully attempts to specify the hierarchy among the ladies by using a different colour (red) for Mehrdokht, while the act of shooting distinguishes her from her maids. While the higher-class maids are on the second floor, the less important stay on the first (Figure 30).[47]

Women play a strong role as primary or secondary figures in the narratives of several paintings.[48] In Persian miniature painting, the garden may be formally or physically divided into male and female areas, emphasizing both the privacy of women and the hierarchy of the people within the scene. This relates to the cultural value of *hijab* and the intimate role of women within the family and society. Painters signal gender segregation by showing women as groups or individuals on the balcony, on the roof, or in isolated areas in the garden. If not physically separated by a barrier, their seating and standing area is fully isolated from the male zone, even when it is adjacent. Being on the balcony enables women to observe events in the garden and whisper amongst themselves without being seen or overheard. In a painting probably made under Behzad's supervision, and based on Mir ʿAli Shir Navaʾi's poems in Chaghatay Turkish, the crazed old Sheykh of Sanʿan and his male followers stand in front of the building and talk to the women who are gathered on the balcony (Figure 31).[49] Common to many paintings, this type of scene shows the gender specificity of garden and pavilion. Similarly, in the story of the fickle old lover from the *Haft Awrang* (Figure 25), the pavilion and the garden are clearly divided into zones: the ground floor for the elderly, the second floor dedicated to women, the roof for the youths who are watching the event, the courtyard for courtiers, and the planted area for the gardener.[50]

Often, the pavilion is allocated to women and the garden to men. In paintings focusing on a narrative based on women the whole space may be defined as a female zone. For instance, in a painting from Nezami's *Khosrow va Shirin* (Tabriz, 1406–10), women are hidden behind the windows and on the second floor. This space could be called a female zone because of the dominance of the female presence in the painting (Figure 32).[51] There is a complete absence of men in a Timurid painting from the *Khamseh* (1494–95) in which the owner of a garden discovers maidens bathing in his pool (Figure 33).

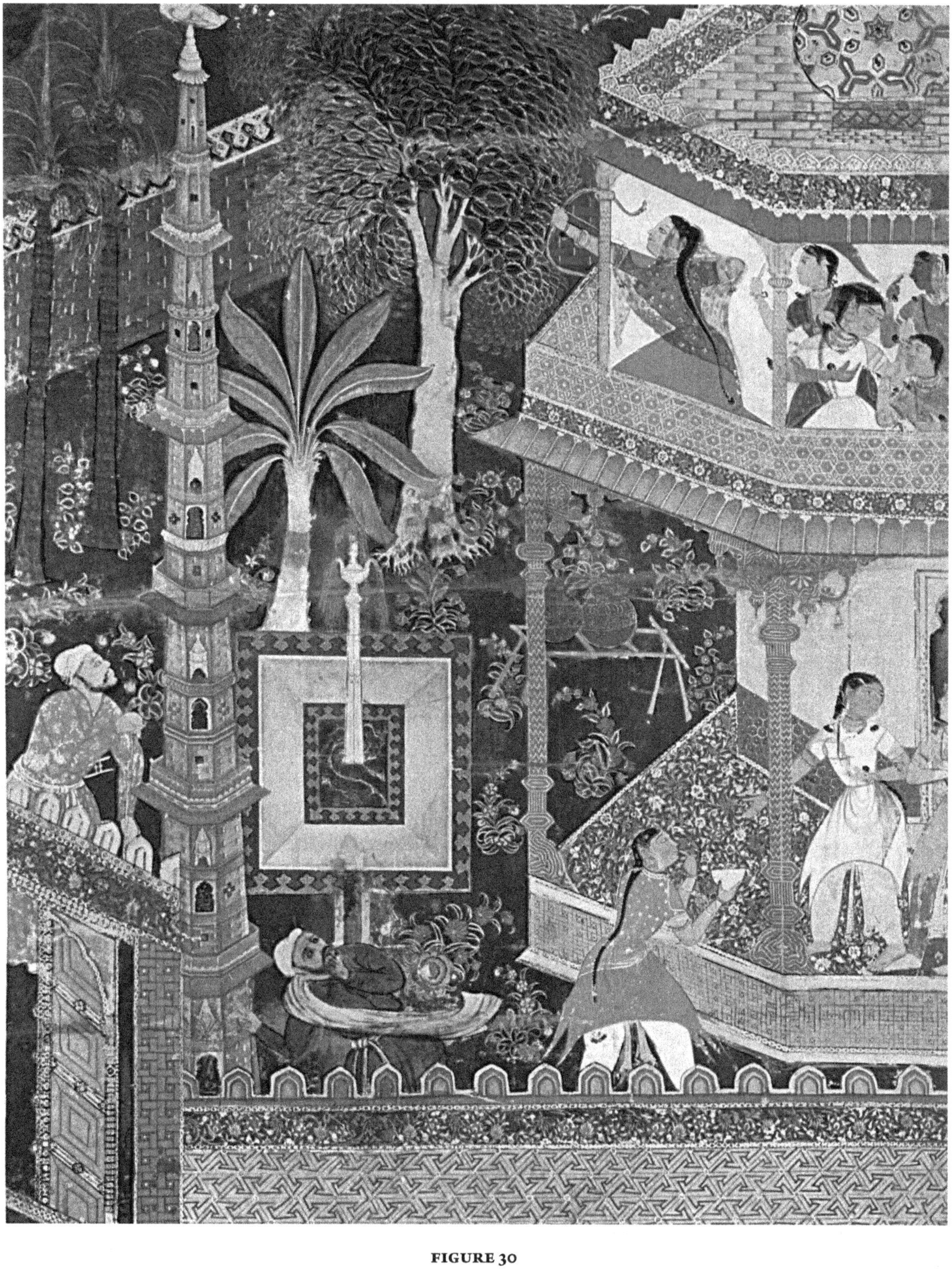

FIGURE 30
Mehrdokht shoots her bow at the ring. From *Hamzenameh,* India, 1564–69.

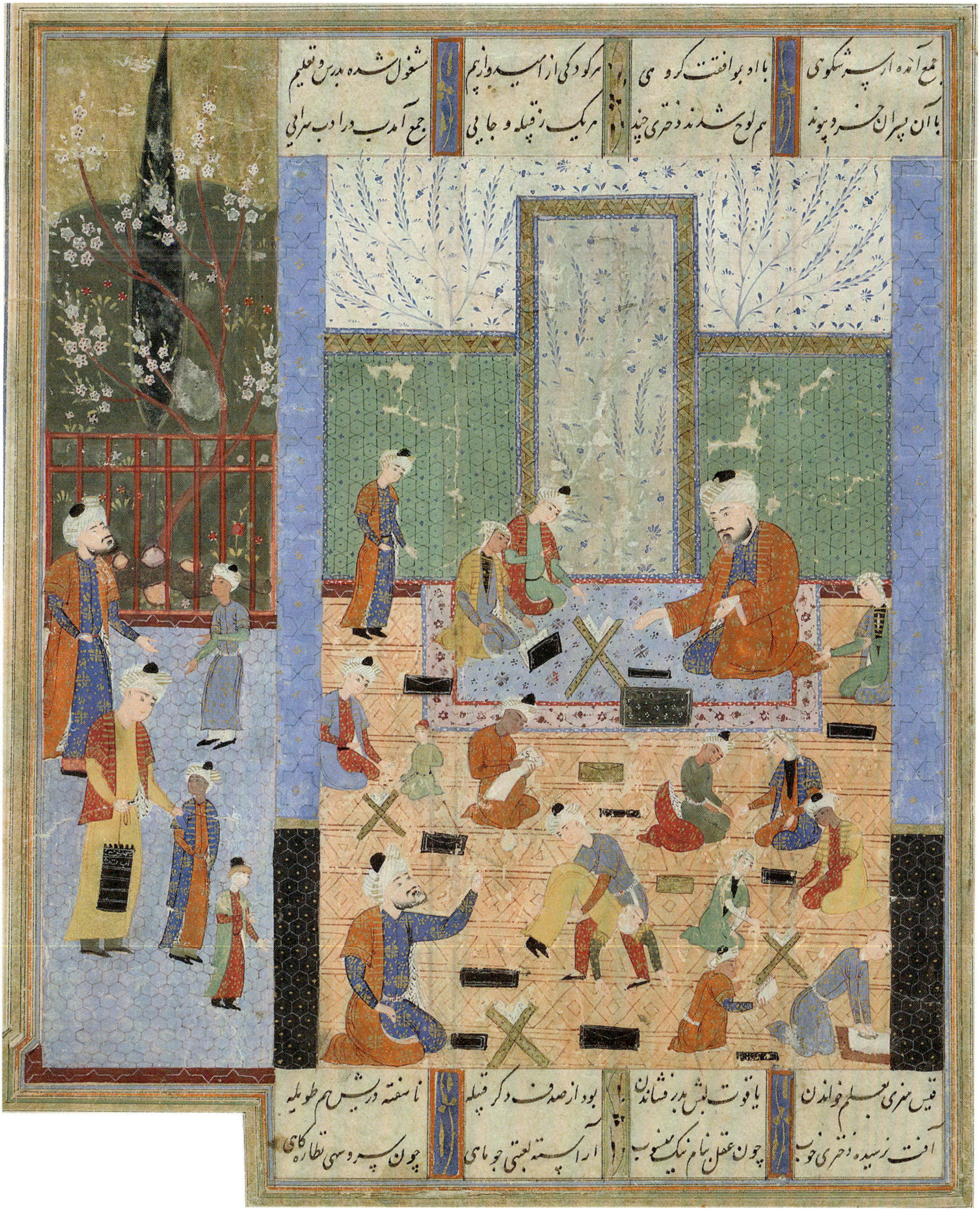

FIGURE 24

Leyla and Majnun at school. From the *Khamseh* by Nezami, Shiraz, 1560.

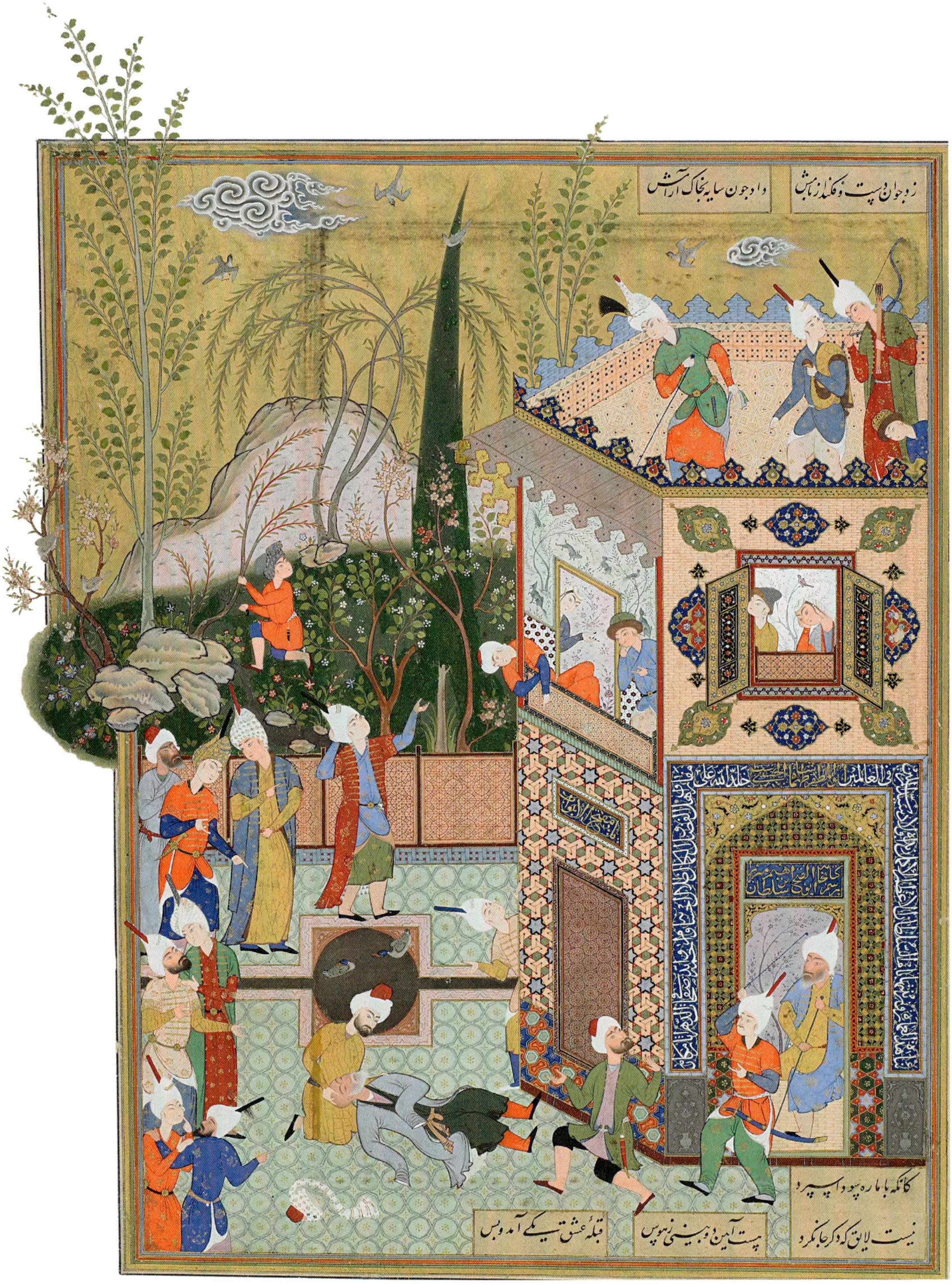

FIGURE 25

The story of the fickle old lover who is knocked off the rooftop of the garden pavilion. From the *Haft Awrang* by Jami, Mashhad, 1556–65.

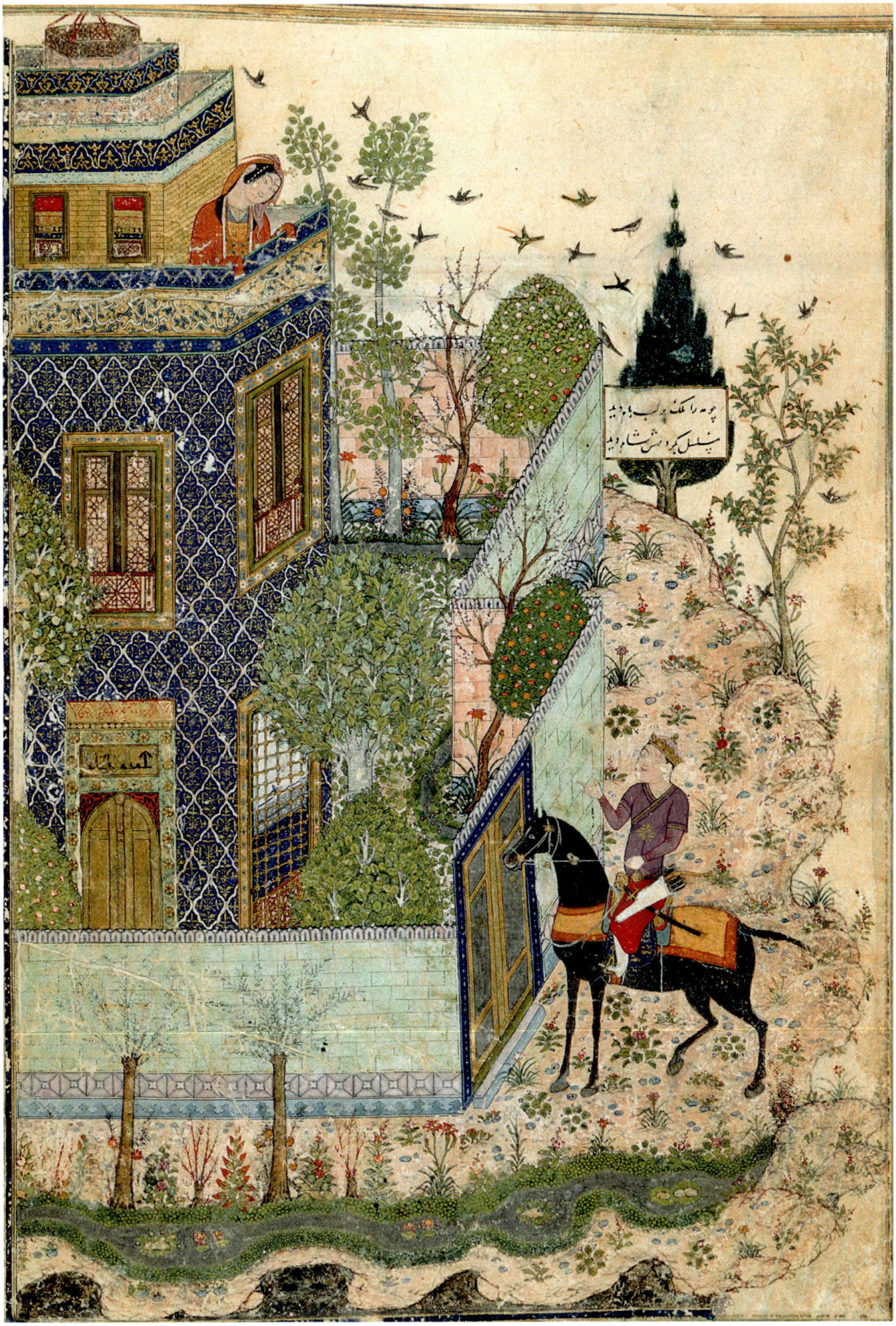

FIGURE 26

Homay at the castle gate. From *Three Poems* by Khaju Kermani, fourteenth century.

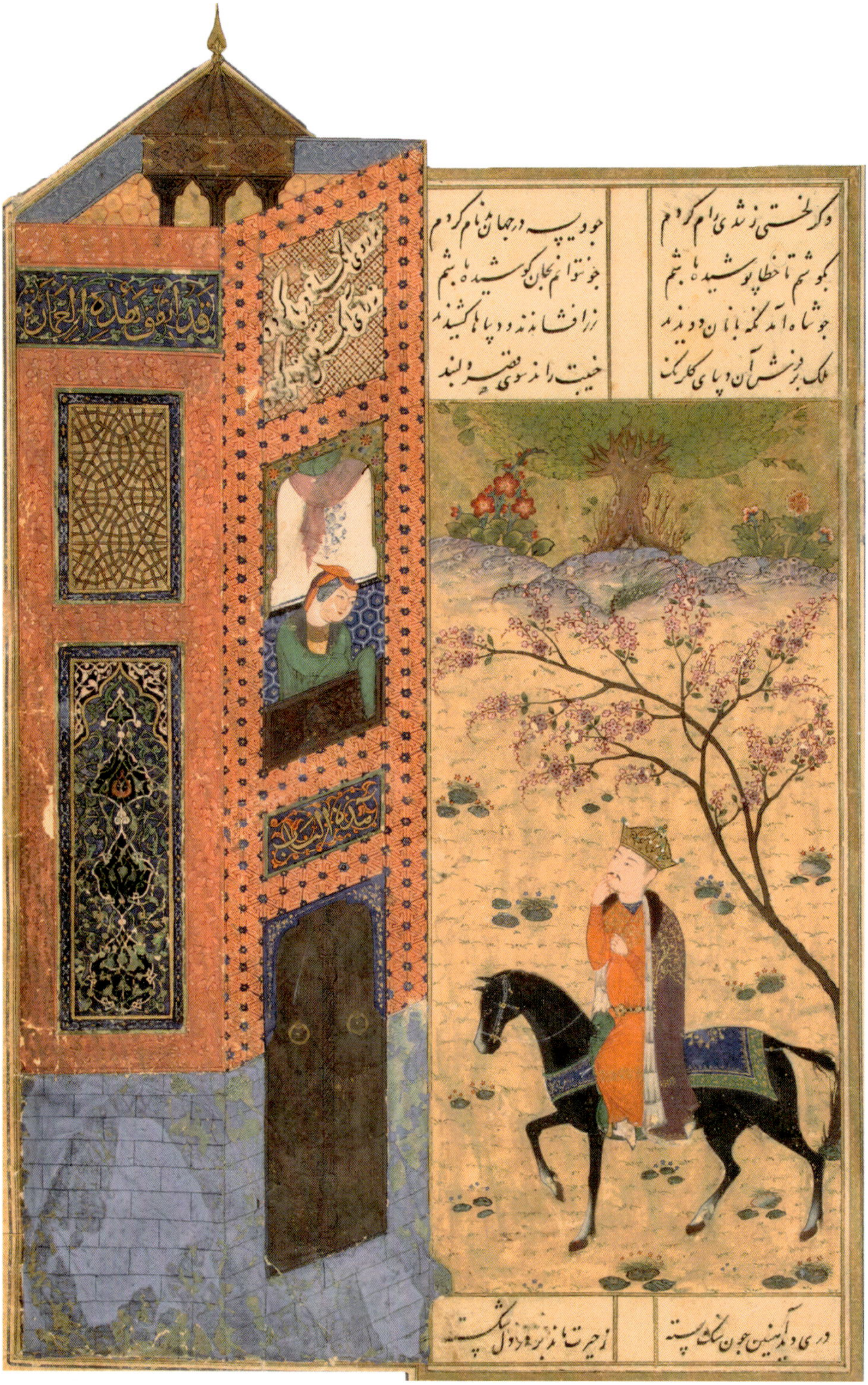

FIGURE 27

Khosrow in front of Shirin's castle. From the *Khamseh* by Nezami, 1431.

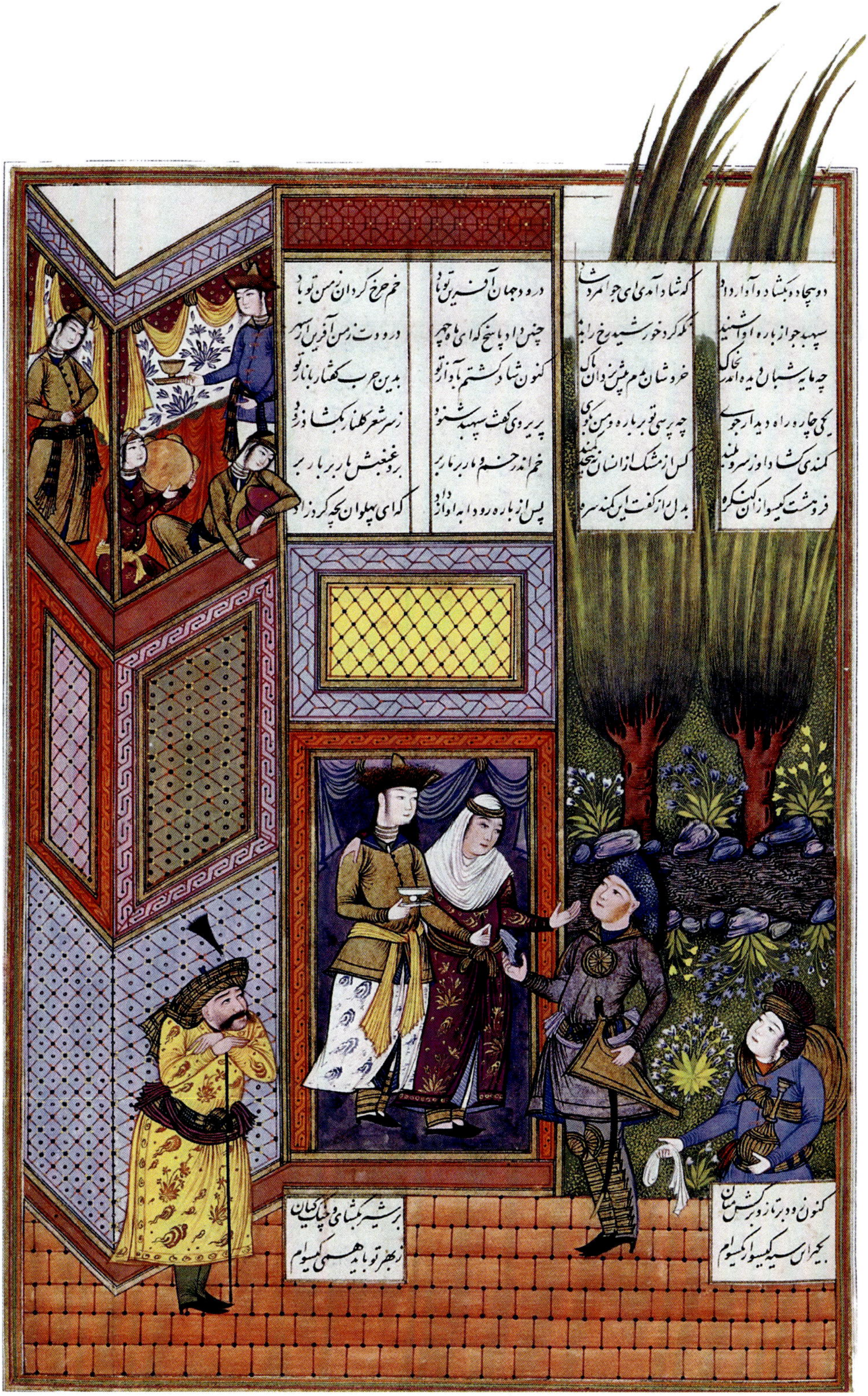

FIGURE 28

Zal and Rudabeh pronounce their marriage vows. From the *Shahnameh*, attributed to ʿAbdol Rashid Deylami, Isfahan, seventeenth century.

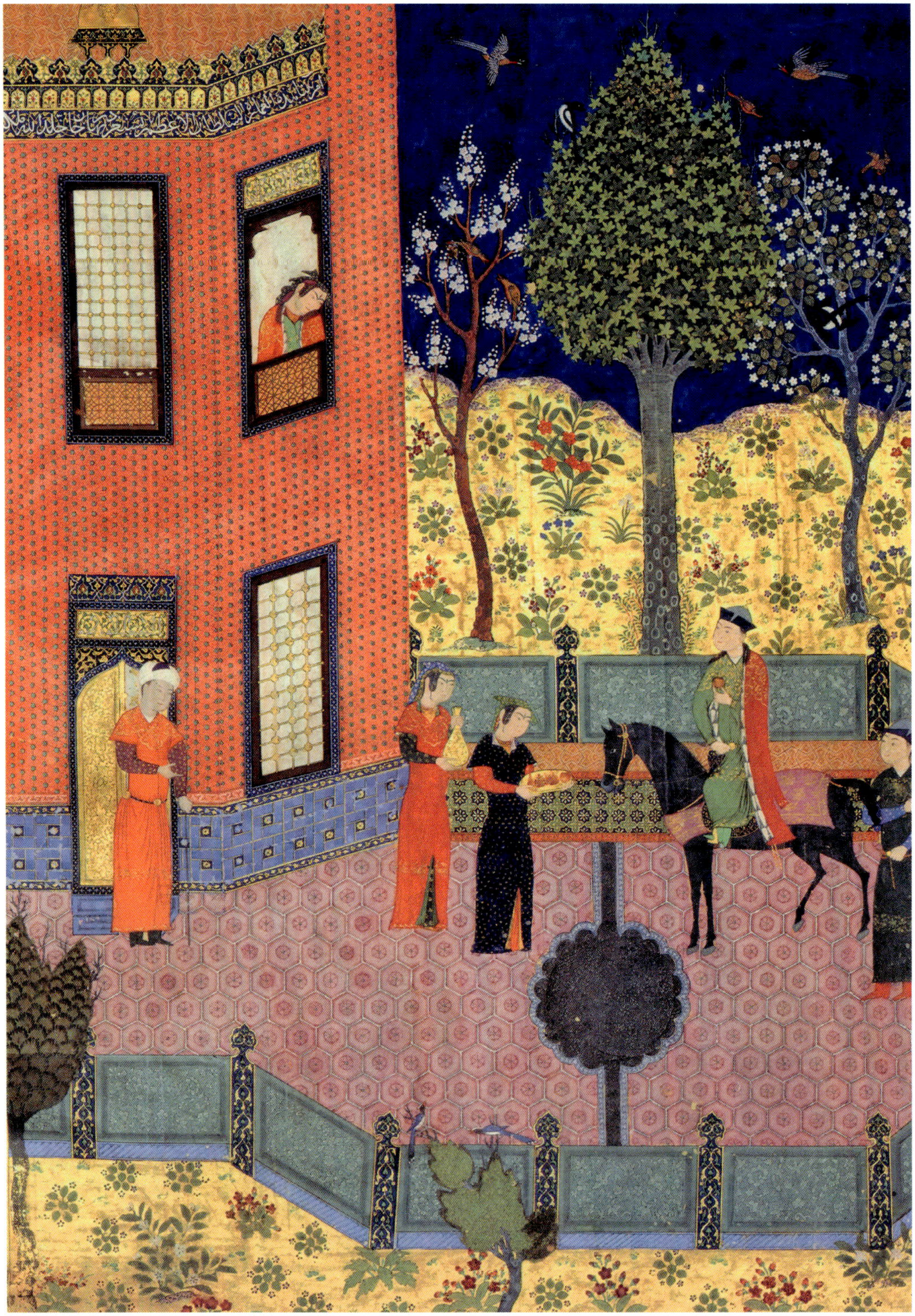

FIGURE 29

Ardashir meeting Ganjvar Ardavan and Golnaz, the maid. From the *Shahnameh* of Baysonghor, 1429.

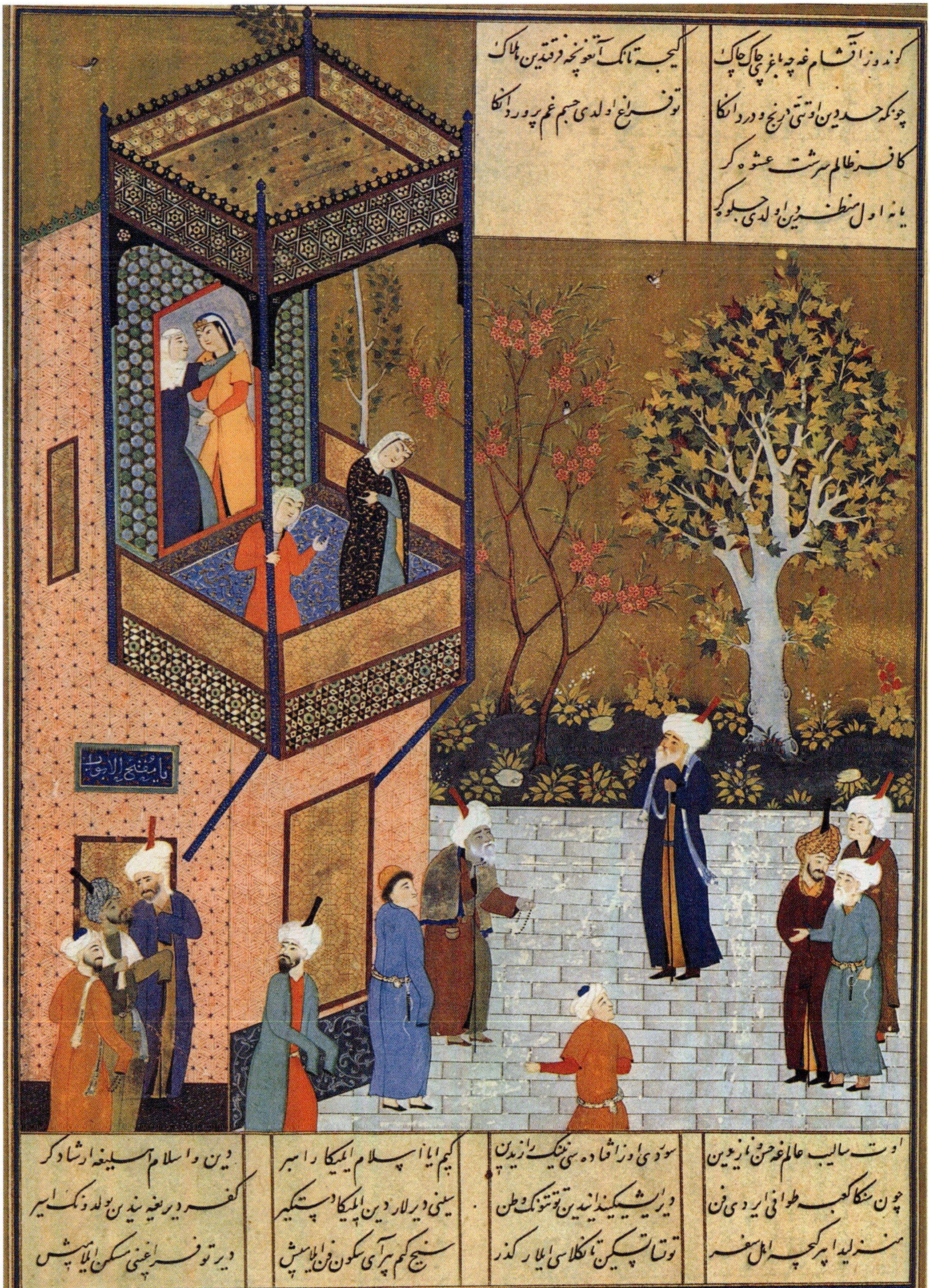

FIGURE 31

The crazed old Sheykh of San'an. From the *Divan* by Mir 'Ali Shir Nava'i in Chaghatay Turkish.

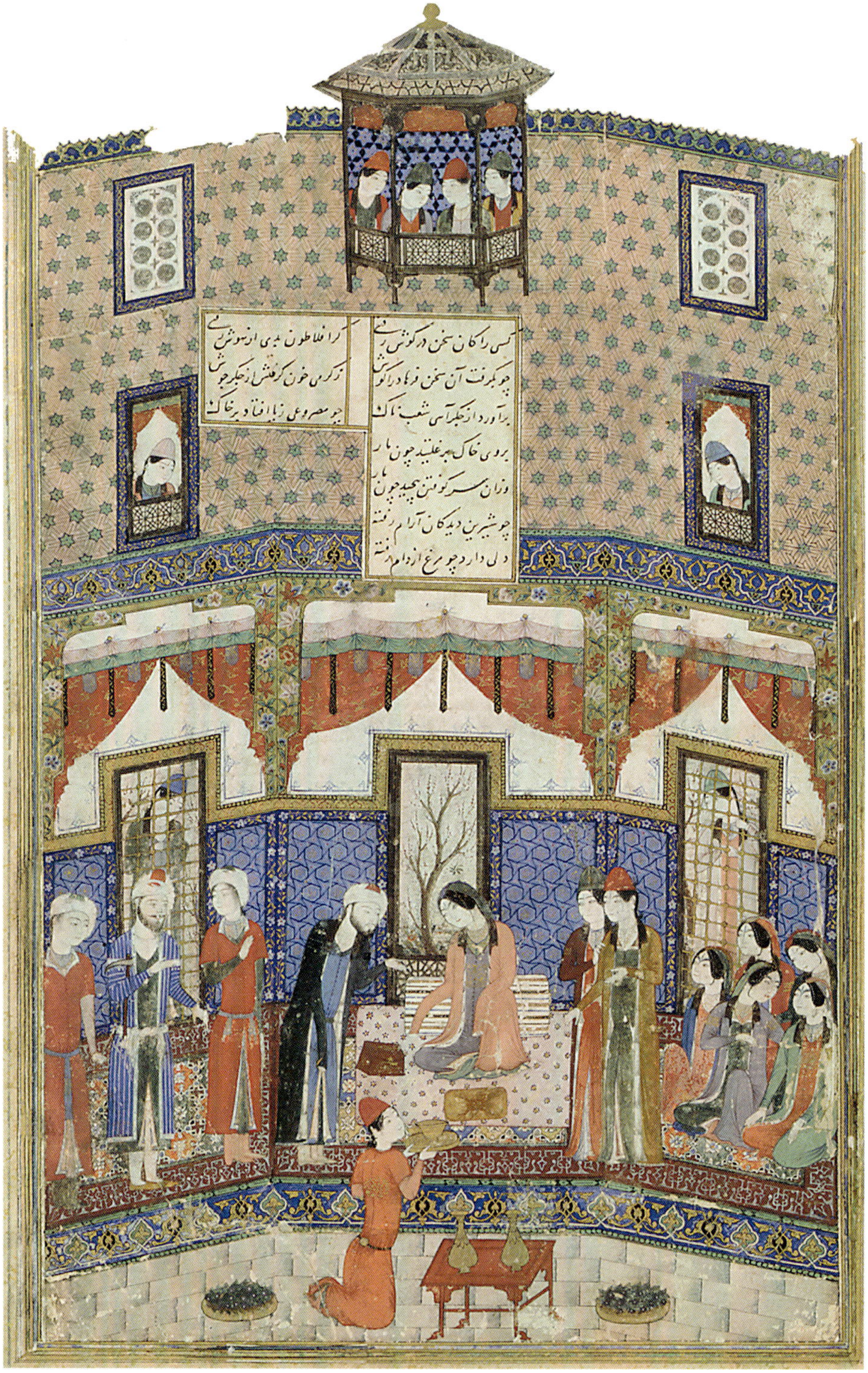

FIGURE 32

Shapur brings Farhad before Shirin. From *Khosrow va Shirin by* Nezami, Tabriz, 1406–10.

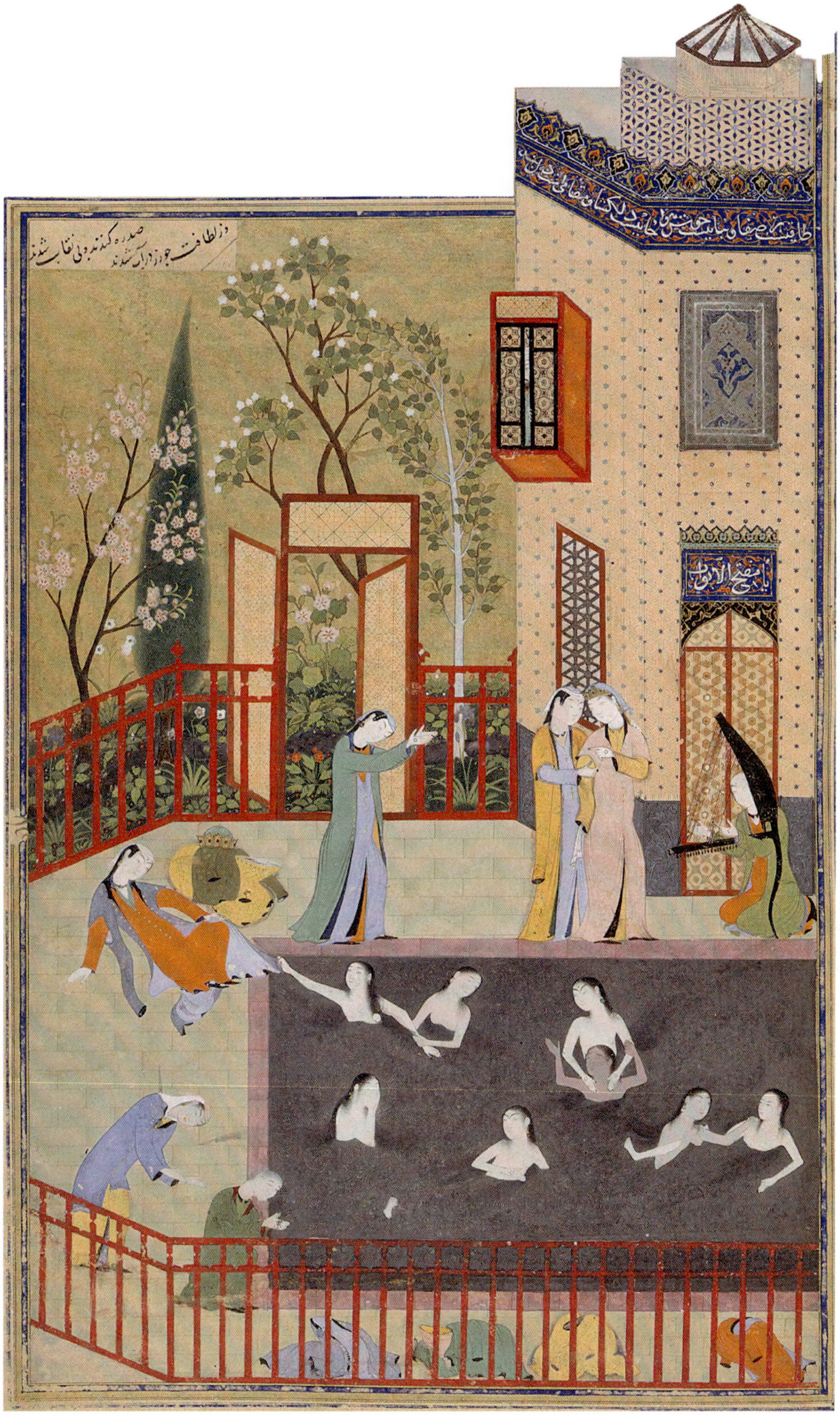

FIGURE 33

Maidens bathing. From the *Khamseh* by Nezami, Herat, 1494–95.

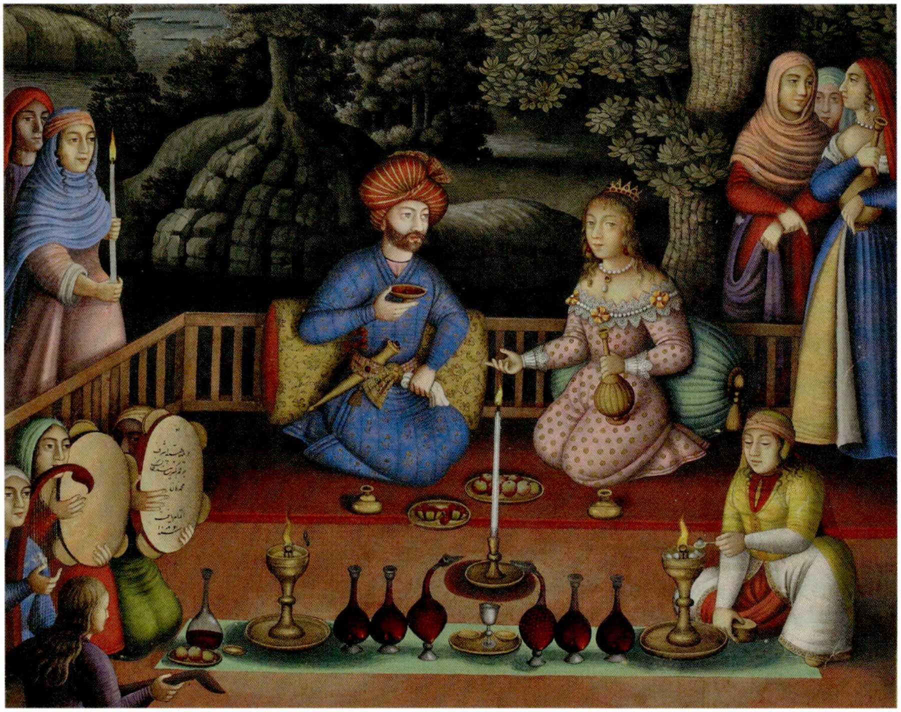

FIGURE 34
The so-called Bahram Gur and the Indian Princess, identified here as Turktazi and the Queen of the Faeries, Turktaz. From the *Khamseh* of Shah Tahmasp, attributed to Muhammad Zaman, 1675–76.

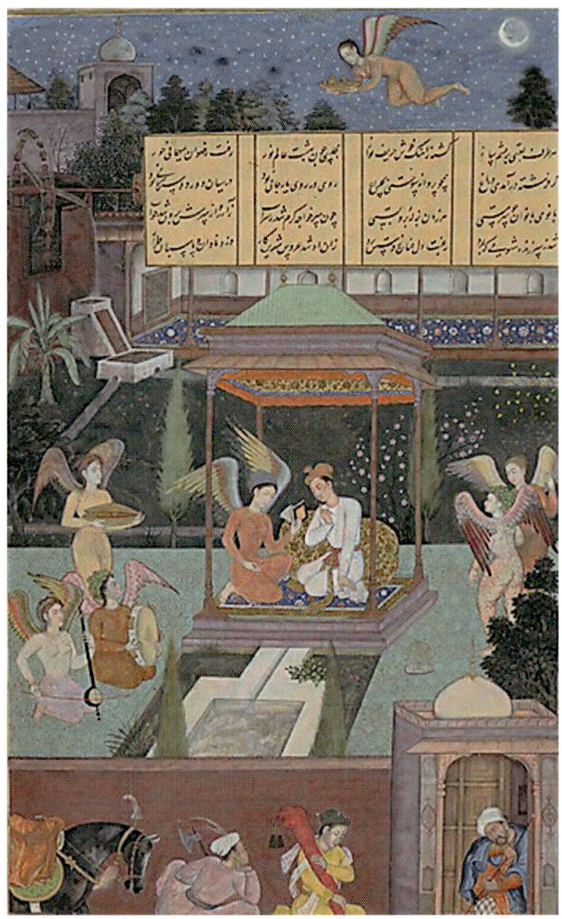

FIGURE 35
The Princess of the Blue Pavilion. From the *Khamseh* (Quintet) of Amir Khosrow Dehlavi, India, 1597–98.

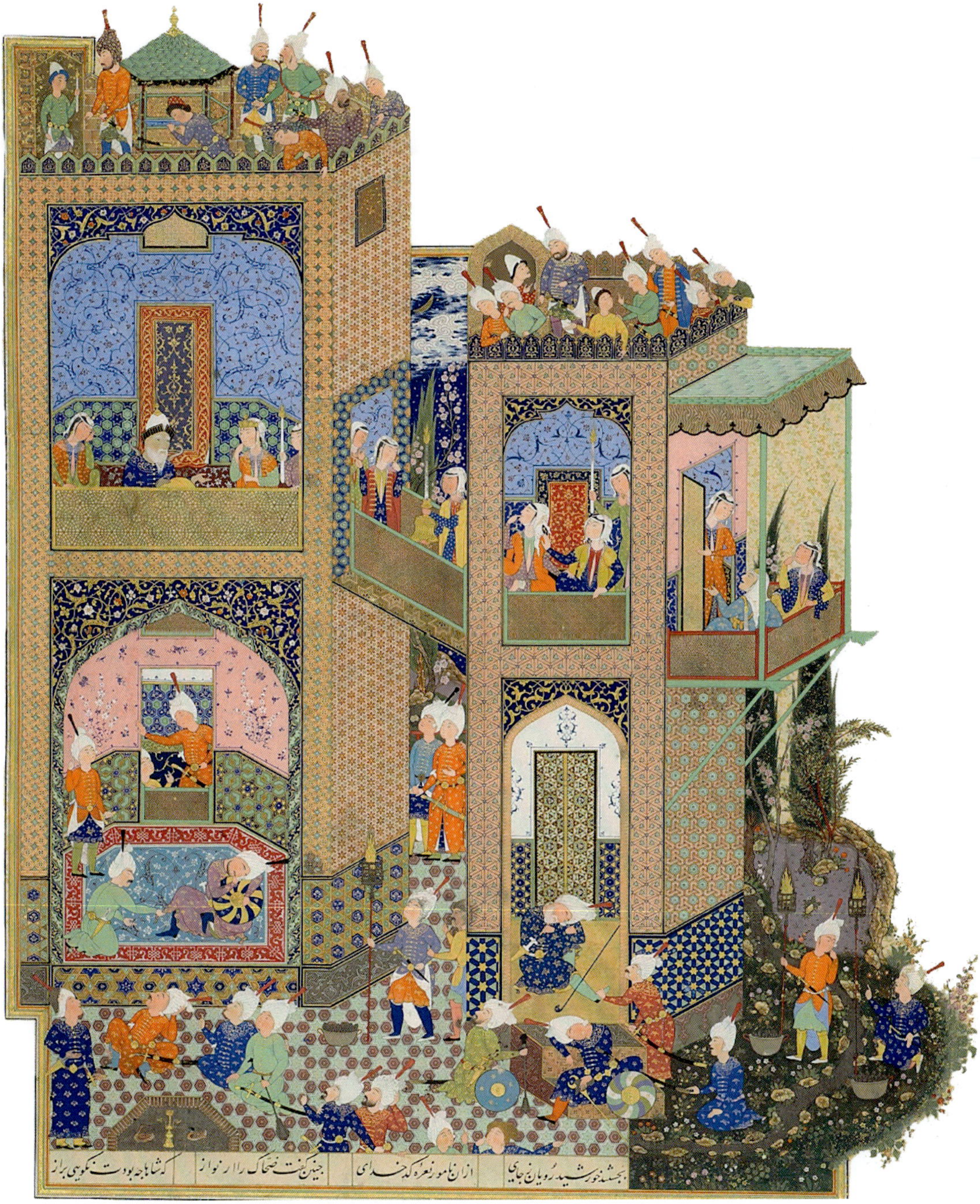

FIGURE 38

The nightmare of Zahhak. From the *Shahnameh* of Shah Tahmasp, Tabriz, 1525–35.

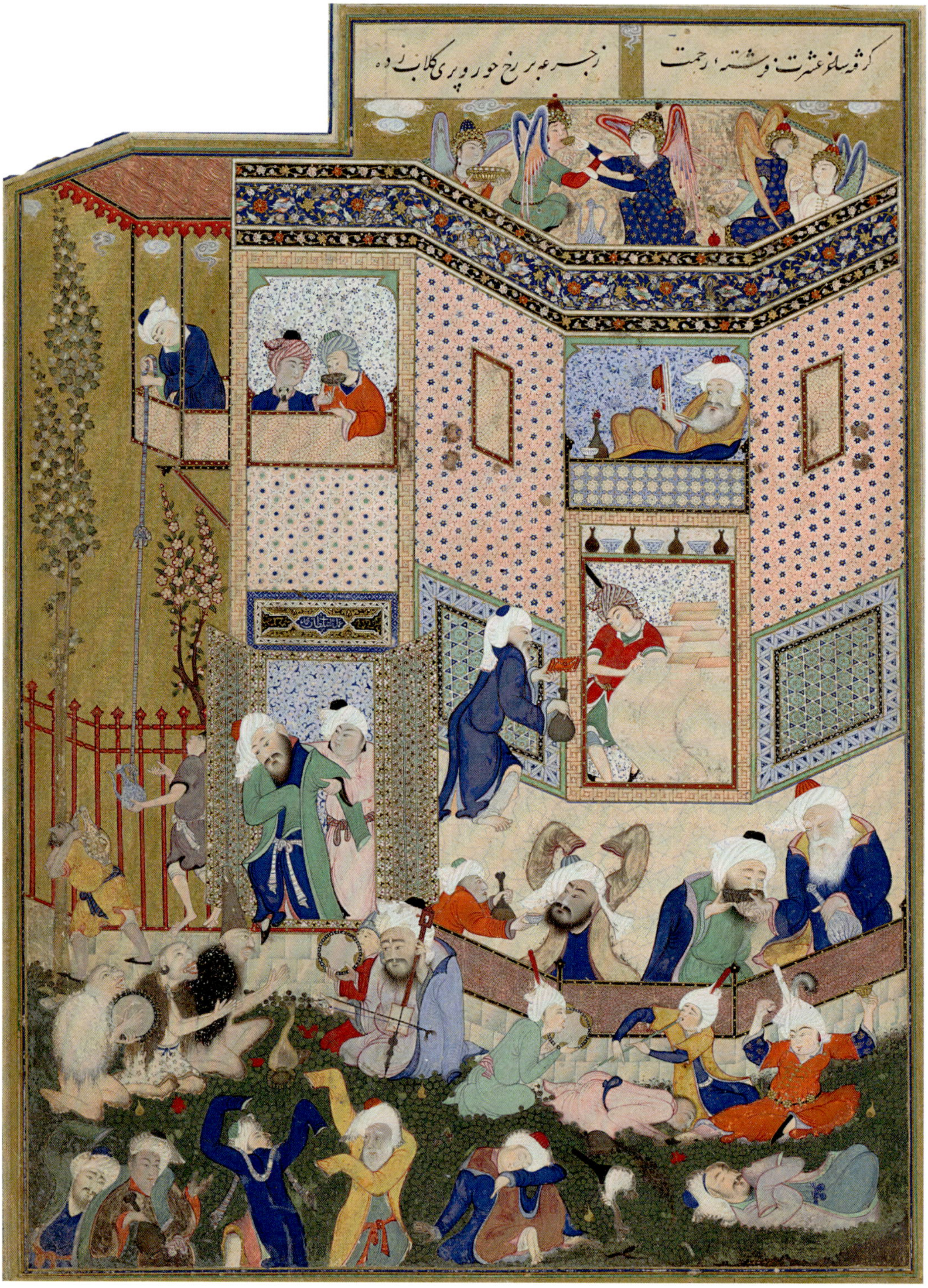

FIGURE 39

Earthly drunkenness. From the *Divan* by Hafez, attributed to Soltan Muhammad, Tabriz, 1526–27.

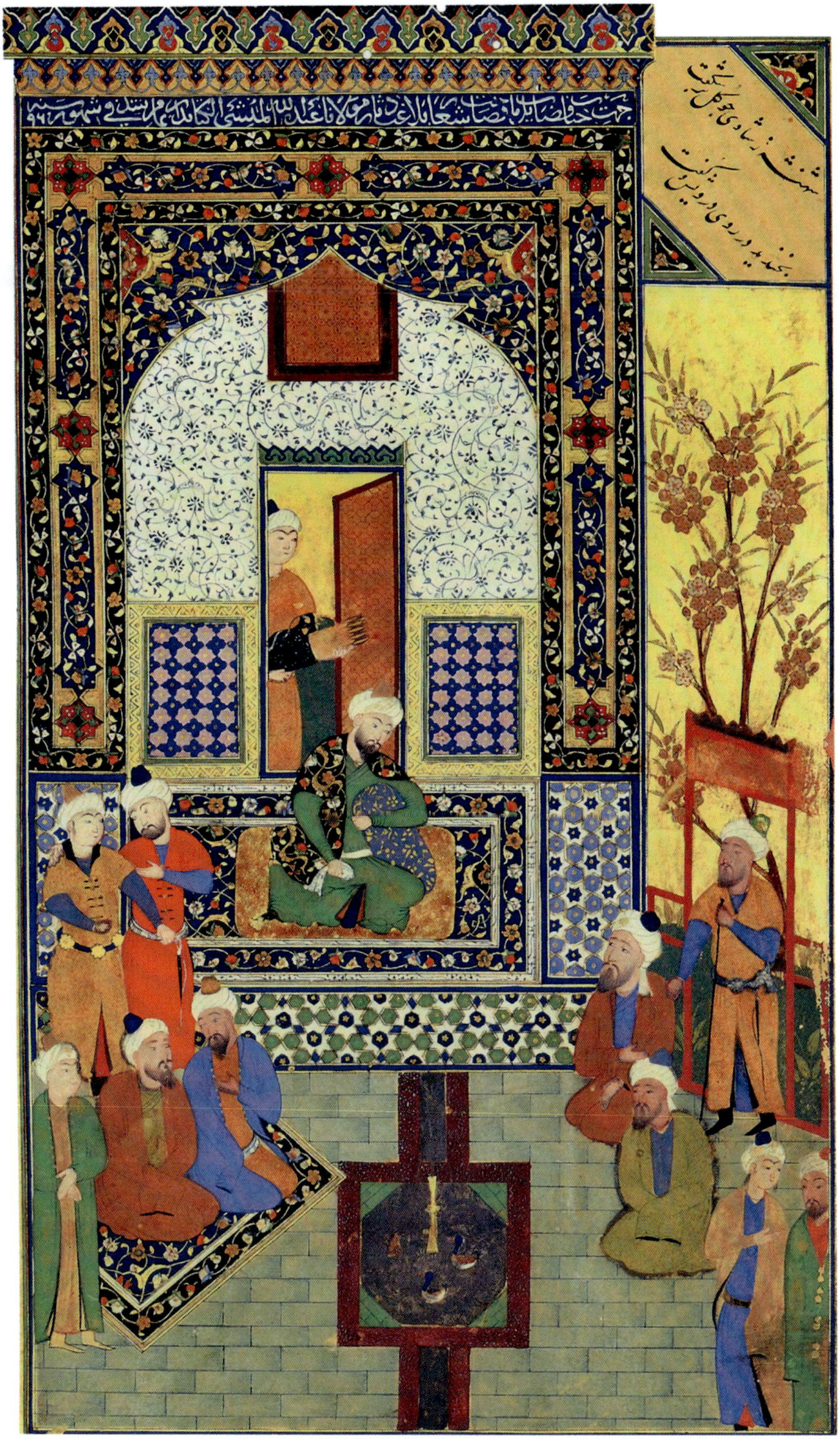

FIGURE 42

The conversation between the king and the dervish. From *Bustan* by Sa'di, 1553.

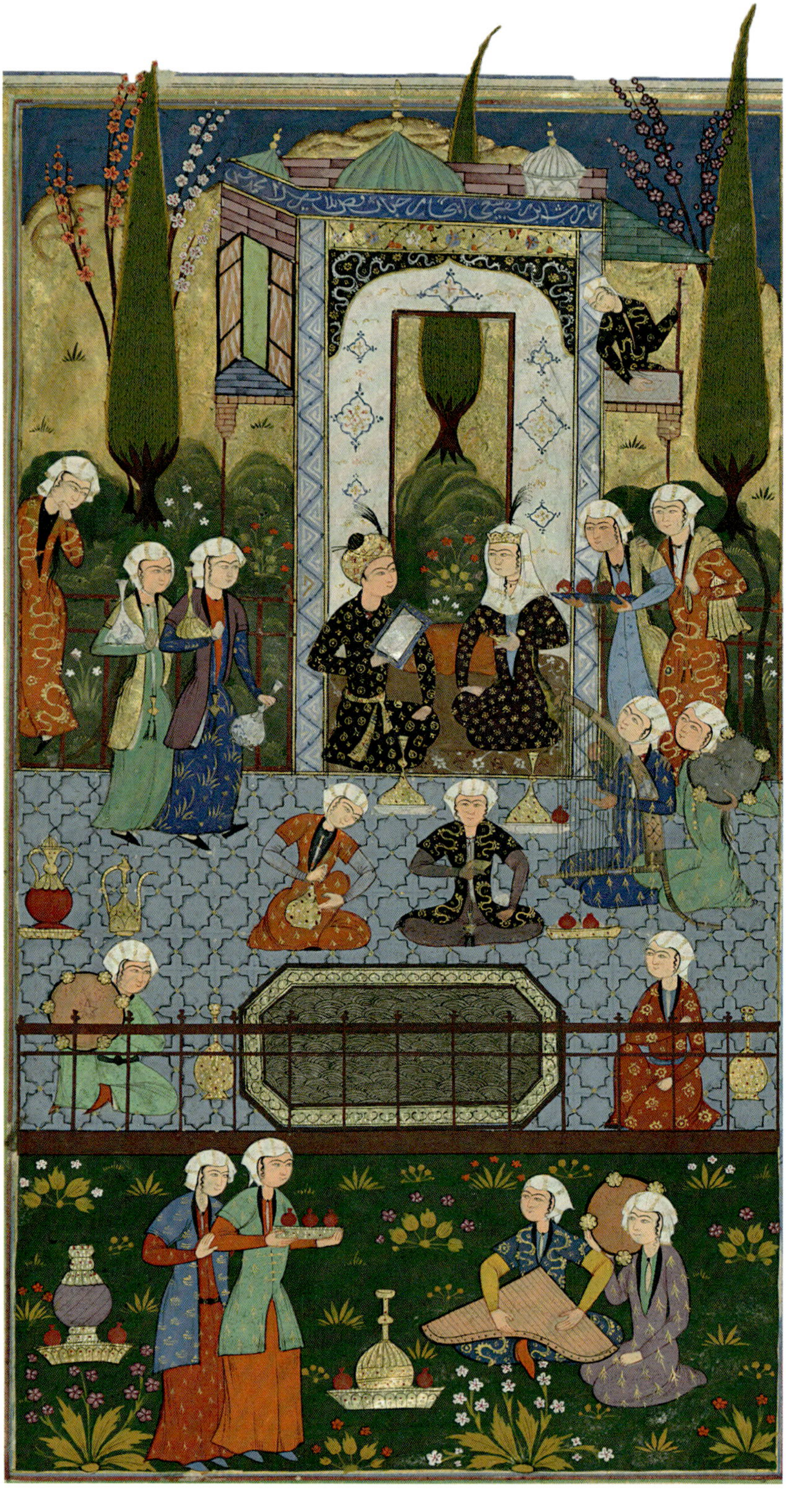

FIGURE 43

Alexander the Great admires his portrait, ordered by Queen Nushabeh.
From the *Khamseh* by Nezami, 1528–29.

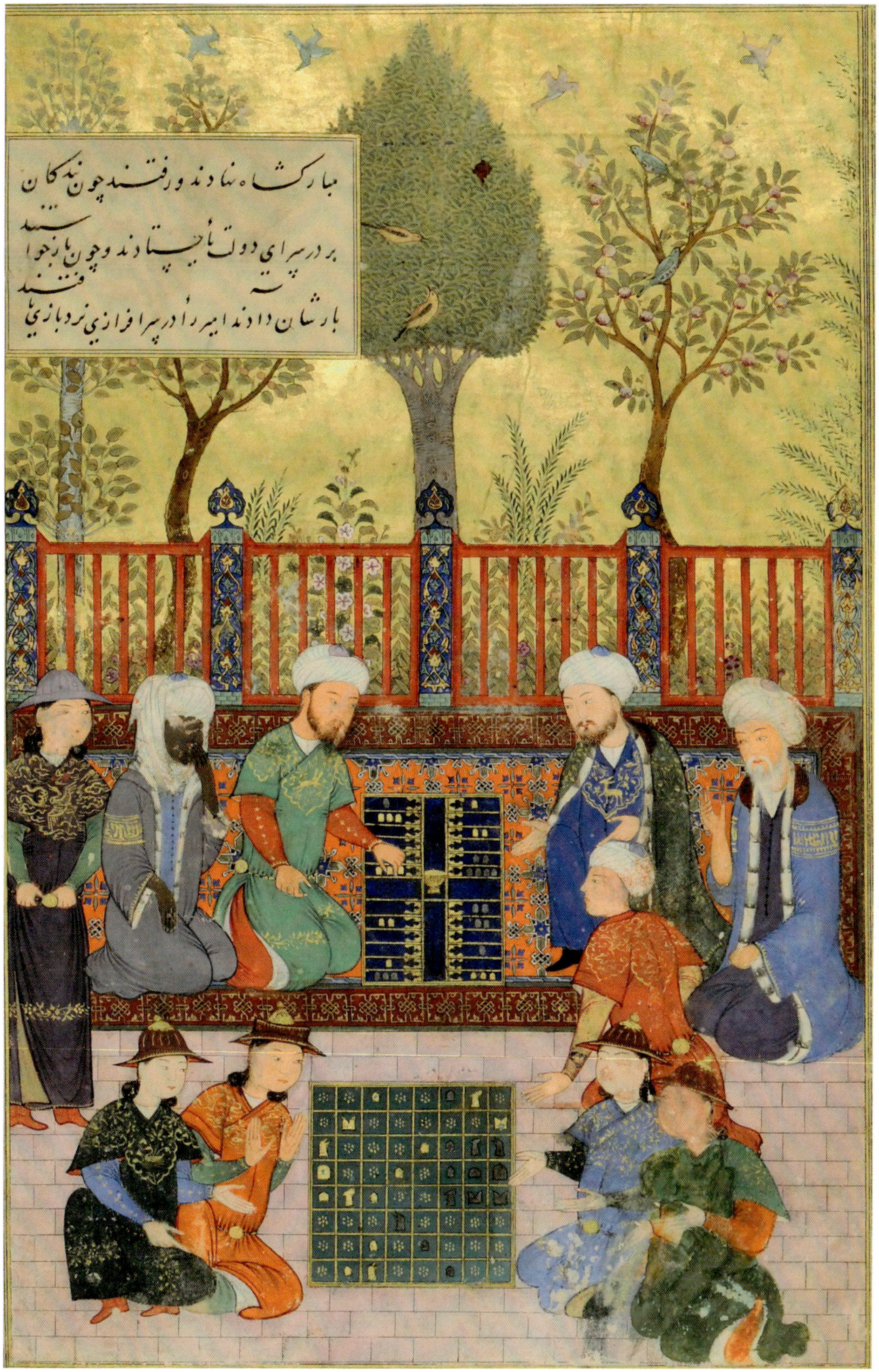

FIGURE 44

The games of backgammon and chess. From the *Anthology* of Baysonghor, Herat, 1427.

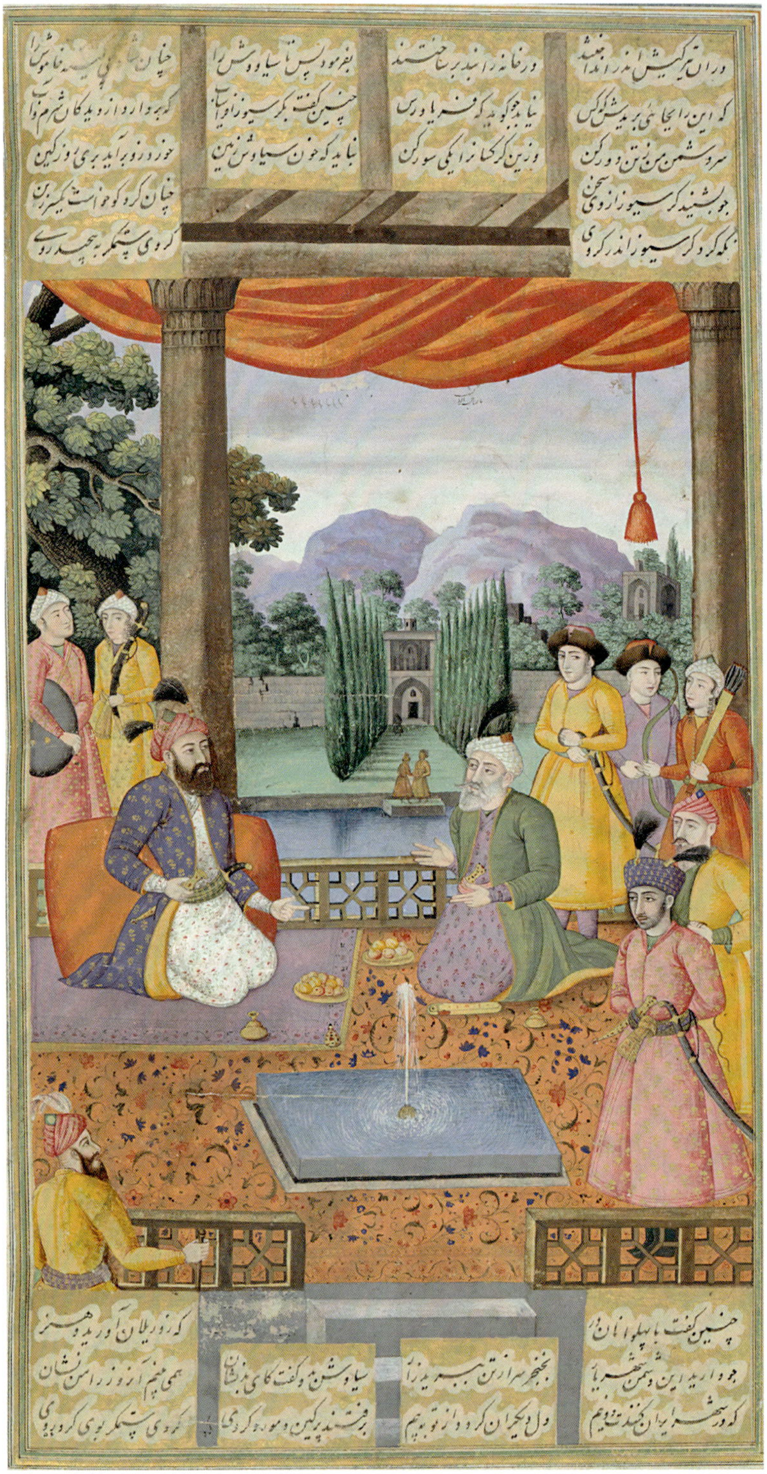

FIGURE 45

Siyavash captive before Afrasyab. From the *Shahnameh*, Isfahan, 1696.

Hierarchy

The royal sponsorship behind the miniature paintings indirectly encouraged artists to apply a hierarchical language in their paintings. This language, depending on the text associated with the painting, highlighted the status of the king, his vizier and his courtiers. Hierarchy within the court may be shown by changing the composition of elements in the painting, the contrast and harmony of colours, the figures' gestures and postures (moving, sitting or standing) and emotions, and people's geographical location in the garden and pavilion. Illustrations portraying the inside spaces of the royal pavilion stress the king's throne as the most significant area and object, while lower-rank courtiers sit and stand around the king, according to their status in the court. The arrangement of furniture and even drinking vessels may be used to help the artist emphasize this hierarchy. For instance, in several paintings discussed here, the throne is placed on one or two carpets while the courtiers sit on a carpet or on the floor, depending on status. The following formula applies: the closer to the throne, the higher the rank of the courtier or guest. This rule, however, should not be over-generalized, especially in the case of paintings which illustrate exceptional events, or even accidents, in which figures may not be arranged in the prescribed order.

This hierarchical order can be observed in Muhammad Zaman's painting (1675–76), depicting a night scene, where the king, seated on the *iwan*, is surrounded by courtiers sitting to his left and right (Figure 34). Zaman's paintings were part of the westernization movement (*farangi-sazi*) in the Safavid age, which is defined by Amy Landau as

> a syncretic mode of painting that blended Safavid artistic traditions with adaptations of European iconography and pictorial techniques, such as linear and atmospheric perspective, modelling and chiaroscuro; it was developed by artists around the 1630s.

She adds,

> By the final third of the seventeenth century, *farangi-sazi* had become a way to signify core themes, values and beliefs of Safavid society in arts of the book: artists used it to depict scenes from Persian literature and religious history and notions of royal power and authority, as well as erotic and Neo-Platonic ideas of love.[52]

In the text, based on Nezami's *Haft Peykar*, the king, Bahram Gur, depicted as King Turktazi (meaning 'Turkish Raider'), welcomes the Indian Princess, depicted as Turktaz, Queen of the Faeries, and asks her about the secret of the city whose inhabitants all dress in black. This rare illustration is quite exceptional as it depicts an uncultivated or so-called natural garden at night. The choice of a night scene probably refers to the king's quest and the mystery behind it.

The Sense of Enclosure

The presence of enclosure has been a significant characteristic of Persian gardens in Pre-Islamic and Islamic eras. This concept is reflected in Persian miniature painting where buildings are enclosed by a light fence or a wall. In some cases, especially house gardens, the wall looks much stronger, probably as protection for the enclosed area. The organic arrangement of natural elements in the garden associated with the pavilion, however, is in contradiction to the presence of enclosure. In other words, in many paintings, the garden itself is not enclosed, but the building (and the paved area close to it) is surrounded by a wall or transparent barrier. The wall becomes a formal device for the artist to frame and capture the events and interactions within the garden. The wall separating the garden from its urban or rural setting is not a common element in Timurid and Safavid paintings; however, it frequently appears in Mughal paintings in which there is a tendency to illustrate the garden as part of a larger urban context. This quality can be seen in a Mughal painting (1597–98) based on the *Khamseh* of Amir Khosrow Dehlavi, depicting the Princess of the Blue Pavilion (Figure 35). The inclusion of the wall, which separates the urban fabric from the garden, as well as the sharp edge distinguishing the paved from the planted area, enhances depth and perspective. In this case, it is interesting to see that these two enclosures divide the main frame into three layers of story, each with its own characteristics.[53] Usually the barrier between the planted and paved areas is light and transparent, allowing a visual connection between the garden and the building. Examples can be found in two paintings discussed earlier: the red fences in the story of the maidens bathing in a garden pool (Figure 33) and Soltan Malek Saleh's *chaharbagh* from Sa'di's *Bustan* (Figure 5).[54]

The Design of the Building

Buildings shown in gardens vary in height, being usually single- or double-storeyed, and in a few cases, three-storeyed. It is difficult to find any rule to relate the height of the pavilion to its typology as a house or palace. Most buildings are two-storeyed and include a balcony that provides a panoramic view of the garden. Sometimes, counting the number of doors and calculating their height (compared to the human scale in the painting) helps in estimating the overall height of the building; mostly, however, the proportions do not appear to be realistic but are the result of a play with forms, shapes and volumes. For instance, in an illustration from the *Khosrow va Shirin* by Hatefi (1498), the proportions of the height of the building and its three storeys seem confusing and do not match the human scale in the painting.[55] The three-storeyed building depicted in this painting follows a pyramidal pattern in which the height of each floor is less than that of the one below. Here, the change of height from the third floor to the first makes the building less realistic and more sculptural.[56] This phenomenon reveals that the artists have come up with a unique proportional system, which does not necessarily match that of the real architectural design. However, it is not a common pattern in Persian painting; for instance, in the contemporaneous painting from Nezami's *Khosrow va Shirin* (Tabriz, late fifteenth century), Shirin's hexagonal three-storeyed pavilion has more realistic and accurate proportions, although Khosrow and his horse still seem larger than other figures (Figure 36).[57] It appears that the change in the scale of figures or building elements is a device to emphasize certain parts of the painting, based on the narrative, and also to make a visual equation. In this case, enlarging the figure of Khosrow allows the artist to balance the monumental palace of Shirin on the right, and Khosrow on the left, and consequently, to highlight the conversation between these two.

As with height, there is much variance in the overall plan of the pavilions. The most common forms are the square and the hexagon. In most cases, the square-shaped plan refers to residential use, whereas hexagonal and octagonal plans are mostly used to portray the monumental aspects of the building, which is usually a palace. For instance, in the last painting,[58] using the hexagonal plan isolates the building from the urban fabric around it, which usually dictates square and rectangular patterns, and establishes a special relationship between the building and the surrounding garden. The same monumental pattern is commonly used in garden carpets, where the pavilion structure is contrasted in the centre of a *chaharbagh*. An early eighteenth-century carpet shows a rectangular pavilion placed in the centre of a large *chaharbagh,* each of its four sectors subdivided by water channels into a number of other compartments (Figure 37).[59]

In some paintings, especially in the late Safavids, the plan seems unclear because of more complicated forms in the design of the pavilion. In such cases, the plan includes a complex series of buildings and façades relating to the narrative behind the painting. For instance, in Mir Musavvir's depiction of the nightmare of Zahhak from the *Shahnameh* of Shah Tahmasp (1525–35), the plan of the buildings cannot be easily recognized (Figure 38). Using this confusing form and volume may also correlate to the main subject, that is, the "frightening nightmare".[60] There is a series of balconies and bridges that show the tension inside Zahhak's court. A garden is chosen as the main setting for the building, even though the poem does not mention it. The bridge connecting parts of the building, and even the second-floor balcony, have probably been added to make the building look more transparent, and as a way to show the interior. Creating such a magnificent illustration, with its complex layers and connectors, is unlikely to be based on daily observations, and is probably the result of the artist's imagination.[61]

This is typical of Mo'in Mosavvar's school of painting, in which the building is usually

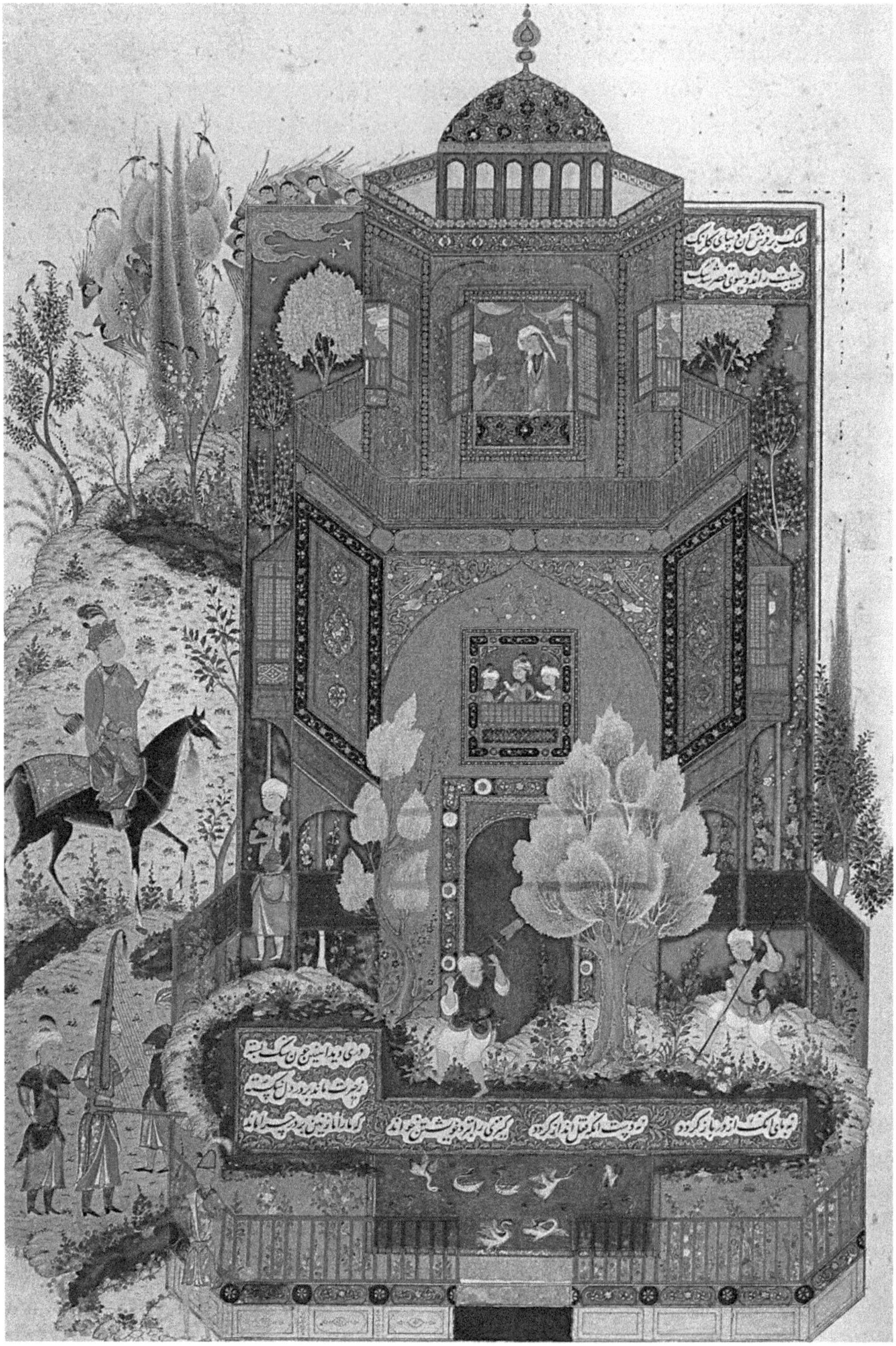

FIGURE 36
Shirin's pavilion. From *Khosrow va Shirin* by Nezami.

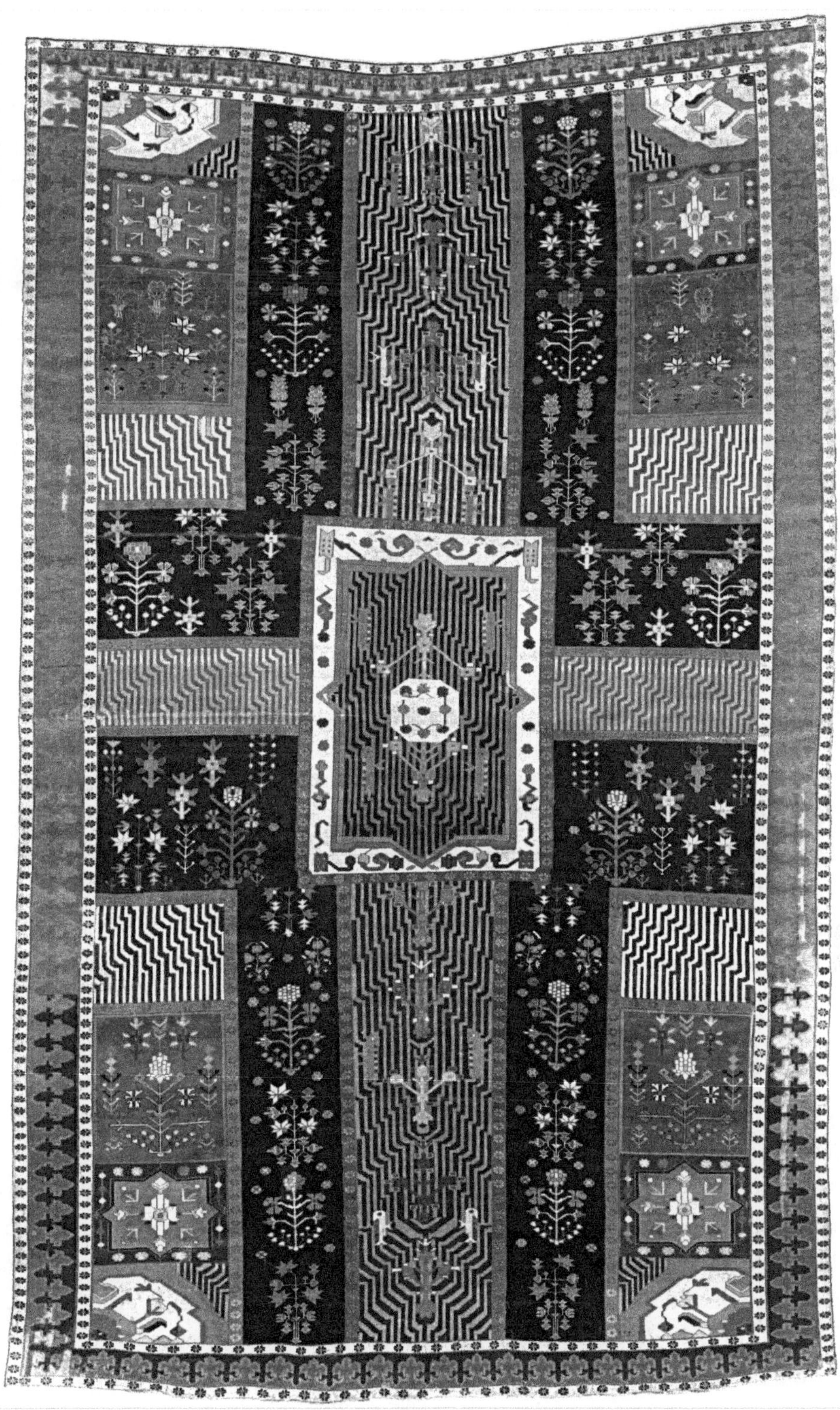

FIGURE 37

Persian garden carpet. Kurdistan, second half of the eighteenth century.

introduced as a layer or a series of layers and not as a volume. These compound compositions enable the painter to capture the complexity of the plan and elevation while summarizing the building in a two-dimensional frame. In other words, these complex forms work as tools to shed light on hidden angles of the building which could not be shown in a two-dimensional façade. This quality is reflected in a work by Soltan Muhammad from the *Divan* by Hafez (1525), which captures the drinking scene inside and outside the pavilion: the (back) hidden side of the façade is pushed forward and opened up in order to include it (Figure 39). The angels on the roof, in contrast to the bucolic scene of the elderly drunkards, underline the metaphysical aspects of the painting. All three types of enclosures (wall, railing and fence) are visible in this painting. This example highlights the formal and two-dimensional value of the building rather than its volumetric quality. A similar approach is taken in a work by Qasem 'Ali (1485) from the story of Majnun coming to the house of Leyla (Figure 40),[62] in which the wall works like a threshold between the garden and the paved area, rather than part of a real building. The *iwan,* which is towards the courtyard rather than the garden, causes confusion about the relationship between outside and inside, and among the building, and the paved and planted areas.

Architectural Elements

The main architectural elements in garden pavilions include the *iwan,* balcony, openings, water channels and fountains, and enclosures. An *iwan,* also called a portico, is a single large vaulted hall walled on three sides and opening directly to the outside on the fourth.[63] It acts as a consistent component of the Persian pavilion, providing a unique opportunity for the king to enjoy the view of the garden while being inside the building. For instance, in one of Qasem 'Ali's paintings (1485), Nushirvan is sitting with a lady on the *iwan,* which is located in the middle of a planted garden that seems to surround the building (Figure 41). In this case, the *iwan* is a place for intimate conversation, while in other paintings the conversation occurs between the person on the *iwan* and the audience in the courtyard. A sixteenth-century painting (1553) from Sa'di's *Bustan* shows a conversation between the king sitting in the *iwan* and the dervish sitting in the courtyard (Figure 42).

In many paintings, the throne is located at the centre of the *iwan,* offering the best view of the courtyard and figures standing there, as we have seen in the early Safavid painting from the *Shahnameh* of Shah Tahmasp (Figure 21). In some examples, two thrones or royal chairs are placed where the king and his special guest are being entertained, while in others, the throne is located in the paved area next to the *iwan,* probably in order to decrease the hierarchical distance between king and courtiers, and to portray the king as more approachable. The *iwan* need not always be the dominant element, as when the artist attempts to highlight the garden behind the building. In an early Safavid painting (1528–29)

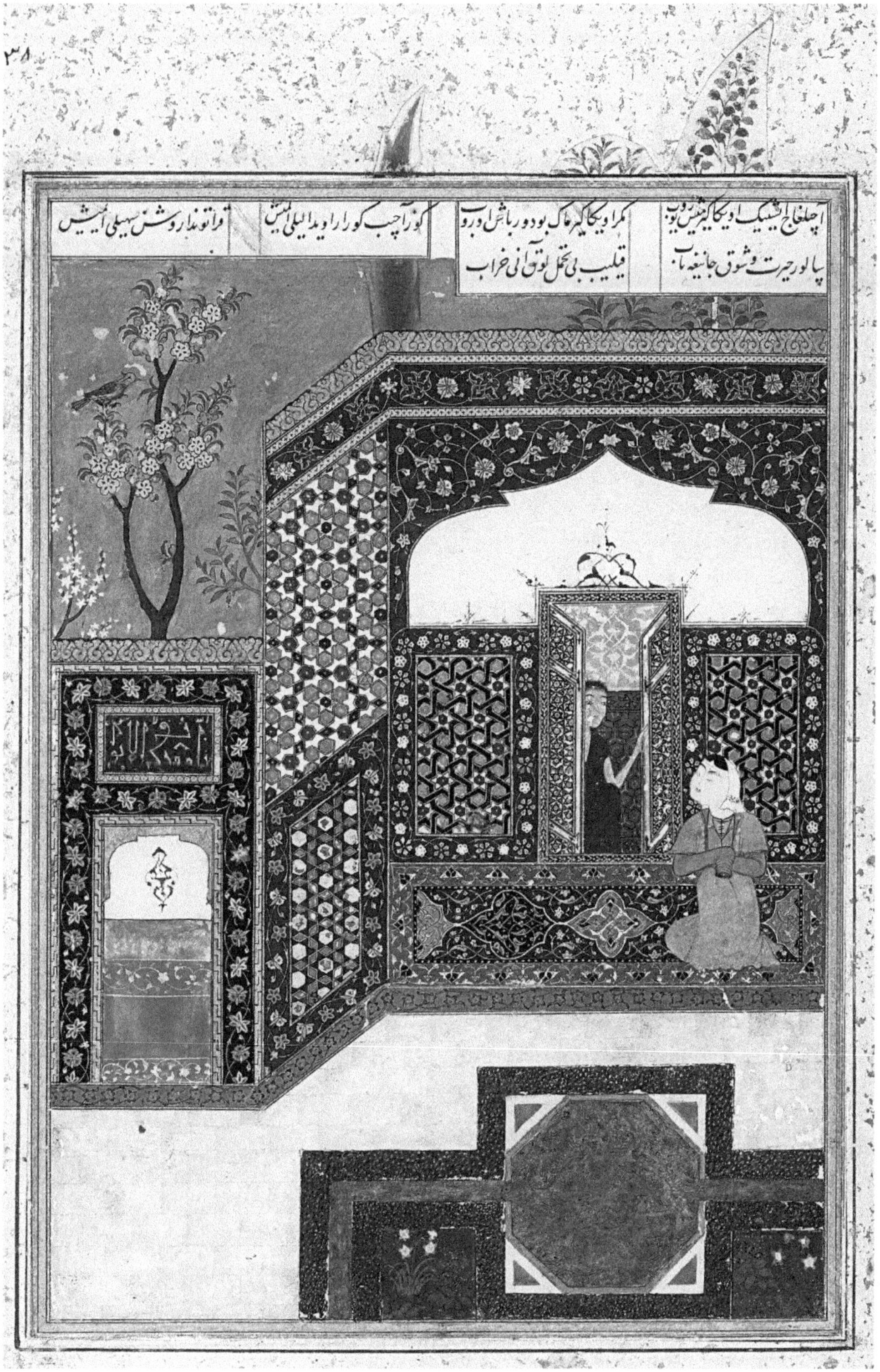

FIGURE 40

Majnun coming to the house of Leyla. From the *Divan* by Mir 'Ali Shir Nava'i in Chaghatay Turkish, attributed to Qasem 'Ali, 1485.

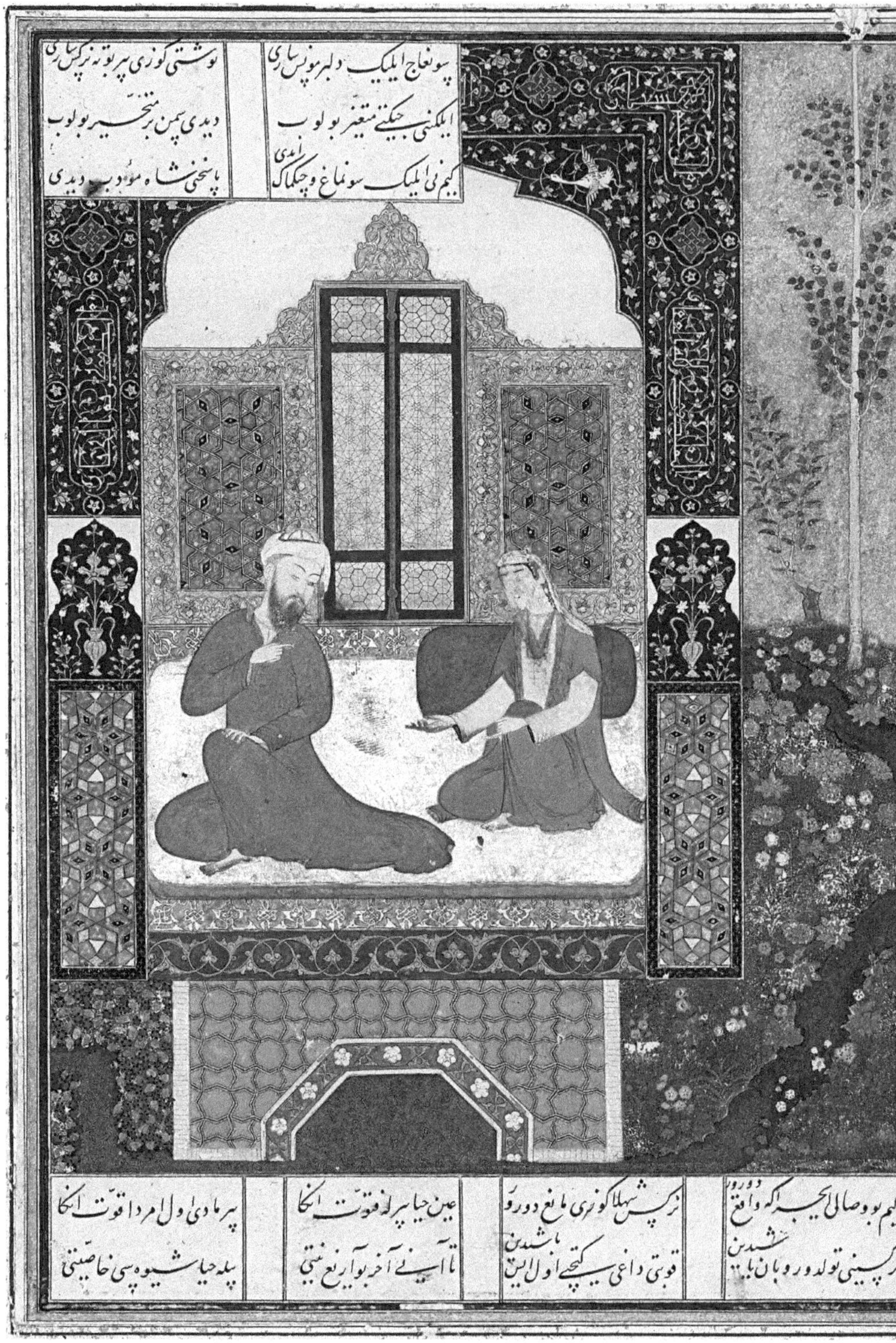

FIGURE 41

Nushirvan with a lady on *iwan*. From *Hayrat al-Abrar* by 'Ali Shir Nava'i, attributed to Qasem 'Ali, 1485.

from Nezami's *Khamseh* that shows Alexander the Great admiring the portrait of himself that was ordered by Queen Nushabeh (Figure 43), the people before the *iwan* create and define a sense of extension from the building to the courtyard and somehow connect the three layers of the painting: foreground garden, built area and background garden.

The *iwan,* being considered a significant transitional space between the courtyard and pavilion, is usually two or three steps higher than the level of the courtyard. Being on this higher level defines the status of the king and special courtiers or members of the harem, and others who are not allowed to enter the *iwan*. Thus, in most paintings only a few specific figures are close to the king's throne in the *iwan*. People facing the *iwan* usually stand in rows in a way that the king could easily observe them. In an illustration from Shah Tahmasp's manuscript of Nezami's *Khamseh* (1427), the painting concentrates on the *iwan,* which is shown as the setting for the backgammon game between the prince and his courtier (Figure 44).[64] The elaborate red railing in this painting emphasizes the game as the focal point. A rectangular or square *iwan* may act as a focal point in some paintings.[65] The semi-octagonal or trapezoid-shaped *iwan,* which appears frequently in Safavid and Mughal paintings, is probably a visually modified version of the *iwan* shown in perspective.[66]

One or three doors usually connect the interior of the building and the *iwan,* but in most cases there is no window to the interior, since showing the background may distract from the story. A painting from the *Shahnameh* shows a different view from the *iwan* (Figure 45). It emphasizes the higher level of *iwan* and its architectural elements such as portico and railing.[67] This work, which could be categorized as one of the earliest examples of what Grabar calls "realism" in Persian painting, is a depiction of seventeenth-century Safavid buildings. It shows Siyavash captive before Afrasyab in the *iwan*. This perspective drawing, definitely done under European influence, shows the garden, the fountain, and rows of trees aligned with the *iwan,* its columns and its fountain.[68] This painting was created after the transmission of perspective techniques from European art, and enabled Safavid artists to show a more realistic connection between the pavilion and the garden and its components.[69] It also shows elaborate columns which are different from the typical thin and undecorated columns, usually made of wood, which enabled people to have the undisrupted view that appears in older, two-dimensional, paintings.[70] The majority of *iwans* in painting are porticos without columns. In that respect, the *iwan* in Persian painting is somewhat comparable to the portico in mosques and *madrasas*. Some Safavid artists, such as Zaman and his successors, depicted the *iwan* as a columned hall in their paintings, probably under European influence.

The balcony appears in paintings when there is a need to establish a connection between the inside and outside of a building; for instance, when people on the inside look out at the courtyard. The balcony is usually a vertical cube with a light roof made of cloth or wood with thin pillars. To some extent, this form is comparable to the structure of the kiosk in painting, which will be discussed later. The similarity is evident in a painting (1526–27) attributed to Sheykh Zadeh, a Herat-trained artist (Figure 31). Here, the balcony appears as a flimsy and isolated structure, and not as an inseparable part of the building. Two thin, weak beams underneath, which do not seem strong enough to support its weight, prove the painter's concentration on its formal role rather than its structural sturdiness.[71] Even in the few cases where the balcony looks more complex, delicate and real, and less imaginary, it is usually treated as an additional and detached part of the building, and one in which a different architectural language is applied.

Openings, doors and windows, are apparently considered secondary elements in Persian painting. Usually, the main entrance of the garden or pavilion is not shown unless the exterior is important in the narrative accompanying the illustration. For instance, the entrance is visible in a Qasem 'Ali painting (1521) based on *Panj Ganj* (Figure 9). Here, the garden is fully separated from the urban context by walls. The stress on the entrance has to do with the focus of the narrative, which is about Yusof attending Zulaykha's party. Openings, in most cases, are bare of any ornamentation; however, in some paintings they are treated as mini-frames for detailed and elegant decorations. The windows and doors in paintings which capture the interior of the building are also devices to control the penetration of light from outside to inside and afford a view of the garden. A quick review of the paintings that depict the interior of a pavilion shows that there are usually limited degrees of visibility from inside to the garden. For instance, in a painting from Nezami's *Khosrow va Shirin*, three windows behind Shirin make a visual connection between interior and exterior (Figure 32).[72] In this case, as in most other paintings, the windows and door are treated as two-dimensional.

The whole concept of the Persian garden and pavilion in reality is linked with water as the main source of life and abundance. The fountains and channels in paintings play a similar role, as a softening element that makes a balance between the natural and artificial areas. There are two types of water channels depicted in miniature painting. The first has an organic and natural pattern, while the second is straight and geometrical. The first type usually belongs to the natural landscape (also called the Chinese garden) captured in the background of several paintings.[73] The second type of water channel, which appears in the foreground, is usually placed in front of the building in the paved area. This type is always a straight channel crossing a pool. The difference between these two types is visible in a sixteenth-century painting attributed to Mirza 'Ali, Soltan Muhammad's son, from the *Khamseh* by Nezami, which shows Barbad playing music to Khosrow. The pool in the paved area is connected to the water in the planted area via a channel (Figure 15). It clearly shows how running water is contrasted and connected between the two different parts of the garden, and the ways in which the design applies geometrical and organic languages.[74]

The pool is usually located in the paved area next to the pavilion, the *iwan*, or close to the throne. It is usually circular, square, rectangular or hexagonal. In some cases, the artist has used a more complex plan, such as a floral pattern, in the design of the pool. This representation of garden and fountain is also used as a prototype on woven textiles from the seventeenth and eighteenth centuries.[75] For instance, the floral pattern is reflected in a carpet made in the late seventeenth century which illustrates the fountain in the middle of the garden (Figure 46). This classical Persian garden is divided into four beds by two intersecting channels of water. The garden is actually depicted from two points of view at once: from above, giving the architectural plan, and from the side, showing the trees and shrubs in profile. In some cases, two planted flowers, placed one on each side, frame the pool for the king who is facing it. In others, the form of the fountain resembles the form of the pavilion (palace or kiosk) before it. It can be seen in the story of the enthronement of Yusof, where the square form of the pool resembles the plan of the kiosk in front of it. In a painting by Mir Mosavvar, the octagonal pool is related to the rectangular shape of the building next to it (Figure 38).[76] The similarity between the plan of the fountain and that of the pavilion confirms that artists design the garden components in such a way that they enhance the connection between the building and the garden.

As I have mentioned, the paved area in the garden is separated from the planted area by a fence in the majority of paintings. This fence is usually a light structure made of wood or metal, which is transparent enough to allow people to view the garden from the pavilion and the courtyard. There is usually a gateway or two to make connections between the planted and paved areas. An instance can be seen in a painting from the *Khamseh* (1495–96), in which the fence and door separate the pavilion (paved) area from the surrounding garden (Figure 47);[77] in another painting, from the *Divan* by Hafez, the white fence separates two areas of the garden with different spatial hierarchies (Figure 18). In the case of private residences, the whole private entity, including the garden, is protected and separated from the public area (street or neighbourhood) by a brick wall. In the painting showing the conversation between Homayun and Homay, the jagged edge of the wall highlights the separation of the building complex and the natural landscape (Figure 26).

THE PAVILION AS A PORTABLE STRUCTURE

The pavilion not only appears in gardens as a building but also as a kiosk or throne. The pavilion as a throne was a movable structure that could be carried by horses, camels, elephants and even humans. The mobile nature of the pavilion has been so dominant that its equivalent

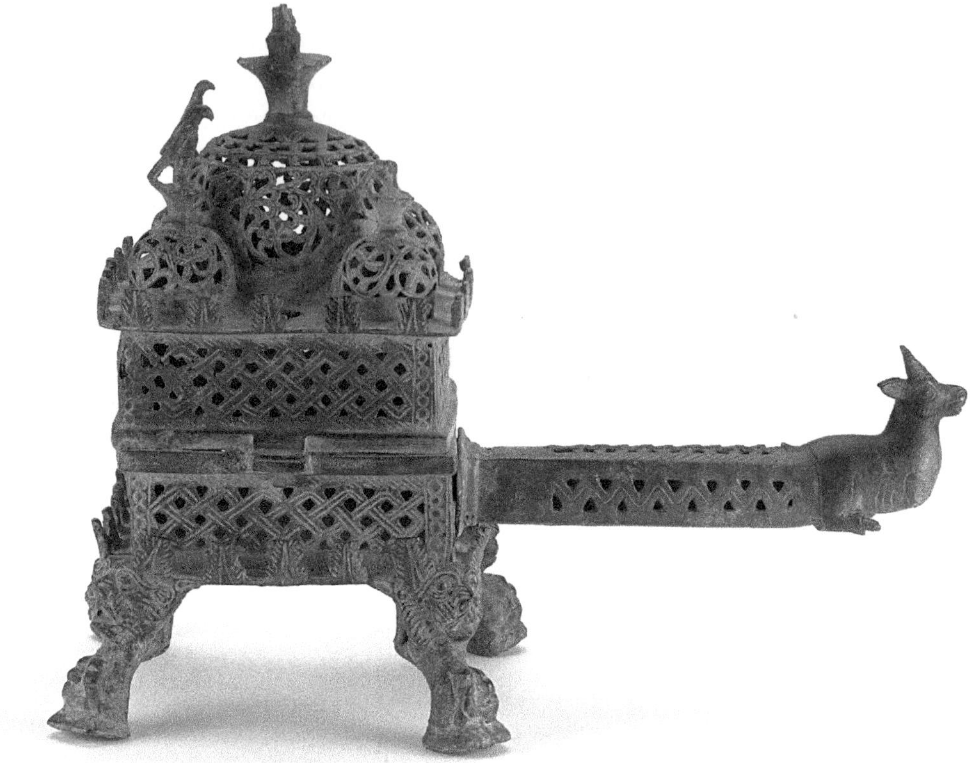

FIGURE 49
Brass incense burner. Eighth–ninth centuries.

term in Persian, *palun,* means 'packsaddle'.[78] The moving pavilion has been depicted in the story of Yusof and Zulaykha in the *Haft Awrang,* where Zulaykha's pavilion is being carried by a camel (Figure 48).[79] This illustration shows Aziz and Zulaykha in their pavilions entering the capital of Egypt, with the Egyptians coming out to greet them. Here the pavilion is a domed hexagonal structure, designed for one person and held on to the camel by strong girths.[80] The subject of pavilions on camels apparently interests artists other than painters, as can be seen from an incense burner made of bronze (Egypt, eighth and ninth centuries CE), which abstracts the subject of the pavilion on an imaginary quadruped animal (Figure 49). This sculpture could be also interpreted as a square structure surmounted by a large central dome, with additional smaller domes placed at the four corners. The piece is really a combination of building and pavilion, while stressing the mobility of the pavilion structure.[81]

The level of design detail usually depends on the status of the pavilion's resident: for example, the royal pavilion of the king or his queen is usually more refined in terms of ornamentation. The pavilion allocated to women is generally enclosed and covered to protect their privacy. This structure, which should not be mistaken for the royal throne, can be transported and placed inside the building or garden. In such cases, the pavilion (throne) has legs and can be placed on ground. The mobility of the pavilion as throne in painting depends on the underlying story and the nomadic or urban context of the narrative. For instance, the pavilion is placed on a boat or ship in several paintings, which depict the maritime or riverine travels of a significant figure. In a rendition of Ferdowsi's parable of the ship of Shi'ism from Shah Tahmasp's *Shahnameh* (1525), the pavilion is located on a boat (Figure 50).[82] Here, the door and the pathway act as the connector between the private areas (kiosk) and the public areas (rest of the boat). It is quite clear that the artist, Mirza 'Ali, uses the same architectural elements – platform, railing and door – that appear in a garden kiosk, in this different location. The same scene is evident in other paintings, such as one by Behzad from the *Hasht Behesht* by Amir Khosrow Dehlavi (1496) which depicts the abduction of the king's favourite maiden (Figure 51),[83] and another from the *Shahnameh* (1618–19) illustrating Key Khosrow crossing Lake Zarah in pursuit of Afrasyab (Figure 52).

This model is also apparent in arts outside the Persianate cultural realm. For example, an illustration by 'Abd al-Latif (1315) from the *Automata* by al-Jazari reflects a domed pavilion which is placed on a boat-like structure (Figure 53).[84] In contrast to the mobile pavilions in

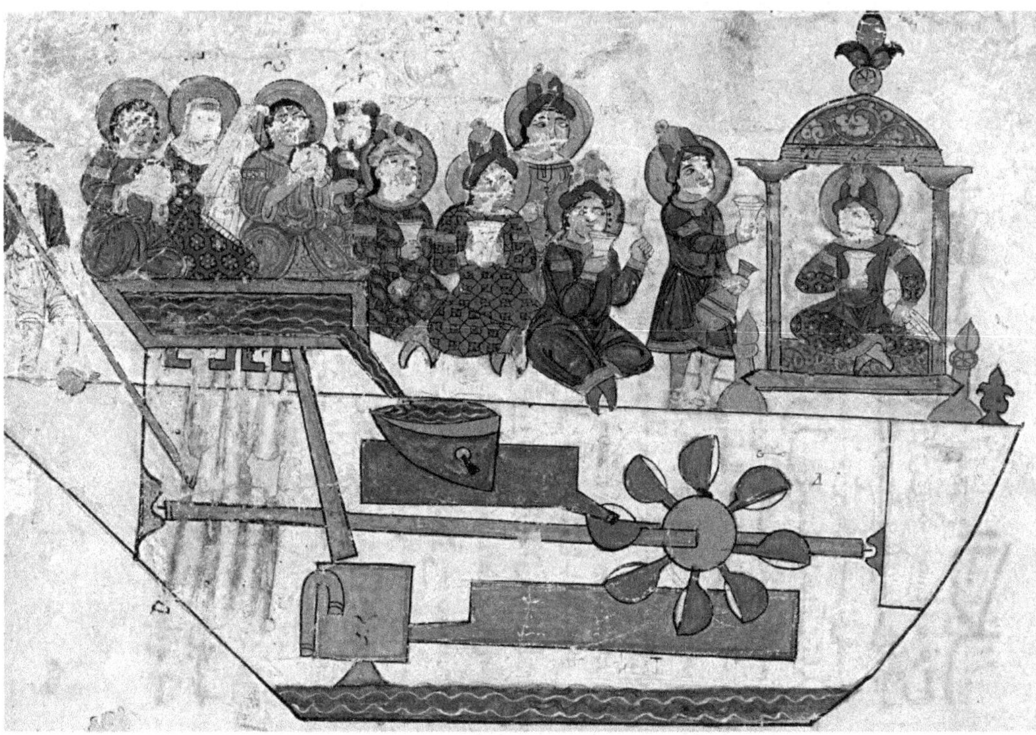

FIGURE 53
Domed pavilion. From the *Automata* by al-Jazari, Syria.

some paintings, the pavilion as a kiosk seems very site-specific and physically inseparable from its setting. For instance, in Meskin's painting (around 1590) based on the story of Noah's ark, the same design is used to define a seating area in the ship.[85] In this case, Noah is sitting on a deck that looks like a kiosk. This kiosk-like structure seems fixed, and physically and visually inseparable from the boat.[86] The focus on the pavilion area could still be interpreted as a signifier of the hierarchical order of spaces in the boat. In other words, sitting in a kiosk is a sign of significance. The kiosk here has four thin columns and is two-storeyed. In a painting by Behzad from the *Khamseh* by Nezami (1494), which illustrates Leyla and Majnun at school, the kiosk is depicted as raised brick platform under a tree close to a fountain (Figure 54).[87] These examples confirm the flexibility of the concept of kiosk, as well as its frequent occurrence in painting regardless of the message and narrative.

The Throne

Royal patronage meant that depiction of court life was a popular subject for Persian painters. This alone probably justifies the frequent appearance of the king's throne, which acts as the focal point in many paintings, especially those that depict the enthronement ceremony. This throne could be as simple as a chair, such as Khosrow's throne in a painting supervised by Behzad from the *Khamseh* by Nezami (1525), which illustrates his enthronement (Figure 19). The placement of the throne at a thirty-degree angle makes it the focal point of the painting. Unlike many other paintings, which place emphasis on the various personages in the garden, with their gestures, emotions and interactions, here the stress is on Khosrow, who is facing the paved area of the garden.[88]

The throne is usually located in one of three places: inside the building, on the *iwan* or in the planted area. Paintings in which the throne is inside usually focus on the interior of the palace and treat the garden as a minor background. Depicting the king on the *iwan,* from either in front or behind, affects the visibility of the garden, but it enables him to have a panoramic view while highlighting him and his status. In a painting attributed to Kamal-uddin Behzad (1529), depicting celebrations marking the arrival of Timur in Samarqand in 1396, the throne is located close to the *iwan* (Figure 55). The musicians play before the king, who is sitting on his monumental throne from which he has a wide view of the courtyard. Another sixteenth-century painting from *Masnavi-ye Jamshid va Khorshid* shows Jamshid and Khorshid sitting on a throne on the *iwan* (Figure 56). While the throne and *iwan* are usually sufficient signifiers of social or royal rank, putting the throne on the *iwan* can be interpreted as a double emphasis on the rank of the figures sitting there. This painting is one of the few in which the throne and kiosk appear simultaneously. While the unattended kiosk allows the throne to function as the focal point of the painting, it appears that the artist envisions

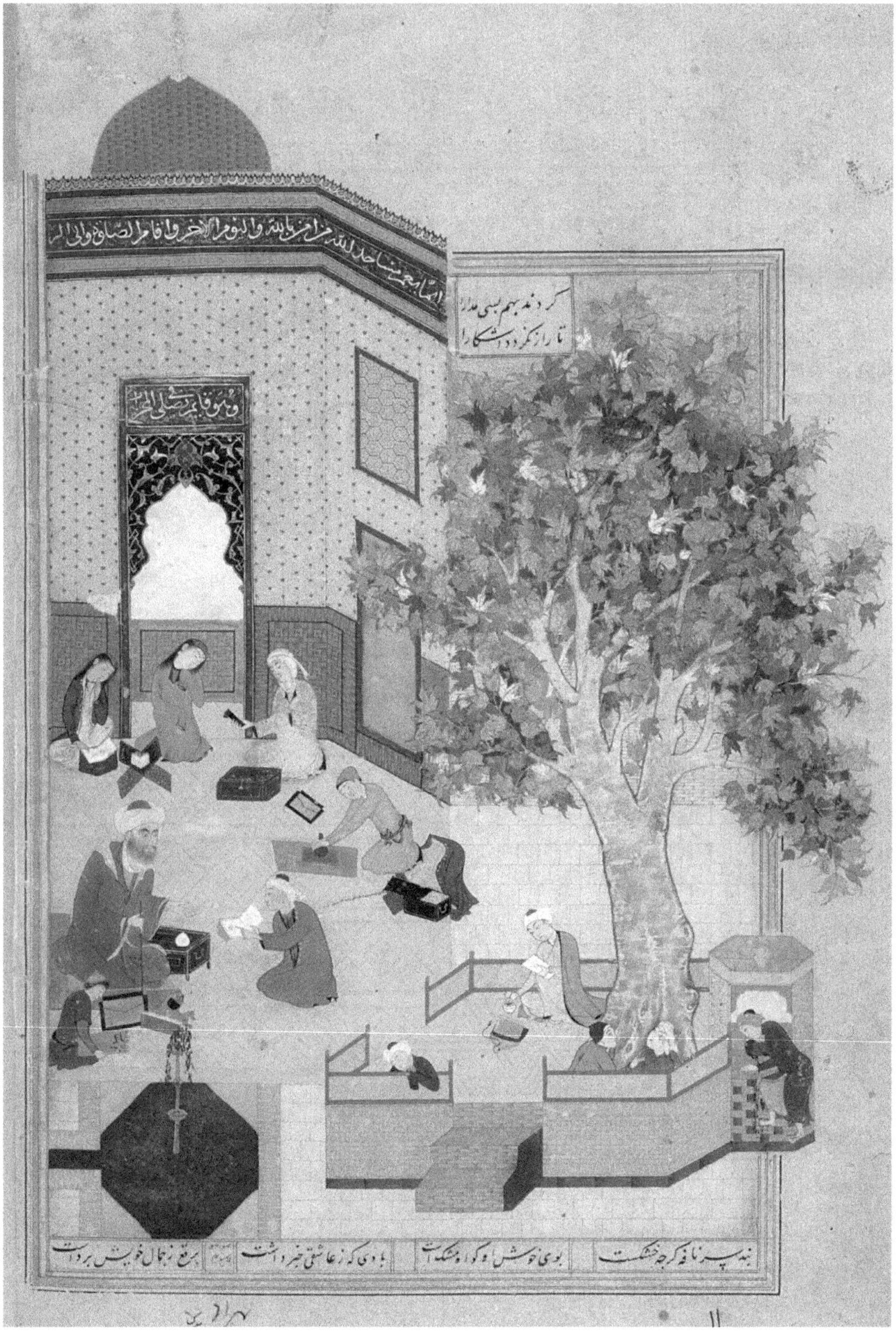

FIGURE 54

Leyla and Majnun at school. From the *Khamseh* by Nezami, Herat, 1494–95.

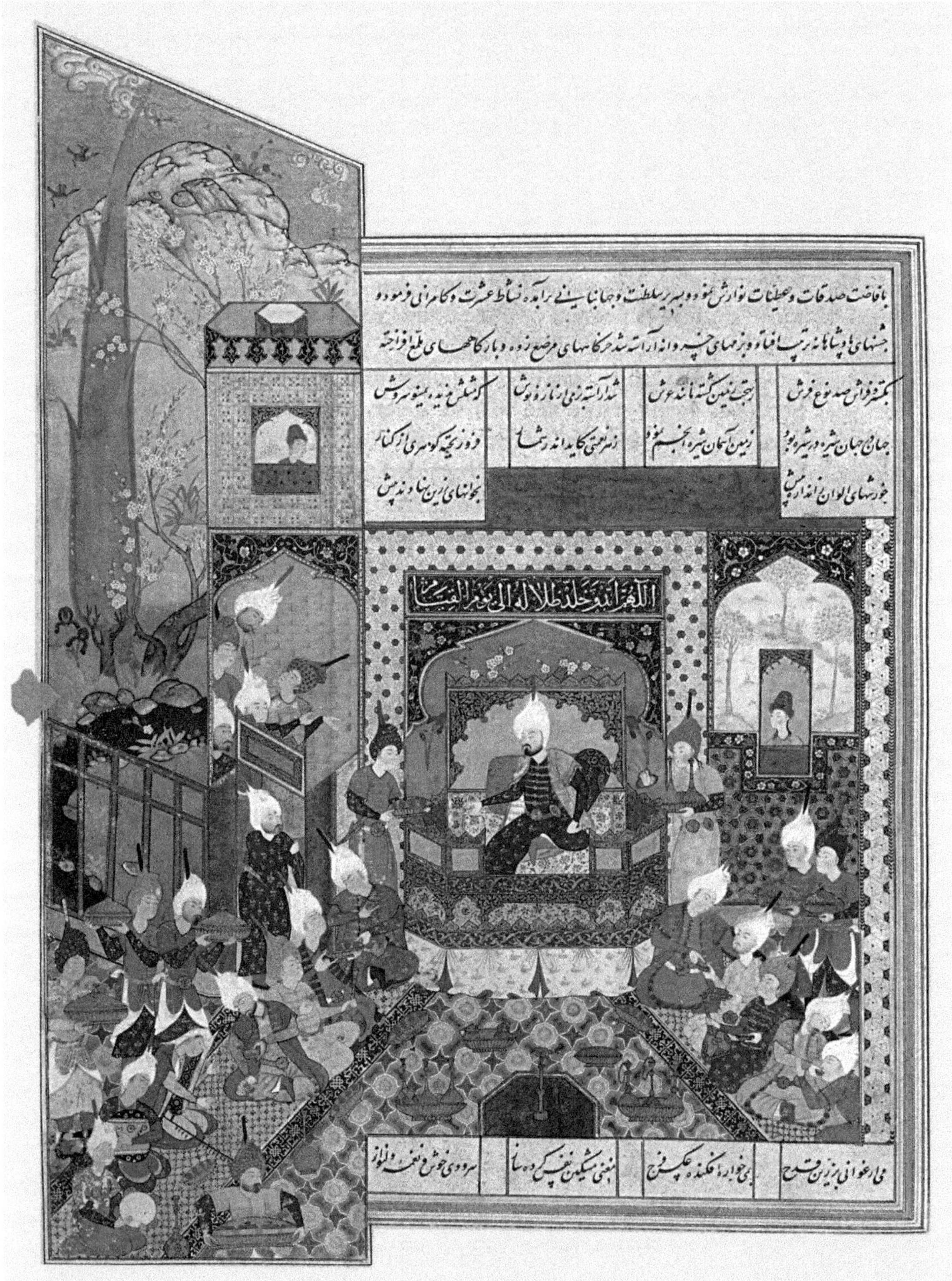

FIGURE 55

Celebrations marking the arrival of Timur in Samarqand in 1396.
From the *Zafarnameh,* attributed to Kamal-uddin Behzad, Herat, 1529.

different roles for them, and one does not simply replace the other. In a Safavid *Shahnameh* (1618–19) depicting Key Khosrow feasting Rustam, the throne is located in the portico in the middle of the garden (Figure 57). The artist makes the throne the focal point by using a hexagonal and monumental form for the throne, emphasizing the centrality of the throne and *iwan,* and using the dome and portal ornamentations to point towards Khosrow's head.[89] The throne on the ground or in the planted area appears in several paintings which depict wars, negotiations or encampments, such as one showing the conversation between Rustam and Isfandyar (1430) before their war (Figure 58). Here, their thrones are located under a tree on a carpet in the planted area of a garden.[90] In this case, the carpet under the thrones highlights the importance of the people sitting there: Rustam and Isfandyar. The carpet also defines a clear boundary between the planted and sitting areas and works as a symbolic barrier to highlight the court, thus decreasing the value of the planted areas. The circular arrangement of figures helps the artist to stress the centre, where the thrones are located.

What is common to all of these illustrations, which demonstrate the presence of the throne in different parts of the garden, is the significance of the throne and its higher position as defined by the judicious application of the elements in the composition. The throne is usually highlighted by placing it on a carpet (and not on the bare ground), on a higher level, on the *iwan,* in front of the pool, close to a significant architectural element, or in between two flowerbeds. For example, in a painting from the sixteenth-century *Shahnameh,* Khosrow's throne is before the door of his tent (Figure 59). It shows Khosrow, enthroned, celebrating Nowruz with numerous courtiers and attendants in a dark green flowery landscape under a tent. The throne in the royal encampment is also visible in the depiction of Shida (Pashang) in the camp of Key Khosrow on a battle plain between Mount Raybad and Mount Kanabad, from Berenson's *Shahnameh* (Figure 60). Afraid of Key Khosrow's armies, the Afrasyab sent his son, Shida, with a peace message, offering to avoid a battle between their armies if the Iranian leader would fight him or his son in hand-to-hand combat. Key Khosrow agreed to fight Shida, and ultimately slew him. According to Bailey, the artist has used this scene as an excuse for a collage of the decorative patterns and pastel colours presented by the tents of the encampment. The grandeur of this quilt-like effect is enhanced by the flowery glade below and the silver stream running through it.[91] In a painting by Ram Das in the Persian translation of the *Baburnameh* prepared for Akbar (1589), Babur is receiving Persian, Uzbek and Rajput envoys in a garden at Agra (Figure 61). Babur's throne is under an awning on two layers of carpet.[92] The tent is located in a garden with a view of the city, a typical scene in Mughal paintings.

The throne is usually wide enough to be used by a person sitting cross-legged, and sometimes long enough for a sleeping person. Despite its significance in the court, special guests are sometimes allowed to sit there. For instance, in a painting from the *Khamseh* (1528–29), both Khosrow and Shirin share the same throne (Figure 62). To put more emphasis on the throne, it is located at the main gateway to the garden in the centre of the frame.[93] This throne is further differentiated by its colour, by being placed in the centre of the frame, and by using a strong geometrical composition to make it the focal point.

The throne, in general, is square, hexagonal, rectangular or circular. In a painting from the *Shahnameh* of Shah Tahmasp (1525), Zal, who is sitting on a large hexagonal throne covered with an awning, is consulting with the Magi in the courtyard (Figure 63). The throne is frequently depicted as a mobile element in paintings from the *Shahnameh*, for instance in the Berenson *Shahnameh* (1535) which illustrates Solomon's throne (Figure 64). Bailey writes,

> This throne is surrounded by animals and *jinns*, while a flock of ecstatic birds and sphinx fly above, forming a canopy to protect him against the sun. The animals are particularly delightful in the variety of their pelts and their animated expressions, as is the pond in the lower part of the image with its ducks and fish. Four dragon-heads grow from his throne, and from behind Solomon's nimbus a talisman appears made up of a gold mask with two birds of gold facing each other.[94]

The scene of the flying throne surrounded by imaginary animals appears in several versions of *Shahnameh* and *Soleymannameh*. In the *Soleymannameh*, an early Ottoman painting produced under Persian influence (1481–1512) by Firdevsi Burusevi and dedicated to Bayzid,[95] the throne of Bilqis (the queen of Sheba) is shown centrally, framed by a rounded arch with plasterwork, under a ribbed dome on a porphyry transitional zone and with a trefoil finial. Above that is the base of an upper dome with deep casements, the shutters of which are open, surmounted by a dome with spiralling ribs.[96]

The Kiosk

The kiosk in Persian painting is a light and open structure, covered, with a raised platform, which can traverse the whole garden. It is a place for higher-rank people to sit, relax and view the garden, eat and drink, talk and observe others. Kiosks do not appear in many paintings; however, we will try to discuss its characteristics based on the existing cases.

The kiosk is usually located in any of three different locations: in the centre of the garden, in the planted area, or on the paved area close to the pool. What is common to these examples is its close connection to natural elements such as water, plants and flowers. In most paintings, the kiosk is either in front of a geometric square pool, close to a natural river or water channel, near flowers and plants, or in the shade of a tree. The kiosk is usually used by the king and his special guests as a place for entertainment and, in some paintings, is large enough to accommodate two or three people or to provide space for drinking or feasting. This

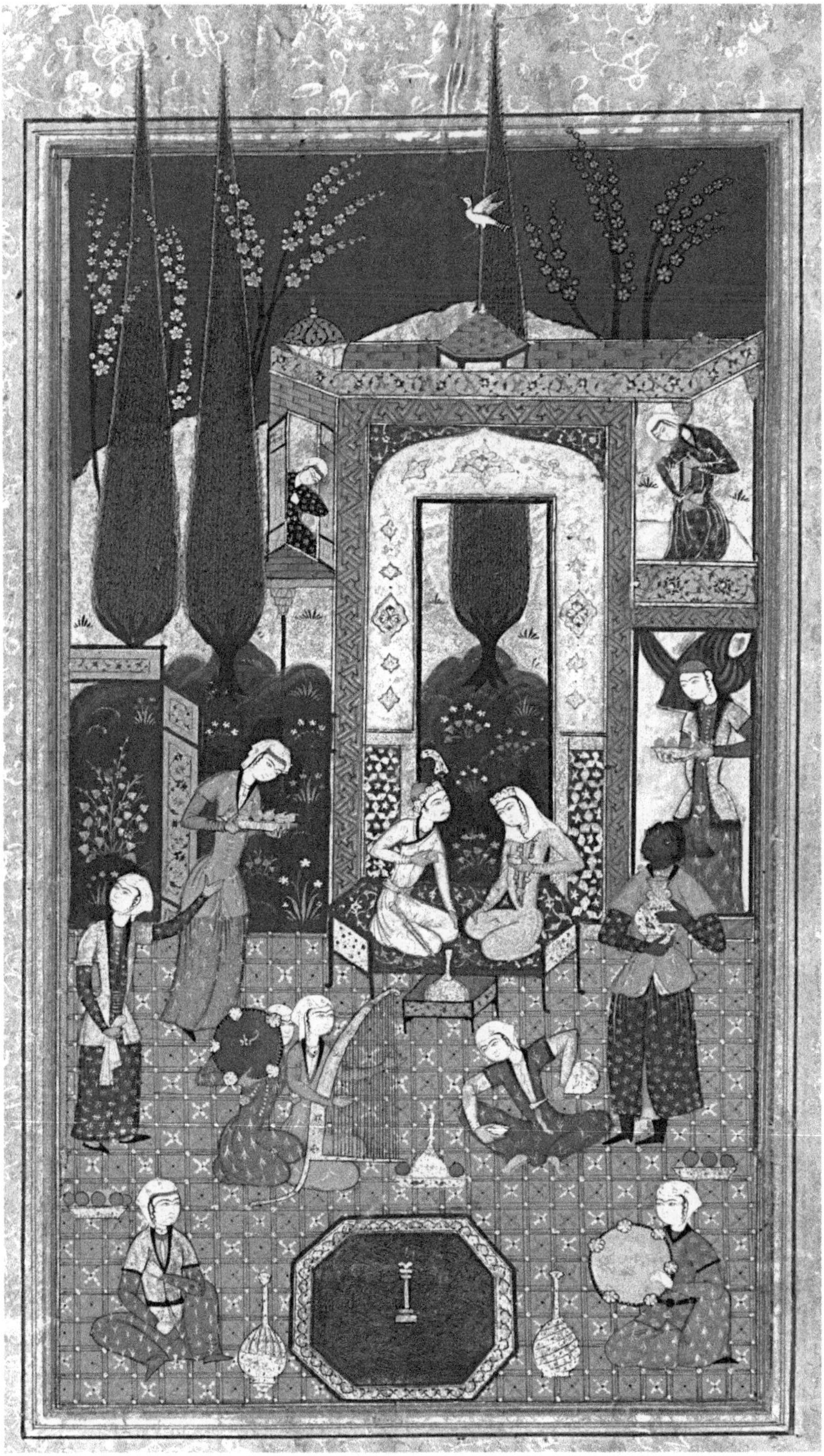

FIGURE 62

Khosrow and Shirin in the palace. From the *Khamseh* by Nezami Ganjavi, 1528–29.

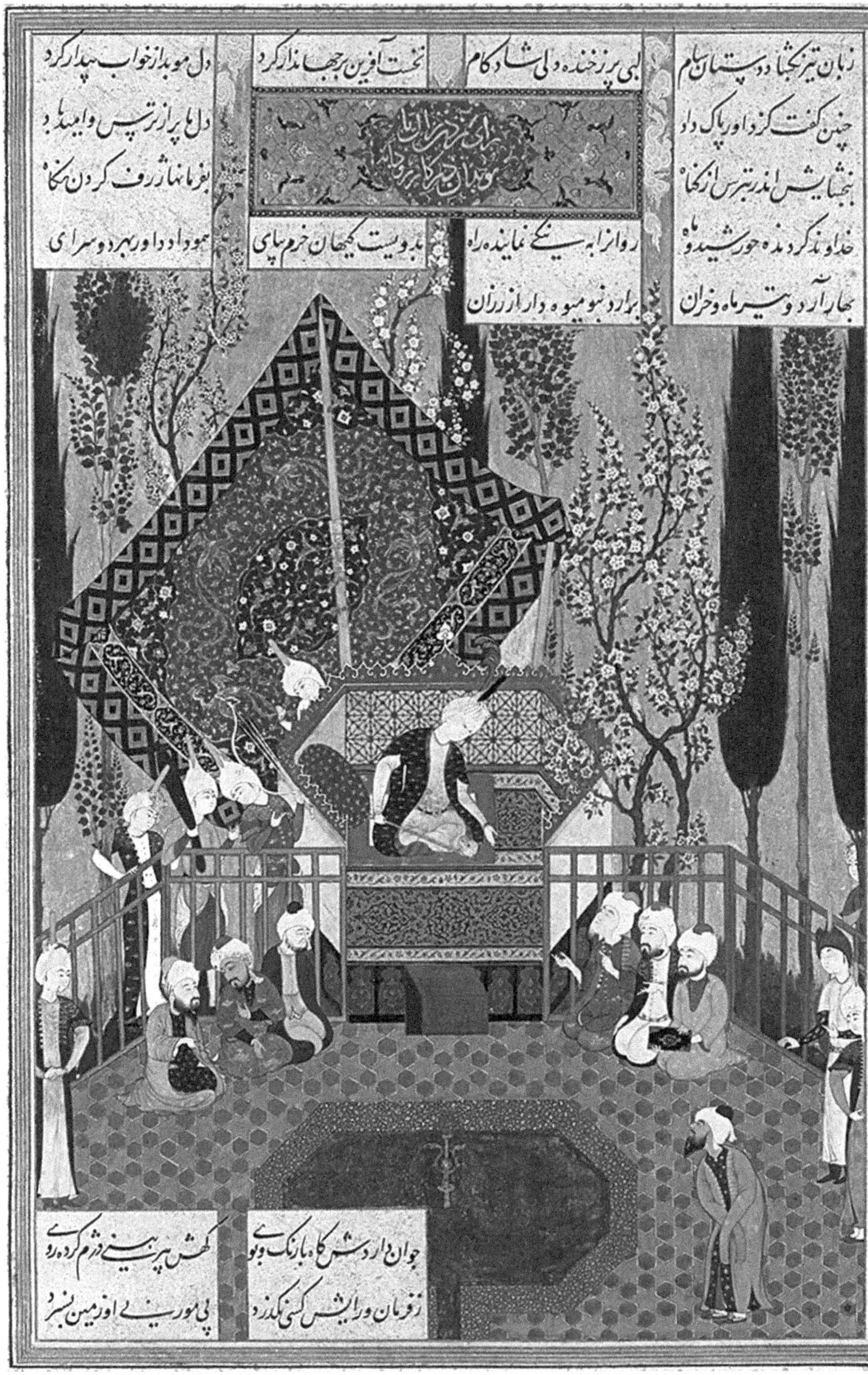

FIGURE 63

Zal consults the Magi. From the *Shahnameh* of Shah Tahmasp, attributed to Soltan Muhammad, Tabriz, 1525.

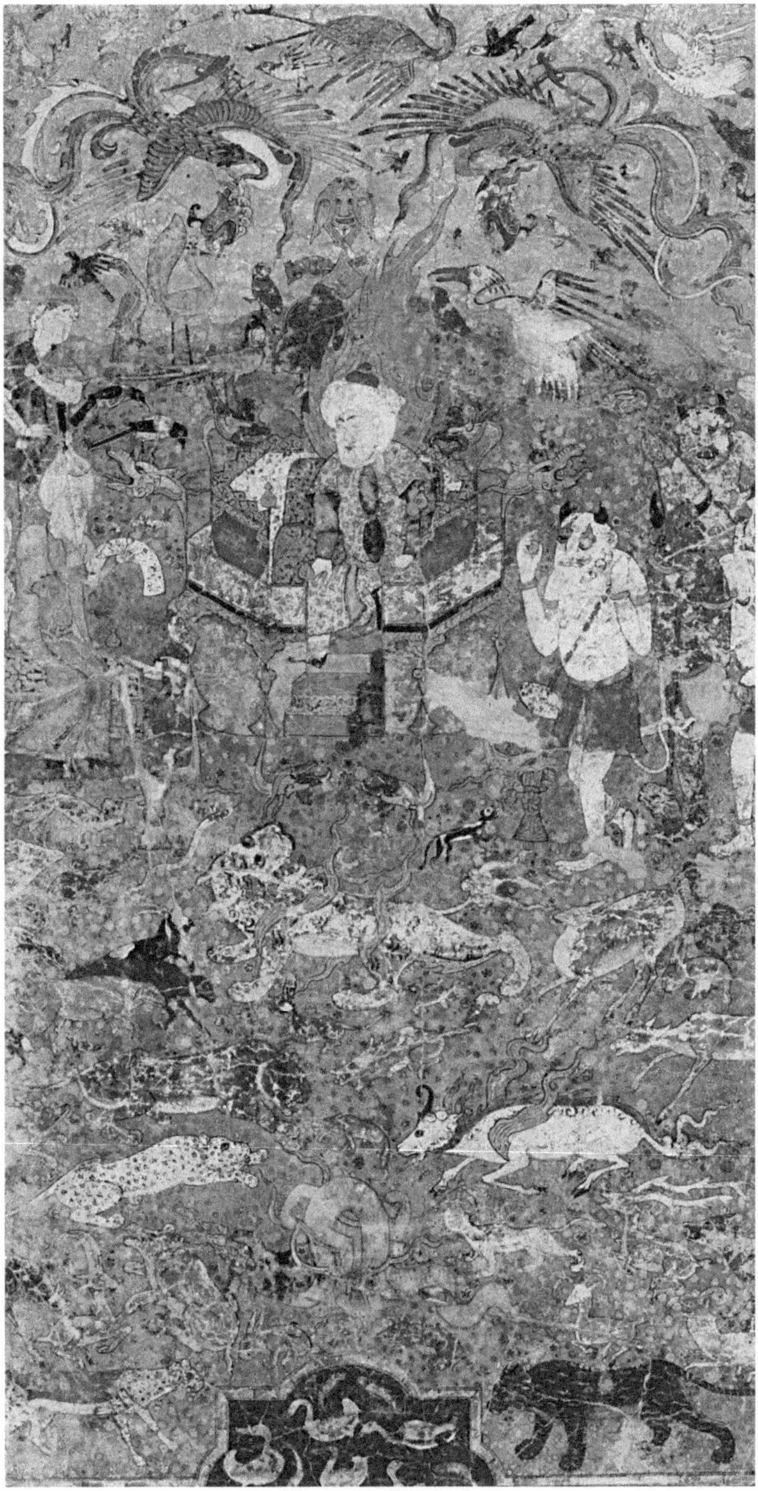

FIGURE 64
Solomon on his throne. From the *Shahnameh,* signed by Mahmud Mozahheb, Shiraz, 1535.

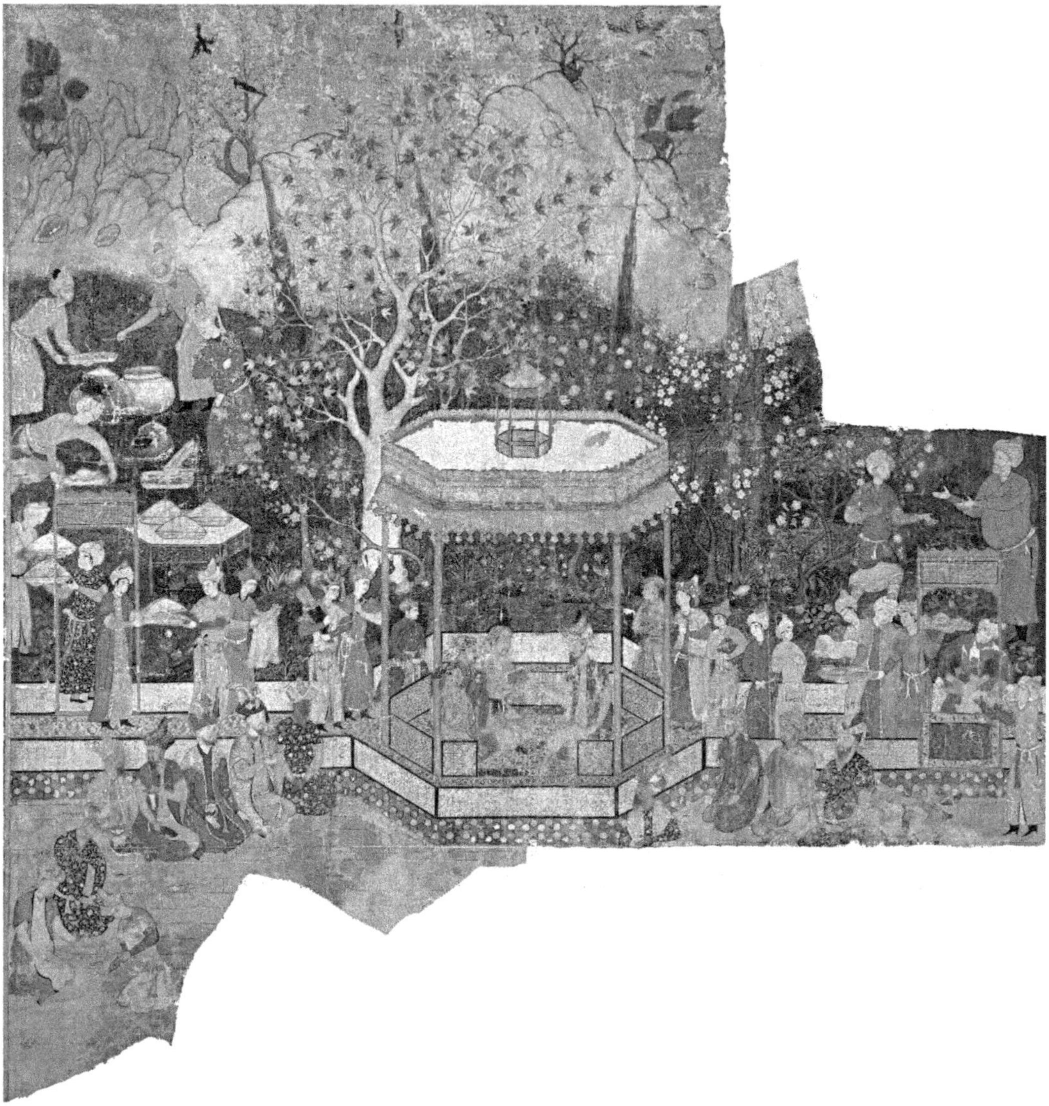

FIGURE 65
The princes of the house of Timur. Made by Mir Sayyed 'Ali, India, 1550–55.

is evident in a painting by 'Abd al-Samad (1550–60),[97] which depicts Timur and his courtiers in his hexagonal kiosk, surrounded by rows of courtiers and ambassadors standing and sitting around the kiosk (Figure 65). This kiosk defines a pathway between the planted and paved areas of the garden. The structure is apparently of wood but the painting is not clear enough to be certain. In a few pictures, an unattended and empty kiosk suggests a lack of hierarchy or a casualness about the meeting going on in the garden, for instance where the Sheykh is teaching his students while sitting on the ground with his students and guests (Figure 66).

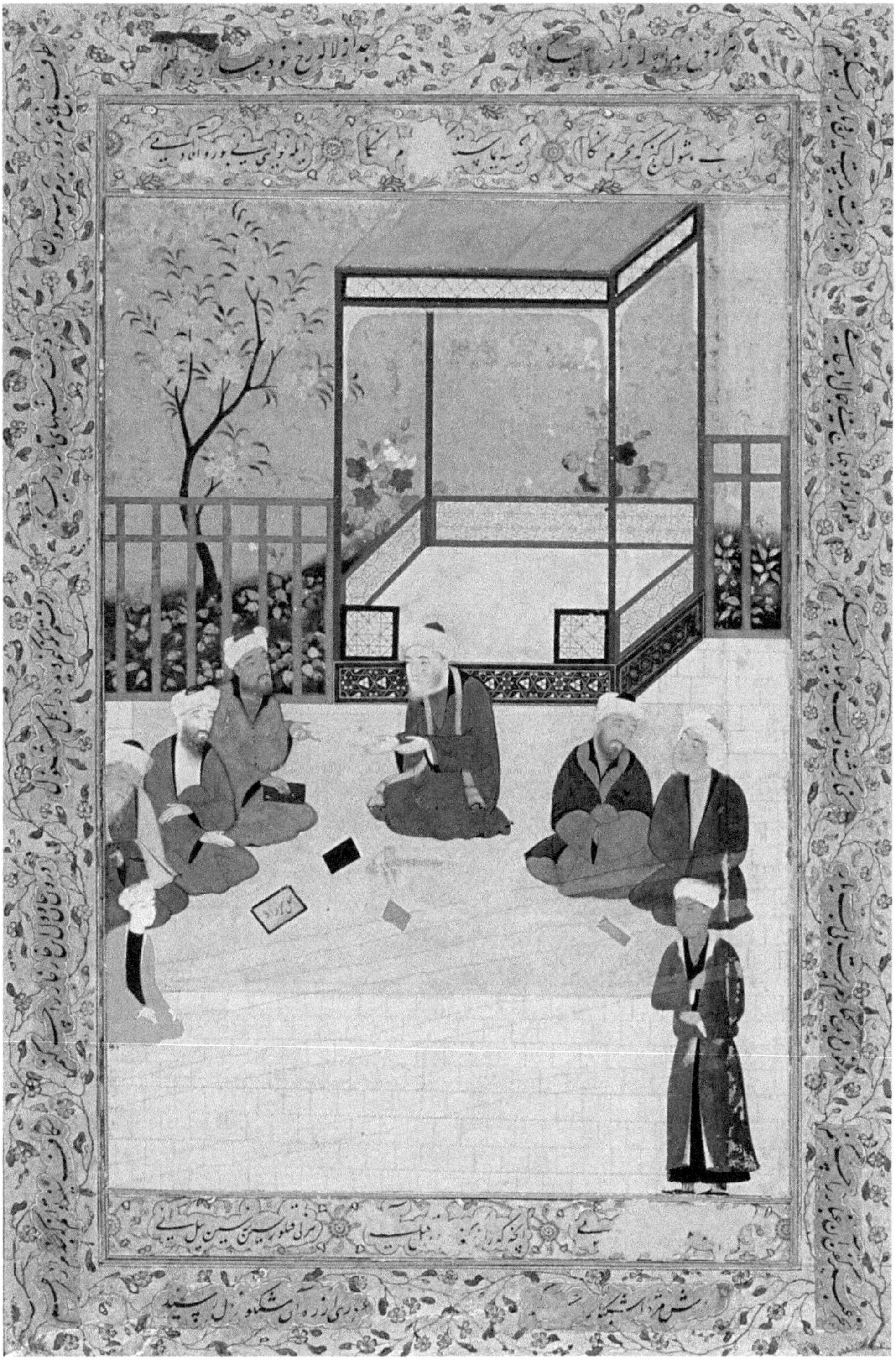

FIGURE 66

An assembly of sages with the poet Jami. From the Gulbenkian *Baharestan* of Jami, Herat, 1525–30.

Ettinghausen avers that several elements of this picture are copied from works in the cycle of Behzad, while the empty kiosk is more problematic, suggesting that this can only be the work of a beginner. It is, however, typical of the composition used by Behzad, with a similar grouping of figures and architecture and landscape elements.[98]

It appears that some artists use the kiosk as a model for other structures in their paintings. In a painting (1526–27) attributed to Sheykh Zadeh Mahmud Mozahheb, the balcony structure resembles that of a kiosk (Figure 31).[99] We have already seen that using the kiosk as a model shows that the artist assumes that the balcony is a light structure and not an integral part of the building. Using wood as its main building material underlines the kiosk's nature as a temporary structure, one which could, if required, be disassembled and moved to other areas while still having the primary objective of being fixed in its location. Another version appears in Meskin's painting of Noah's ark, in which the same kiosk design is used to define a seating area in the ship.[100] The kiosk appears frequently in Mughal painting, mostly integrated with reality. For instance, in an illustration from the *Khamseh* (Quintet) of Amir Khosrow Dehlavi (1597), the Mughal princess is in the blue pavilion (Figure 35).

The Throne versus the Kiosk

Several similarities between the kiosk and the throne, in terms of plan, height and location in the garden, reveal strong connections between these structures. Such correspondences lead to a significant question: is the kiosk in Persian gardens a developed (or modified) version of the throne? In some cases, the strong resemblance between throne and kiosk in terms of height, plan, form and size makes it difficult for an observer to differentiate them.[101] The difference between the kiosk and throne lies in their use and their mobile nature. While both structures are made of light material, the throne could be easily moved and placed in different parts of the garden in contrast to the kiosk, which is usually a fixed structure whose location is much less fluid. Another difference between the kiosk and throne is their size: the kiosk is usually large enough to be used by two or three people, while the throne is usually designed for one person. Moreover, the throne is usually non-roofed or covered by temporary umbrellas held by servants, whereas the kiosk is in most cases roofed and covered, serving as a shady, semi-open area, where people can sit and sleep while being protected from the hot sunshine.[102]

A Timurid painting from Shiraz (1438) from the *Tarikh-e Jahan-Goshay* of 'Ata Malek ibn Muhammad Joveyni depicts Kuyuk the Great Khan, grandson of Genghiz Khan, at the moment of his enthronement with courtiers and attendants surrounding him (Figure 67). This event took place at his camp near Qaraqorum. Kuyuk sits on a gold throne and felt blanket, sipping from a ceramic cup. To the left, two men kneel on a blanket with their eyes lowered, while a bearded man strums a typical Persian rabab below. In the centre a kneeling man offers Kuyuk a gift. This entire scene takes place under an open tent on a green hill ornamented with foliage. The throne is under a large awning, which is held on a single column.[103] Comparing it with a Safavid painting from the *Shahnameh* (1602) which shows a domed and roofed kiosk located in the middle of a garden (Figure 68), may clarify the temporary and permanent natures of the roof structures.[104] This painting depicts Zal and Rudabeh celebrating their wedding night in a kiosk. These examples also confirm that the portability of the throne in contrast to the fixed kiosk (as their main distinction) should not be over-generalized. This kiosk, which is located in a natural setting, has legs and temporary stairs, and seems completely portable.[105]

The Relation of the Throne and Kiosk to the Garden

The kiosk or throne is usually the focal point of the painting, especially when the underlying story refers to the king and his courtiers around him. Generally, the stories take place right in front the throne or kiosk. Depending on the underlying narrative, the throne may be inside the building, which is located in the garden, on the *iwan* or before it, or in the planted or paved areas. The location of the throne on the *iwan* or in the interior typically reflects the artist's emphasis on the building instead of the garden. In some illustrations, the kiosk or throne are located on the *iwan* or close to the main gateway.[106] The placement of Siyavash's throne on an *iwan* in a painting from the *Shahnameh* of Tahmasp, is a tool to emphasize his royal status when he is receiving gifts from agents of Afrasyab who are offering peace and friendship (Figure 69).

In contrast, there many instances where the throne is located on the planted areas and no building is involved. Depending on the story, the kiosk as connector in the garden is either a fixed or movable structure, light enough to be transported to another location. The kiosk or throne can be situated in natural fields rather than gardens, as we see in some Turkaman-style paintings in which the portable throne is an unornamented and simple chair placed among trees and flowers, often close to a creek.[107] A painting in the *Haft Awrang* by Jami (1556–65)[108] shows the roofed hexagonal kiosk in the middle of the garden next to a big tree (Figure 70). The height of the platform and a low railing provide visibility for people inside the kiosk.[109] The components of the kiosk, such as its low railings, thin columns and its roof, which is apparently made of cloth, are highly decorated. The unique composition of postures along with elongated bodies enhances the rhythm and movement in this painting. The artist also shows the garden within the urban fabric by revealing the garden walls, probably because the accompanying poem tells how the garden is seen by a young city dweller, who desecrates it by plucking the apples and pomegranates and trampling the blossoms and boughs.[110]

Planted areas as the main settings for thrones or kiosks are usually either in royal gardens, or are encampment areas in deserts or fields or natural parks. However, most thrones or kiosks are placed near the royal palace or in the intersection of paved and planted areas. In other words, the kiosk sits between the planted area, which is usually in the background of the painting, and the paved area, which is usually the foreground and the main setting for the narrative. This significant phenomenon clarifies the cultural implications of the kiosk as the connector between the paved and planted areas in the garden. It is evident in numerous Safavid paintings, such as one attributable to Aqa Mirak, from the *Khamseh* by Nezami (1539–43), depicting a duel between physicians (Figure 71). This kiosk is close to the door and acts as a mediator between the planted and paved areas. It stands completely within the paved area, as if defining the boundary with the planted area, while the water channel overstresses the horizontality of the composition. The inscription over the door reads, "May this court always be opened in prosperity" and over the pavilion: "Even though the dignity of our threshold may not become lofty, nevertheless the sun sets its feet on our house. May Allah perpetuate his kingship and sovereignty forever." Welch believes that this painting implies a real setting at Shah Tahmasp's court.[111]

If the kiosk works as a connector between garden and building or between planted and paved areas, so too the fence to the garden, which is different from the wall, can divide the paved area from the public and private areas, dedicated to men and women respectively.[112] In a work by Mirza 'Ali, Shah Tahmasp's artist, from the *Khamseh* by Nezami, the throne is between two areas in the garden (Figure 72). The story talks about the moment when Nushabeh recognizes Eskandar from his portrait. The artist depicts the monumental throne, facing the building with its back to the garden. The huge throne-back blocks Nushabeh's view of the trees, plants, flowers and the water channel in the garden behind. The throne has a hexagonal plan and faces the main fountain, with a floral pattern, to allow the queen to enjoy the sound of splashing water. This area is enclosed by a fence, which separates the working people and women from the male members of the court, who are sitting and standing before Nushabeh.[113] Soltan Muhammad (1517–40)[114] puts the throne of the prince in front of the building so that the prince faces the garden and the courtiers inside it (Figure 18). Here, the throne works as a mediator between the garden and the building.[115]

In a sixteenth-century painting from the *Divan* by Amir Khosrow Dehlavi, the artist attempts to frame the whole garden with all its components such as entrance, building, kiosk, enclosing wall, fence, *iwan* and planted areas (Figure 73).[116] The trapezoid plan of this kiosk is simply a deformation of a rectangular plan in perspective. Another zoomed-in view is visible in a Safavid painting in which the young prince drinks wine in the kiosk (Figure 74).[117] This kiosk is close to the planted part while being open to the built area. Such enclosure emphasizes the paved area as the main setting for the narrative.[118]

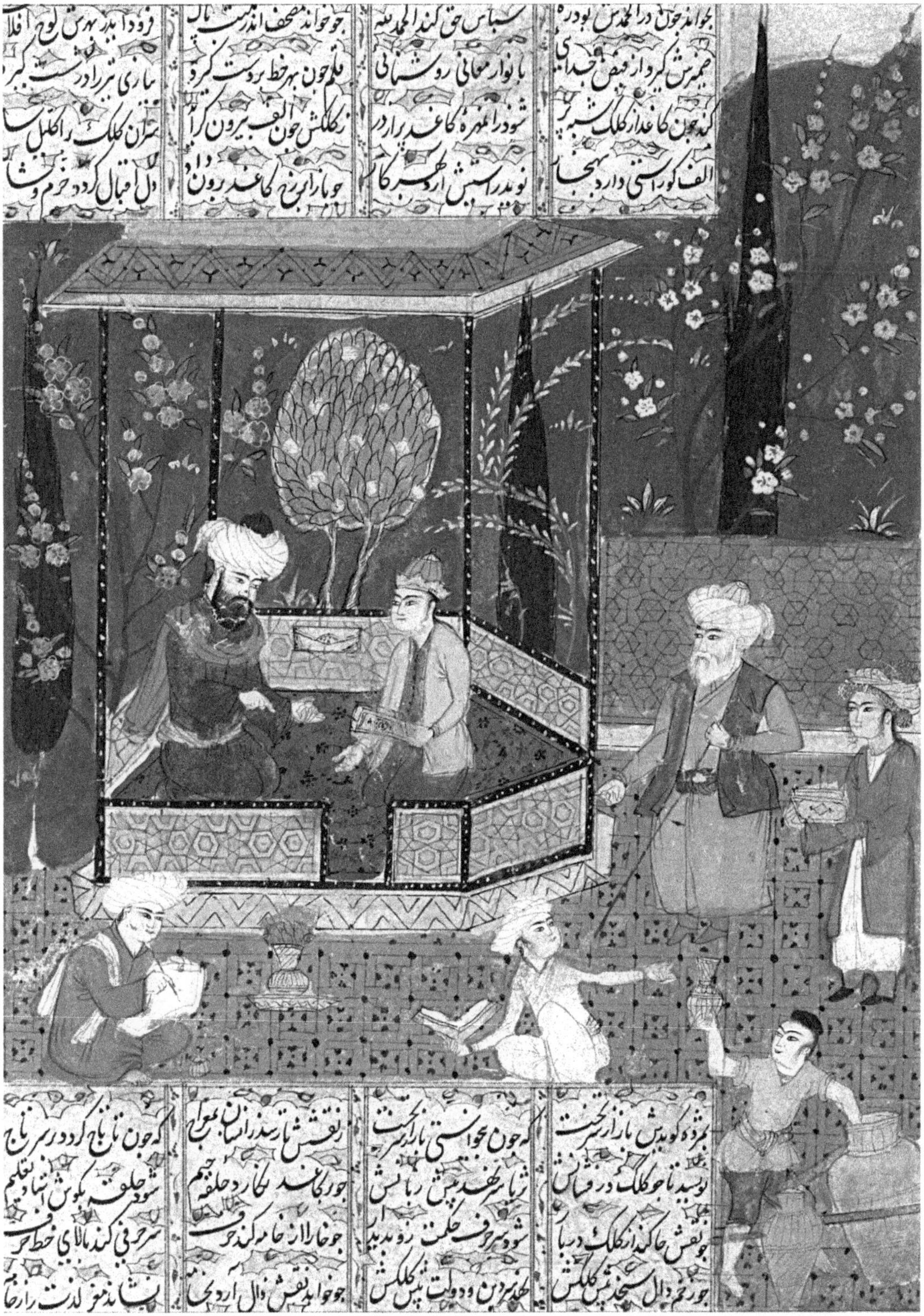

FIGURE 73

School scene. From the *Divan* by Amir Khosrow Dehlavi, 1609.

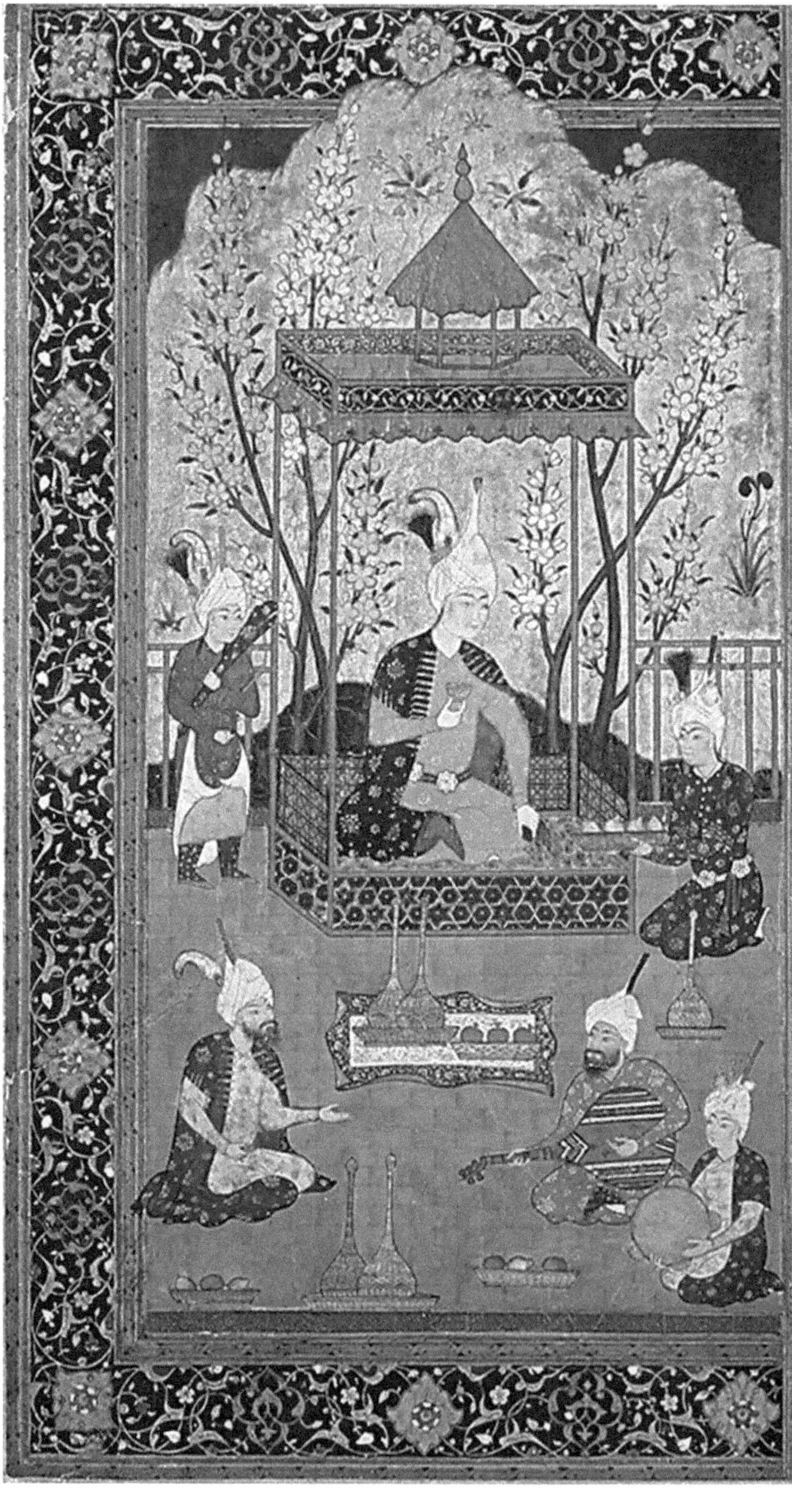

FIGURE 74
Prince in a garden courtyard. Tabriz, 1525–30.

The kiosk between the paved and planted areas can also create a path. We can see this phenomenon in a damaged and repainted painting by 'Abd al-Samad (1550–60), which depicts the house of Timur; here, the hexagonal kiosk defines a route between the paved and planted areas of the garden (Figure 65).[119] This kiosk is located in the middle of a pathway where special courtiers and servants can walk through, while other courtiers and ambassadors sit before the kiosk. This kiosk is a fixed structure that is connected by a long path to two gateways to the right and left of the painting. One of these doors connects the planted area to the 'kiosk area', while the second connects the paved area and the building to it. Using an aerial view in this unique painting enables the artist to offer a wider view of the garden and people inside it[120] and refers to the artist's perception of the kiosk as the point from which the user can view garden and building at the same time. The person seated in this location can control and supervise people and observe events while being able to enjoy the garden. Putting the kiosk between the building and garden may symbolize the king's role as the moderator between the ideal world (paradise, nature) and the real world (earth, man-made). A painting from the *Shahnameh* (1486), which shows Zal and Rudabeh embracing, supports this hypothesis. Here, the throne or kiosk works as a metaphoric separator and connector between inside and outside (Figure 75). Proving this hypothesis requires further research, but Sufism and mysticism exercised considerable influence on Persian poetry and painting.

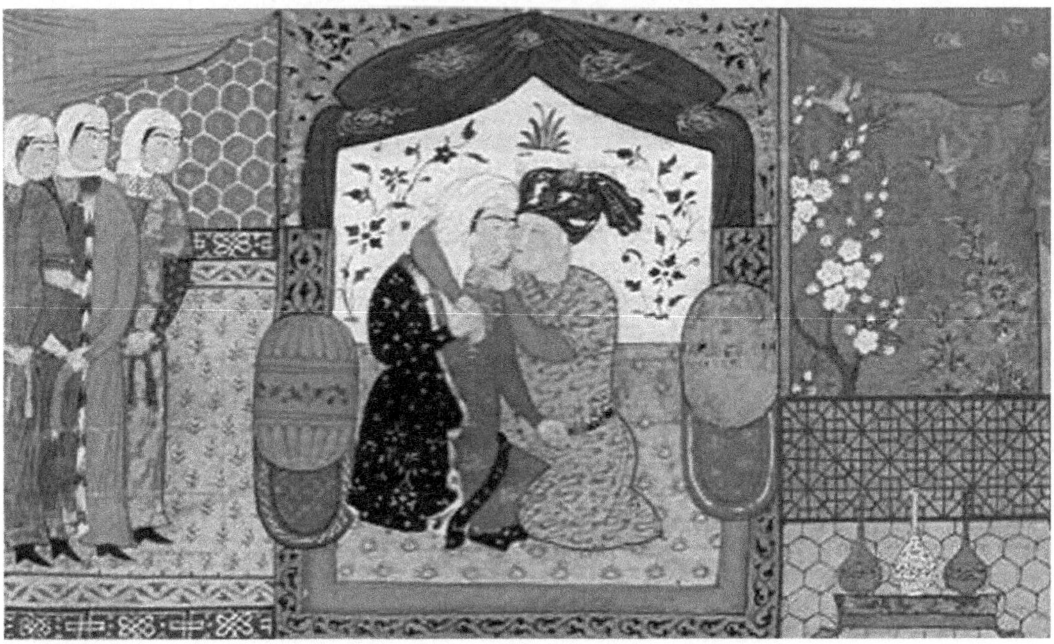

FIGURE 75
Zal and Rudabeh embracing. From the *Shahnameh*, 1486.

The Design of Thrones and Kiosks

As we have seen, thrones and kiosks are usually square, rectangular, hexagonal or octagonal. Among these forms, the octagon rarely appears in paintings, while the hexagonal form is quite frequent, especially for thrones. Using the square and rectangular forms, which are somehow in resonance with the geometric plan of the buildings or the courtyard, enables the artist to connect the throne and kiosk to the garden in a stronger fashion. In contrast, the hexagonal form dictates a monumental character for the throne or kiosk and underlines it as an exalted structure. In some cases, the hexagonal form of the throne is a reflection of the pavilion or the garden design. For instance, in the scene of Zulaykha tempting Yusof (1533) from Jami's *Yusof va Zulaykha*, the hexagonal plan of the throne reflects the hexagonal plan of the pavilion in which it is located.[121] We can also see this resemblance in the form of the fountain, which sometimes mimics the form of the kiosk or throne in front of it. In a story from *Bustan*, the square shape of the kiosk is correlated to the square-shaped fountain before it in a *chaharbagh* (Figure 5).

The throne is usually designed for one person because it is considered a private area, while the kiosk is large enough to accommodate more people. For instance, in a story from the *Khamseh* by Nezami (1549), Alexander and Queen Nushabeh sit in the same kiosk (Figure 76). This kiosk is not roofed and is open on four sides, with a view of the paved area rather than the planted one. In contrast, some thrones in paintings are large enough to accommodate two people, probably to highlight the intimacy between them. For instance, in the *Haft Awrang*, Solomon and Bilqis sit together on the same throne and converse about Solomon's findings (Figure 77). This kiosk-like throne is located among trees before the pool in the garden.[122] Another difference between throne and kiosk is that people usually sit cross-legged in the kiosk, while in the throne they can put their feet on the platform which acts as a step in front of it. The kiosk is large enough to be used as a drinking and eating area, while the throne is too small to accommodate plates of fruit or wine jugs and glasses. In contrast to thrones, most kiosks have cloth or wooden roofs to provide shade for the space underneath. The throne, meanwhile, may have a temporary umbrella held by a servant. The kiosk roof is usually supported by four thin columns, which allow a visual connection to the garden. The level of detail and ornamentation on the surfaces and roof of the kiosk is usually related to the degree of elegance of the painting.

The throne and kiosk are normally three or four steps higher than ground level. To go up to the throne, the king uses a step placed close beside it. In comparison, in most paintings, there are no steps in front of the kiosk even when it is placed on a platform or foundation. A painting from the *Kalileh va Damneh* (1429) shows Borzuyeh taking this book to Anushirvan (Figure 78). It shows that a platform is needed to step down from the kiosk.[123] Being on the higher level enables the user have a wider view of the garden and people around the throne, while highlighting the supremacy of the king. In other words, height usually correlates to the enhancement of view, the status of the user, the function of the throne as a place for sitting or drinking, the location in the garden, and the size and plan. The kiosk's roof can be unrealistically high in some paintings and not harmonious with the proportion of the human figures, and this, too, is probably to emphasize the hierarchy of the users.[124]

The height of the kiosk and throne varies, then, depending on the hierarchical order, as well as the level of exaggeration in the painting style.[125] A low level in these structures may equally be interpreted as underlining any hierarchical order.[126] The throne is usually open on two or three sides, which enables the user to observe the areas around it. It usually faces one side, while the kiosk has no particular direction, and, in that sense, is neutral in the garden. Closing the throne or kiosk from any side helps the artist define the hierarchy and even define the direction of the garden. Moreover, adding a back provides protection and security for the person seated on the throne while permitting the emphasis of his status though the application of ornamentation. The degree of openness also depends on whether the kiosk is to be used as a sitting place, an entertainment area for special guests, or for drinking, eating and feasting. The last four uses require a full view of the garden to enjoy the view and the feeling of being part of the carefully constructed 'natural' setting, so larger kiosks are usually open on four sides. In a painting from the *Khamseh* which illustrates Zal consulting the Magi, his hexagonal throne is also open on all sides (Figure 63).[127] This throne is fixed and heavy, in contrast to Bilqis's throne depicted in the *Shahnameh,* which is a mobile (and visually light) structure defining a more personal space while emphasizing her status.

The kiosk was such a fascinating object that it engaged artists' imaginations. While most kiosks and thrones are single-storeyed, there are a few cases of two-storeyed kiosks in painting. One of them appears in a painting (1540) illustrating Prince Akbar presenting portraits by the royal artist, 'Abdol-Samad Shirinkar, to his father, Homayun. This double-storeyed hexagonal kiosk is placed within an ornate garden (Figure 79). There is a staircase connecting two gateways on the first and second floors. These gates work as signifiers to define new 'realms' in the whole structure. It is also interesting to see the large degree of interaction between this kiosk and its surrounding environment. The tree, which is growing inside the roof of the second floor, unifies the setting (garden) and the object (kiosk).[128]

The same concept for the design of a kiosk is used in an early sixteenth-century miniature painting illustrating the garden of the fairies. The kiosk here, which is a hexagonal platform, has been moved up onto the branch of the tree as a way to emphasize the idealistic setting (Figure 80). Putting it here makes it look like a tree house.[129] All of these examples reveal that the frequent appearance of the throne and kiosk relates to their symbolic weight in any illustrated garden, as well as their potential to reflect the hierarchical order within. Comparing the early Timurid paintings with the late Safavid ones also shows the level of

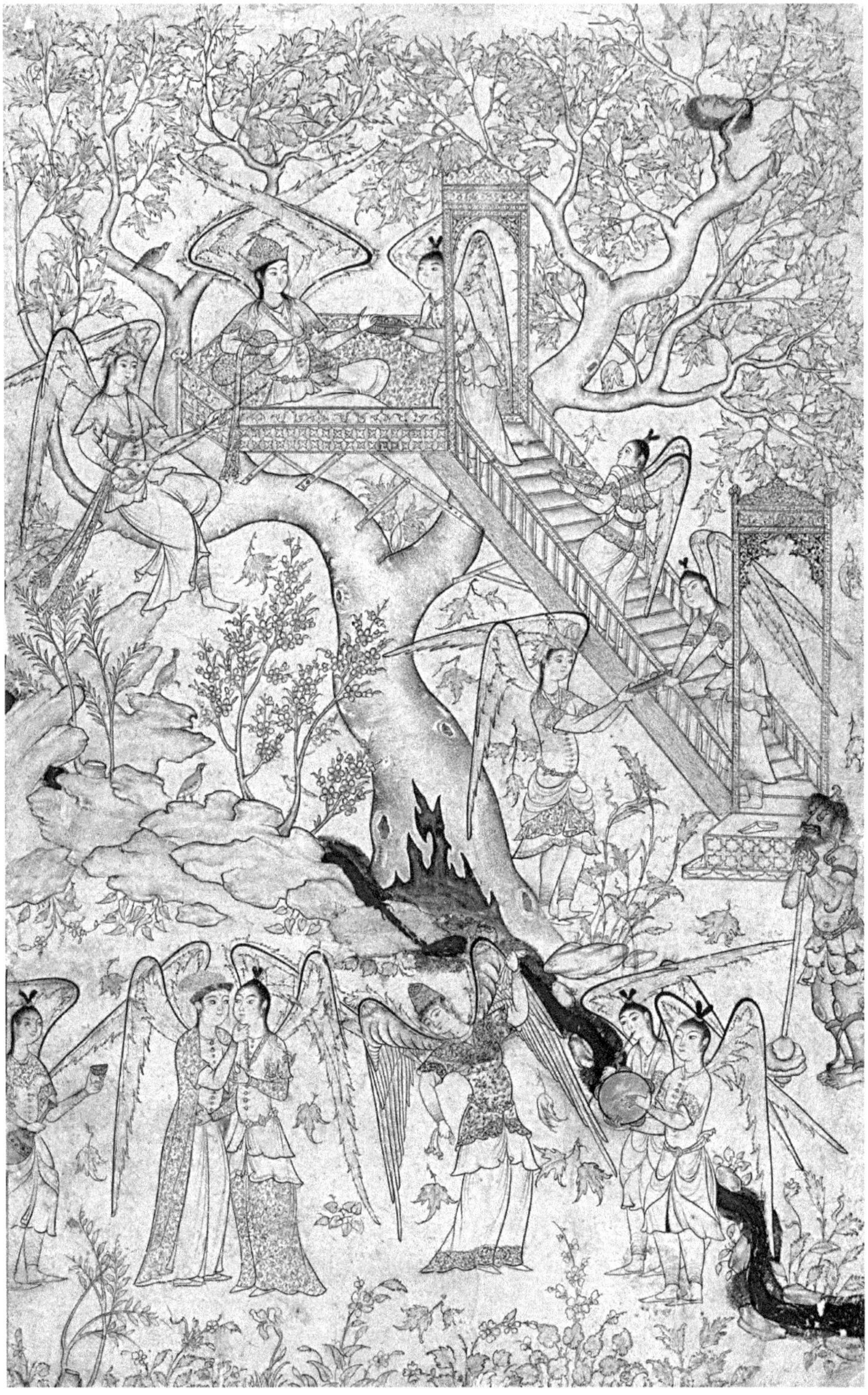

FIGURE 80
The garden of the fairies. Early sixteenth century.

elaboration and development and the ways in which they gradually become a stable part of garden imagery, not necessarily as the depiction of real gardens but as constructions of the artist's imagination and creativity. The kiosk or throne plays a crucial role in linking garden and building and also in connecting people to the natural environment around them in the garden.

THE TENT IN THE GARDEN

The Iranian plateau has, at different eras, been used as a pathway for nomadic tribes such as the Turks of Central Asia, the Arabs and the Mongols. The increasing trend towards nomadism in this region encouraged the use of the tent as a portable form of a palace and pavilion.[130] The evident impact of this nomadic culture is the common use of tents instead of buildings. In other words, sometimes tents took the place of garden pavilions. This permitted greater mobility for the court, which allowed them to defend the boundaries of their territories. Behzad (1480) shows tents being pitched in the garden of Hoseyn Bayqara, the ruler of Herat between 1468 and 1506 (Figure 81).[131]

The tent structure not only provided shelter but was flexible in terms of structure and form. It even entered the Islamic imagination, where the Prophet Muhammad perceiving 70,000 tents close to the throne of Allah, each as large as the world, was depicted in Timurid paintings (1436).[132] Furthermore, as indicated in various chronicles, tents were frequently pitched in gardens and worked with buildings as shelters. A painting from the Freer *Haft Awrang*, depicting Yusof giving a royal banquet in honour of his marriage, shows this symbiosis between buildings and tents (Figure 82). Since many accounts are not specific in terms of description, miniature paintings can be used to reconstruct these tents. There are four forms that can be traced in Persian gardens: umbrella, conical, yurt and pyramidal. The main differences between these types are form, size and the level of complexity.[133] The first three forms appear frequently, while the pyramidal tent, probably because it is so complex, seems to be unpopular with artists.[134] It was common to add architectural features, like doors, to tents. The most elaborate tents followed floor plans dictated by architectural tradition. Some of these tents, which were described by Clavijo and other travellers, included built elements such as walls in such a way that they were described as castles.[135]

The simplest form of tent, and the one closest to the kiosk, is an awning that provides an open view on all sides. It appears in several paintings, such as an illustration (1440) in which Timur's grandson, Ulugh Beg, is enthroned beneath a white canopy decorated with a text in blue and supported by an armature of red coloured poles (Figure 83). Ulugh Beg's wives and a retinue of attendants, including guards, food bearers and falconers, are

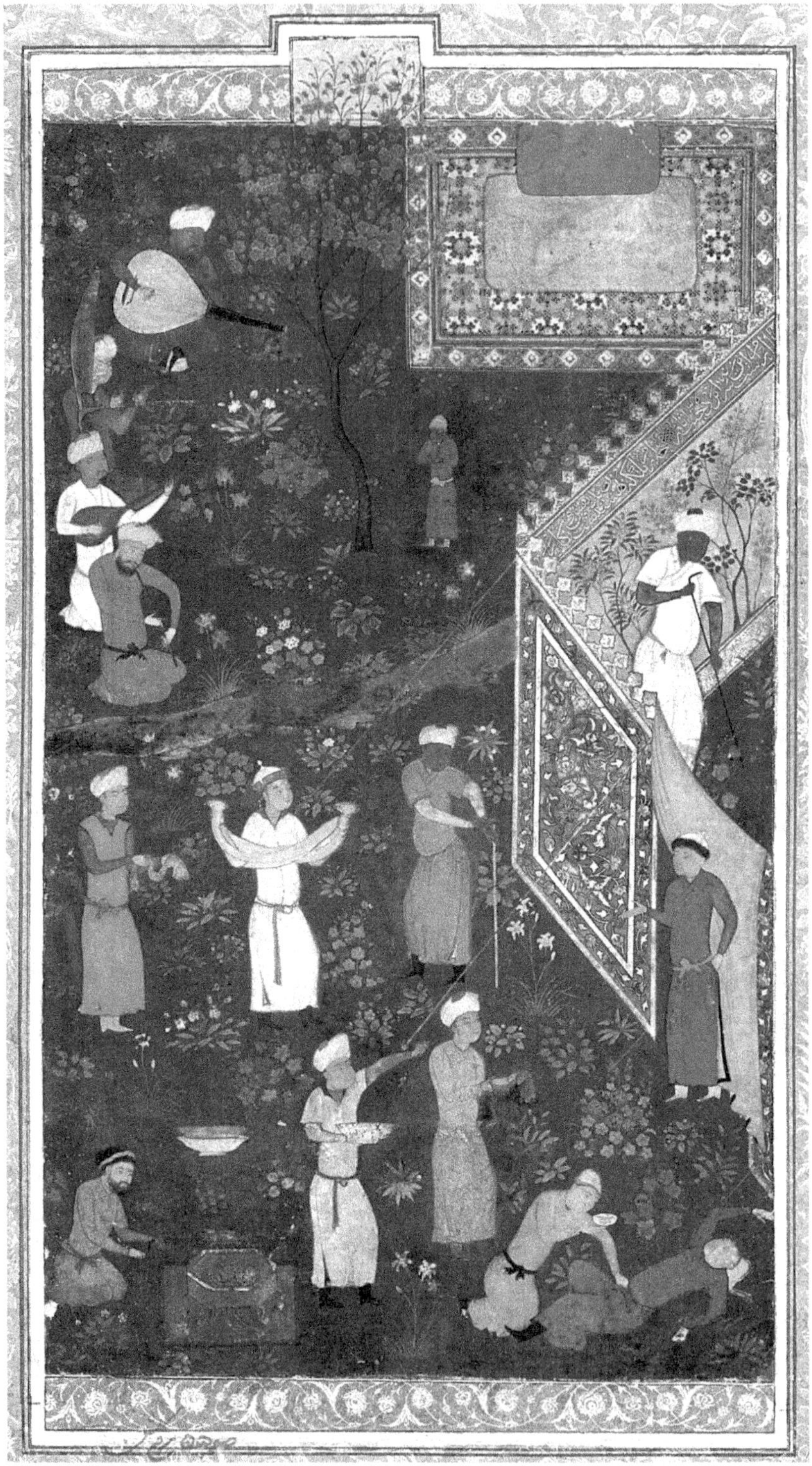

FIGURE 81

Soltan Hoseyn Mirza in promenade. From *Moraqqa' Golshan*, attributed to Kamal-uddin Behzad, late fifteenth century.

positioned along one side.[136] This canopy functions like an awning with a rectangular crown on top and is a combination of built elements such as a dome, poles and fabric arranged in an unrealistic fashion.[137]

The awning is also evident in several paintings illustrating excursions in a natural setting or a garden. For example, in a painting by Soltan Muhammad from the *Divan* by Hafez (sixteenth century), two picnicking lovers are sitting under an awning in a garden (Figure 84). Here, the tent has a very simple form without much ornamentation. The decoration of the roof resembles the arrangement of flowers and plants in the garden.[138] This form appears frequently in other sixteenth-century paintings. In the scene of Khosrow celebrating Nowruz (1560), the large throne of Timur is located under an awning. Here, Khosrow celebrates with numerous courtiers and attendants in a dark green flowery landscape under a tent (Figure 59). The focal point is Khosrow himself, while the garden is pushed to the background. This example suggests that the size of the tent (or umbrella) depends on the size of the throne.[139] In another painting from the *Shahnameh* (1444), the umbrella and platform form a temporary kiosk, which is placed over the water channel (Figure 85). The ropes connect the tent to the surrounding trees. This interaction between water and kiosk developed gradually in gardens in Mughal India and Ottoman Turkey and probably resulted in the creation of the concept of the water-kiosk, that is, a kiosk located on water. The more developed version of this concept (an awning on a platform) appears in a late Mughal painting (1822) from the *History of Akbar Shah* that narrates and illustrates events in Akbar's court (Figure 86).[140] In *Khosrow va Shirin* by Yusof Nezami, where the return of Shapur to Khosrow is depicted, the tent is just a shadow-caster with a wall behind it (Figure 87).[141] The nomadic life of the court in tents is depicted in an illustration from the *Tarikh-e Jahan Goshay* by 'Ata Malek Ibn Muhammad Joveyni (1438), in which Kuyuk Khan receives gifts from his nobles in his camp after his enthronement (Figure 67).[142] In this case, the tent is completely open but offers total shade.[143]

Another common form of tent is the conical type, usually held up by one or two poles. The more developed versions included a disc on top of the centre pole to hold out the tent and to increase the interior volume, and may have had up to eight or ten sides.[144] This type of tent is illustrated in some paintings. In a painting by Mir Sayyed 'Ali from the *Khamseh* by Nezami (1540), Majnun is brought in chains to Leyla's conical tent by a begging woman (Figure 88).[145] The natural field is the main setting for conical tents and yurts, which are laid out in an organized fashion.[146] Other instances of the conical tent in a natural setting, which symbolize nomadic life, appear in several sixteenth-century paintings in the Freer *Haft Awrang*, where the tent is pushed to the background of the painting.[147] Another painting, from the *Jami' al-Tavarikh* (1596), depicts the ceremony held to celebrate the victories of the Mongol ruler, Ananda, in Iran and Central Asia. Here, Ananda sits on a throne near the tents (Figure 89). Two areas of the encampment – residential and administrative – are separated by a red fence. While the residential area is placed in the background of the painting with less emphasis, the administrative or royal area depicting the court of Oghuz is the focal point. The plain ground, as well as the porticos on the right of the frame, define a built area in the camp that seems totally different from the natural area.

In Central Asia, the conical tent gradually evolved into the yurt, which offered more space. It can be seen in miniature paintings from as early as the fourteenth century and appears in *Khosrow va Shirin* by Nezami (fourteenth century), where Khosrow and Shirin sit next to their yurts (Figure 90). The tents are not well decorated here, which leaves the main stress on the conversation between the figures and the music party.[148] Gender segregation within the encampment (*ordu*) is also reflected in paintings. In several illustrations, the male zone is separated from the female one. In a painting by Kamal-uddin Behzad from the *Zafarnameh* (1528), the whole *ordu* is occupied only by men. It shows European ambassadors bringing Morad, the captive son of the Ottoman king, to Timur's court (Figure 91).

Not all tents are located in natural settings. A scene from the *Guy va Chowgan* by Arefi (1523) shows a tent pitched on a water channel immediately in front of a hexagonal pool (Figure 92). It is one of the rare examples which combine tents with the geometric layout of the garden.[149] Sixteenth-century paintings apply a more delicate ornamentation for the tents: here the dome of the tent is highly decorated, as it would be if it were on a building. Mir Sayyed 'Ali's illustration of the camp scene (1539–43) from *Leyla and Majnun* of Nezami shows two types of tents in a natural setting: yurt and conical (Figure 93). Although these tents are similar in terms of structure, the main tent is distinguished by its different colour.[150] While the key figures sit on two layers of carpet, the courtiers simply sit on the uncarpeted, planted area.

In an illustration from the sixteenth-century *Shahnameh* of Tahmasp, the story of Kaveh tearing Zahhak's scroll, the tent is located in the paved area of the garden with a natural background (Figure 94). The elaborate decoration and detailed patterns on the roof and walls, and the addition of a wooden door, all serve to make the tent look like a permanent structure. In some paintings, the tent apparently works as a sleeping area.[151] In these cases, the seating area is separate, and it seems that the tent is only used for sleeping.[152] A yurt may denote social significance: in a painting from Sa'di's *Bustan* (1488) illustrating a gathering at the court of Soltan Hoseyn Bayqara in Herat, the throne is located at the door of the yurt, which is formally differentiated from the awning behind it although both have very elaborate decorations (Figure 16). The level of ornamentation of the tent usually depends on the rank of the person living there.

The appearance of the tent in any form – awning, conical or yurt – has to do with the prevailing nomadic lives of kings and rulers in the Ilkhanid, Timurid and Safavid ages. The tent is usually located in a natural setting, which usually includes trees, plants and creeks. What is noteworthy is that, even when the poetry associated with the painting is silent

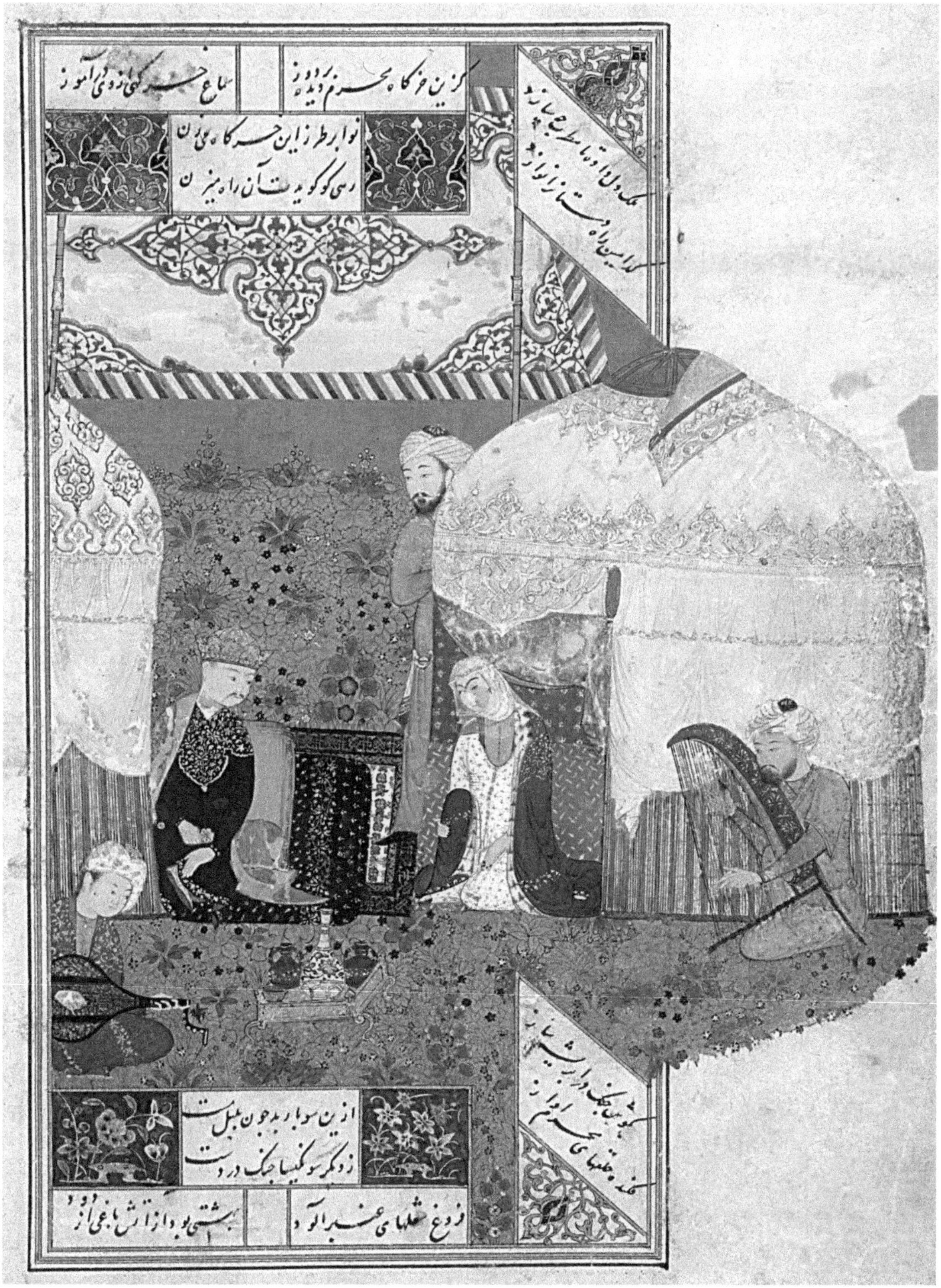

FIGURE 90

Khosrow and Shirin in front of their tents. From *Khosrow va Shirin* by Nezami, Iran, 1431.

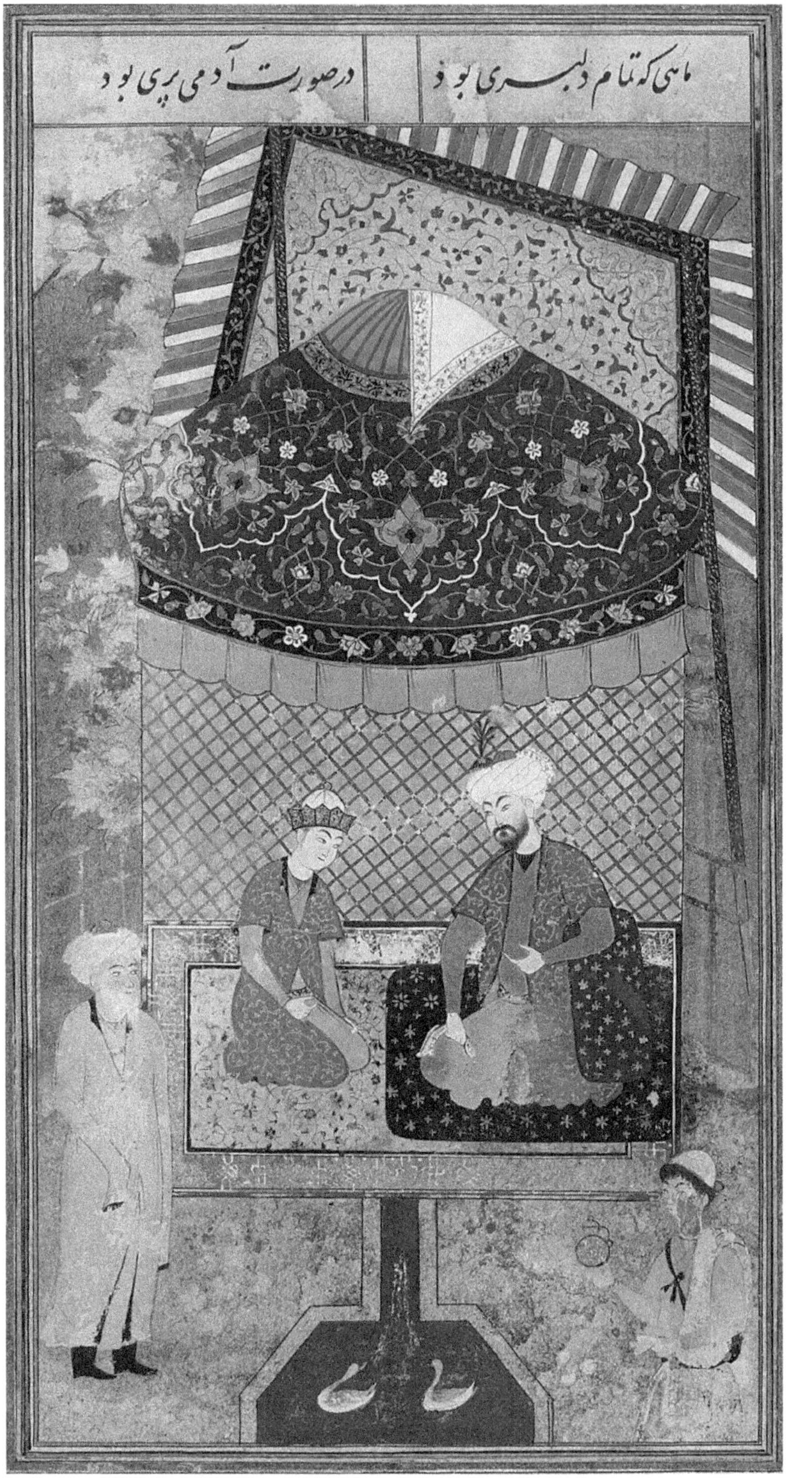

FIGURE 92

The king and his young son. From *Guy va Chowgan* by Arefi, Herat, 1523.

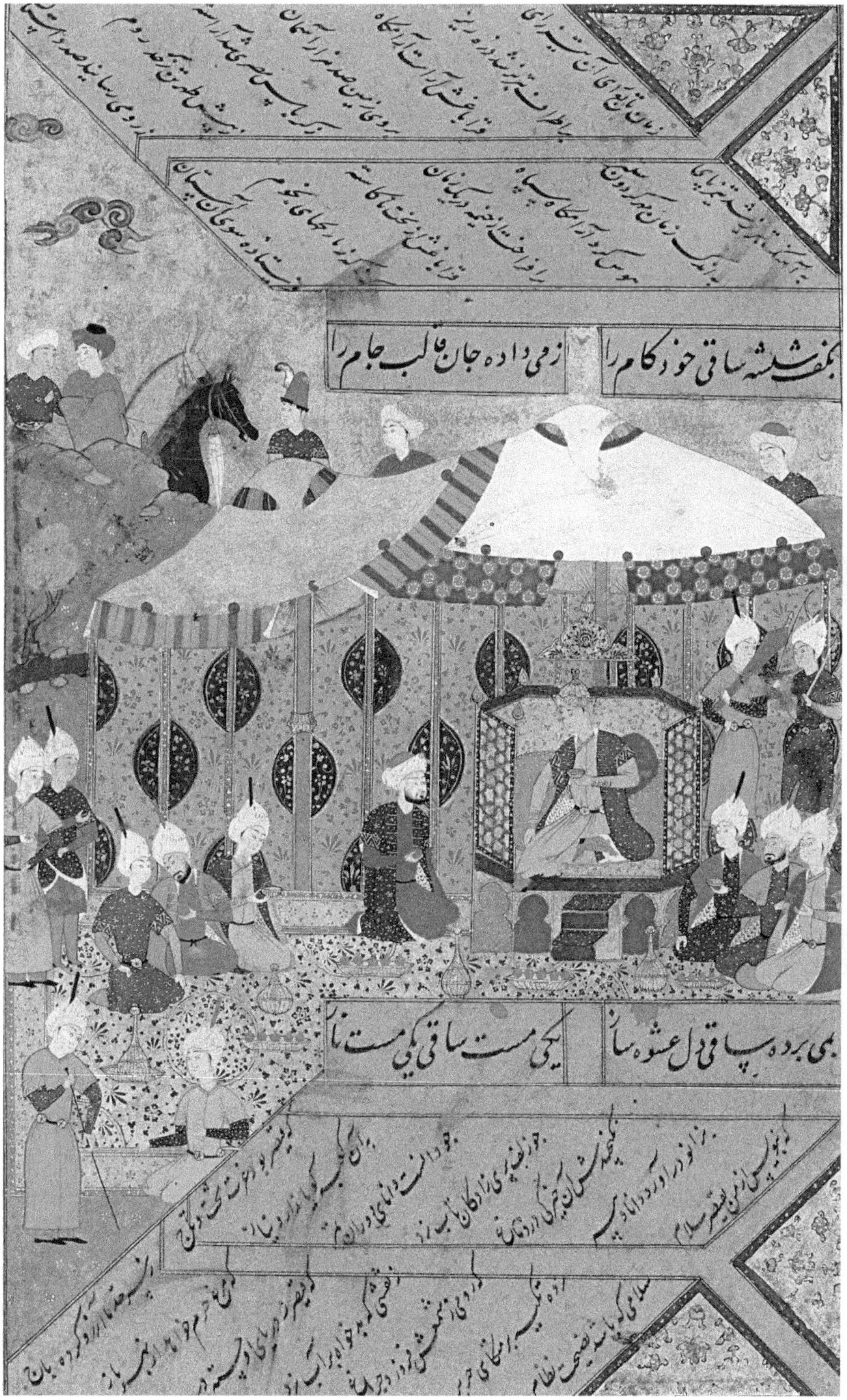

FIGURE 94

Kaveh tears Zahhak's scroll. From the *Shahnameh* of Shah Tahmasp, attributed to Qadimi, sixteenth century.

about the location, the artist still chooses the tent as the main setting for the narrative. In the case of certain stories from Ferdowsi's *Shahnameh* and Nezami's *Khamseh*, both tent and building are depicted as the main setting for the narrative. This is because the poetry, and especially the terminology applied in it, is ambiguous enough to allow the artist to illustrate it the way that they prefer and to develop a style that reflects their observations. The tent in a formal garden, especially in association with other buildings, appears infrequently in Persian paintings, although the remaining examples confirm that tents were, on occasion, pitched in formal gardens.

CONCLUSION

The garden is consistently used as a setting for narratives illustrated in Persian paintings produced between the fourteenth and eighteenth centuries. The garden is usually accompanied by a man-made structure, the pavilion, which varies in scale. Depending on the story behind the painting, the style and focus of the artist on the pavilion appears in various forms which differ in terms of permanency and mobility and include the building, kiosk, throne and tent. The building can be viewed from inside or outside, depending on the goal of the artist and the function of the pavilion as private (house) or public (palace). A house is usually depicted as a pure volume (double-storeyed building with a square plan), while the pavilion as a palace is treated as fragmentary and is most often illustrated from the front, with an emphasis on the *iwan* as the focal point of the painting. This treatment highlights the function of the *iwan* as the connector between the building and garden. The *iwan* also provides the best setting for the royal throne, from which the king and courtiers have a panoramic view of both the garden and the people inside it. The throne, on or in front of the *iwan*, serves as a visual link between the building and the garden in the painting. The Ilkhanid, Timurid and early Safavid artists used a two-dimensional language to show the pavilion while the late Safavid artists, under European influence, employed perspective techniques to capture the three-dimensionality of the spaces, especially the *iwan*.

In addition to the building, kiosks or thrones were extensively depicted in gardens. Perhaps the text accompanying the painting is silent about the presence or absence of pavilions, or the terminology used is ambiguous; either condition is enough to let the artist interpret the pavilion as he imagines it. Both kiosk and throne are used by the king and his guests to enjoy the view of the building, garden and people. While the throne is usually a monumental structure and is differentiated from its setting, the kiosk is more closely related to the building and garden in terms of form and plan. In contrast to the kiosk, which appears fixed and unmovable, the throne seems portable and flexible and lacks a permanent roof.

Being occupied by a high-ranking male, the kiosk and throne are usually placed in areas separated from the female zones (which are typically associated with the building, either on the balcony, inside, or on the roof). The kiosk is usually large enough to be used by two people, whereas the throne can normally accommodate only one. Both kiosk and throne are in close relationship to natural elements such as water, flowers, trees and plants: usually facing a fountain, and placed between the paved and planted areas, they connect the garden and building. In some paintings, the kiosk is integrated into a pathway that separates the garden from the pavement.

The tent, on the other hand, is rarely associated with any building in Persian painting. This is because the majority of tents in paintings are placed in natural landscapes, villages, deserts, or fields, and not in 'designed' gardens. The tent, appearing in three forms – awning, conical and yurt – is always in close relation to water, plants, trees and flowers. Artists treat the tent as a flexible structure with a unique capacity to be open or closed. This allows the mysterious life inside to be emphasized; in effect, the artist stimulates the curiosity of the audience by offering a privileged, inside view, while highlighting the social function of the tent as a place for public meetings. Varied degrees of visibility are possible, demonstrating the significance of the view out into the garden and its activities for the tent's inhabitants. Changing its transparency into a canopy or yurt lets the artist enhance gender segregation in the garden while providing greater degrees of privacy for the female residents. The levels of ornamentation and decoration, including the number of carpets, especially those under the throne inside or next to the tent, signify the status of its residents. The tent, as an awning or canopy typically connected with a platform, stands in place of a kiosk and is therefore usually situated next to, or even on, a water channel.

4

The Garden and Pavilion through the Lens of Travellers and Historians

LOCAL historians and European travellers who visited the Persian world frequently refer to gardens as the main settings for social and political events. While these travel and historical accounts may be diverse in terms of origin, accuracy and chronological and cultural context, they have something in common: they are based on real and personal observations and experiences, from the differing perspectives of the insider (the historian) and the outsider (the traveller). This difference stems from the writer's cultural background – European or Persian – and the context in which the document was written. Current scholar J.D. Gurney summarizes the issues of coverage and perspective that result from the use of extant sources:

> With few surviving chronicles and loss of almost all of the state archives, historians, especially of the later Safavid period, have to rely to a disproportionate degree on the accounts of European travellers. Fortunately some of these, such as Chardin, Tavernier and Olearius, have left pre-eminent examples of genre, but even so, few attempts have been made to explore their preconceptions, prejudices or the extent of their understanding of Persian society.[1]

The main difference between historians' and travellers' writings lies in their point of view. Since most travellers voyaged for a defined purpose, as merchants, diplomats, military advisors or religious missionaries, the information that they recorded was determined by these preoccupations. As a matter of fact, travellers rarely reached levels of Persian cultural and intellectual life beyond the court and did not pose the kind of questions that interest historians and local travellers.[2] Europeans, as foreigners, were more concerned with the description of people and places, whereas native historians and biographers often reported events.[3] The notes of foreign travellers were usually more descriptive and concentrated on the details of space, design of gardens, and even the people inside them. In contrast, historians or local travellers were generally less interested in descriptions, and focused more effort on recording historical events in gardens and pavilions, sometimes with a bias derived from the royal patronage.[4]

In this chapter I aim to reconstruct the ideas behind gardens and pavilions by considering the accounts by European travellers who visited the Persianate world between the fourteenth and seventeenth centuries, such as Ruy González de Clavijo, Michele Membre, Thomas Herbert, Pietro Della Valle, Jean Chardin and Samuel Gottlieb Gmelin, and the chronicles and history books written by local historians such as Abul-Fazl Beyhaqi, Adib Shahab-uddin, Khajeh Rashid-uddin, Hasan Romlu, Babur and 'Abdi Beyk Shirazi, Jafar ibn Muhammad ibn Hasan Jafari, Qasem Abu Nasr Haravi and Eskandar Monshi.

As the observations of historians and travellers are different in terms of origin, context, patronage and writing style, they complement each other and answer questions not addressed in other documents, especially when we consider that documents that describe gardens in detail are scarce in Persian historical literature. Descriptions in history and travel accounts cannot necessarily provide an inclusive restoration of the image of historical gardens and pavilions, but they do allow us to examine the garden as a complex of layers of social interactions, spaces and physical elements. In addition to clarifying the origins, evolution, functionality and design concepts of gardens and pavilions, using these documents enables us to examine the relationships between gardens, pavilions and the city from a broader perspective, rather than restricting our focus to purely architectural design. However, accuracy depends on the authors' degree of familiarity with the context; this, as well as the reliability of names and dates, must remain an area of concern, and requires critical analysis.

THE ISSUE OF TERMINOLOGY

The wide range of terminology used in naming gardens and pavilions highlights both the cultural importance of gardens and pavilions in Persian society and their functional diversity.

The significance of this terminology lies in the varied vocabulary, which reflects cultural views about gardens and the man-made structures within them and encapsulates the diverse designs and functions of gardens and pavilions.

The major challenge lies in linking the terms used with actual designs since most of the gardens and pavilions which we will be considering here no longer exist. To compound our problems, the same word can point to two or three different meanings in different periods. Three categories of words are used to refer to gardens in Persian historical documents. The first two refer to gardens as economic resources and places for pleasure respectively, while the third refers to the garden as a whole. The garden used as a resource for cultivating fruit and other crops is referred to using the terms *khormastan* 'palm grove', *raz* 'vineyard', *marghzar* 'green field or lawn', or *mazra'eh* 'farm', while 'pleasure gardens' are *bustan* 'flower garden', *ferdows* 'enclosed paradise', *golshan* or *golestan* 'flower garden', and *khazra'* 'area of greenery'. Khosrow, in his travelogue the *Safarnameh*, uses *bagh, bostan* and *mazra'eh*[5] to differentiate gardens used for pleasure, fruit production and other types of farming, respectively.[6] He also notes the palm groves (*khormastan*) in Tabas[7] and pleasure gardens (*basatin*) in Arzan that have running water in channels.[8] Similarly, Beyhaqi uses an abundance of terms to describe the garden and pavilion in his chronicle. In addition to Khosrow's word *bagh,* he uses *khormastan, baghcheh* 'small garden', *golshan* 'flower garden', *bustan* 'flower garden', *ferdows* 'paradise',[9] *raz* 'vineyard' and *khazra'* 'green field'.[10] Pinder-Wilson argues that after the Seljuk period the word *bagh* was widely used to denote any entity comprising both palace and garden.[11] However, this hypothesis requires reconsideration in light of writings by both poets and historians in which the majority refer to the garden and residence as separate entities.

Persian historians use three categories of words for pavilions. The first category refers to the use of pavilions as private, semi-private and public residential areas. The second refers to spaces or areas inside buildings. The final category refers to the function of a pavilion as a semi-open space within a garden. Terms which denote pavilions used as private or public residences are *kushk* 'kiosk', *divan* 'office', *khaneh* 'mansion', *qasr* 'palace, castle', *'emarat* 'building' and *sarai* 'palace'. *Khaneh* and *sarai* usually refer solely to private houses, while the other terms denote semi-private residences owned by high-ranking people. However, in most historical documents the precise differences in meaning between these terms seem unclear. For instance, Beyhaqi refers to various Ghaznavid palaces using the terms *kakh, sarai, kushk* and *khaneh* without distinguishing his meaning further.[12] He refers to the Kushk-e Mahmudi, Mahmud's palace in the city of Ghaznin, and the *sarai* and *kushk* in Shadyakh Garden in Nishapur.[13] These terms are frequently used by other historians. 'Abdi Beyk uses *sarai* to denote a royal building (Sarai-e Shahi) in a garden used as a place in which to receive God's mercy and kindness (*manzelgah-e rahmat-e elahi*).[14] He also calls this building a *qasr*[15] 'palace, castle', describing it as "the space of the royal court".[16] The second category refers to spaces within buildings such as *hoz-khaneh* 'fountain room' and *bala-khaneh* 'second floor'.

For instance, in the *Tarikh-e Yazd*, Jafar ibn Muhammad ibn Hasan Jafari uses the term *hoz-khaneh*, meaning 'guest room with a fountain in the centre'. In some cases these terms are even used to denote whole buildings. Jafari uses *hoz-khaneh* to denote a guest building that is separated from other buildings within gardens. In the *Tarikh-e 'Alam Aray-e 'Abbasi*, Monshi uses several different words to identify buildings or structures in gardens; these terms include *iwan* (originally meaning verandah but also used as 'palace'), *bala-khaneh* and *'emarat*.[17] The use of the word *iwan* implies the significance of a view of the planted areas in the design of any structure in a Safavid garden. Monshi uses *iwan* when he writes about a large ceremony in the Keif Palace (Iwan-e Keif).[18] Monshi's use of *ravaq* 'portico' is comparable in meaning to *iwan*.[19]

The third category of words refers to the use of pavilions as semi-open spaces in gardens; these spaces are called *soffeh* 'summer-house', *iwan* 'verandah', *dokkan* 'platform and bench', *ravaq* 'portico', *sabat* 'roofed corridor', or *tonob* 'tent's rope'. The most widely used term is *soffeh*. Linguist 'Ali Akbar Dehkhoda indicates that *soffeh* would refer to "a roofed *iwan*, an intermediate space between *ghorfeh* 'room' and *dehliz* 'corridor'". Beyhaqi describes a *soffeh* as a platform on which tents are pitched[20] or where the throne is located.[21] Beyhaqi refers to the *Soffeh-ye no* ('New *Soffeh*') in the Bagh-e Khass in Balkh, describing it as a "high [tall] and wide" structure located in front of an area of greenery and close to a fountain and a wide courtyard.[22] The term *soffeh* involves ambiguity since it is used variously to refer to a building (*divan*) within the garden, a building close to the *soffeh* (the platform or *iwan*), or a building close to pitched tents. It is also used by Beyhaqi's contemporaries: the famous poet Farrokhi Sistani, in his *Divan*, refers to the *soffeh* as a "semi-open space and a domed building",[23] while Khosrow uses the word to refer to spaces within a building such as the *ghorfeh* or the *iwan* of the *divan* (the main guest room of a house), to a wooden house, or to a *bala-khaneh*.[24] Beyhaqi even specifies the use of *soffeh*, confirming that this term was used to refer to a setting used for administrative purposes: "And [Bunasr] went to the *divan*. It was a very cold day. He sat on the *soffeh* of the Bagh-e 'Adnani. The wind was blowing very harshly. He went to the king [amir] and showed five or six letters and then came back to the *soffeh* and answered [the letters] and then left."[25] In his writings Beyhaqi also refers to a *dokkan*, indicating a platform or couch placed in a garden. This type of platform appears to be similar to a kiosk but is not necessarily roofed. For instance, he refers to a *dokkan* in the Shadyakh Garden in Nishapur: "In the middle of the grass there was a *dokkan*, on which they [Amir Mas'ud and Bunasr] sat and had a long chat."[26] The purpose of this type of platform was to provide a place to sit where one could enjoy the view of the garden. Beyhaqi writes that Mas'ud sat on a throne in the middle of the garden and entertained his guests.[27] Jafar ibn Muhammad ibn Hasan Jafari, in his descriptions of these gardens in Yazd, uses two other terms: *sabat* and *tonob*.[28] These rarely appear in other historical documents. Unfortunately, today no physical evidence of the gardens in Yazd survives that could throw light on the meanings in the sixteenth century of *sabat* and *tonob*, but both are used to refer to roofed areas and kiosks in gardens.

GARDENS AND CITIES

The analysis of pavilions requires an understanding of the relationship between cities and gardens, which is addressed in historical documents. Two types of garden are observed and described by travellers and historians in terms of their location either inside or outside the city, although the majority of texts refer to royal gardens outside cities. This is because such gardens provided a wider range of opportunity for use. Before analysing the multiple functions of gardens, however, we need to consider two aspects which profoundly affected the relationship between pavilion gardens and cities: the flexibility of gardens in terms of accommodating new structures (such as kiosks and other buildings), and the role of gardens in the growth of cities.

Gardens as Living Cells

Despite the common perception of the Persian garden as a single defined territory, some texts, such as the *Tarikh-e Beyhaqi* and the *Tarikh-e Yazd,* confirm that there could be different stages in the construction of pavilions which were not necessarily based on a master plan. Abul-Fazl Beyhaqi praises Mas'ud's knowledge of geometry and claims the latter's palace in Ghaznin, Kushk-e No-ye Mas'udi[29] – which was designed and constructed by Mas'ud – is a "world" in itself.[30] Beyhaqi then mentions that over a period of twenty years after the palace's construction, additional buildings were erected inside the garden; while the claim that Mas'ud designed these buildings and gardens himself might be merely an exaggeration by Beyhaqi as a court historian, what is important here is the suggestion that some of the buildings were added not on the basis of a master plan, but rather in an organic manner based on contingent need.[31] Beyhaqi claims Mas'ud himself also designed a new *soffeh,* other buildings, a fountain and a pool, and even suggested renovation of old buildings in the Bagh-e Khasseh.[32]

According to Jafari in the *Tarikh-e Yazd* (fourteenth–fifteenth century CE), the army general Amir 'Emad-uddin Mojtaba similarly added new buildings to the Bagh-e Taghanshahi, which had originally been built by Atabak Taghanshah, including a *sabat,* water channels, a *tonob,* a fountain room (*hoz-khaneh*) and an *'emarat* (building).[33] Later, when Amir Mortaza came to Yazd, he added another office (*divan-khaneh*) and a fountain to the middle of this garden.[34] The governor Shah Yahya also built an excellent *sabat* and mosque at the entrance to this garden. According to Jafari, the Bagh-e Amir Shahi in Yazd, originally constructed by Khajeh Amir Shah, included buildings (*'emarat*), a house (*khaneh*), an entrance (*dargah*) and a kiosk (*kushk*). When Amirzadeh Eskandar took power, he ordered the construction of a new palace (*qasr*) along with a fountain room and wind-catcher (*badgir*).[35] Similarly, the Bagh-e Layestan, a vast garden built by Shah Yahya, included a kiosk (*sabat*) at the entrance, another building close to the entrance (*kushk-e bar bala-ye dargah*), a lake and a three-storeyed pavilion (*kushk*). When Amir Chakhmaq came to power he erected a new palace for himself, while all his courtiers also built houses for themselves to stay in during the summer.

Gardens and the Growth of Cities

Population increase and the associated problems of adequate space within the bounds of city walls meant that cities gradually needed to expand. This issue is discussed by Masashi Haneda with regard to the Ilkhanid cities,[36] by Heidi Walcher with regard to Safavid Isfahan,[37] and Manu Sobti with regard to the cities of Central Asia.[38] The problem was also commented upon by travellers and historians. For example, Clavijo, who categorizes gardens on the basis of their location inside or outside cities,[39] highlights general concerns over the increase in the population of the city of Samarqand and the concomitant lack of space, which forced people to live outside the city under trees and in caves.[40] This, along with other factors necessitating the growth of cities, such as shortages of land and the need for new buildings and public spaces, encouraged kings and administrations to extend the boundaries of capital cities. What is important to our study is the influential role that both existing and new gardens played in master plans for urban development. These were not necessarily considered to be individual, isolated and private entities, but dynamic parts of the city as a whole that would become part of the public realm, would change the orientation of the city, or would accelerate urban development.[41]

Three examples of such gardens merit further consideration. First, there is the Bagh-e Mahmud outside Ghaznin, which eventually became Mahmud's mausoleum, and which completely changed its role from being a private royal garden to a public space (because Mas'ud ordered the removal of all trees and other plants). Second, there is the Hezar Jarib garden in Isfahan, which was designed during the reign of Shah 'Abbas specifically to enhance Chaharbagh Street as the main recreational axis of the city of Isfahan, the new Safavid capital. Finally, there is Uzun Hasan's garden at Nasriyyeh, which served as the focal point for the new Ilkhanid dynasty. In the latter case, Uzun Hasan attempted to shift the entire city centre to this new neighbourhood, which included a piazza, garden and palace, mosques and a hospital.[42] This developed neighbourhood was no longer merely a place to pitch camp or pursue recreational activities, but a new urban quarter serving the whole city.[43] These three examples demonstrate that, at least in the pre-Safavid period, gardens located outside cities were considered to be territories which could be incorporated into the city proper as needs dictated. Urban expansion relates not only to the size of gardens, but also to their use and functionality. In other words, gardens could not only be developed and converted into urban quarters, but could also undergo a radical change from private into public spaces. Furthermore, the shortage of land within cities and the frequent use of gardens as sites for military and royal encampments encouraged planners to use gardens outside cities as significant cells for urban growth. This trend impacted the flexible definition of the pavilion as a building, kiosk or tent, which in turn was related to the multiple functions of gardens.

THE USES OF GARDENS

In social and cultural studies, limited attention has been devoted to the analysis of gardens, although they have widely served as cultural centres in Western and Eastern civilizations. Contemporary scholar John Dixon Hunt has referred to the necessity for research on the cultural and social life of gardens, arguing vigorously that gardens have never been 'marginal' elements in reality.[44] The marginality of gardens in academic studies is also a consequence of underestimating their complexity throughout history. Such ignorance can be seen in many Persian and Islamic studies in which the formal aspects of gardens are highlighted over other elements. While there is no doubt that spiritual and religious factors have played a role in the development of the *chaharbagh,* the fourfold garden, a recent review of Persian literature indicated the materialistic and worldly value of gardens and pavilions.[45] Nevertheless, it appears that the dominant emphasis placed on the aesthetic and ideological value of gardens has led to an oversimplification of the concept behind them. Such a narrow view diminishes the historic role of gardens to artistic objects and places for delight rather than as dynamic components of Islamic cities.

The concept of Persian gardens originated in Mesopotamia and Achaemenid royal hunting parks and pleasure gardens. Although the tradition of hunting parks declined after the advent of Islam, the design of pleasure gardens, which represented the Qur'anic paradise, was pursued by political authorities and the wealthy. Their primary function as places for recreation, leisure and joy, however, overshadowed their lesser-known advantages as sites for political, social and cultural events, although historical documents make numerous references to the centrality of gardens and their buildings on such occasions. Indeed, the simultaneous use of gardens as places for restoration, political meetings, parties, ceremonies, encampments and pilgrimage made them vital parts of the urban design. Closer examination of historic and travel accounts will shed light on the practical qualities of Persian gardens and attest to their multifunctionality in the Medieval Age, although it should be noted that this exploration does not address the impact of functional flexibility on the design of gardens and their placement outside or inside cities, subjects that deserve to be explored in future studies.

Gardens as Sources of Income and Pleasure

In any study of Persian gardens, a distinction should be made between agricultural and fruit gardens and those that are solely devoted to delight. However, in most cases, gardens can have dual or multiple functions. Gardens as sources of income in the Persian world were observed by travellers such as Naser Khosrow, Ibn Battuta and the Frenchman, Jean Baptiste Tavernier (1605–89). Tavernier compared gardens to caravanserais (*ribat*) and bazaars in terms of their economic benefit,[46] while Battuta (1304–68), a Maghribi traveller, wrote about his observations of the fruit gardens inside the city of Baghdad and in Oshtorgan (near Isfahan).[47] Battuta also compared Shiraz to Damascus, explaining that Shiraz was more beautiful because it had several fruit gardens.[48] Masashi Haneda, scholar of Persian history, in his studies on Ilkhanid gardens outside Ghazan and Tabriz, discussed their role in supplementing urban life by supplying vegetables and fruit for the inhabitants of those cities.[49] Similarly, the gardens around Samarqand also served as bazaars for selling food and fruit, and included specific platforms where the sale of garden produce took place.

'Abdi Beyk, a historian of the Safavid court, named several fruits and vegetables grown in Shah Tahmasp's royal garden of Sa'adat Abad in the city of Qazvin, indicating that royal gardens were intended to be productive.[50] Moreover, due to their economic value, gardens were considered significant properties in administrative contracts. Adib Shahab-uddin wrote that two-thirds of the gardens of Nowruzi and Firuzi and the Khan Maleki Bazaar were dedicated as dowry and a bridal gift to a newly married couple who were the children of the political rulers (Sa'd's daughter and Hulagu's son).[51] While the majority of gardens contributed to their owner's income or larder, they also played a significant role as recreational settings for private and public use. This dual purpose of gardens is also reflected in the terminology: for example, the word *bagh* (literally meaning garden) refers both to pleasure gardens and agricultural fields.

The eleventh-century historian Abul-Fazl Beyhaqi, in his famous chronicle, mentioned several pleasure gardens owned by Amir or his courtiers which were located outside cities.[52] He also stressed pleasant views as a main recreational aspect of Ghaznavid gardens: "Amir [Mas'ud] arrived in the Bagh-e Firuzi and sat in the courtyard with a view of the greenery".[53] In Timurid documents, such as the *Ahsan al-Tavarikh,* the Bagh-e Zaghan is referred to as the largest garden in Herat; it was located outside the city and was apparently used by a royal family.[54] Like their Ghaznavid, Ilkhanid and Timurid predecessors, Safavid kings

(1499–1736) owned many pleasure gardens, mostly outside cities, which were used for meetings, gatherings and ceremonies.[55] One of these was the Sa'adat Abad Garden outside Qazvin.[56] Babur, who was contemporary to Shah Tahmasp, used his gardens for recreation and relaxation, especially after wars: according to Hasan Romlu, when Babur finished quelling the rebellion in Balkh, he went to the Bagh-e Sefid to rest and prepare for the next war.[57]

Babur's notes illustrate his passion for different kinds of amusements in gardens: "under the shade of the trees of the same garden, and sitting on the top of the eminence which overhangs the river, we set some men to wrestle before us for amusement".[58] The restorative use of these royal gardens does not conflict with their productive function, although, unlike Mughal Indian gardens, it appears that the fruits produced in Persian royal gardens were only used by the members of the royal family or given as imperial gifts to guests visiting the court.

Administrative Meetings and Ceremonies

The administrative uses of gardens and the pavilions inside them are consistently mentioned in documents compiled by writers and travellers such as Beyhaqi, Monshi, Babur, Clavijo, Herbert and Chardin.[59] In his description of the administrative affairs in the garden of Shadyakh in Nishapur, Beyhaqi narrated that the Caliph's ambassador came from Baghdad to bestow the *khal'at* (caliphal robe of honour) upon the Amir, Mas'ud. Mas'ud faced the *qibla* and put on the robe, and then army musicians blew trumpets in the garden, following which the Amir and his courtiers began drinking.[60] He also noted that Amir Mas'ud took his administrative materials with him onto the *soffeh* (the *iwan* or the platform), where he could have a clear view of the garden in the Bagh-e Shadyakh,[61] and pointed out that when Mas'ud's father, Mahmud, travelled to his gardens, all his *divan* (offices), including the furniture and his entire personnel, were moved to the garden in order to take care of official affairs.[62]

Beyhaqi referred to several administrative meetings in the Ghaznavid gardens in Khorasan, writing, for example, that after hearing some news "he (Amir) asked for a meeting with his courtiers and soldiers and nobles and asked their opinion".[63] He also observed law enforcement in gardens, such as the sentencing and execution of prisoners.[64] Apparently, some Ghaznavid gardens, such as the Bagh-e Sad-Hezareh, were close to hunting parks and were primarily used for the king's feasts after hunting.[65] The Timurid garden of Zaghan (the Bagh-e Zaghan) in Herat was occasionally used as a residence for Mirza Muhammad Heydar,[66] and Romlu repeatedly refers to this garden as the main administrative centre for the Timurids.[67] In addition, the ambassadors of Dai Ming Khan and the emperor of China came to Herat and met Qara Yusof Turkaman (the governor) in the Bagh-e Zaghan in 1413. This garden was also the setting for the enthronement ceremony of Shahzadeh Mozaffar in

1456;[68] Soltan Abu Sa'id's celebration of the birth of the prince (Shahzadeh Baysonghor) in 1464,[69] and for the meeting of Soltan Muhammad Mirza, his army and courtiers, and Homayun Shah in 1544.[70] Similarly, Khunji in the *Tarikh-e 'Alam Aray-e Amini* mentioned several royal parties in this garden, such as the party held for the circumcision of the son of Mo'ezz al-Dowla 'Abd al-Qazi Soltan Bayqara in 1487.[71]

'Abdi Beyk, in his description of the garden outside of the city of Qazvin, clearly explained that the pavilion (*qasr*) was not only intended to be used as a residence for Shah Tahmasp and his family, but also as the main location for his administrative affairs. Shah Tahmasp's son, Shah 'Abbas, developed the city of Isfahan by adding several gardens and pavilions along the new street of Chaharbagh. He also used gardens in Qazvin and Herat for his administrative ceremonies before settling in Isfahan. Shah 'Abbas's biographer, Eskandar Beyk, however, only offered vague details about the official use of gardens and their pavilions, although he did describe Safavid kings and their courtiers camping in gardens.[72] He also referred to royal parties,[73] official meetings,[74] and receptions of foreign ambassadors in the palace[75] of the Bagh-e Sa'adat Abad.[76]

Whereas these writings illustrate the nomadic mentality of the king and his perception of a garden as a temporary place, Babur's memoirs express his passion for enjoying his gardens – he wrote about sitting near water, drinking wine,[77] and fishing there[78] – while, at the same time, regarding them as appropriate venues for administrative meetings. The garden is temporarily transformed into a bit of wilderness, yet bureaucracy, administration and government affairs inhabit the same space (Figure 95). Babur also referred to passing the month of Ramadan in the Bagh-e Hasht Behesht[79] and described himself as having afternoon communal prayers in his garden and palace in Agra.[80]

Cultural and social behaviour within royal courts and gardens is usually neglected by historians, but these examples show that it has been carefully described by travellers such as Clavijo, Membre, Herbert and Chardin. Their descriptions illustrate the cultural use of the pavilion, people's actions and interactions inside it, and the relationship between the pavilion and the social hierarchy within the court. The significance of this social organization lies in the fact that it directly results in the visible or invisible division of spaces inside the pavilion. Michele Membre, a visitor to the court of Shah Tahmasp in Tabriz in 1539–42, described the hierarchical order in the court. The king gave audience in his 'pavilion' in the centre of the garden, his throne surrounded by four tiers of spectators who sat in an order dictated by their rank. These tiers (based on their closeness to the king) included vassals, governors, courtiers of lower rank and *qurchis* (cavalrymen). Those who were more honoured had large parasols for protection from the sun.[81] This scene could be compared to Clavijo's description of Timur's court, where the cross-legged Timur sat on silken carpets in a portal in front of the entrance to his palace, with a fountain before him.[82] Clavijo explained the interaction between ambassadors, *meerzas* (courtiers and nobles) and Timur:

> As soon as the ambassadors saw the lord they made a reverential bow, placing the knee on the ground and crossing the arms on the breast; then they went forward and made another, and then a third, remaining with their knees on the ground. The lord ordered them to rise and come forward; and the knights, who had held them until then, let them go. Three Meerzas who stood before the lord and were his most intimate councillors, named Alodalmelec Meerza, Borundo Meerza, and Noor Eddin Meerza, then came and took the ambassadors by the arms and led them forward until they stood together before the lord. This was done that the lord might see them better, for his eyesight was bad, being so old that the eyelids had fallen down entirely.[83]

The linear seating order in Timur's court is comparable to the organization in the court of Shah 'Abbas in the Ashraf pavilion, described by British traveller, Thomas Herbert: "round about the room were also seated several tacit Mirzaes, Chawns, Soltans, and Beglerbegs; who, like so many inanimate statues were placed cross-legged, joining their bums to the ground, their backs to the wall, and their eyes to a constant object."[84] Herbert also explained the strict behaviour policy in the court of Shah 'Abbas: "To speak one to another, sneeze, cough, or spit in the Pot-shaw's [king's] presence being…held to good breeding; nor they offend the king, who by the fulgor of his eye can dart them dead as soon as speak the word."[85] Herbert described the shah, who sat at the top level and was "beloved at home, famous abroad, and formidable to his enemies".[86] Similarly, Babur described his reception in his garden at Agra. He sat in the newly built octagonal kiosk on the northern side and faced his courtiers who sat to his right and left. Nobles, governors, clergies and Qur'an readers sat on both sides about five or six yards away. Babur's descriptions show that high-ranking people sat closer to him, while *mollas* and Qur'an readers were farther away. The *qizilbash* (Safavid envoys) and Uzbek sat about seventy or eighty yards away under two awnings on Babur's right and left sides, respectively. He had also selected two of his commanders to sit beside each group of ambassadors and take care of them.[87]

These accounts from the courts of Timur, Shah Tahmasp, Shah 'Abbas and Babur clarify the hierarchical order applied in all royal meetings, whether they were inside or outside the pavilion or gardens. The king always occupied the upper position, either at the end of a rectangular hall like Shah 'Abbas in Ashraf, or in the centre as in the case of Shah Tahmasp. They also show the special reception intended for ambassadors in royal gardens and reveal their predetermined position in the court. Thus, the king sat on a roofed pavilion (a throne or kiosk) in order to be differentiated from all others, including special guests.

Encampments

While some gardens in the Persian world were planned as extensions to cities, some served as refuges from them. The design of gardens outside cities was also the result of the nomadic life of sovereigns who were either disinclined to stay in cities or afraid of being trapped within their walls, especially as cities were under constant threat from external enemies or internal rebellions. Several references to encampment gardens during the Ilkhanid and Timurid periods verify this point. Haneda discussed the common tradition of designing gardens outside Ilkhanid cities to function as nomadic camps. He exemplified Sharuyaz as ideal summer pasturage with rich supplies of water and grass and also mentioned the vast garden on the outskirts of the Soltaniyyeh, built by Uljeitu's vizier, Taj-uddin 'Ali Shah, in the early fourteenth century.[88] Clavijo's account also confirms the influence of the nomadic mentality on the design of gardens by noting that Timur always preferred to stay in gardens outside the city of Samarqand, such as the Bagh-e Delgosha.[89]

Bernard O'Kane explored the impact of pastoral nomadism on the concept of place for royal courts in medieval Persia. He referred to Safavid and Timurid historic accounts, such as the *Tarikh-e 'Alam Aray-e 'Abbasi* and Clavijo's travel notes, to demonstrate imperial encampments (*ordu*) during different periods and to investigate the use of gardens for such camps. These historic texts imply a lack of desire to stay in palaces inside cities and a dominant tendency to stay in tents that provided greater mobility.[90] O'Kane wrote that the *ordu* was, in many respects, a mobile city: "An elaborate ceremony accompanied the camp every time it moved; a strict formation based on military rank was observed, with the drummers, trumpeters and pipers of each unit occupying prominent positions." Mosques and bazaars were located in each encampment, although prices were high because of the difficulties of transport. The ruler and his household formed one camp and each of his wives had a camp of her own, as did army generals and viziers.[91] Historian Monika Gronke pointed to the concept of *ordu* and how Timurid and Safavid historians never referred to capitals as fixed places.[92] In his description of the Albares, Clavijo says that people do not possess anything but their tents, nor do they live in cities or villages, but on the open plains in both winter and summer.[93] The Uzbek ruler, Sheybani Khan, in response to his chronicler, Fazl Allah Khunji, who spoke about several capitals of the world, said, "Let our capital be our saddle".

Khunji, the biographer of the fifteenth-century ruler Aqqoyunlu Soltan Yaqub, explained the benefits of nomadism: "[Soltan Yaqub] was not a town dweller affected by dirty habits, as was the case with many rulers of Khorasan, Fars, and Kerman, but followed the seasons wandering in open spaces going from summer quarters to winter quarters."[94] Similarly, Joveyni, author of the history of the Mongols, wrote: "The capital of Ogetei, the heir-apparent, during his father's reign was his yurt (tent) in the region of the Emil and the Qaboq."[95]

Gronke intelligently points out that Romlu, who worked in the Safavid court, and Eskandar Monshi never discussed the change of capitals, mainly because the word "capital as a fixed territory does not have any meaning for them and refers to the royal encampment". Building on Gronke's observation, it should be noted that not only does Romlu fail to identify cities as capitals, but he rarely refers to palaces as the main setting for administration. Instead, he frequently speaks about travel between gardens, in some cases without mentioning the names of cities. For example, he writes that, in 1422, King Shahrokh travelled from the Bagh-e Zaghan to Azarbayjan;[96] in 1455, Soltan Mirza Babur decided to travel from the Bagh-e Sefid to the Bagh-e Mokhtar; Mirza Shah Mahmud went from the Bagh-e Mokhtar to the Bagh-e Zaghan,[97] and that Soltan Hoseyn Mirza travelled from the Bagh-e Zaghan to a garden in Astarabad.[98] These examples demonstrate a dominant cultural view in which the city, as the main administrative centre, was replaced by the garden. In other words, gardens were always points of departure and destination and automatically signified cities.

Although Gronke and O'Kane called *ordu* a Mongol tradition, Beyhaqi's account of the Ghaznavids sheds light on its roots in this region during the pre-Mongol age. Describing the use of Ghaznavid gardens in Khorasan as encampments outside cities, he wrote that Amir Mahmud, his son Amir Mas'ud, and their courtiers usually stayed in the royal gardens for two or three nights on their way to and from the city of Ghaznin.[99] Such use confirms the functionality of these gardens as caravanserais for the king before or after war. Beyhaqi's notes show that Mas'ud and Mahmud never stayed in their royal gardens in Balkh, Ghaznin and Herat for long periods of time because their final destination was the royal palace (*kushk* or *kakh*) inside these cities. In other words, while the gardens were treated as intermediate residences by the Ghaznavid kings, they were considered to be more than a temporary residence for nomadic rulers, such as Khans and Timur.

Military Purposes

Ilkhanid documents, such as *The History of the World-Conqueror*, the *Tarikh-e Ghazani* and the *Tarikh-e Vassaf*, confirm the use of gardens for encampments and reveal their strategic function in wars. These accounts show how gardens played a logistical role in defending cities against Mongol attacks and in initiating invasions. According to the *Tarikh-e Ghazani*, which outlines the history of the Ilkhanids (1265–95), the Mongols attacked Shiraz from the Bagh-e Piruzi. The author of this text, Khajeh Rashid, even clarified that the invaders chased their horses from the gardens.[100] Similarly, in the *Tarikh-e Vassaf*, Adib Shahab-uddin wrote that when the Mongols attacked Khwarazm, citizens had gathered in the Bagh-e Khorram in order to fight against them. Mongol troops caught them by surprise in the garden and, after a general massacre, attacked the city, looting and destroying buildings.[101] According to Shahab-uddin, the governor of Shiraz, Atabak Sa'd, kept Mongol soldiers and envoys in his garden outside the city in order to keep them unaware of events inside the walls. Sa'd transferred his administration to the garden and ordered his courtiers (*arkan-e dowlat*) to stay in their houses next to it.[102]

Additionally, Romlu's *Ahsan al-Tavarikh* confirms the strategic role of Timurid gardens in local and regional confrontations and rebellions. For instance, the Bagh-e Chenar, outside Samarqand, was used as a camp in military expeditions during the Timurid age (around 1450).[103] In some cases, attempts were made to invade the royal gardens located outside cities in order to diminish the defence forces, as when in 1470 Turkaman's army attacked the Bagh-e Zaghan outside Herat before invading the city. This was significant as it was the main seat for the king and, therefore, the actual capital and symbol of power.[104] Similarly, in 1520 Uzbeks attacked this garden before attacking Herat, as it was the main army encampment. Romlu also wrote about a battle inside the Bagh-e Sarafraz in which 300 soldiers were killed.[105] In 1512, the soldiers of Beyk Soltan used the Bagh-e Sefid as a camp to attack the city and, because they could not succeed, returned to the garden.[106] This garden was also later used as a camp by Uzbek troops for their expeditions in 1523.[107]

Gardens, because of their role in administrative settings, were also used for major rebellions. Romlu recounted that Amir Shir Haji invited Tarkhani courtiers to his pavilion (*kushk*) in the Bagh-e Zaghan with an excuse that he was holding an advisory meeting, but actually intending to murder them.[108] Even Marco Polo, who travelled to China and through Persia in the thirteenth century, described the garden in the Valley of the Assassins as the biggest and most beautiful garden ever seen. This garden was used as a preparation camp for assassins to be sent to different parts of the country to terrorize Isma'ili's enemies, such as Khajeh Nezam al-Molk. It was later invaded by Genghiz Khan's grandson, Hulagu, in 1526, when he besieged the mountain fortress and put 'Ala'-uddin to death. Marco Polo also discussed the notion of paradise and how it was used as to motivate the assassins:

> [the Sheykh] used to put some of these youths in this paradise, four at a time, or ten, or twenty, according as he wished. And this is how he did it. He would give them draughts that sent them to sleep on the spot. Then he had them taken and put in the garden, where they were awakened. When they awoke and found themselves in there...they believed they were really in Paradise. And the ladies and damsels stayed with them all the time, singing and making music for their delight and ministering to all their desires...when they awoke, they believing they had been in Paradise and longing for it, were willing to go out and kill, and looked forward to the day of their going. In this way he was able to send out the assassins where ever he might wish and that if they died on their mission they would go to Paradise all the sooner.[109]

The involvement of gardens in war required the presence of defensive structures nearby. While most documents are silent regarding the existence of these kinds of structure, Romlu confirmed the presence of a (watch) tower built near the Bagh-e Morad in order to protect the garden.[110] In addition to the need for new structures, the use of gardens as encampments to accommodate hundreds of people affected their size and required that they encompass huge territories. According to Beyhaqi, Ghaznavid gardens in Khorasan were usually big enough to contain the whole court and many soldiers. For instance, the Bagh-e Khasseh was so extensive that 500 soldiers once hid in the garden in order to ambush 300 Indian soldiers.[111] Beyhaqi stressed that the garden was so long that the whole army could assemble there.[112] These gardens, therefore, were immense complexes with several buildings and vast open areas. Clavijo also makes clear that Timurid gardens were much larger than surviving gardens, such as the ones in Isfahan and Shiraz, since they were used to lodge large portions of the army and its equipment.[113]

Sites of Pilgrimage

Gardens were not only used for encampments and administrative affairs, but also had the flexibility to become pilgrimage sites. The type of mausoleum gardens in which the tomb element was an afterthought should not be mistaken with mausoleum gardens which were constructed as a complex based on a predetermined design. The conversion of gardens into pilgrimage sites is mentioned in few documents, and historians before the tenth century are somewhat silent about gardens as places for prayer and pilgrimage. Beyhaqi should be credited as one of the earliest historians to highlight this usage. He wrote that Mahmud of Ghazneh was buried in his favourite garden (the Bagh-e Piruzi) in 1030 after a communal evening prayer.[114] Mahmud's burial in this garden probably gradually modified its nature and use, converting it from a place for pleasure to a pilgrimage site. Beyhaqi confirmed this hypothesis in his narrative: when Mahmud's son, Mas'ud, came to the garden to visit his father's tomb, he ordered the removal of all flowers and plants in order to make it purely a place for pilgrimage. To justify his command, Mas'ud said: "My father liked this garden and that is why he left his instructions to bury him here. I forbid myself to come into this garden [again] except to come as a pilgrim. The greenery and other plants should be removed so that no one comes here [again] for sightseeing."[115]

Beyhaqi's account indicates that Mahmud's wish to be interred in his garden was not his own innovation, but an existing tradition for those of high rank; his vizier, Bunasr, was also buried in his garden outside the city of Ghaznin. In both cases, caravanserais were constructed close to these gardens after the funerals – in the Bagh-e Piruzi by Mas'ud as an endowment for his father's soul, according to Mahmud's will.[116] Although Beyhaqi's text does not clarify whether these caravanserais were located inside or outside the walls of the gardens, both examples clearly illustrate that the gardens, which were originally private places for pleasure, were transformed into public spaces after the construction of tombs and mausoleums.

Constructing a public building in a garden was also associated with the cultural tradition of conducting funerary rituals for high-ranking people. Romlu narrated a story about a ceremony in Bagh-e Sefid in which the Timurid king Shahrokh, with his courtiers, servants and high-ranking people attended communal prayers after the death of Mirza Baysonghor. The corpse was then sent to the Gohar Shad Beygom Madrasa and buried there.[117] Nevertheless, it appears that funeral rituals in gardens were not a common tradition in Persia until the Ilkhanids: Ibn Battuta, for example, did not refer to gardens as settings for tombs and mausoleums in the fourteenth century. An exception in Battuta's text is the mausoleum of the poet Sa'di in Shiraz, which was located inside a garden that included a restaurant for pilgrims and small marble pools that were watered by creeks derived from the river in the city.[118]

A developed version of this concept appears in the Ilkhanid cities in the north-western regions of Persia, where new urban quarters were formed around mausoleum gardens. These districts were gradually converted into cities and were labelled as 'pastoral cities' by Haneda, who analysed urban development in the cities in the north-western regions of modern Iran, Ghazaniyyeh, Soltaniyyeh and Nasriyyeh, in order to highlight the central role of the mausoleum in the growth of Ilkhanid cities.[119] The development of urban quarters based on mausoleum gardens was an innovative idea, because the erection of monumental mausoleums was not a common tradition among the Mongols. They always kept the location of the body of their leader, Genghiz Khan, unclear.[120] Even Khajeh Rashid, the Ilkhanids' historian, explains that there is no rationale to building tombs.[121]

The question is, how did the Ilkhans become interested in constructing mausoleums? Haneda believes that Ghazan Khan determined to build a tomb for himself after his conversion to Shi'ism and his pilgrimage to the Shi'ite mausoleum of Imam Reza in Mashhad.[122] Ghazan Khan chose to construct his tomb in a garden so that he could not only be laid to rest in a splendid and well-managed mausoleum, but also initiate a charitable institution that could take advantage of his wealth.[123] Ghazan was concerned to create a city that included areas of greenery.[124] Perhaps that is why he chose the Bagh-e 'Adeliyyeh on the south-west outskirts of Tabriz as the main site for his mausoleum which, according to Adib Shahabuddin, included a quarter with all facilities.[125]

BUILDINGS IN GARDENS

Despite the common use of gardens as encampments, the accounts written by historians and travellers confirm the existence of buildings in most royal gardens. Since most of these gardens no longer survive, our knowledge about them depends primarily on historical material. Historians discussed in this chapter who refer to buildings in gardens include Mafarrukhi, Beyhaqi, Jafari and Eskandar Monshi. 'Abdi Beyk, due to the nature of his work, is an exception because he does not simply mention buildings but instead carefully describes the royal pavilion in Sa'adat Abad in Qazvin. Travellers' accounts also provide precious information about buildings in gardens that no longer exist. For instance, Clavijo's descriptions of the palaces in gardens at Kesh and Samarqand[126] draw a clear picture of the pavilions' placement, design and ornamentation. Similarly, despite various exaggerations, the Venetian merchant, Della Valle, and the correspondents Herbert and Chardin provide valuable detail not only of the design of garden pavilions, but also the cultural context behind their construction and design. The primary questions which must be addressed here concern records of the existence of buildings in gardens, their use as houses or palaces and their architectural design.

Buildings in gardens are cited in a number of Ghaznavid, Seljuk, Timurid, Safavid and early Mughal documents. One of the earliest writers to talk about buildings in gardens is Beyhaqi, who worked as a historian in the Ghaznavid court and mentions gardens in Ghaznin, Herat, Balkh and Nishapur. Although he is sometimes silent about the presence of palaces, in the case of the Bagh-e Piruzi, the poems of his contemporary Farrokhi confirm the existence of one (Kakh-e Piruzi) in this garden.[127] This reveals that the lack of references to buildings does not necessarily prove their absence.

The Seljuk king Malek Shah is credited by the historian Mafarrukhi[128] with the creation of four gardens in Isfahan when he succeeded his father Alp Arsalan in 1072; each was a thousand *jarib* in extent.[129] The Bagh-e Bakr was fragrant with narcissus, myrtle and saffron, and its pavilion was provided with luxurious seats from which to enjoy the magnificent views to the accompaniment of the cooing of doves and cooling breezes. The Bagh-e Falasan possessed a lofty pavilion (*qasr*) variegated in colour, with a high tower (*sarh*) commanding a fine view over the garden of Ahmad Siah with its beds of bay and myrtle, meadows (*riyad*) with pools, and places for sitting. The Bagh-e Karan was planted with fruit trees and rows of pines and cypresses, and is described as having two pavilions, one overlooking the Zayanderud River, the other in front of the city square (*meidan*). In Seljuk gardens in Isfahan, the pavilion, with its commanding prospect, was a prominent feature, and plants were selected equally for their decorative and aromatic qualities.[130]

Mirza Muhammad Heydar in the *Tarikh-e Rashidi* names the most famous kiosks that he has heard of: "Among the vast kiosks of the world are: in Tabriz, the Hasht Behesht kiosk of Soltan Yaqub; in Herat, the Bagh-e Khan, the Bagh-e Sefid and the Bagh-e Shahr; and in Samarqand, the Kuk Sarai, the Ak Sarai, the Bagh-e Dilkushai and the Bagh-e Buldi".[131] He even writes, "though the Rajan is more lofty and contains more rooms than all these, yet it has not their elegance and style. It is nevertheless a more wonderful structure."[132] Similarly, in the *Tarikh-e Yazd*, Jafari names several gardens in the Yazd vicinity, without dating them. In his description of the garden of Firuzi, built by Sayyed Majd-uddin, he talks about three buildings: house (*'emarat*), entrance (*dargah*), and fountain room (*hoz-khaneh*). Similarly, Eskandar Monshi in the *Tarikh-e 'Alam Aray-e 'Abbasi* talks about "excellent buildings" (*'emarat*) in gardens even though he does not always clarify their function and never describes them.[133] Ibn Battuta talks about the existence of public buildings inside the gardens he visited in the Persianate world, especially the ones in Shiraz. On that trip, he observes a *khanqah* (Sufi shrine) located in the middle of a garden through which a big creek, surrounded by trees, runs. In this case, he writes that the *khanqah* is big enough to include spaces such as guesthouses.

Likewise, Babur refers to his stays in houses and palaces located in gardens. He writes about his visits to the tanks, gardens and the palace at Dhulpur,[134] his residence in houses at the Bagh-e Sefid (Tarab-khaneh) and the Bagh-e Jahanara (Susani-khaneh),[135] and his overnight stay at a house in the garden of Ulugh Beg Mirza.[136] Babur refers to all these buildings as houses (*khaneh*), thus suggesting their residential function. Fryer mentions that Persian gardens and summer-houses were located outside the town of Shiraz.[137] He provides a complete description of a royal Safavid garden:

> Here grow the loftiest Cypress-Trees in the universe; nor do they want bodies proportionate to their height, one of which is said to be set by Shaw Abas [Shah 'Abbas]. These set in order make majestick walks, under whose shelter thrive the under woods; which were they removed from the first rank of the quarters, whether our countrymen would allow the rest to be wilderness, orchard, or garden, would be a question; since these, with the water-courses make the whole design of the perspective; in which promiscuously are included philberts, hazelnuts, pistachios, sweet almonds, cherries of both sorts, peach, apricot, prunellas, figs, prunes, grannet, chestnut, nectorines, quince, and all those we call wall-fruit, without any assistance: oranges and limes begin to flag here, rejoicing more where cold is less felt.[138]

He mentions that

> in the midst of all a banqueting-house or house of pleasure, with this convincingly, that which side so ever we cast our eyes, most grateful greens refresh our prospect, and cooling springs feed spouting fountains, till they unite in a full sea, and thence are diverted into pleasant streams, both for diversion and benefit of place."[139]

He also gives us other information about the ponds near which coffee houses are located, offering sherbet and smoking tobacco.[140] Here, it is significant that we are able to differentiate pavilions (as houses or palaces) from other buildings designed in gardens.

Entrances to gardens were often built structures worthy of mention. For example Beyhaqi, in reference to Sarai-e 'Adnani in the Garden of 'Adnan (Bagh-e 'Adnan), mentions that it is located close to the entrance and people should go through this building in order to enter the whole garden.[141] In this case, even though the building is referred to as a *sarai* (house/palace) it works as the gateway.[142] Another example appears in Clavijo's description of the entrance building at the Delgosha garden: "The entrance to this garden was very broad and high, and beautifully adorned with glazed tiles, in blue and gold. At this gate there were many porters, who guarded it, with maces in their hands."[143] The entrance is apparently huge enough to allow the entrance of six elephants with wooden castles on their backs.[144]

The placement and form of the pavilion in the garden depends on several factors such as the size of the garden, the topography of the site and its relation to any other buildings and structures. In order to clarify the relationship between the city, garden, pavilion and its inhabitants, we shall discuss five garden pavilions, developed in the Ilkhanid, Timurid and Safavid periods. The selection of these examples is not just based on the availability of historical material, but was also made to highlight the typological diversity of buildings in gardens. These cases fall into two general categories. The first includes a garden and pavilions which were designed to a master plan for a new city or urban quarter, such as the pavilions in the Garden of Nasriyyeh and the Dargah pavilion in the city of Isfahan. While these garden pavilions were designed in different historical periods and geographical contexts (Ilkhanid Tabriz and Safavid Isfahan), they shared a common feature: they were not regarded as isolated pavilions inside secluded gardens but were designed to be part of a new urban quarter. The second category includes pavilions constructed in gardens (or garden complexes) as secluded entities, such as the Timurid pavilions in Samarqand and Safavid pavilions in Sa'adat Abad and Ashraf. It should be noted that the intention here is to depict the diversity of pavilions in the Persianate world and the contexts behind them; each of these cases deserves an in-depth examination in future studies.

The Palace Garden in Nasriyyeh

The account of travels by an anonymous Venetian merchant provides a detailed description of the Hasht Behesht palace complex, which was built for Uzun Hasan, ruler of the White Sheep Turkman (1466–78 CE), and was located in his new quarter in the immediate outskirts of his capital of Tabriz. Developing this new quarter, called Nasriyyeh, which was shaped around his mausoleum, allowed Uzun Hasan to extend the borders of the city. The Ilkhanid historian, Hasan Romlu, writes that when Hasan died, his corpse was buried in this garden.[145] Haneda calls it a mausoleum city and believes that it served as a model for two other mausoleum cities developed in the Ilkhanid period.[146] Uzun Hasan encouraged people to use this new quarter by constructing public areas such as a market, *madrasa,* mosque and hospital, and at the same time erecting a private palace garden for himself. The significance of the garden complex in this quarter is that it was not designed as an isolated realm but as the focal point for urban development. The garden has three entrances, one each in the south, the north and the east. Beyond the main gateway, there is a fine paved road which leads to the royal palace. The eastern door, which is quite simple, stands on an immense piazza (*meidan*), and leads into the garden. This door has a wall of bricks in the form of an arch, three yards high and two broad, without any decoration, but simply whitened with plaster; through it there is a fine large fountain. There is also a large edifice with many rooms, and a covered hall overlooking the garden. The garden in the royal quarter included four structures: the palace, royal harem, summer-house and gallery.

The palace, an octagonal structure of two storeys on a stone dais, is located in the centre of this garden, which is divided into parts by a running stream.[147] The palace is thirty paces high, and about seventy or eighty yards around.[148] The *iwan* (terrace) is paved with marble and has steps leading to the garden. In the middle of the *iwan,* there is a channel for a streamlet, paved and skilfully lined in marble. This streamlet, according to the author, is four fingers broad and four deep, and flows in the form of a vine or a snake. It rises at one part, flows around and where it rejoins the water is conducted away elsewhere.[149] There are gutters on all the angles of the building from which water spurts.[150] This huge building has four entrances, described as a yard and a half high and five yards wide, which open onto an *iwan.*[151]

There is a central domed hall embellished with paintings and surrounded by four rooms, each of which has its own anteroom connecting it to the entrance.[152] Staircases lead to the second floor and the dome.[153] The paintings on the ceiling of the central hall, represented in gold, silver and ultramarine blue, depict general stories, such as battles between the Persians and the Ottomans, and others related to Uzun Hasan's life, such as his hunting expeditions[154] and the Ottoman ambassadors in his court.[155] The hall seems quite dark, only receiving light from windows to the anterooms and chambers; consequently, the magnificent paintings only become distinct when these doors are open. The beautiful silken carpet in the hall is apparently woven to the measurements of this hall, and not on standard modules.[156]

In addition to the palace, there are three other buildings/structures which are in a lower level of the garden's hierarchy. These are the harem (building for royal women) and two semi-open spaces allocated to the king and courtiers. The harem is a large, one-storeyed building which has a central hall surrounded by several chambers.[157] Through the centre of this gallery flows a stream of pure water, "a cubit in breadth and as much deep". The doors of these rooms are well decorated with patterns and calligraphy in blue and gold and pearls. The walls and ceiling are decorated with plaster and ornamented with gold, ultramarine and many other colours.[158] Two other structures in this garden, the summer-house and gallery, will be discussed later, in the section on kiosks.

Safavid Pavilions in Isfahan

Shah ʿAbbas (1587–1629 CE), the most powerful of the Safavid monarchs, moved his capital from Qazvin to Isfahan because of its strategic and natural advantages.[159] He invited scientists and artisans from other areas to convert Isfahan into an international centre for business, science, art and architecture.[160] Safavid planners reorganized the plan of Isfahan to create a new city. As a result, it became one of the most important in the world. Isfahan, which was also called "half of the world", included a new city centre, several gardens and new residential quarters with their local bazaars, a grand bazaar, and a famous boulevard, Chaharbagh, along which several gardens (including pavilions) were located.[161] The Safavid garden pavilions are reflected in most accounts by travellers who visited Persia from the seventeenth century onwards, such as Herbert (1628), Tavernier (1632), Chardin (1660s–70s), Fryer (1677), Kaempfer (1684–1685), and Binning (1847–49). For instance, Fryer refers to the houses located in orchards and gardens along Chaharbagh Street, most of which belong to the emperor and define the borders of his court.[162] Fryer's text proves the existence of several garden pavilions, which he calls "summer-houses", on both sides of Chaharbagh Street, which are no longer extant. According to Fryer, these summer-houses face ponds and offer a delicate sight to their inhabitants.[163] Apparently, however, they looked very strange to Tavernier because he writes that you can never find gardens and pavilions in Persia![164] Three major garden pavilions described by travellers are ʿEmarat-i Dargah, Hasht Behesht and Saʿadat Abad.

Tavernier writes that Chaharbagh Street begins from a "kiosk" which is about forty feet square.[165] According to Tavernier, this pavilion, called ʿEmarat-i Dargah, is located behind the palace of the king, and has narrow corridors and four halls, which he calls *iwan*.[166] The water channel in Chaharbagh Street, derived from the Zayanderud River, runs through this kiosk.[167] This two-storeyed building has several windows with wooden openings (*moshabbaks*). He also mentions that at certain times, only the king and his family are allowed to walk in this street.[168] Another pavilion in Chaharbagh Street, which still exists, is Hasht Behesht, described by Fryer as a "sweet summer-house" crossed by two channels.[169] The paintings of the central hall show ships and boats in a naval scene of war.[170] This explains the interior design of this pavilion:

> The summer-house is built entirely of polished marble, the arch of cupilo is inlaid with massy gold, upon the walls are painted the famous actions of their heroes, the tank in the middle is all of silver, the posts are stuck with looking-glasses, reflecting the postures of the body, and the figures of the whole fabrick, an hemispherical turret presses on four pillars, which are the main supporters.[171]

Fryer's description of this pavilion is particularly valuable for the restoration and preservation of the ornamentation, because comparing it to the current condition of this building can show the original decoration before the addition of other layers in the Qajar period. Robert Binning, who visited Isfahan in the nineteenth century, also describes the Hasht Behesht pavilion, without mentioning its name.[172] He has heard that it is one of the seven palaces (Haft Dast), which formerly stood in different gardens beside each other on Chaharbagh Street. According to Binning,

> this suite (Hasht Behesht) comprises a palace, two storeys high, containing a vast number of apartments, none very large or handsome, built round a court laid out in garden beds...one of the chambers in the lower story, ornamented with a Tabriz marble (*hizara*) daubed with flowers, and a cistern of marble in the floor.[173]

Binning describes another Safavid pavilion on the west of Chaharbagh Street, which no longer exists.[174] He mistakenly locates it on the eastern side, but tells us that it was built by the last Safavid king, Shah Tahmasp.[175] According to him, this palace resembles Chehelsotun and has an open façade with a flat roof supported by twelve pillars inlaid with mirrors and ornamented chambers within.[176] This palace consists of an open polygonal hall below, and some rooms above, much tattered and tarnished (Figures 96, 97, 100).[177]

The Timurid Garden Palaces in Samarqand

Timur's capital, Samarqand, was apparently full of gardens and pavilions. Although these gardens no longer exist, Golombeck and Wilber were able to approximate their location in their book.[178] Clavijo explains that in Timur's royal complex at Kesh, called Talicia, the palaces/pavilions were located on a hill overlooking the garden. To ascend the hill, there were two bridges on opposite sides, and two doors which opened upon flights of stairs leading up to the summit of the hill, where the palace stood. In this garden there were deer and many pheasants. Beyond it there was a great vineyard, as large as the garden, which was also surrounded by a mud wall, and all round the wall there were rows of tall trees, which looked very beautiful. The tents of the ambassadors were pitched on the grass, near a stream of water. The pavilion had chambers very richly ornamented with gold and blue polished tiles.[179] The foreign ambassadors were invited by Timur to his chamber, which he had set apart for feasting and for the company of his women. Clavijo also talks about his experience in the house in Bayginar (Bagh-e No) gardens:

> On Monday, the fifteenth of September, when Timur travels to Bayginar Garden, the ambassadors follow him. This garden had a very lofty and handsome entrance, made of

> bricks, and adorned with tiles in blue and gold, arranged in various patterns. On this day the lord ordered a great feast to be prepared, and sent for the ambassadors, and many other people, both men and women. This garden is very large, and contains many fruit, and other trees, which give shade. Amongst them there were avenues, and wooden terraces, on which the people walked. In the garden there were many tents, and awnings of red cloth, and of various coloured silks, some embroidered in various ways, and others plain.[180]

In a village near the city of Kesh, Clavijo and his companions had dinner at a great house in a plain near the banks of a river, and in the midst of a large and very beautiful garden.

Clavijo talks about a cross-shaped "house" in the centre of Bayginar Garden and describes its ornamented interior. In the middle of this house there were three chambers in which beds and carpets were placed. There was a silver-gilt platform (as high as a man and three arms broad) opposite the entrance in the largest of the chambers. On the top of this there was a bed of silk cloths, embroidered with gold, placed one on the top of the other, and here the lord was seated. The walls, which were covered with glazed tiles, were hung with rose-coloured silk cloths, ornamented with plates of silver gilt, and set with emeralds, pearls and other precious stones. There were pieces of silk above these ornaments, from which tassels of various colours hung. There was a huge arch, which formed the entrance to the chamber, and silk cloths raised up by spear poles kept together by silken cords, with large tassels which hung down to the ground. Two gold tables were placed in the centre of the house, opposite the main door.[181]

Clavijo's description of the gardens in Samarqand reveals their significance not only for Timur and his successors, but also for ordinary people. The idea of gardens and pavilions was later applied to another urban setting when Timur's successor, Baysonghor, transferred the capital to Herat. Unfortunately, the lack of archaeological evidence and historical studies does not allow us a clear picture of the evolution of gardens in the Timurid age, but a valuable document, written by Qasem Abu Nasr Haravi, confirms the dominance of the concept of the pavilion in the Chaharbagh in Timurid Herat.[182] His book, the *Irshad al-Zira'ah,* includes eight chapters, each of which is called a *rawdha* (paradise). The eighth chapter is devoted to *chaharbagh* and building design (*tarh-e chaharbagh va 'emarat*). The elements of such buildings, which should be oriented north-south, are the *iwan, chaharbagh* and high *ravaq* (columned hall). The building should also face a pool, which is twenty *zar'* away from the foundation of the building.[183] In contrast to his brief description of the building, he provides detailed information on the kinds of trees, plants and flowers which should be sown in specific parts of the garden.[184] The building should be surrounded by fruiting plants and trees and should provide a pleasant view of several plots, each devoted to a specific flower. Although Alemi interprets the layout of the *chaharbagh* in Haravi's text as four parallel plots (and not a cross-shaped plan), it should be stated that Haravi's text does not specify a layout for the *chaharbagh* other than the established fourfold pattern (Figures 98, 99).[185]

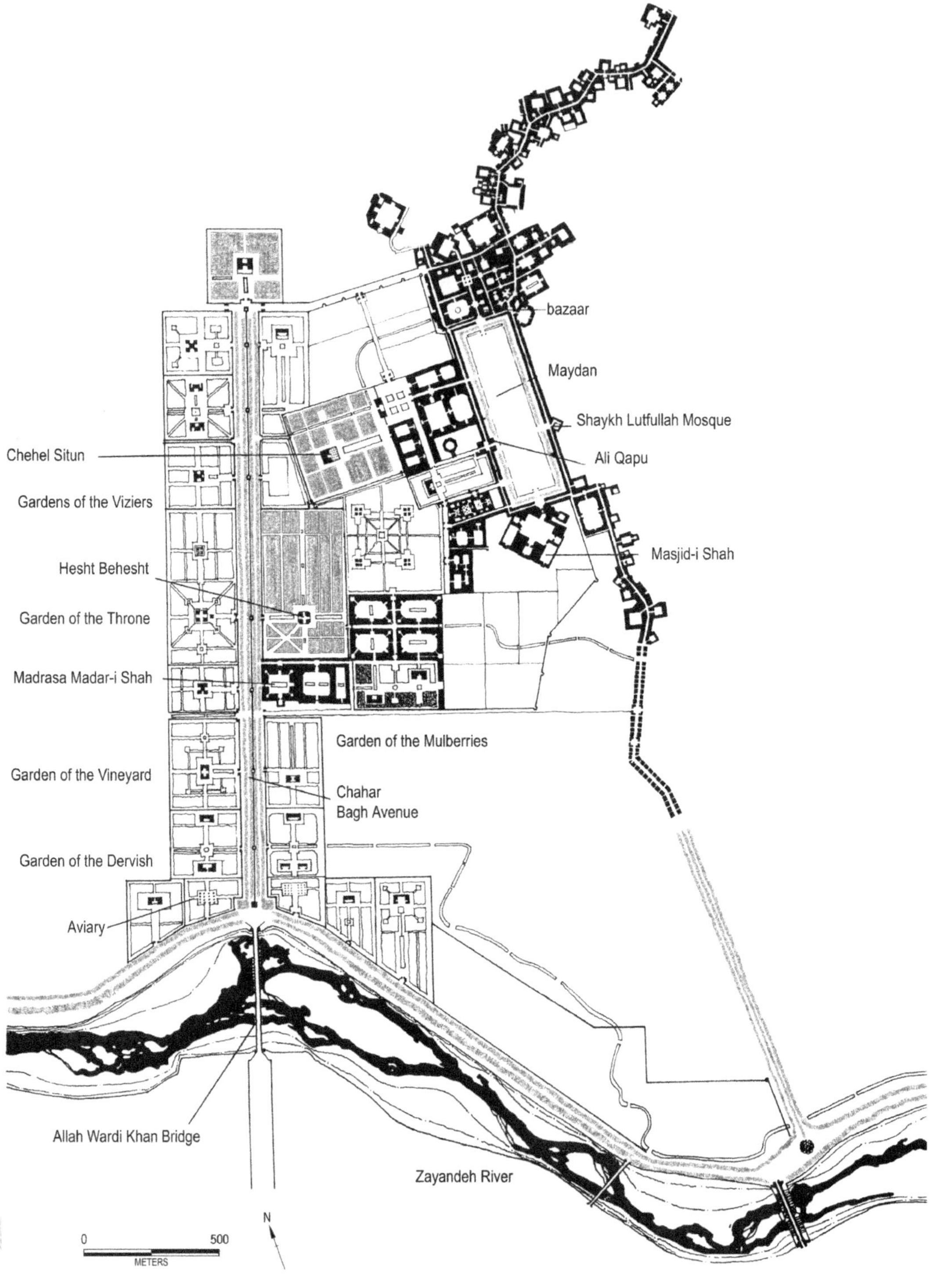

FIGURE 96

Chaharbagh Street in Isfahan.

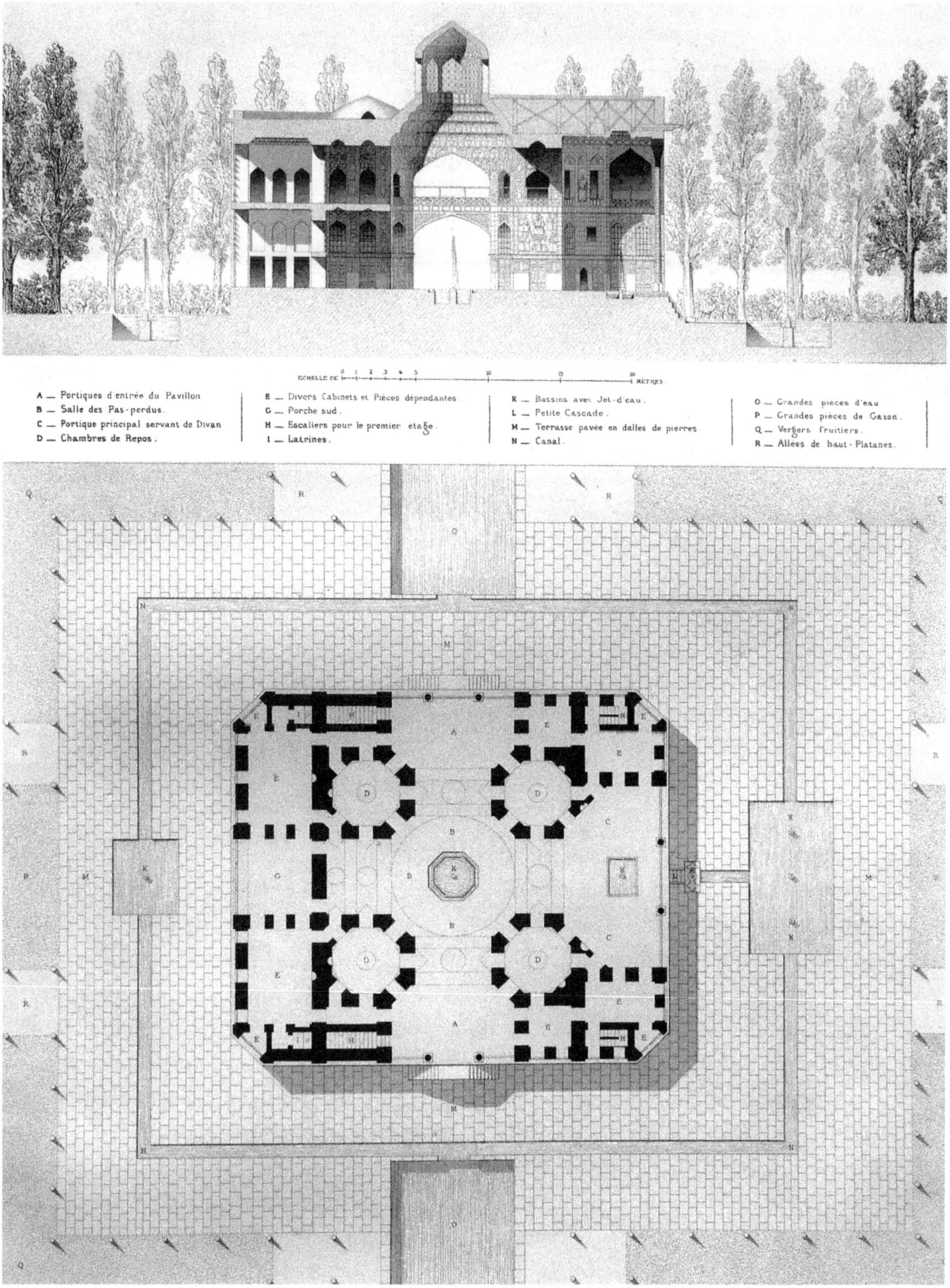

FIGURE 97

Hasht Behesht and the Bagh-e Bulbul, 1867.

The Sa'adat Abad Palace in Qazvin

'Abdi Beyk is one of the few writers in the Safavid age to describe a real garden.[186] According to the author, his work was commissioned by Shah Tahmasp and his four books of poems, which are essentially a description of the garden in Jafar Abad[187] outside the city of Qazvin,[188] provide extensive information on the economic aspects of gardens and the typology of fruits and flowers and their use in Safavid Persia. 'Abdi Beyk talks about the presence of a royal building (Sarai-e Shahi) in the garden and mentions that the architect had a meeting with Shah Tahmasp after its construction to celebrate the building, in 1558.[189] Beyk calls this palace (*qasr*)[190] a place to receive God's mercy and kindness, and describes it as the site for royal administration.[191]

This building is located in the middle of the garden of cypress trees surrounded by a transparent layer of reeds.[192] 'Abdi Beyk talks about the presence of a bathhouse[193] in this paradise (garden) as a *waqf* (donated) building.[194] He also describes the doors of the interior space of the building, which he calls *keryas*.[195] The pillars are tall and the ceiling bears decorative patterns.[196] There is an *iwan* on the front face of the building with a door decorated with many patterns in gold and blue.[197] He talks about shadow in a couple of verses, which shows the importance of shaded areas in garden. 'Abdi Beyk speaks of the unity of inside (*batin*) and outside (*zahir*), a reference to Sufi religious values:[198] although he does not explicitly relate this concept to the design of the pavilion, he indirectly discusses the connection between inside and outside by talking about the transparency of the pavilion.[199]

This building, according to 'Abdi Beyk, has tall pillars and several windows. He does not describe these openings but mentions that the inside space is very light.[200] From his description, it remains unclear whether the roof is domed, or just a transparent ceiling.[201] He also mentions that the foundation of the building "touches" water. Does this mean that the building is surrounded by water or that water runs through the building? The second option is less likely because, in his description of the interior space, he does not talk about the presence of water. A transparent ceiling carried on tall columns admits light to the inner space.[202] 'Abdi Beyk also mentions that there are arches and domes decorated in blue colour with delicate ornamentations. It is not clear whether he is talking about real paintings or tiles, but since he does not mention the use of tiles, it is possible that these are actual paintings similar to those drawn in Safavid palaces of 'Aliqapu and Chehelsotun, a hypothesis supported by subsequent verses in which he describes scenes of feasts (*bazm*) and war (*razm*) in different rooms.[203] In the *bazm* hall, which is being used by royal ladies, there are pictures of famous lovers in Persian culture, such as Yusof and Zulaykha, Leyla and Majnun, and Khosrow and Shirin. The hall of war has paintings depicting battles between early Muslims and others. There are also illustrations of the swords of Imam 'Ali, which are signs of the Shi'ism of the Safavid king. These descriptions remind us of the interior space of the hall in Chehelsotun palace in Isfahan, in which almost the same topics (war and love) are evident.

The Palace Garden in Ashraf

Sir Thomas Herbert, the English traveller and author, who visited Persia in 1627–29, provides an extensive description of Shah 'Abbas's court and garden at Ashraf. He writes, "the palace is large, and looks into very pleasant gardens, albeit the building itself be not very regular, but rather confusedly divides itself into four *mohols* [*mahal* = quarter], or banqueting-houses, which be gorgeously painted. Were these united, they might better delight the eye, and cause the architect to be commended – but more of it at the ambassador's audience." According to him, Shah 'Abbas is proud of his garden and calls it "his own garden".[204] Herbert writes about his entrance to the court:

> At our alighting an officer bade us Hosh-goldom (welcome) and ushered us into a little house which stood in the centre of a large court, wherein was no other furniture save a few Persian carpets, which were spread about a white marble tank filled with water. Here we reposed, and for two hours were entertained with polo and wine; nothing so good as the material they were served in, flagons, cups, dishes, plates, and covers being all of gold.[205]

Herbert explains that, after his exit, he passed a spacious garden, which was "curious to the eye and delicate to the smell", and then proceeded to another "summer-house," which was rich in gold embossments and painting. From this pavilion, they had a delightful view of the Caspian Sea to the north.[206] He describes the large, square chambers with arched and richly gilded roofs and carpets of silk and gold. There are also tanks and fountains full of water in the middle of the space as well as goblets, flagons and cisterns filled with perfumes, rose water, wine and flowers. From these chambers, Herbert and his companions were later guided into another large upper-chamber, where according to him, "the roof was formed into an artificial element, many golden planets attracting the wandering eye to help their motion".[207] The picture that Herbert portrays could be completed by looking at Chardin's travel notes from his visit to Ashraf more than thirty years later: "those invited were made to come through the gardens by an avenue of large trees under which a dozen horses were to be seen making one of the main spectacles of royal celebrations...".[208] Chardin describes the royal throne which is at the back of the room:

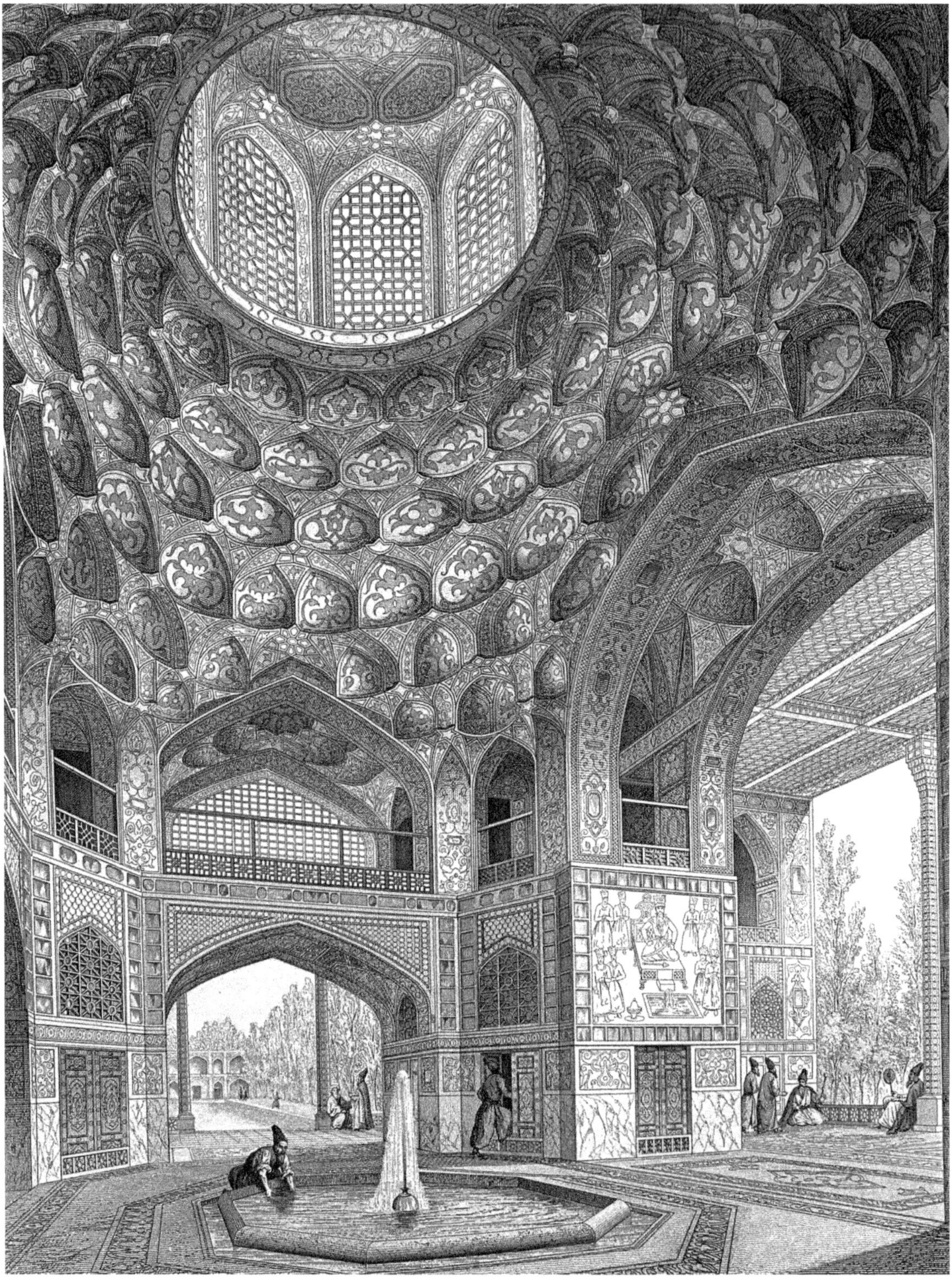

FIGURE 100
The interior of Hasht Behesht in Isfahan, 1867.

> It is square, about 8 feet across and 2 or 3 inches high, covered with a white fabric on which were embroidered pearls, and gold and silver very richly woven in the centre. A large high cross-bar covered with precious stones served as the back of the seat having two cushions at the sides, also covered with precious stones...on the right of the Shah ['Abbas II], having at his waist a little golden box full of handkerchiefs and scents for the use of the Shah if requested. Along the sides of the room are the royal officials in rank.[209]

Pietro Della Valle, the Roman traveller who also visited Shah 'Abbas's court in the summer of 1618, gives one of the few accounts of the Safavid court in Ashraf.[210] He describes their circulation inside the garden:

> after the little courtyard [located beyond the first door] we passed a second door, with its covered atrium, through a small one with a few more guards; and immediately inside stretched the garden, square, not very big, in the process of being planted, and situated behind the palace, where the level ground ends at the foot of the hills clothed with woods. On these hills, the king has also planned, and already started to build, some pavilions and loggias, which will be part of the garden.[211]

Then he describes the inside of this royal pavilion, which is called *divan-khaneh:*

> in the middle of the level square below is the *divan-khaneh,* namely a loggia three times as long as it is broad, all open at the front, but behind and along the sides encircled by a wall, filled with windows, down to the ground, as is the custom here. This loggia is raised two steps from the ground; and its open front, one of the long sides, faces the north and has the entrance door, from which leading directly to the *divan-khaneh* is a wide shady path, all paved with stone in their usual way.

There is a stream of water which runs in the middle of this pathway and springs from a little fish-pond in front of the *divan-khaneh.* According to Chardin,

> Behind, the same pathway continues as far as the hills; and at the end of the garden, and in the middle of the *divan-khaneh,* in the part behind the wall to the south, is a communicating door, aligning the avenue in front and the avenue behind. In the *divan-khaneh,* which, as is usual, is also covered with very beautiful carpets, are to be found many of the leading men of the court seated on the floor.[212]

Gmelin (1770 to 1774 CE), who travelled to northern Persia and visited Safavid palaces in Ashraf more than a century after Della Valle and Herbert, writes: "Shah 'Abbas the Great, who left behind so many tasteful monuments, also had Ashraf built and embellished it with a beautiful palace or rather with many pleasure houses built in an almost Italian style."[213] Perhaps he calls them Italian style because the houses and gardens incorporate a "symmetric plan". He continues, "It is situated about half a mile from the sea and abuts west to mountains, which consist of forests." According to what he has heard from other people, he writes that the Shah's plan

> was not to build a large town or a fortified place. According to the Shah's intentions, only nature should reign. Innocent rustic delights should be presented. Therefore Ashraf consisted of nothing but unaffected farms that were scattered disorderly in the forested plains that run from the mountains until close to the coast.[214]

He adds:

> Here the peasant worked; here nature triumphed. The pleasure houses with their gardens are about half a [German] mile in circumference and have been built in the best garden locations."

He mentions that the garden complex in Ashraf was violently destroyed and became an abode for wild animals as a result.[215]

Binning, who visited the Safavid garden in Farah Abad in the nineteenth century, similarly writes:

> Here Shah Hoseyn had a splendid palace, of which scarce a terrace remains. The ground is occupied by long streets of desolate and hideous ruins; often serving as lurking-places for thieves, who sally forth by night to rob unwary travellers. South of these melancholy ruins, rises a high precipitous mountain, on the summit of which is perched a ruin.[216]

Gmelin's description of garden houses in Ashraf is very informative:

> The royal houses, of which each one has its own name, are 2 and 3 storeys high and built with square stones and quarry stones. The walls of the houses as well as of the floors consist mostly of marble and alabaster. Each storey has a large hall on both sides and a few smaller rooms. In the middle of each hall there is a fountain. The marble walls are partly whole and uniform, partly cut out to form recesses. They are mostly decorated with paintings, both with a coarse brush and pictures in Chinese taste. It is peculiar that the Persians betray their inclination to licentious living in all

parts. One can imagine nothing more scurrilous and despicable than the different licentious variations that appear in the pictures.

Gmelin, who is apparently shocked at seeing so many beautiful and elaborate paintings in these houses, asks whether these are exhibited for public viewing.[217]

These travel accounts prove that the garden complex at Ashraf, despite its remoteness from the Safavid capital, Isfahan, served as the major setting for administrative meetings. In spite of the lack of archaeological evidence, they serve to demonstrate the nature-oriented approach that was taken by Safavid designers in the selection of these specific sites and in the design of palaces. Several references to the view of the Caspian Sea and the surrounding mountains are witness to this claim. The spaces in these gardens were arranged linearly to emphasize the hierarchy within the court and decrease the accessibility of the main hall (*divan-khaneh*), in which the king's throne was located.

KIOSKS IN GARDENS

In addition to enclosed built spaces, there are usually semi-open spaces in gardens, which are used for various purposes. Although these spaces are widely reflected in visual media such as paintings, they rarely appear in accounts by travellers and historians. This absence seems to be because most travellers are more interested in explaining their experience in enclosed spaces like buildings and tents, which are usually more complex structures and therefore more appealing in terms of ornamentation. Even the *Irshad al-Zira'ah*, which is a manual on gardens in the Timurid era, does not refer to semi-open areas or kiosks in gardens. Yet this silence should not be taken as evidence for the absence of kiosks in gardens. A few descriptions in chronicles and in travellers' accounts point to the presence of three types of kiosks in gardens: the kiosk as a built or installed structure, as a platform with temporary roof, or as a movable structure.

The kiosk as a built structure is described by Beyhaqi, Babur, and the Venetian merchant. Beyhaqi, in his description of the Bagh-e Jannat in Ghaznin, writes that in one of the corners of the rectangular pool in front of this building (located in the middle of the garden), a roofed seating area (kiosk) is located. According to Beyhaqi, this seating area has four columns and provides a good view of the water from three sides. This kiosk is apparently very similar to that mentioned in some historical accounts. According to Falsafi, in a royal ceremony Shah 'Abbas ordered that carpets should be spread around the pool for the courtiers and guests,[218] while he and his special guest, the Spanish ambassador, were also taking part in the festivities.[219] Babur's notes shed light on the use of the kiosk (as a built structure) from the perspective of a user and not just an observer or historian. In the *Baburnameh,* there are several notions of the kiosk as a free-standing structure in the garden, belonging to high-ranking people and allocated for royal purposes.[220] Babur mentions that after the communal prayers, he went to the kiosk in order to write some official letters. Suddenly, a storm blew up and spread his papers about. The storm was so fierce that it knocked down the screen that surrounded the kiosk and tore the roof into pieces.[221] The structure of the roof fell down on Babur's head but did not injure him.[222] From Babur's description, we can assume that the kiosk is a very light and transparent structure, which has flexible elements (probably grass) on the roof.[223] In another narrative, Babur talks about the octagonal kiosk in the garden: "On Saturday the 6th, I had a feast in the garden. I sat in the northern part of it, in an octagonal pavilion that was recently erected, and covered with grass for coolness."[224] He writes that after the exchange of gifts and the serving of dinner, the Hindustani jugglers were brought in and performed their tricks.[225]

As already mentioned, the Venetian merchant, in his description of the palace garden at Nasriyyeh, talks about two semi-open structures that are located in the same garden. One is the four-yards-square summer-house, which is close to the harem, and is beautifully decorated with patterns in enamel, gold and ultramarine blue. This semi-open summer-house is used by the queen and her maidens for doing traditional needlework while enjoying the view of the garden.[226] It is probably far from the palace and close to the harem in order to provide privacy for the women. The other semi-open structure in this complex is a gallery in the south-west corner of the garden, which is connected to the palace by a paved avenue. It has seats made of marble and a railing ornamented with colourful plasterwork.[227] The roof is supported by marble columns and decorated with gold and plaster. It faces a marble fountain which is as long as the gallery. This fountain, which always has four or five couples of swans, is surrounded by rose trees and jessamine. The location of these semi-open spaces identifies and confirms their gender specificity.

Despite his abundant references to Timurid buildings and tents, Clavijo does not talk about kiosks in Timur's gardens. However, in his description of the Talicia garden at Samarqand, he points to a platform which is located in the middle of the garden. He writes:

> On Sunday, the 31st of August, at dawn, the ambassadors were taken to this garden, which was surrounded by a mud wall, and might be about a league round. It contained a great number of fruit trees of all kinds, except citrons and limes; it was traversed by many channels of water, and a large stream flowed through the centre. These channels flowed amongst the trees, which were large and tall, and gave a pleasant shade. In the centre of the avenues formed by the trees, there were raised platforms, which traversed the whole garden.[228]

The construction of kiosks as a combination of platforms and awnings (parasols) apparently has been a dominant tradition in gardens in hot climates such as that of Yazd. Jafari, in the *Tarikh-e Yazd*, reveals the existence of these structures (which he calls *tonob* and *sabat*). He describes the Bagh-e Sabat as a garden with several old and new buildings (*'emarat*), a house, and a kiosk, which is called Tonob-e Bu-Sa'idi.[229] He mentions that Soltan Jahangir ibn Shah Yahya has built an excellent kiosk (*tonob*) close to the entrance, under which water runs. There is also another awning (*sayeban*) close to the other door and to the new bathhouse. He refers to an excellent lake at the centre of the garden with a pavilion (*qasr*) in the middle. Some of these kiosks are unroofed platforms and are referred to as *soffeh*. For instance, in the Bagh-e Mehtar 'Alishah-e Farrash, there is a *soffeh* in the middle of the garden and a *pishgah* and big courtyard in front of it. Jafari also talks about a kiosk (*tonob*) which is close to the main entrance.[230] His text proves that some of these kiosks or roofed platforms (*soffeh* or *tonob*) were erected much later than the construction of the garden and buildings inside it. This shows that the kiosk (in any form) may be perceived as an afterthought in the design.

This hypothesis is confirmed in another part of the *Baburnameh* when Babur writes about the octagonal platforms in the middle of pool:

> On Monday, the seventh of the first Rabi, I mounted and rode to Sikri. The octagonal platform, which I had ordered to be built in the midst of the tank, being finished, we went over [in] a boat, raised an awning, and had a party, when we indulged in a *majun*.[231]

Nevertheless, the kiosk as a fixed structure was not always for private use, and in some cases it was employed as part of the urban quarter. For instance, Khajeh Rashid-uddin, in the *Jami' al-Tavarikh*, talks about the public use of the kiosk in the garden complex in Ghazaniyyeh. Here, the kiosk in the mausoleum garden was used every Friday evening to supply food and soup for the visitors.[232]

It is vital to note that the kiosk is not always a fixed structure. It might also be a decorative throne (pavilion) that could be carried by servants and placed in any part of the garden or inside the buildings. Membre writes how several camels were loaded with pavilions in the *ordu* of Shah Tahmasp in Tabriz.[233] He also mentions that, on 1 February, when the king holds a festival for three days (probably to celebrate the end of Ramadan):

> They place pavilions in rows and the entrances of the pavilions are towards the east. For it there are most beautiful pavilions with columns gilded and with many figures. The pavilions are white outside but inside they are designed with much better labour, and they lay fine carpets, and the king mounts, and in the *meidan* (piazza) he gallops his horse and plays at the wooden ball with the wooden bat, galloping on his horse.[234]

The king was seated upon a *takya-namad*, which was of great price, with his sword beside him.[235] Membre describes this fancy structure as an *otaq* (room),

> which is made of sticks of gilded wood in form of a dome and covered over with scarlet. Upon the cloth is foliage, cut out and sewn with silk. Within, on the ground there was a red felt, lined with a kind of woollen canvas, and over the said felt there were very fine carpets of silk, on which appeared figures of many animals and foliage.[236]

Unfortunately, Membre's account is one of the few describing the kiosk as a movable structure. However, these examples, despite their diversity in terms of form and architectural quality, verify the use of the kiosk as a setting for high-ranking people such as the king and his guests.

TENTS IN GARDENS

Political instability, external threats and internal rebellions, especially after the advent of Islam, did not allow most administrations in Persia to settle in one place. These mobile courts used gardens as places for military encampments, royal ceremonies or administrative affairs. The need for constant travel, and the nomadic mentality dominant among the Turks of Central Asia and the Mongols, required the use of tents as portable palaces. Even though most kings had palaces, they still preferred to live in their tents.[237] Khajeh Rashid-uddin is one of the earliest historians to provide precise information about the location of royal tents in gardens. According to the *Tarikh-e Ghazani*, which chronicles the history of the Ilkhanids (1265–1295 CE), when Arghun Khan became sick in the Garden of Aran, he stayed in his yurt (tent) for several months. Attempts by his doctors and servants to heal him failed and he died. His family and courtiers mourned in their tents for three days and then sent his coffin to another city.[238] Rashid-uddin writes that, in order to prepare for the festivals in a square area which was enclosed by a wall, tanks and cisterns were installed to feed rivers and streams. Avenues were also planted round the edge with willows to provide a passage for the populace who had to be confined to the periphery of the walled enclosure. The central area of the garden was reserved for the golden pavilion (*khargah-e zarrin*), the golden throne and surrounding tower, baths and lofty buildings.[239] Ghazan Khan, who had large buildings and palaces on the grassland (*marghzar*) on the outskirts of Ujan, used his golden tent (*khargah-e zarrin*) in the garden as his main residence.[240] Similarly, Rashid-uddin talks about pitching tents in the grassland in Sham, which was used as the source for water and grass, and at the Bagh-e 'Adeliyyeh.[241] Haneda believes that this camp was used as a military base for Ghazan Khan.[242] Pinder-Wilson explains that this type of garden was developed by the Mongols for a purpose peculiar to their own traditions and usages: "The assumption of royal power required a garden setting for the nomadic encampment; the existing Persian *bagh* was adapted to the requirements of the Ilkhans."[243]

The *Tarikh-e Beyhaqi*, which often refers to the encampments in Mahmud's and Mas'ud's gardens in Khorasan (two centuries before the Ilkhanid period), contradicts the common belief regarding the Mongol origins of the concept of *ordu* in gardens. Beyhaqi provides valuable information about encampments of the Ghaznavids in the gardens of Khorasan. According to him, when Mahmud and his son moved to new gardens they had not only to move the royal kitchen, dress rooms (*jameh-khaneh*), treasury (*khazaneh*), administrative offices (*davit-khaneh*) and so on, but also to provide special spaces for royal women (harem), slaves (*gholams*) and nobles. Most Ghaznavid gardens mentioned by Beyhaqi included buildings, but since they were not enough to accommodate all of the people, they still needed to pitch tents.[244] For instance, in the description of the encampment in the Bagh-e Piruzi, Beyhaqi writes: "Amir went to the garden and to the pitched royal tent (*sarapardeh*) and stayed there for two days. When everyone left, they removed [all] the tents."[245] We can imagine the difficulty of carrying all of these tents and court furniture between gardens. This phenomenon was observed by Anthony Jenkinson (1529–1610/11), the British traveller who recorded his observations of a mobile *ordu* in Central Asia and estimated about a thousand camels drawing carts with houses upon them like tents, looking from far off like a town.[246]

Tents remained the main residences even centuries after the Mongols and the Timurids. The Safavids, who were more settled and civilized than their predecessors, still maintained the habit of camping in gardens. The Venetian traveller, Michele Membre, provides great detail about Shah Tahmasp's royal encampment in Tabriz. In contrast to some Europeans, he had sharp eyes and avoided generalization. He provides valuable information on the royal camp of the court of Shah Tahmasp, where the king was lodging with his *ordu* in the meadows, with his army in 5000 tents.[247] Shah 'Abbas's historian, Eskandar Monshi, also refers to the royal encampments in Safavid gardens. For instance, he talks about a royal ceremony in the garden of Sa'adat Abad in which more than 760 people stayed in the tents.[248] Even though estimates of the number of tents in travellers' notes are usually exaggerated, these documents prove the dual life of their inhabitants as well as the symbiosis between the temporary settlements (tents) and permanent residences (buildings). Clavijo observes this in the Delgosha garden, where ambassadors were received in silken tents and rich palaces:

> This house and garden, where the lord received the ambassadors, in it there were many silken tents, and the lord remained there until the following Friday, when he went to another garden, where there was a very rich palace, which he had lately ordered to be built, called Bayginar.

Although there were palaces (called *sarai* or *khaneh*), Timur preferred to stay in his fancy tent.

The Placement of Tents

Accepting the existence of *ordu* and the use of tents as regular settlements raises the question of the practicality of erecting hundreds of tents in huge plains and gardens. Moreover, the fact that the *ordu* was mostly occupied by soldiers leads to other questions regarding social organization, culture and discipline within the *ordu*. Pitching and organizing the tents was apparently a quick process. Clavijo mentions that the assembly of tents for about twenty thousand men did not usually take more than three or four days.[249] The placement of tents in large fields and gardens apparently followed a pre-designed plan based on the rank of courtiers and soldiers. The first pitched tent belonged to Timur and it is likely that higher-rank courtiers and army leaders were then closest to Timur's tent. Clavijo confirms this: "When the tents of the lord were pitched, each man knew where his own tent should be pitched, and every one, high and low, knew his place, so that the work was done without confusion or noise." Clavijo also describes the organization of the tents of Timur's wives in the garden: "The first wall and tents were for the use of the chief wife of the lord...and the other was for his second wife." Apparently, they joined walls (called *zalaparda*)[250] to surround an area filled with many tents and awnings which were distinguished by their colours.[251] This area had a lofty and large tent in the centre, which was inhabited by the royal family.

Clavijo's notes show the separation of male and female areas in the *ordu*. The issue of gender segregation is also highlighted by Ibn Battuta, who refers to the separation of women's *ordu* from the men's tents in Baghdad. He confirms Clavijo's observations regarding the significance of hierarchy in his description of Abu Sa'id's camp (*ordu*), saying that the formation of the camp is based on military rank. Abu Sa'id's camp includes mosques and bazaars and contains smaller quarters (*mahalleh*) for the king, his wives, viziers and courtiers. Ibn Battuta's observations of the encampment of Soltan Abu Sa'id outside the city of Baghdad also show that the *ordu* is divided into several quarters allocated to women and courtiers:

> When they encamp, the Soltan and his mamluks occupy a camp by themselves, and each of his khatuns occupies a separate camp of her own, each of them also having her own imam, mu'azzens, Qur'an readers and bazaar. The viziers, secretaries and officials [of the finance department] encamp separately, and each amir also has his own camp. They all present themselves for duty after each afternoon prayer, [returning to their camps] with torches carried before them.[252]

He explains that his lodging was arranged in a special location among rushing streams and lofty trees.[253] In contrast, Timur's grandson, Babur, describes his experience in encampments from the point of view of a resident, not an observer. For instance, Babur refers to his tent which is pitched in the middle of the garden.[254]

Likewise, Monshi writes that Shah 'Abbas's tent, which was called the "administrative tent" (*kheyme-ye dowlat-khaneh*) in the royal encampment (*ordu-ye homayun*) in the garden of Sa'adat Abad was differentiated from the other tents by its size.[255] Depending on the availability of open space inside gardens, the tents could be located either inside or outside the boundary. In some cases, the placement of the tent was not necessarily the sign of position and hierarchy. For example, Timur's tent was pitched outside the garden of Delgosha, while some of his soldiers dwelled inside the garden. Using vast plains to organize these temporary micro-scale cities required a clear and advanced layout which could prevent chaos, rebellion and conspiracy.

The organization of the *ordu* should have the capability to define public, semi-public and private realms in very clear fashion. The rows of tents created streets and avenues in which were distributed the various businesses that provided services and goods to the residents, especially the troops. Clavijo's descriptions draw a clear picture of temporary streets where different guilds, such as bakers, cooks and butchers, were located. There were even areas where public services were offered, such as huts that were used for hot baths and contained boilers for heating the water.[256] Ibn Battuta's notes indicate that keeping discipline was a major concern in the royal camp. He writes:

> It is their custom to set out with the rising of the dawn and to encamp in the later afternoon. Their ceremonial [on setting out] is as follows: each amir comes up with his troops, his drums and his standards, and halts in a position that has been assigned to him, not a step further, either on the right wing or the left wing. When they have taken up their positions and their ranks are set in perfect order.[257]

Ibn Battuta, similarly, explains the administrative organization within Abu Sa'id's *ordu*, where the secretaries and officials of the finance department had to present themselves for duty each afternoon.

The Interior Design of Tents

Despite the widespread use of tents, there are fewer records of their structure and design than they deserve. Fortunately, Clavijo provides detailed and comprehensive descriptions of Timurid tents, which were somewhat comparable to their Mongol precedents. In his report of Timur's *ordu,* he writes about a huge pavilion (tent) in which several tents were located:

> Within the wall there were many tents and awnings pitched in various ways, amongst which was a high tent, not drawn out by cords. The walls were of poles, a little larger than a lance, which crossed each other like a net, and on the top of these poles there were others forming a high capital. These poles were secured by broad girths to each other, and to stakes fixed near the walls of the tent. The tent was so high that it was wonderful how it could be secured with these girths, and the top was covered with a crimson cloth, and the walls were lined with cotton, like a coverlid, so that the sun could not penetrate. It had no ornaments or figures whatever, except that there were some white stripes all round the outside. These stripes were covered with silver-gilt bezants, as broad as a man's hand, which were adorned with precious stones. Between these stripes there were others, which went all round the tent, folded in small folds like the skirts of a robe and embroidered with gold threads. When there was any wind, these folds moved backwards and forwards, and looked very beautiful. The tent had an entrance, with doors of very small canes, covered with red cloth.[258]

It is evident from his description that within this huge area, covered streets of tents were located. Within the wall there were many smaller tents as well as a large tent made of silk, with windows at intervals, which were separated from the passage by silken nets. In the centre of the space formed by this wall there was another high tent, with the same red cloth and silver-gilt bezants.[259]

In the event of big ceremonies and feasts, Timur ordered his relatives and women, his sons and grandsons, his councillors and all the people who were scattered round, to assemble at his royal neighbourhood in the garden,[260] which included streets of royal tents, closely pitched on the banks of the river. Following Timur's command, the courtiers and soldiers should be present in their tents with their wives in order to attend any festivals.[261] Clavijo describes the royal neighbourhood:

> In front of these gardens there was a vast plain through which a river flowed, and many smaller streams. On this plain the lord ordered many tents to be pitched for himself and his women, and that all his host, which was scattered in detachments over the land, should be assembled together, each man in his place, and that their tents should be pitched, and that they should come there, with their women, to be present at the festivals and marriages which he wished to celebrate.[262]

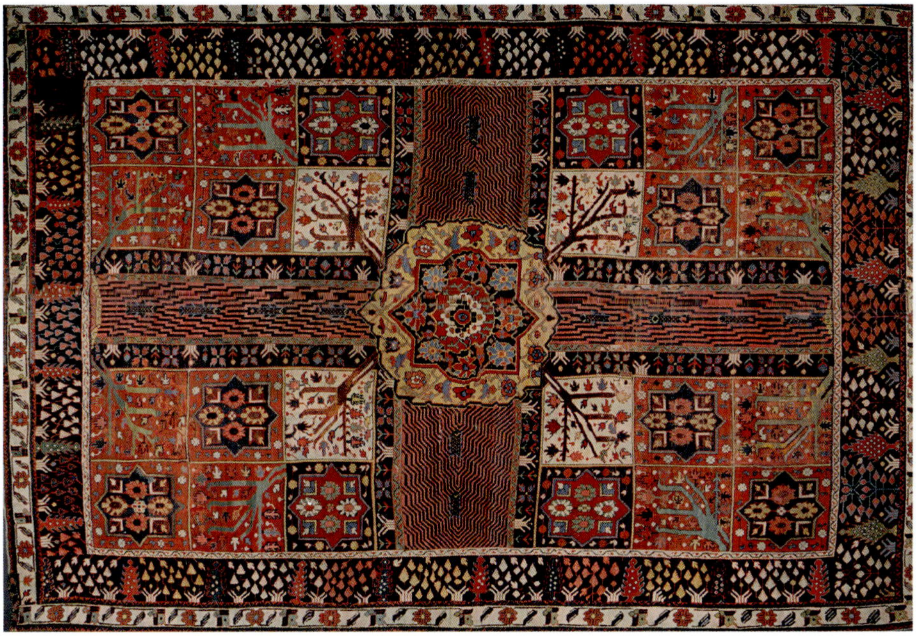

FIGURE 46
Hand-knotted woollen carpet.
Iran, late seventeenth century.

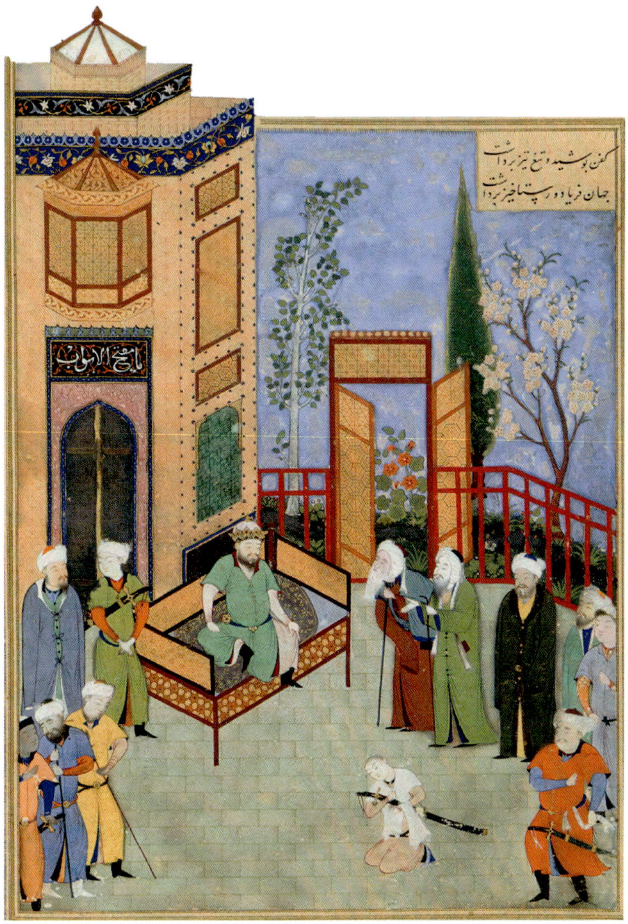

FIGURE 47
Elders pleading with
Hormozd. From the *Khamseh*
by Nezami, Herat, 1494–95.

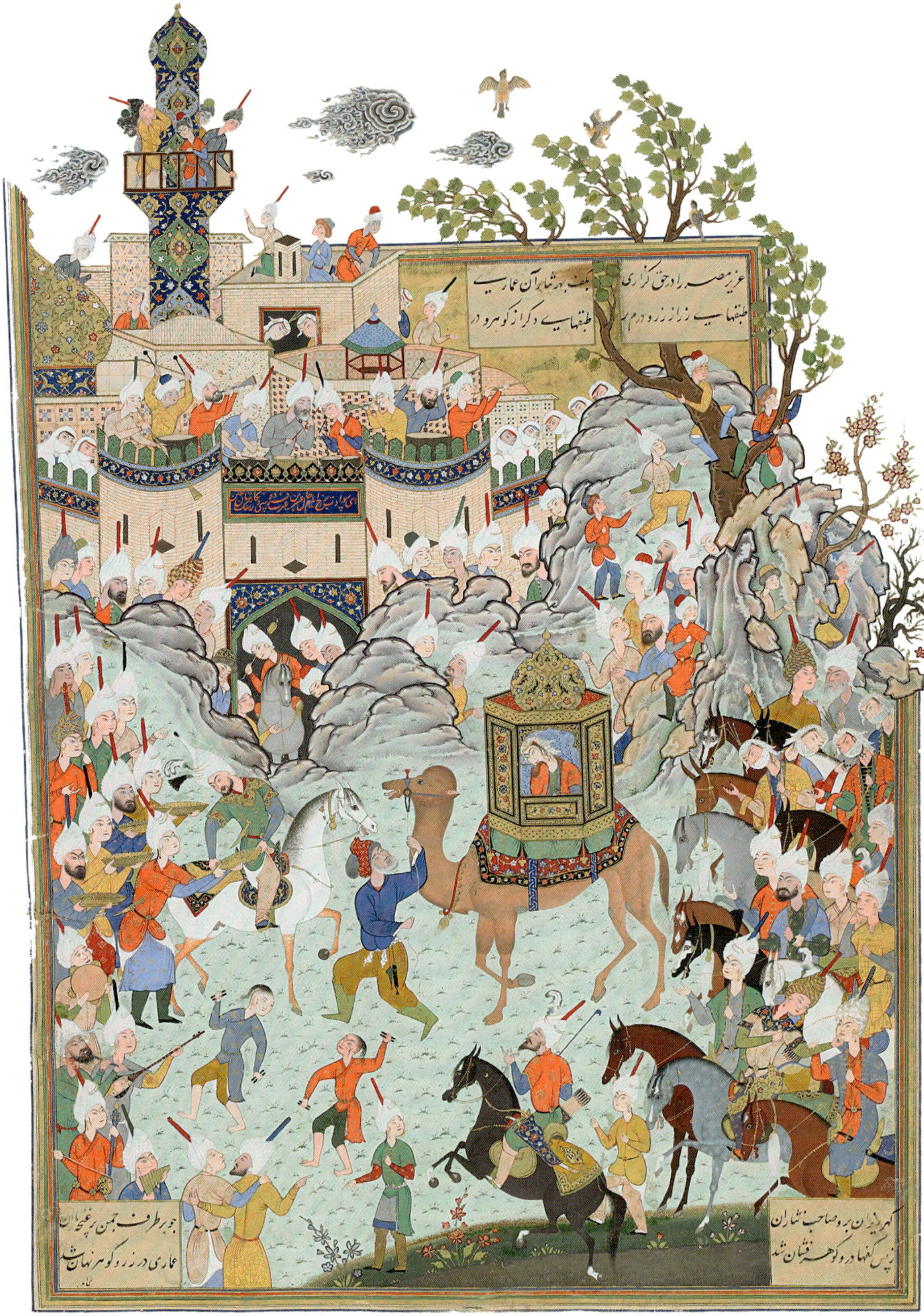

FIGURE 48

The ʿAziz and Zulaykha enter the capital of Egypt and the Egyptians come out to greet them. From the *Haft Awrang* by Jami, Mashhad, 1556–65.

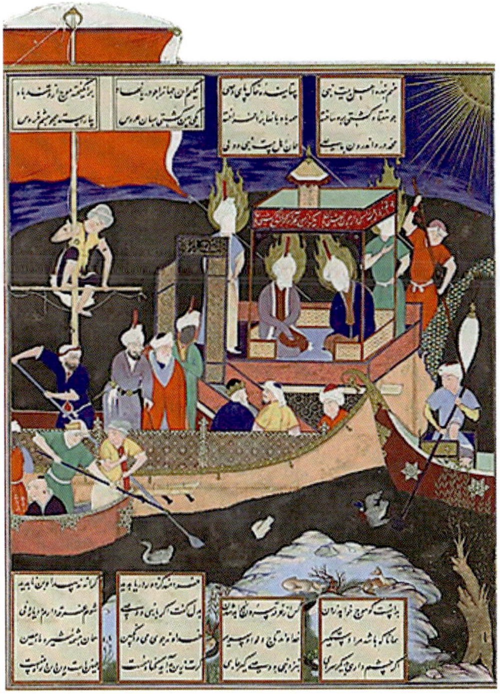

FIGURE 50
Ferdowsi's parable of the ship of Shi'ism. From the *Shahnameh* of Shah Tahmasp, attributed to Mirza 'Ali, Tabriz, 1530–39.

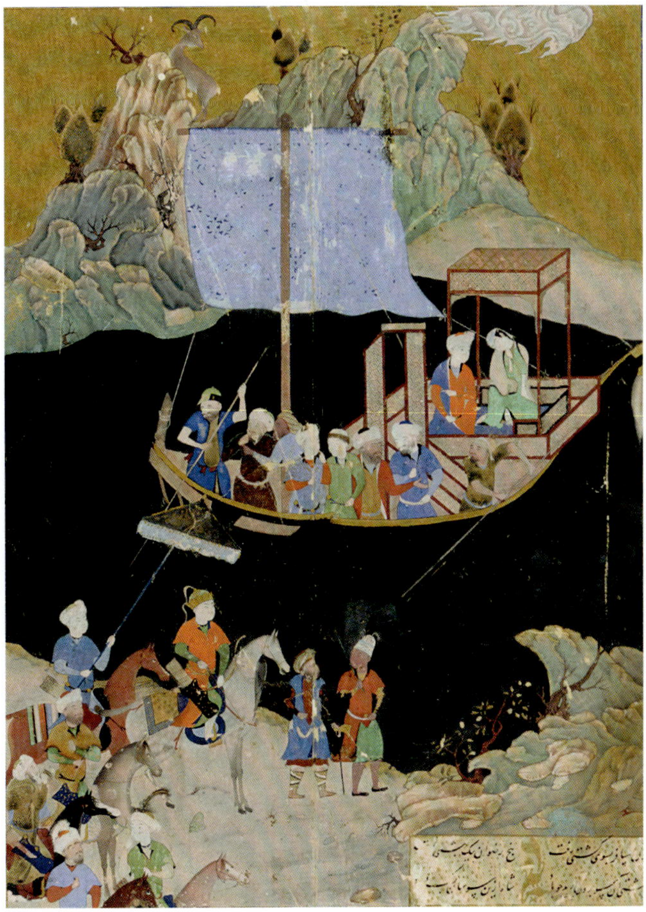

FIGURE 51
The abduction of the king's favourite maiden. From *Hasht Behesht* by Amir Khosrow Dehlavi, attributed to Mirza 'Ali.

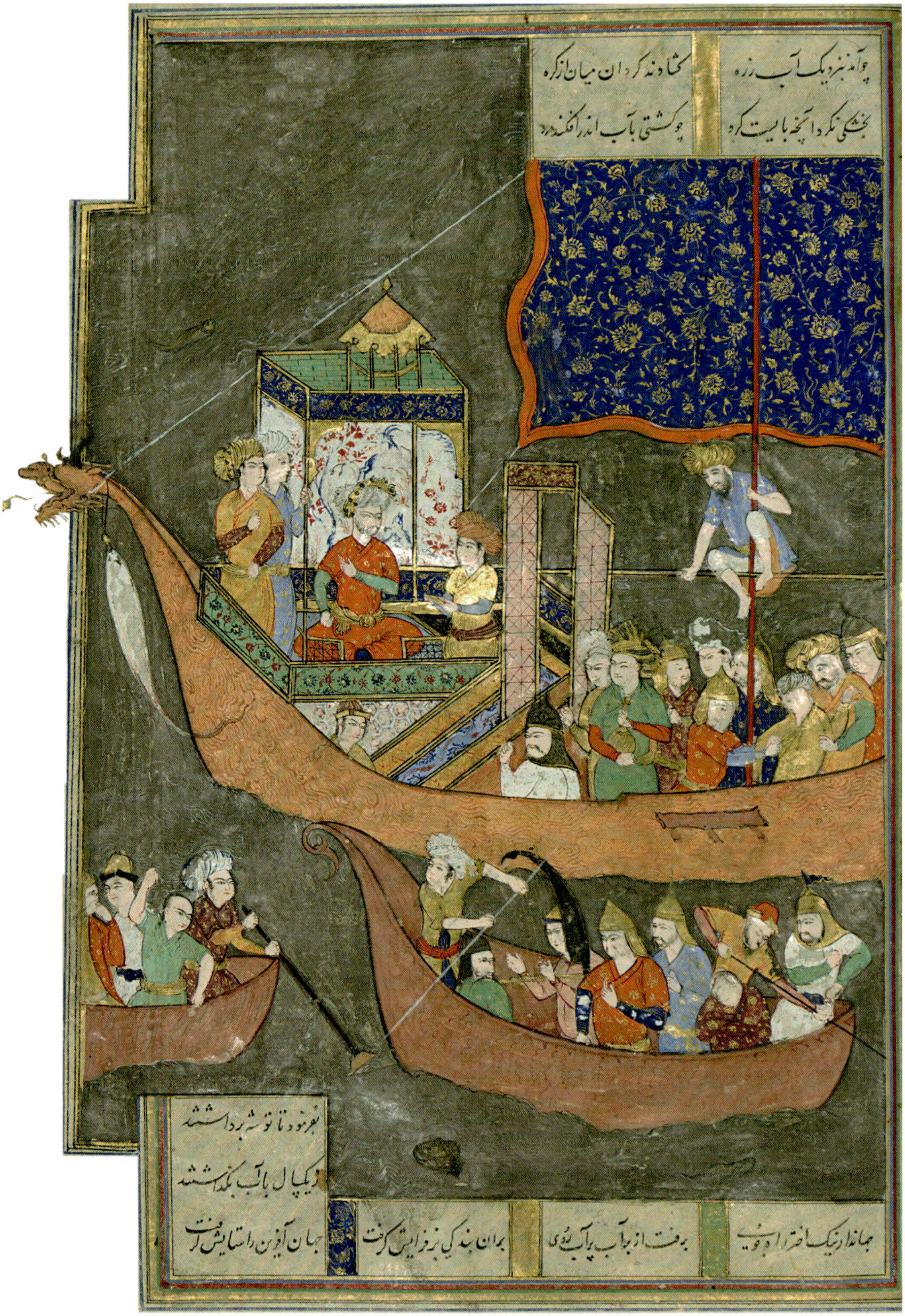

FIGURE 52

Key Khosrow crossing Lake Zarah in pursuit of Afrasyab. From the *Shahnameh,* Herat, 1618–19.

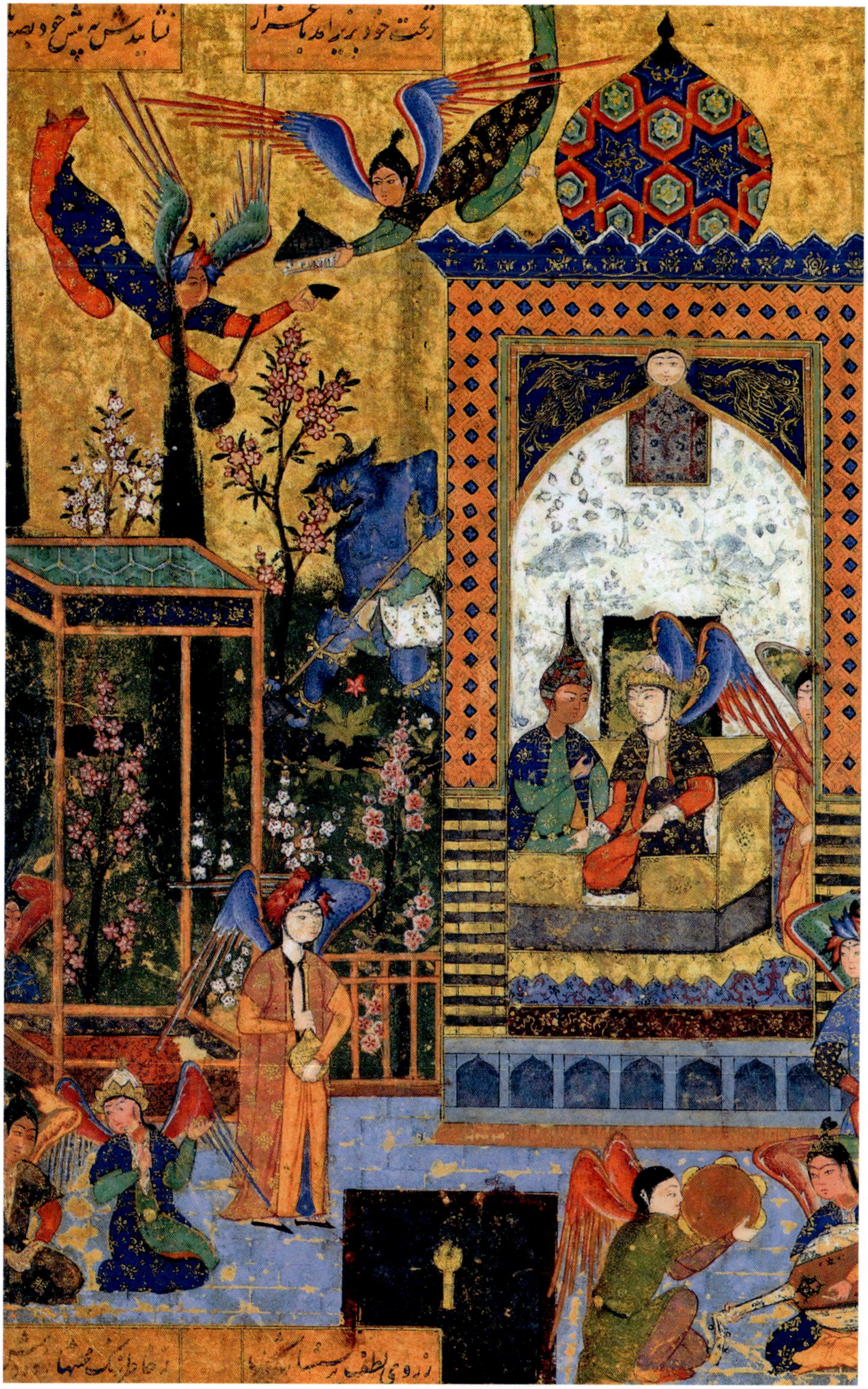

FIGURE 56

Jamshid and Khorshid on a throne. From *Masnavi-ye Jamshid va Khorshid,* sixteenth century.

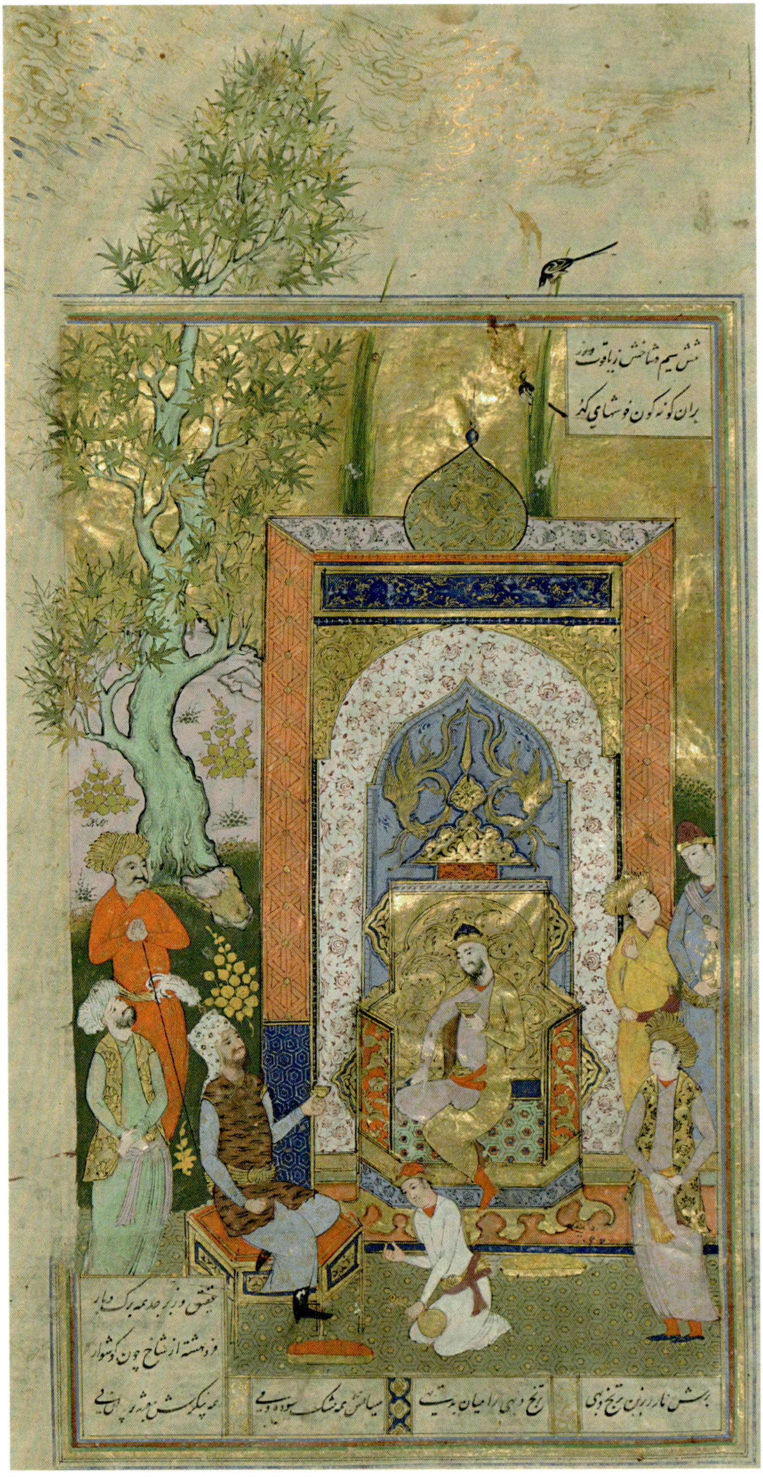

FIGURE 57

Key Khosrow feasts Rustam. From the *Shahnameh*, 1618–19.

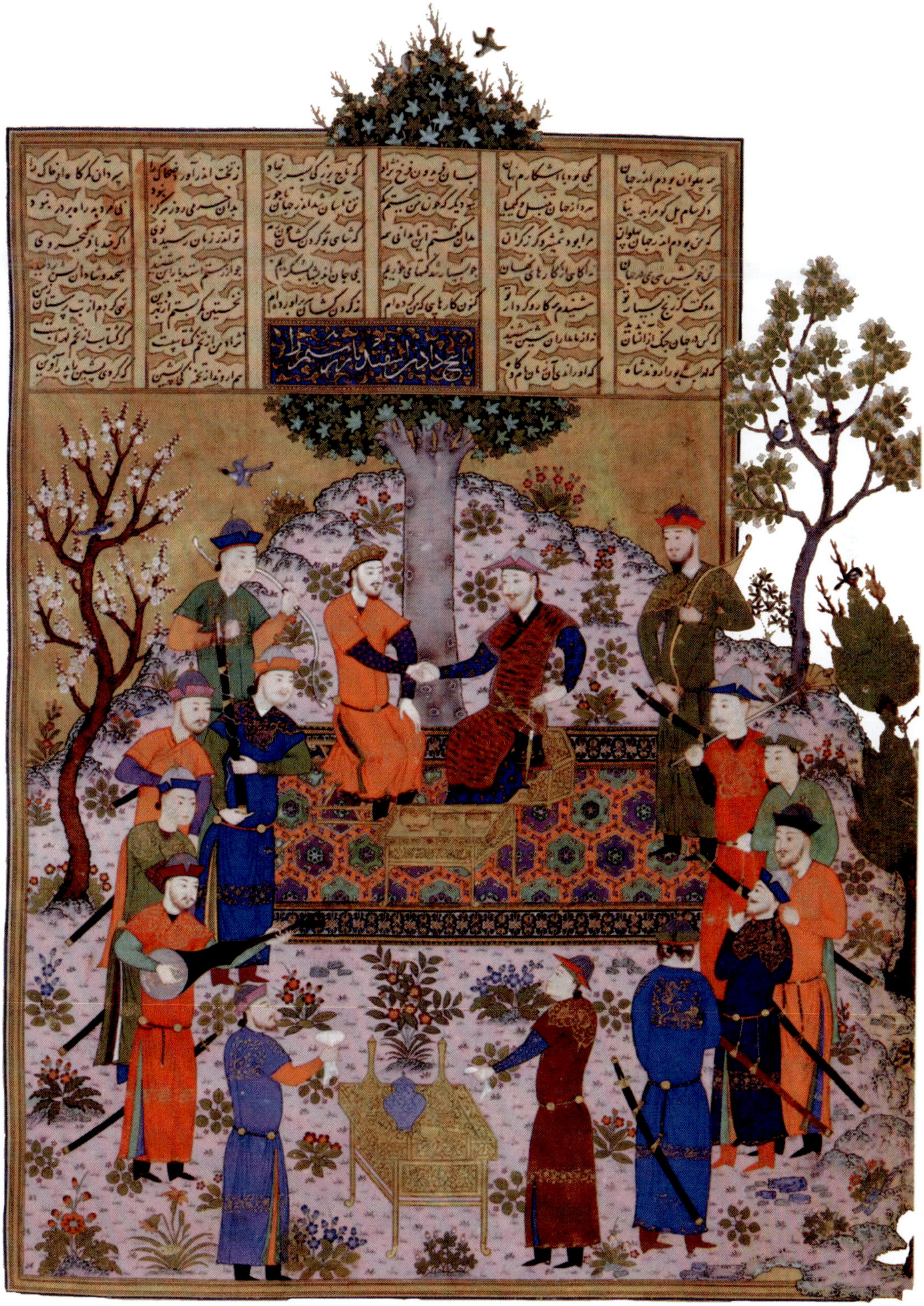

FIGURE 58

The conversation between Rustam and Isfandyar. From the *Shahnameh* of Baysonghor.

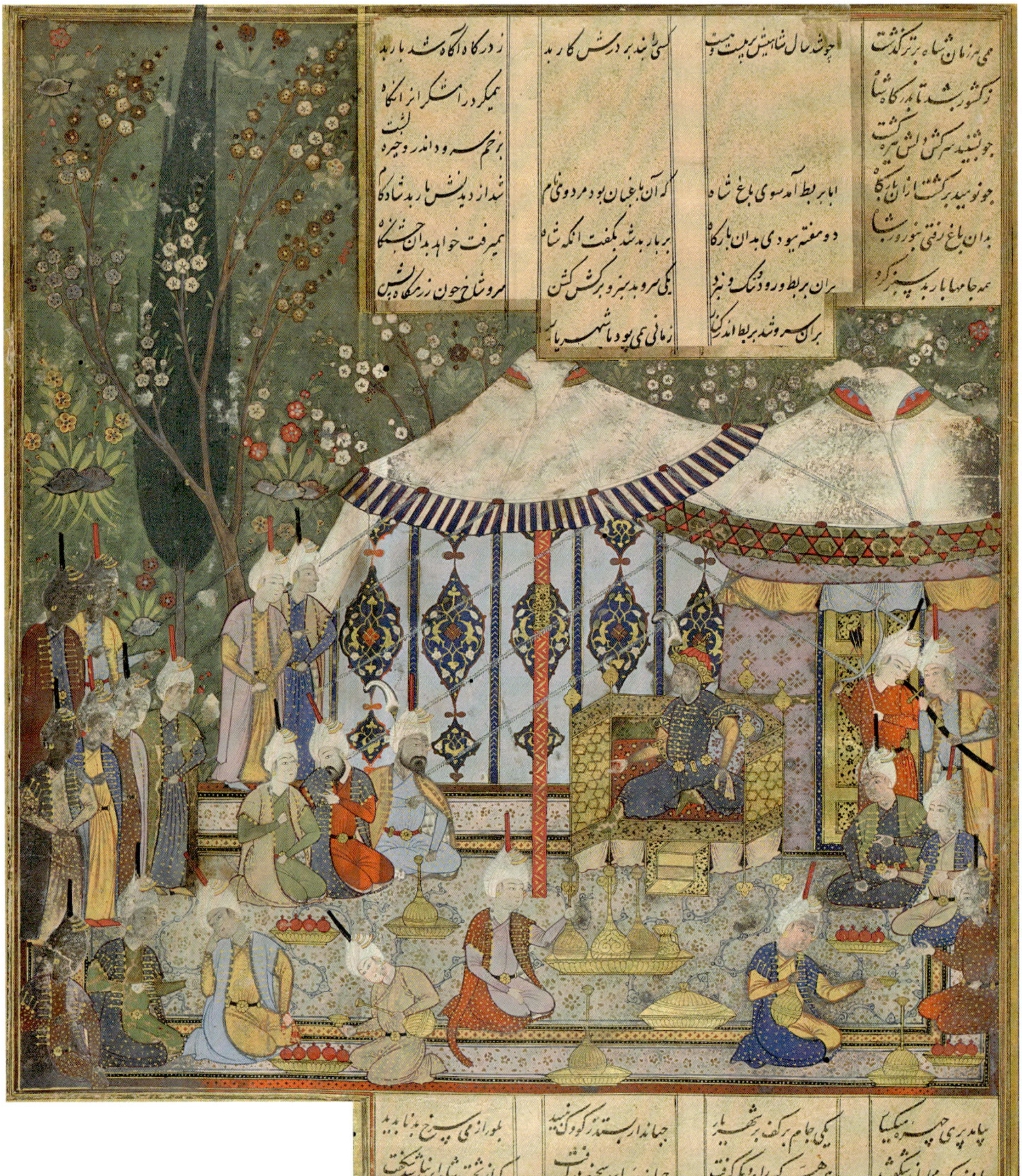

FIGURE 59

Khosrow celebrating Nowruz. From the *Shahnameh,* Shiraz, 1560.

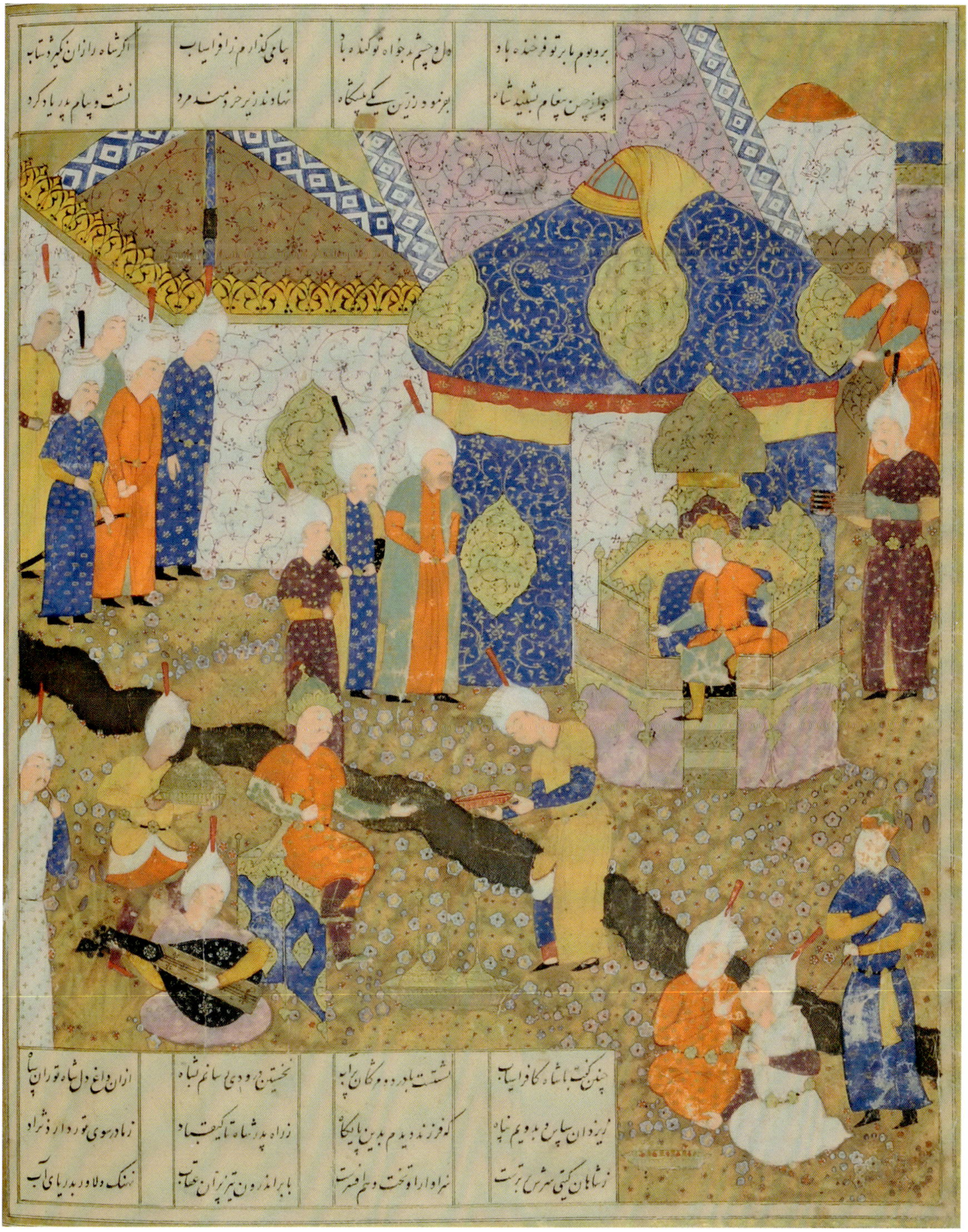

FIGURE 60

Shida in the camp of Key Khosrow. From the *Shahnameh*, Shiraz, 1535.

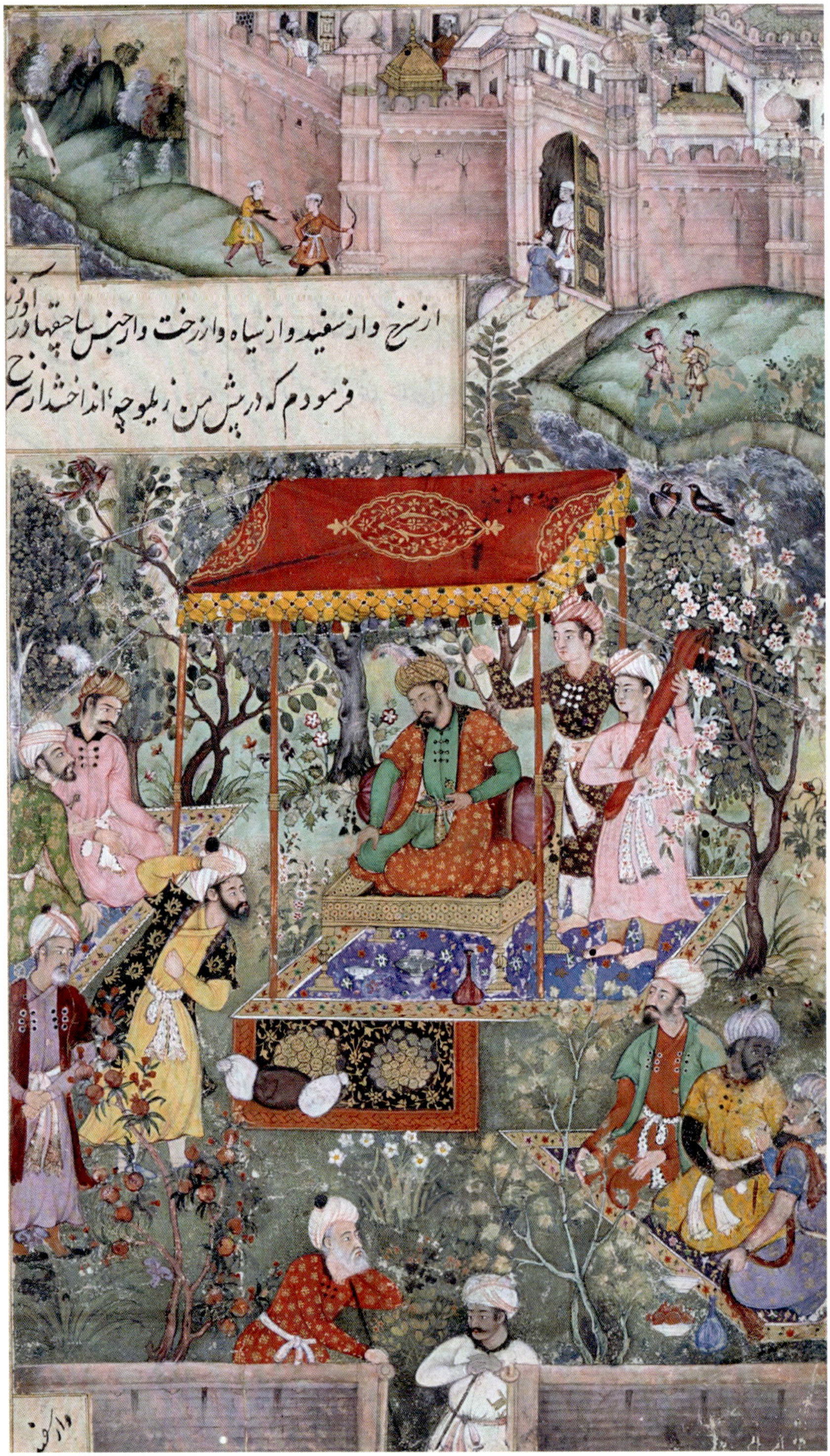

FIGURE 61

Babur receiving Persian, Uzbek and Rajput envoys in a garden at Agra. From the *Baburnameh,* 1589.

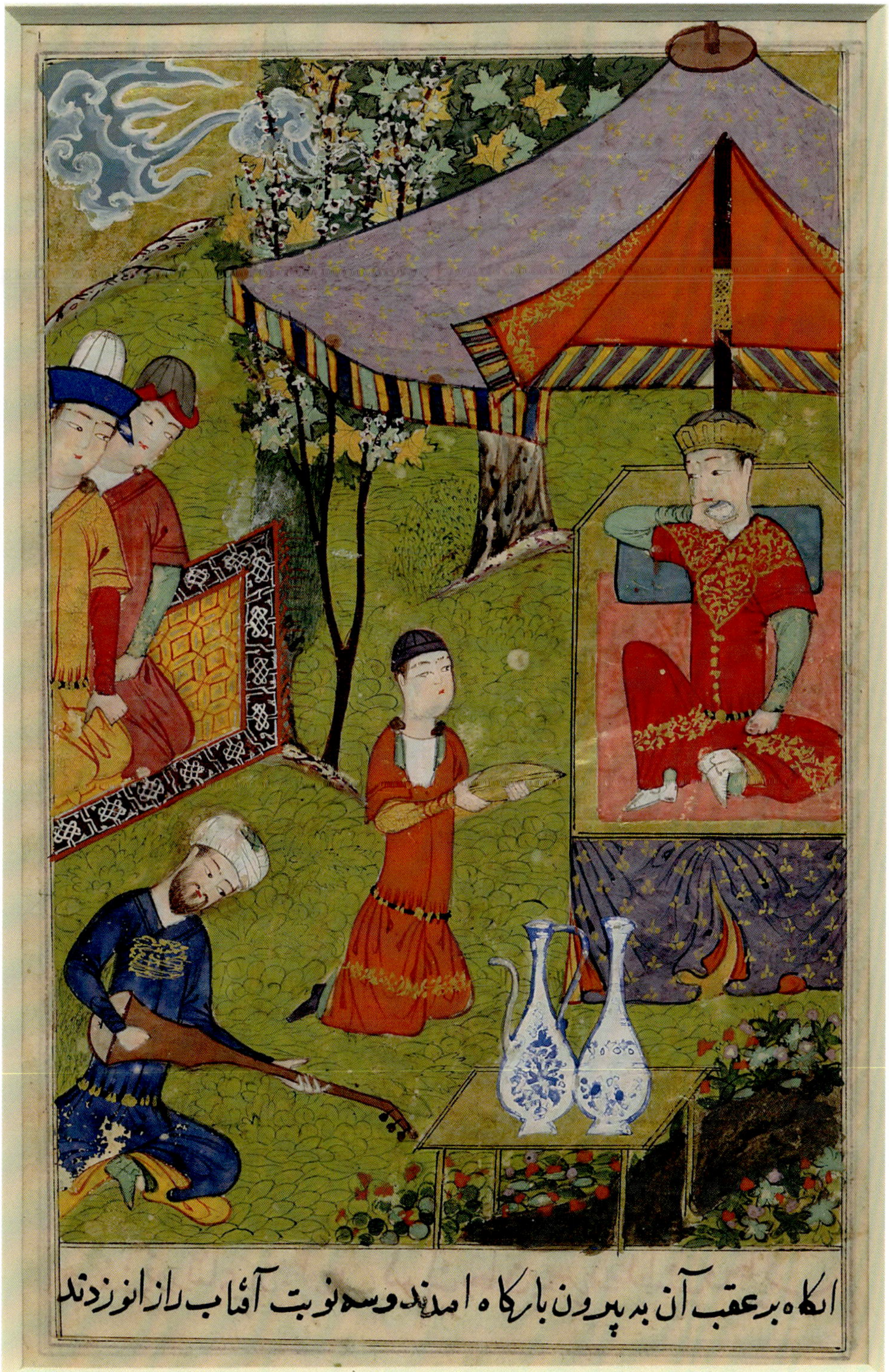

FIGURE 67

Kuyuk receiving gold, silver, jewels and other gifts from his nobles. From the *Tarikh-e Jahan-Goshay* by ʿAta Malek ibn Muhammad Joveyni, Shiraz, 1438.

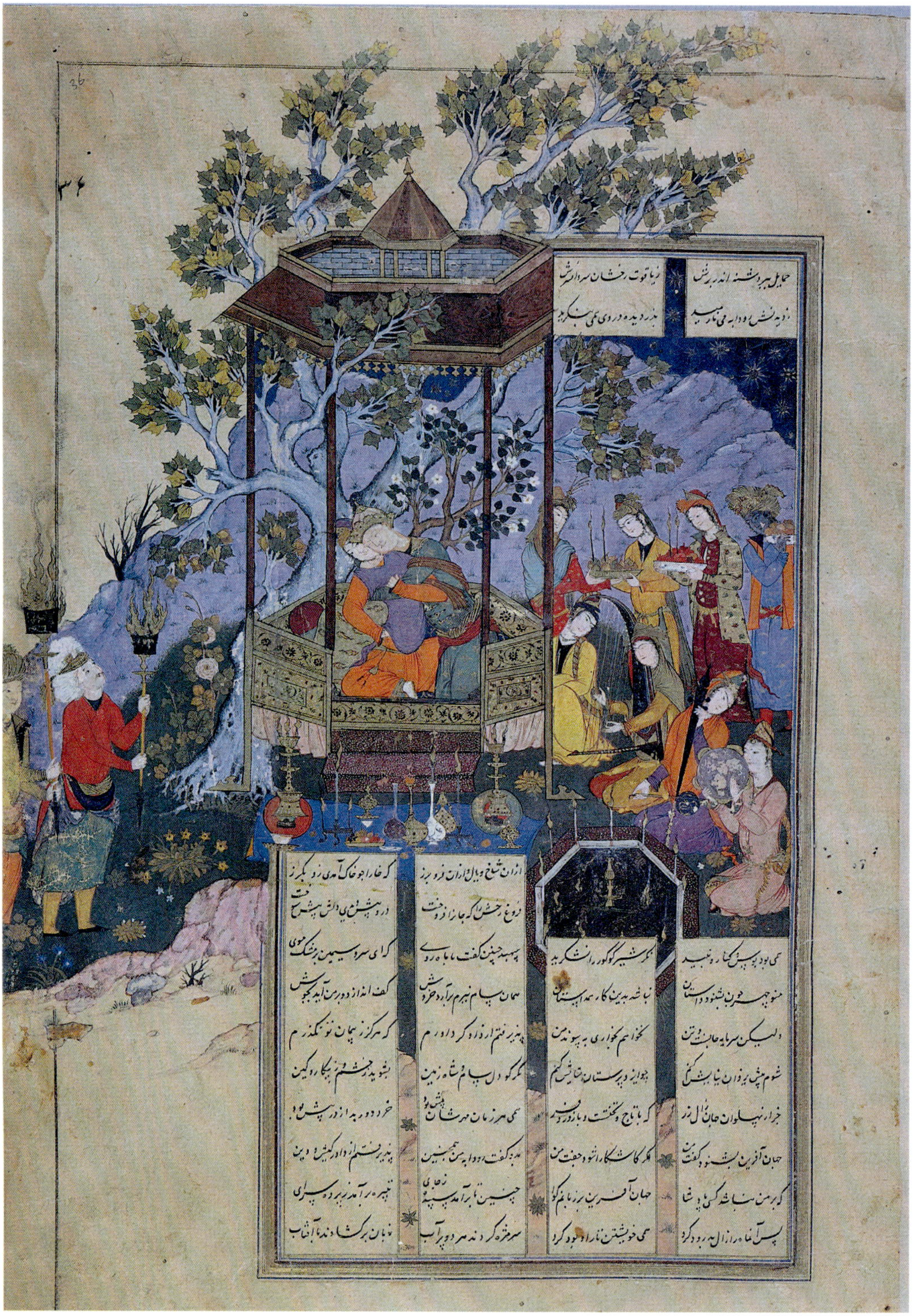

FIGURE 68

Zal and Rudabeh celebrating their wedding night. From the *Shahnameh*, Herat or Isfahan, 1602.

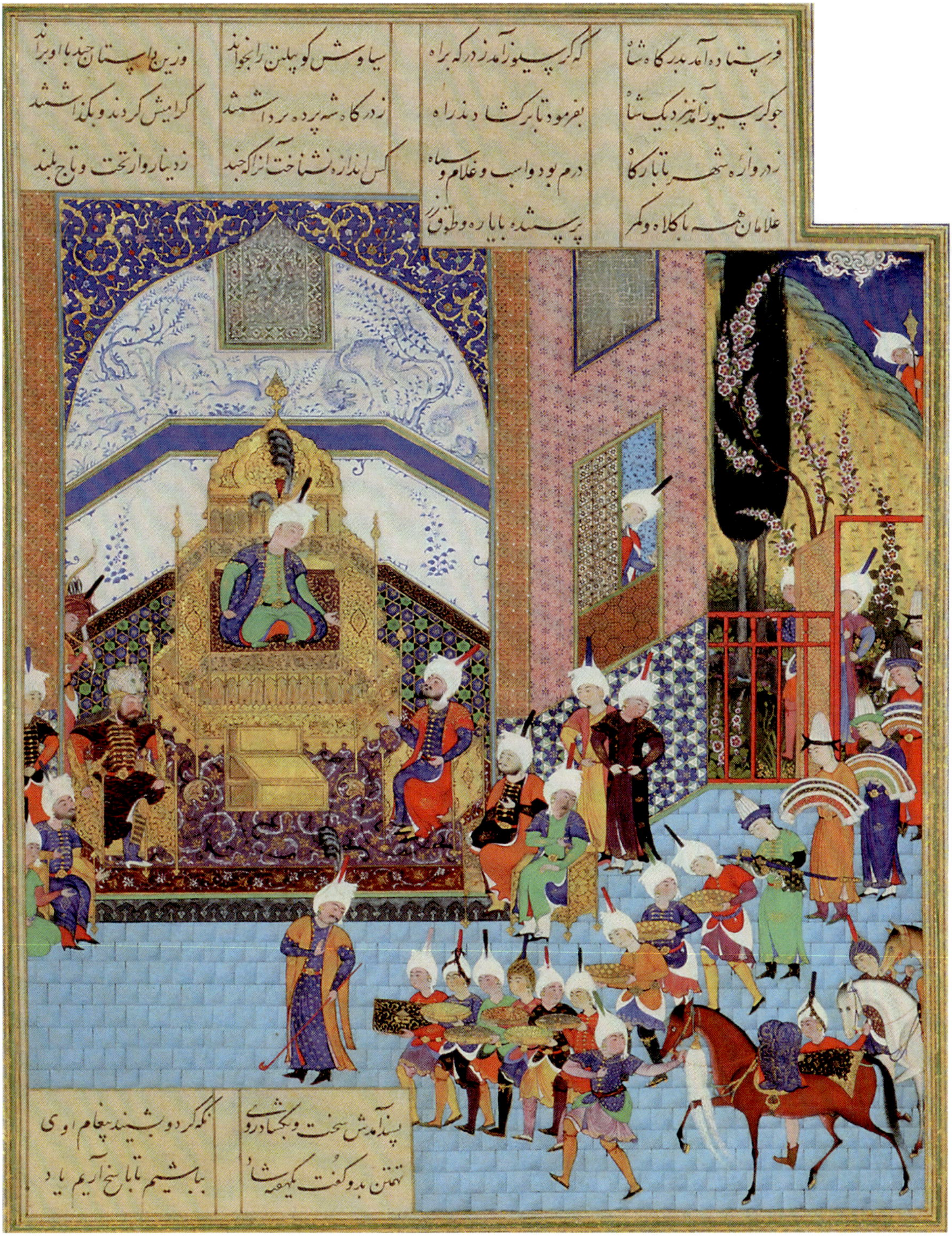

FIGURE 69

Siyavash receives a gift from a peace envoy. From the *Shahnameh* of Tahmasp, attributed to Qadimi, sixteenth century.

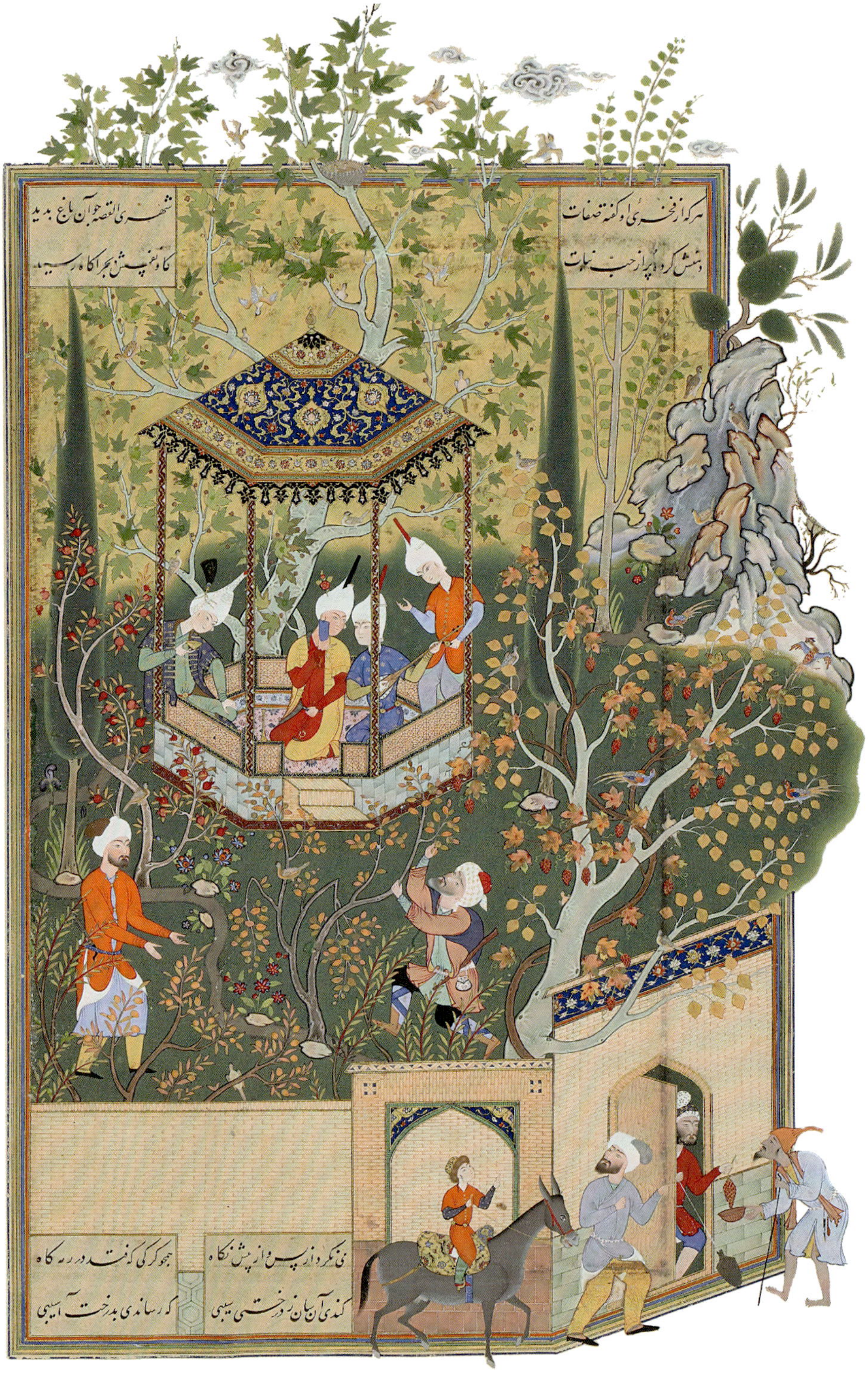

FIGURE 70

The townsman robs the villager's orchard. From the *Haft Awrang* by Jami, Mashhad, 1556–65.

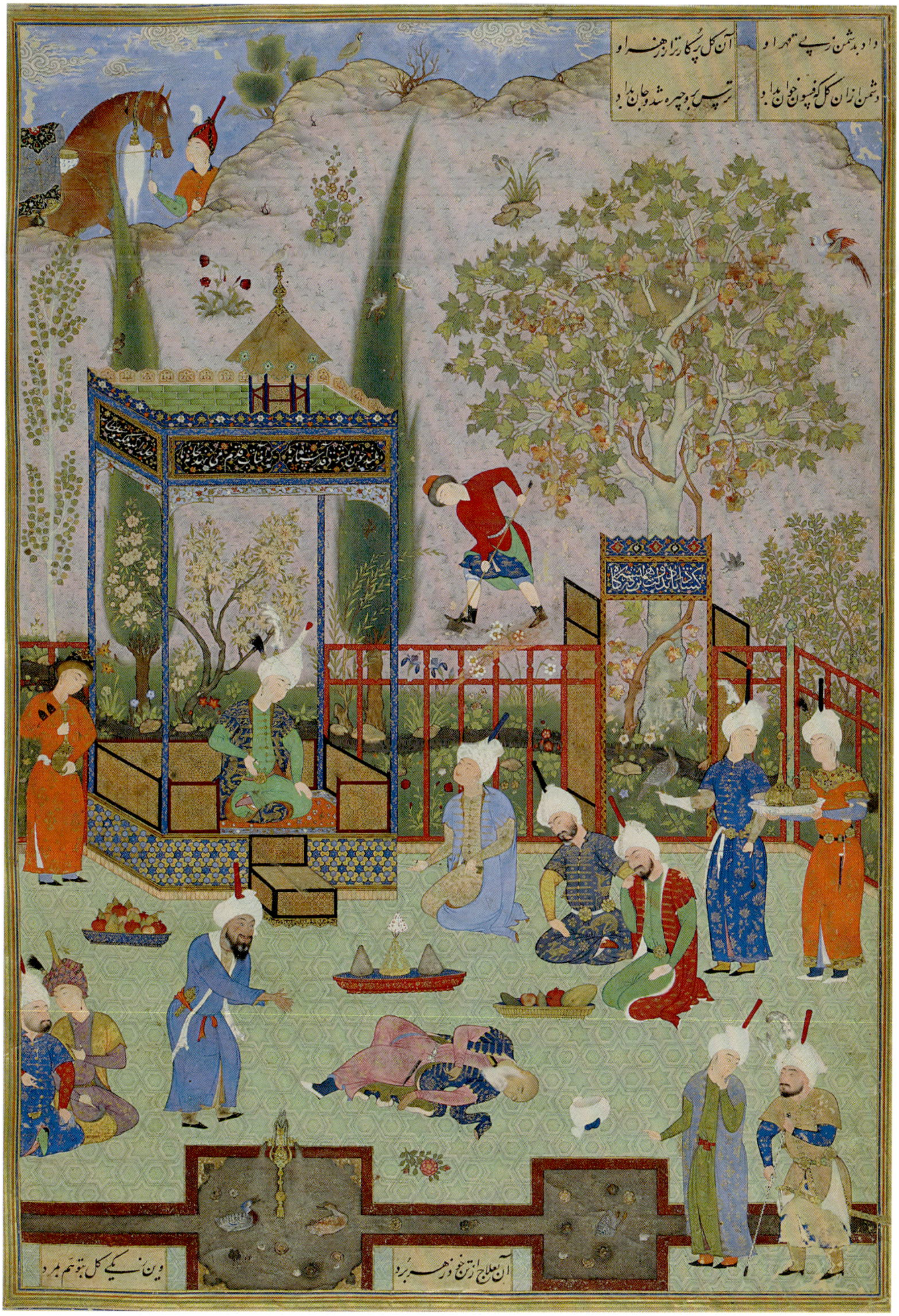

FIGURE 71

The duel of physicians in the royal garden. From the *Khamseh* by Nezami, 1539–43.

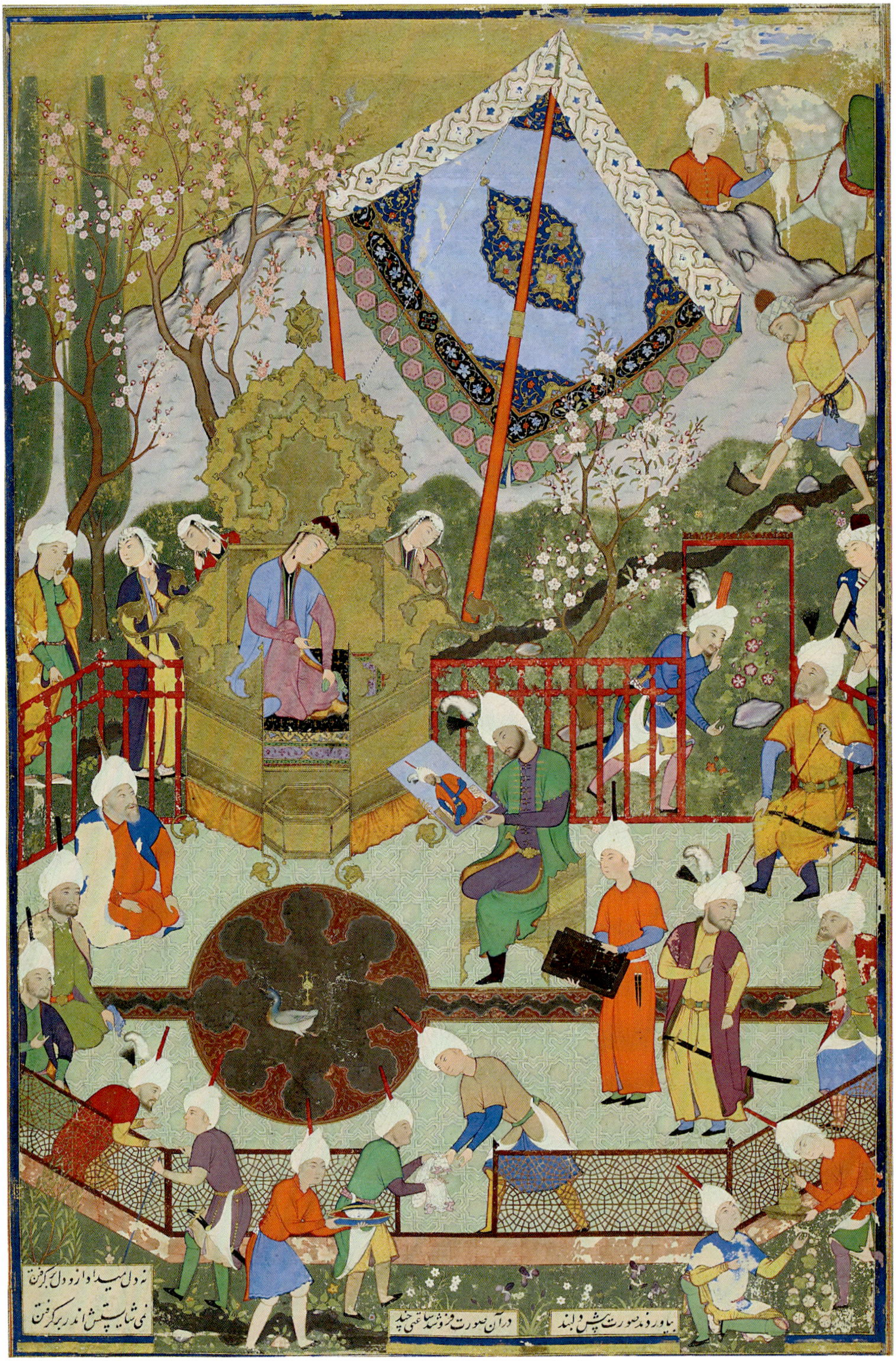

FIGURE 72

Shirin sees Khosrow's portrait. From the *Khamseh* by Nezami, 1539–43.

Clavijo's notes, despite their comprehensive nature, are not sufficient to categorize tents in terms of design. However, we can refer to two significant Ilkhanid documents, *The History of the World-Conqueror* and *The Successors of Genghis Khan*, which provide a clear picture of the tents of Genghiz Khan, used as models by his successors. Ghengiz Khan used to go to mountains every July,[263] where he dwelled in "a *Khitayan* pavilion, whose walls were made of latticed wood, ceiling was of gold while its embroidered cloth, and it was covered all over with white felt: it is called Shira-Ordu. In these parts are cool waters and much grass."[264] The Shira-Ordu is described by Rashid-uddin as "a great tent which held a thousand persons and was never struck. The outside was adorned with gold-studs and the inside covered with nasij (golden embroidery)."[265]

John de Plano Carpini, as one of the first Europeans who visited the court of Genghiz Khan around 1246 CE, speaks of three different types of pavilions, which have different degrees of complexity and ornamentation based on the rank of their residents. These types are:

> *Sira-orda* which is a great tent made of white purple, which in our opinion was large enough to hold more than two thousand persons; and around it a wooden paling had been made, and it was ornamented with divers designs... The Golden-*orda*, which rested on pillars covered with gold plates, fastened with gold nails and other woods, and the top and sides of it were covered with baldakins; the outside, however, being of other kinds of stuff... And a wonderful tent, all of red, purple, a present of the Kitayans.[266]

Carpini and his companions were taken first to the *Sira-orda*, where they remained for four weeks. After the four weeks the whole assembly left the *Sira-orda* and rode to a place "three to four leagues [9–12 miles] distant, where there was a fine large plain near a river flowing between mountains."[267] They set up the Golden-*orda* to hold the enthronement ceremony, which was to have taken place on 15 August but, because of a violent hailstorm, it was postponed to the 24th.[268] Gengiz Khan's Golden-*ordu* could have served as a model for his descendant, Timur, whose tent was called a "castle" by Clavijo, because of its huge size.[269] This lofty pavilion, which had a square plan, was three lances high and hundred paces broad. It was pitched against twelve poles, made of gold, blue and other colours, each of which was as large as a man. Clavijo even describes the pitching process:

> When they pitched the tents, they used wheels, like those of a cart, which were turned by men, and they have ropes fixed in various directions, to assist them. From the vault of the ceiling of the pavilion silken cloths descended, between each of the poles, which were fastened to them, and when they were fastened, they made an arch from one side to the other.[270]

Shah Tahmasp's tent in his *ordu* in Tabriz, which is described by Membre, was not apparently much smaller in size and had a similar structure:

> there was a cord as thick as a finger, with which was formed a complete circle, like a courtyard surrounded with a wall, and having two entrances. Every three paces there was a wooden stake on the cord; on the top of the said pole was an iron point, which was fixed in the ground. The said poles were half-a-rod long. Within the said cord were his [the Shah's] pavilions, and in the first part, on coming through the entrance in the said cord, over against it, is the palace where he gives audience, one behind the other, and the second pavilion is very large.[271]

Clavijo refers to joined porticos outside the square pavilion. These porticos were supported by twenty-four poles (while the tent has thirty-six poles), which were smaller than the central ones. He describes the interior and exterior of the tent:

> From this pavilion at least five hundred red cords were extended, and inside there was a crimson carpet, beautifully ornamented with silken cloths of many colours, and embroidered with gold threads. In the centre of the ceiling there was the richest work of all, and in the four corners were the figures of four eagles, with their wings closed. The outside of the pavilion was lined with silk cloths, in black, white, and yellow stripes. At each corner there was a high pole, with a copper ball, and the figure of a crescent on the top, and in the centre, there was another tall pole, with a much larger copper ball and crescent, and, on the top of the pavilion, between these poles, there was a tower of silken cloths, with turrets, and an entrance door; and when the wind blew the pavilion about, or made the poles unsteady, men went on the top, and secured anything that was loose. Within the pavilion there was, in one part, a chamber covered with carpets, for the use of the lord, and on the left hand there was another carpeted chamber, and another beyond that.[272]

The huge round walls, encircling the pavilion, were about three hundred paces across. These colourful walls, which were made of silk, had cords and poles inside and outside them for support. There was a wide gate, made like an arch, which was as high as a man on horseback,[273] and on the top of it there was a tower with turrets.[274]

Everyone had to pass two main gates in order to get to the royal tent, which was in the centre of this enclosed space. The second gate was even more decorated. Above this door, there were three silver-gilt falcons, with extended wings. All these ornamentations were made to impress the guest and show off the power of the resident of the tent, Timur. There was a silken awning on the door in order to protect the guests and the entrance area from the sun. Clavijo describes this highest part of the royal tent:

> [In the] latter tent there was a very large silver-gilt eagle, with wings displayed, and a little below it. Above the door of the tent, were three silver-gilt falcons, with extended wings, and heads turned towards the eagle, which seemed to wish to attack them. These figures were very well made, and were so placed as to present a very beautiful effect. Above the door of the tent there was a silken awning of many colours, which made a shade before the door, and protected it from the sun, and it was made to move, so that the rays of the sun could never enter the tent.[275]

The royal tents seem to have been large enough to accommodate hundreds of people and pavilions (thrones) for the king and his special guests. Moreover, vertical (curtains) and horizontal elements (awnings) worked as a separator of zones inside and outside tents and also as gender signifiers in the *ordu*. The number of gates and entrances depended on the degrees of control necessary outside the tents. In other words, both Timur's and Tahmasp's tents were located in the centre and the visitor had to pass several entrances to get there. The tents were also highly decorated because they served as the main setting for many administrative meetings and for receiving foreign ambassadors.

CONCLUSION

Both local historians and European travellers who visited the Persianiate world frequently refer to gardens as the main settings for cultural and political events. Even the vast terminology they use to name gardens and pavilions serves to highlight the cultural significance of gardens and pavilions in Persian society. The multiple uses of gardens as recreational areas, encampments and for administrative affairs and pilgrimage affect the nature of the gardens and, consequently, influence the presence, function and design of pavilions. The common use of royal gardens outside cities as sites for encampments, especially in the pre-Safavid age, shaped the perception of gardens as places for temporary stays, as camping zones rather than permanent places for leisure. This phenomenon was due to the nomadic life of the court and the tradition of living in gardens far from city centres, probably to protect their capitals against external attacks or internal rebellions and revolutions. This function of gardens as the setting for encampments converted them from elegant enclosures into huge territories for hundreds of tents. These gardens served as the main settings for administrative affairs, for initiating wars, or for the defence of the cities next to them. The gardens, especially those used for encampments, had the capability to be expanded based on new social, political and urban demands. In other words, at least in the pre-Safavid age, their development was based on new spatial demands and their expansion was not only in terms of size but also use, function and physical components. Two main rationales behind the development of gardens outside cities were the lack of urban land and the common use of gardens as military and camping sites. The flexible nature of gardens also led to a wide definition of the pavilion structure as a building, kiosk, or tent.

Being diverse in terms of geographical location and chronology, the pavilions as buildings were usually octagonal, hexagonal, square or rectangular in plan. A pavilion in the middle of the garden emphasizes the hierarchy of its owner while providing a high degree of accessibility and visibility to the rest of the garden. The levels of transparency of the buildings depend on the geographical and cultural contexts of the pavilions. In contrast to the garden palaces, such as the one in the Safavid garden in Ashraf, which are defined and almost closed entities inside enclosed gardens, some pavilions were defined as parts of the urban neighbourhood (for example, Emarat-e Dargah) and, naturally, included more openings and stronger connections to the garden surrounding them. Water, as a sacred, restorative and decorative element, plays a significant role in the design of pavilions and their connection to the gardens. The running channels pass through some pavilions, such as that of Saʿadat Abad, while fountains, usually rectangular or square, were located in front of garden pavilions. Fountains inside the pavilion are, in some cases, physically disconnected from the fountain outside, treating water as a pure ornamental element. Pavilions as buildings are usually highly ornamented with tiles, paintings and carpets to show off the wealth and power of their owners. Within some pavilions, such as the Ilkhanid Hasht Behesht, the paintings on the interior walls and ceiling highlighted the status of the king by depicting him entertaining foreign ambassadors or battling with enemies.

The kiosk in the Persian garden is a semi-open area, usually in close connection to planted areas and buildings. The kiosk appears in three different forms: platforms covered with temporary roofs and awnings, built structures with permanent roofs, and movable structures (or the developed version of a throne). Although these structures are rarely described because of their simplicity and openness, their use and functionality inside gardens is discussed by a few historians, such as Beyhaqi. Despite their range in terms of form, all types of kiosks have some kind of roof or umbrella to protect their inhabitants from the sun. The placement of the kiosk depends on four factors: view, water, hierarchy and gender. The location usually provides a panoramic view of the rest of garden and its residents. It is also usually in close physical and visual connection with fountains, creeks or water channels. The kiosk could be used only by high-ranking people such as the king and his special guests or courtiers, and often denotes a gender-specific zone for female or male members of the royal family.

The common function of gardens as encampments required the use of tents as temporary structures along with buildings and kiosks. The huge number of residents in the *ordu* demanded the application of organized layouts for tents to enhance social order, prevent crime, provide larger degrees of mobility, and enable residents to pitch and remove tents quickly. The placement of tents within the *ordu,* as a temporary city in the garden, was based on the social or military rank of the residents, the need for privacy for the women, and the distribution of the public services. In most cases, the royal quarter was located in the centre in order to enhance the security of the king and his family. The women's quarter was visually and physically isolated from the male areas. Each camp was a mobile town which could provide all types of public services to its residents. Regardless of its location, the *ordu* consisted of administrative quarters as well as markets, bathhouses and mosques. The size of each tent and its decorations usually depended on the status of its inhabitants. For instance, the king owned the largest tent, which was highly ornamented with elaborate decorations, while the troops' tents were modest and simple in terms of scale, design and ornamentation.

5

Conclusion

THE study of pavilions requires a profound understanding of their settings, Persianate gardens, and their emergence, evolution and integration with man-made structures. The literature examined in Chapter 2 indicates the deep spiritual value of natural elements such as rivers, plants and flowers, and relates them to the story of creation. The *Story of Genesis* develops this further, offering a comprehensive view of nature fully integrated with the Garden of Eden and heaven, while the reflection of heaven in Zoroastrian texts of the Sassanid age shows the widespread influence of this concept in the region. The Qur'an not only integrates ideas of paradise as a garden and the Garden of Eden, it also offers a clear description of the paradise garden, *firdaws*, as the reward of the righteous. The Qur'an also discusses pavilions (buildings and thrones) as specific places where people could enjoy a pleasant view of the garden.

The development of the garden and pavilion as an expression of paradise resulted in a cultural synthesis in Persian literature, especially poetry, as I show in the second part of Chapter 2. Most useful for my argument is the wide and complex terminology used by Persian poets and historians to highlight the cultural significance of gardens and pavilions in Persian society. This rich and specific lexicon enables historians and poets to refer to them both literally and metaphorically. Moreover, these terms draw a clear boundary between the garden and different types of pavilions, specify their use, and clarify design concepts and features. The garden pavilion in Persian literature most often appears as a palace and is seldom referred to as a kiosk or tent. The reflection of the garden and the pavilion in poetry is related to their spiritual and symbolic value in terms of wealth and power. Mythological, religious and literary writings highlight the cultural association and development of gardens and pavilions, especially after the advent of Islam, although they do not specifically clarify the design concepts, features, or the structure of a pavilion in relation to the garden. They do, however, offer an ideal image. In contrast, the historical and travel accounts examined in Chapter 3 provide a clearer picture for three types of pavilions: buildings, kiosks and tents. These particular structures resulted from a cultural need for permanent, semi-permanent and temporary spaces reflected by the use of gardens for recreational, military, economic and social functions. These accounts complement one another. Historians usually refer to the function of pavilions from a historical, political and social perspective while travellers most often provide descriptions of their design features, their ornamentations and of cultural behaviour. In effect, these two viewpoints complement each other by filling in the gaps of the individual accounts.

The frequent use of royal gardens outside cities as sites for encampments, widely reflected in travellers' accounts and rarely reflected in painting, has shaped the perception of gardens as temporary residences. This function converted gardens from elegant enclosures into huge territories with sufficient open areas to pitch hundreds of tents. Gardens were used as a setting for many of the narratives illustrated in Persian paintings between the fourteenth and eighteenth centuries and were usually depicted as containing a man-made pavilion of variable size. Depending on the style, focus and story behind the painting, pavilions appear in different forms of permanency and mobility, that is, building, kiosk, throne or tent.

As buildings, pavilions are usually transparent structures strongly connected to the garden surrounding them, as my discussion of paintings in Chapter 3 shows. Water plays a significant role here, with running channels and fountains inside pavilions treating water as a sacred and decorative element and linking them to the exterior. Ornamented with tiles, paintings and carpets, pavilions as buildings were used to show the wealth and power of their owners who were typically significant political figures. Such pavilions are widely reflected in Persian art and often show the palace in fragmented images. As a palace, a pavilion usually includes at least one *iwan* serving as the connector between the building and garden and providing a setting for the royal throne from which the king and courtiers have a panoramic view of the garden and the people inside it. Ilkhanid, Timurid and early Safavid artists used a two-dimensional language to depict the pavilion while those of the late Safavid period, influenced by European styles, employed varied perspectives to capture the three-dimensionality of the spaces, especially the *iwan*.

The kiosk, mentioned by only a few historians and travellers, is a semi-open area usually in close connection to planted areas and buildings. My studies on kiosk structures confirm that they take three forms: platforms covered with temporary roofs and awnings, built structures with permanent roofs, and movable structures (or the developed version of a throne). Because of their simple architectural design, lack of ornamentation and open nature, travellers have given these structures little attention, but their use inside gardens has occasionally been discussed by historians. According to historical accounts, the placement of the kiosk in gardens depends on four factors: view, water, hierarchy and gender. The location frequently provides a panoramic view of the rest of garden and its residents. It is also in close physical and visual connection with fountains, creeks or water channels. The kiosk can be used only by high-ranking people such as the king and his special guests or courtiers.

Paintings, even more than historical writings, emphasize the kiosk as the main domain of the king and as a place for royal receptions from where they can view the landscape and events facing the courtyard. The kiosk examples discussed in Chapter 3 show that the design of the kiosk in art relates to the courtyard as its main context and often reflects the form and plan of the palace. It functions as a connector between the garden and building and is sometimes integrated into a pathway separating the garden from the pavement. The image becomes so dominant that it even works as a model in paintings which are not related to gardens. Surprisingly, although the depiction of the kiosk becomes increasingly fashionable in Persian painting, the poetry which accompanies the painting rarely refers to the kiosk itself as a setting. Common to both painting and historical writing about kiosks are gender specificity, the high status of residents, and a strong connection with the garden and its natural components.

As mentioned in the discussion on tents in Chapter 4, travellers' accounts relate the large number of residents in royal encampments, or *ordu*. The pre-designed layouts for tents helped to enhance social order, prevent crime, provide larger degrees of mobility and enable residents to pitch and remove tents quickly. The placement of tents within these temporary cities was based on social or military rank, privacy for the women, and distribution of public services. The royal quarter was located at the centre in order to enhance the security of the king and his family, while the women's quarter was visually and physically isolated from the male areas. Each camp was a mobile town that provided all types of public services (such as markets, bathhouses, mosques, etc.) to its residents. In contrast to the kiosk and throne, the tent is rarely associated with any building in Persian painting. This is because most tents in paintings are placed in natural landscapes and not in 'designed' gardens. Artists typically treated the tent as a flexible structure with the unique capacity to be either completely open or closed, and used levels of ornamentation and decoration and the number of carpets to signify the social position of residents. In some paintings, the tent as a canopy is used as a kiosk, in which case it is usually placed next to or over a water channel.

Most studies of Persian gardens neglect pavilions as significant features; this is due, in part, to the dearth of archaeological evidence, especially in the case of kiosks or tents, and also to the common perception of gardens as open fields rather than as integrations of built structures with paved and planted areas. In addition, pavilions have often been categorized as architecture – that is, not specifically as part of garden design. My research, however, confirms the unification of gardens and pavilions as components of a single architectural construction, the paradise garden. It also considers the influence of the relationship between urban fabric and garden on the typology and design of pavilions. The patronage behind the design and construction was also examined, taking into account architectural qualities such as order, space, and circulation in relation to structural mobility and stability.

Although the historical pavilion may, in reality, have been different from its reflection in painting or literature, my research serves as a foundation for subsequent studies. These might focus on visual and literary images of pavilions in specific eras in order to clarify the degree of idealism versus realism. Referring to archaeological evidence in order to study the evolution of each typology (building, kiosk, tent or throne) could make a significant contribution to this field and may, for instance, reveal whether the design of buildings in gardens was under the influence of specific styles or local movements during each period or whether, as Pope suggests, it follows a logical order.

Any further studies on pavilions, especially as royal settings, require an investigation of cultural behaviour in gardens and its influence on the design of spaces in palaces and kiosks. A geographical categorization of the division of spaces may be possible through comparison of the plans of garden palaces from various regions of the Persianate world. My research on the use of gardens as pilgrimage sites in Chapter 4 provides a setting for future studies to focus on the conversion of the pavilion from a palace to a mausoleum, especially in the Ghaznavid period, and its indirect impact on early Mughal mausoleum gardens. The gap in the information on kiosks might be filled with an analytical review of the plans of gardens drawn by contemporary scholars and archaeologists, matching them to historical accounts in order to locate semi-open spaces such as platforms and kiosks and even movable pavilions and thrones. Further research is also needed to clarify the evolution of tent design in central Asia in order to shed more light on the temporary residences and quarters in Timurid gardens discussed in the final chapter.

Finally, a note on the three matrices which follow, and which are designed to summarize the major findings of my research. They are devoted to the three types of document discussed in the second, third and fourth chapters: literature, visual material, and the accounts of travellers and historians. Each matrix includes five rows: *context*, *function*, *time*, *experience* and *design*. The *context* section investigates the relationship between the different types of pavilion and the city, garden and nature. The differentiation between garden and nature is crucial because in some documents the natural setting is the main context of the pavilion, rather than a designed garden. The *function* section indicates the use and users of pavilions. *Time* demonstrates whether the pavilions in their different forms, and in specific documents, are considered permanent or temporary. The *experience* section highlights the social, cultural and individual significance of pavilions, while the last explores the *design* of pavilions with regard to their location, scale and structure.

It should be noted that these matrices are based solely on the material discussed in the preceding chapters. Moreover, their terminology is based on the wording used in the original documents. For example, since in the Qur'an the house in paradise is promised to the "righteous", the same term appears in the matrix. It is clear, then, that with the investigation of new documents, the matrix could be developed further and perhaps even modified to include new terms and themes. Another significant feature of the matrix is the presence of blank cells. These confirm the silence of some documents regarding specific aspects of the pavilion and reveal how detailed its image becomes in the historical documents, as compared to the Zoroastrian texts. This phenomenon allows us to see the chronological development of the concept of the pavilion reflected in the nature of source documents.

Matrix

		Literature (Zoroastrian)		Literature (The Qur'an)			Literature (Persian poetry)	
	Typology	*Palace*	*Throne*	*House and palace*	*Platform*	*Tent*	*Building*	*Tent*
CONTEXT	City						Inside or outside cities	
	Garden			Garden superior	Garden superior		Garden superior, garden and pavilion separated	Garden superior
	Nature				Under trees, close to river, close to water (as a throne)			Close to trees, among flowers
FUNCTION	Use	Residence	Travel	Residence	Temporary stay	Temporary stay	Temporary stay but full of furniture	Temporary stay
	User	Righteous	Souls of the faithful	Righteous	Righteous	Companions	Wealthy and powerful people	Ordinary people
TIME	Permanency	Permanent	Permanent but portable	Permanent	Permanent	Temporary	Permanent	Temporary
EXPERIENCE	Social						Ceremonies and public events	
	Cultural	Representing heaven	Sign of hierarchy	Religious value	Religious value		Sign of property, wealth, and power	Temporary shelter
	Individual		Exploration	View	View		View of all sides of garden	Isolation, relaxation
DESIGN	Location	Between the earth and heaven	Variable	Middle of the paradise garden	In garden		Middle of garden	Planted area
	Scale	One thousand times the height of a man		High			Large and high, tall *iwan*	
	Structure	Firmly established	Golden beams and canopy	Located on a high terrace, transparent	Raised platform		Placed on a platform, includes *iwan*, well-decorated	

		VISUAL (PAINTING)			VISUAL (CARPET)
	Typology	*Building*	*Kiosk and throne*	*Tent*	*Building*
CONTEXT	City	Outside city	Inside or outside cities	Outside cities	
	Garden	Primary element	Secondary element	Secondary element	Central element
	Nature	Close to water	Visually and physically connected to water and trees	Close to trees, plants, and creek	Surrounded by trees and water channels
FUNCTION	Use	Private, semi-public, royal	Sitting area	Meeting, hiding area	
	User	King, royal family	King's beloved, special guests	High-ranking courtiers, royal family, guests	
TIME	Permanency	Permanent	Permanent, portable or fixed	Temporary	Permanent
EXPERIENCE	Social	King, royal family, private affairs	Guest entertainment, social events in garden	Social meetings and events	
	Cultural	Privacy, hierarchy	Signifier of gender or royal hierarchy	Gender segregation, privacy	Signifier of hierarchy
	Individual	View from *iwan* or window	View of building and garden	Sleeping, meeting	Movement
DESIGN	Location	The middle of the garden	Between building and garden (paved and planted areas), in planted areas (portable kiosk and throne), on *iwan* (throne)	Natural landscape, planted area of garden	Centre of garden
	Scale	Usually based on human proportions	Based on figural proportions	Humanistic (realistic)	Based on the proportions of the planted plots
	Structure	Usually on a platform, includes *iwan*, two- or three-storeyed	Transparent, light structure, includes thin columns and light roof	Umbrella connected to a platform, yurt, conical	Hexagonal, octagonal, or square shaped plan

		TEXTUAL (HISTORIANS AND BIOGRAPHERS)			TEXTUAL (TRAVELLERS)		
	Typology	*Building*	*Kiosk*	*Tent*	*Building*	*Kiosk*	*Tent*
CONTEXT	City	Inside or outside cities		Outside cities	Outside or inside cities		Outside cities
	Garden	Primary element	Secondary element	Secondary element	Primary element	Secondary element	Primary element
	Nature	Close to water	Best view of the natural elements of the garden		Integrated with water, surrounded by water	Close to water, surrounded by greenery	Close to water and trees
FUNCTION	Use	Administrative, royal	Administrative affairs, recreation	Royal encampments	Administrative	Private	Royal encampment, administrative
	User	King, courtiers, guests	King, courtiers	High-ranking people	Courtiers, guests, members of harem	Royal family	All people depending on the hierarchy
TIME	Permanency	Permanent	Temporary and permanent	Temporary	Permanent	Permanent	Temporary
EXPERIENCE	Social	Ceremonies, meetings	Ceremonies, parties, and administrative affairs	meetings	Administrative meetings	Public, entertainment	Market, mosque, administrative offices
	Cultural	Symbol of political power	Sign of hierarchy	Gender and hierarchy signifier	Hierarchy	Gender signifier	Privacy, hierarchy
	Individual	View of garden	View	Sleeping	Movement and view	View	Sleeping
DESIGN	Location	Middle of garden	Close to entrance, in centre of garden, hidden in garden	Inside or outside gardens	Centre of garden	Middle of garden, hidden in garden	Inside or outside garden
	Scale	Impressive	Humanistic	Depending on the social rank	Detailed description	Humanistic	Depending on the hierarchy of residents
	Structure	Located on platform, includes *iwan*	Pillared area		Square, hexagonal	Located on a pillared platform	Shira *ordu*, Golden *ordu*

Glossary of Terms

Amir	King, army leader, governor
Badgir	Wind-catcher. Common architectural element in the central and southern regions of Iran; used to cool the air of the interior of buildings
Bagh	An enclosed garden where trees and flowers are planted
Baghcheh	Small garden
Bagh-e jennat	The garden of paradise
Bala-khaneh	The room on the second floor
Bazaar	Marketplace
Beyt	House, room
Bina'	Any kind of building which could be used by humans and animals
Bustan	The garden where fragrant flowers are planted; fruit garden
Chaharbagh	Fourfold garden
Dargah	Main entrance, gateway, royal *iwan*, royal palace
Dehliz	Corridor; long, narrow pathway
Descripto	Description of places, people, time, and objects

Divan-e rasa'el	The office (ministry) of official communications; part of the administration in medieval Persia and in charge of writing and receiving letters and foreign affairs
Divan-khaneh	Ministry of justice, administration house; physical seat of administration office/ministry
Divan	Reception hall; ministry, office, administration
Dokkan	Platform, wooden couch in garden
'Emarat	Building (to build)
Ferdows	Paradise
Fiqh	Islamic jurisprudence based on the Qur'an and Sunna (the Way of the Prophet)
Gardesh	Movement, rotation, walking and exploration, sightseeing
Ghorfeh	Room, separated part of a hall
Gholam	Slave
Golestan, Golzar, or Golshan	Garden full of flowers
Harem	Interior of the house; the residence of female members of the family
Hashtbagh	Eightfold garden
Hijab	Dress for women, covers the body and hair in public
Hijri	The immigration of the Prophet Muhammad from Mecca to Medina set as the first day of the Muslim calendar
Hoz-khaneh	Fountain room, usually located in the basement of the building
Houri	Young companions in the paradise afterlife
'Illiyun	The highest level of paradise; rooms in paradise
Iwan	Vaulted hall open to the garden and walled on three sides. It is connected to the interior of the building through doors and windows
Jannat	Paradise, garden
Jannat al-khalid	Eternal paradise

Kakh	Palace; outstanding building
Keryas	Interior of the house or the royal palace; the cleansing room in the upper floors of the building
Khalifeh (caliph)	The leader of the Islamic state. Usually refers to Umayyad and 'Abbasid leaders
Khanqah	Sufi shrine
Khargah-e zarrin	Golden tent
Khazaneh	State treasury
Khazra'	Greenery
Kheymeh	Tent
Khormastan	Palm grove
Ketab-khaneh	Library; painting workshops in the Safavid period
Kushk	Tall building, palace, kiosk
Madrasa	Religious school
Mahalleh	Urban quarter
Meidan	City square, courtyard
Marghzar	Thicket, grove
Masjid	Mosque
Mazra'eh	Agricultural farm
Meerza	Prince, noble, secretary
Me'rajnameh	The story of Prophet Muhammad's ascension to the heaven
Mu'azzin	The person who calls for the prayers
Molla	Clergy, theologian
Monshi	Secretary
Moshkuy	Harem; female zone in palace or house
Ordu	Royal encampment

Palun	Packsaddle
Piruzi	Victory
Pishgah	The area in front of the palace; the place in a room where high-ranking people sit
Qasr	Palace
Qasr-e shahi	Royal palace
Qawarir	Crystals, glasses
Qibla	The direction towards Mecca where Muslims should face during prayer
Qizilbash (Kizilbash)	Safavid army (literally means "Red Head"); Turkic and other tribes that followed the early Safavid Sheykhs
Qurchi	Soldier, weapon maker
Ravaq	Portico, verandah
Rawdha	Paradise, garden
Raz	Grape vine
Ribat	Caravanserai; hostels inside or outside cities; places where caravans stay overnight which includes rooms for trade, storages, and places for animals
Ridhwan	Paradise
Rihla	Journey
Sabat	Roofed entrance, corridor, or platform. The roof closed to the entrance on which grape branches are placed
Safarnameh	Travel account. Also refers to Naser Khosrow's travel notes during his journey from Khorasan to Egypt
Sarai	House
Sarapardeh	Temporary residence made of tent and cloth; interior of the tent where women reside
Sardaq	Big tent
Sarh	Large palace

Sayeban	Umbrella or roof; the temporary or permanent structure which is installed or held by servants
Senf	Guild
Shabestan	Columned hall, bedroom, harem
Shah	King
Shahnameh	History of kings; the title of the famous mythological epic by Persian poet Ferdowsi (around 1000 CE)
Shahr	City
Soffeh	Roofed *iwan* or platform
Taq	Arch, *iwan*
Takht	Throne, couch
Talar	Guest room, columned hall
Tamasha	Sightseeing, spectacle
Tonob	The rope of the tent; temporary roofs, kiosks
Tarab-khaneh	The house of joy, a place for party
Tarikh	History
Vahishto	Heaven
Waqf	Islamic legal institution of religious endowment whereby properties such as buildings and lands were tied to charitable purposes

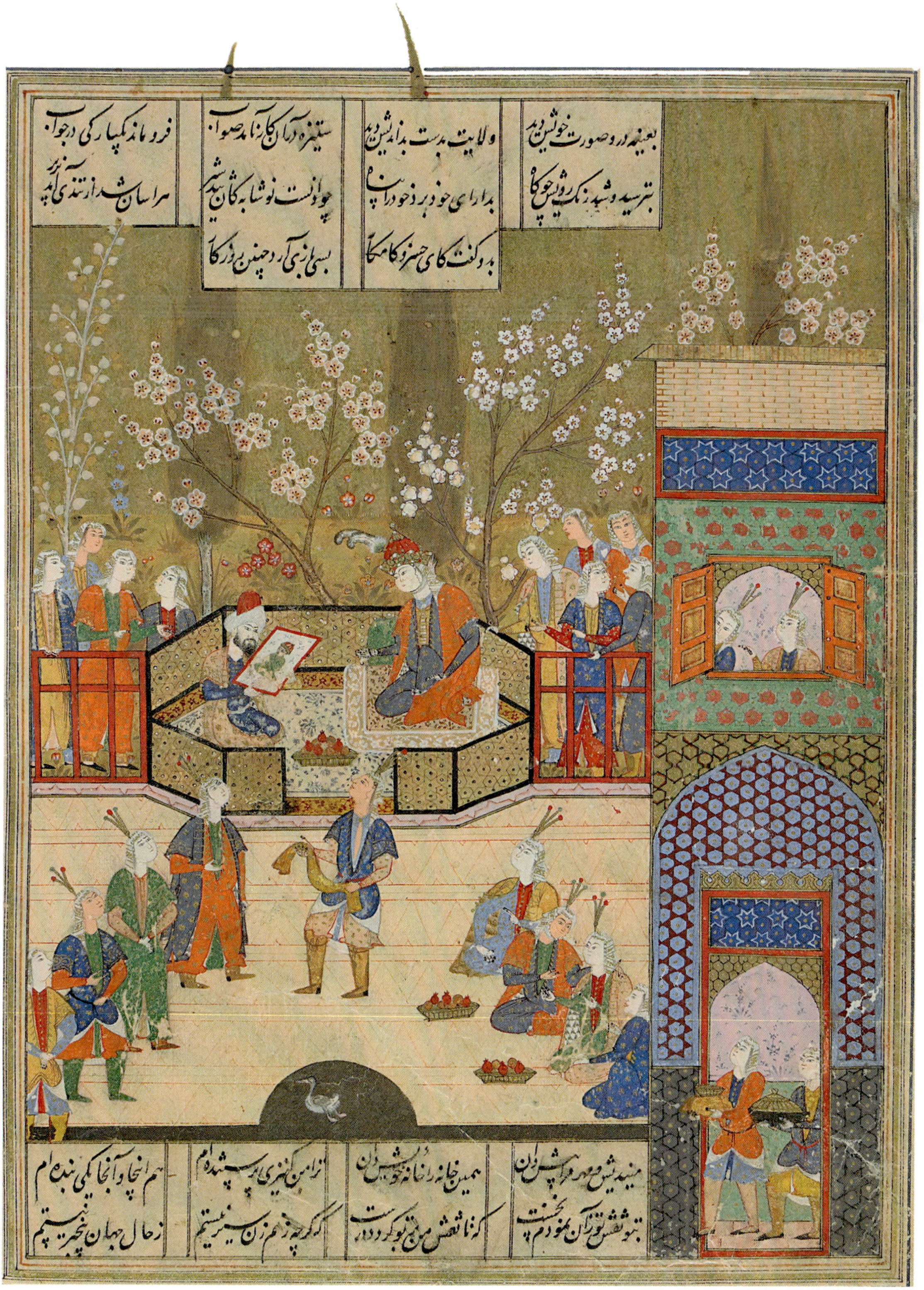

FIGURE 76

Alexander is recognized by Queen Nushabeh. From the *Khamseh* by Nezami, Shiraz, 1549.

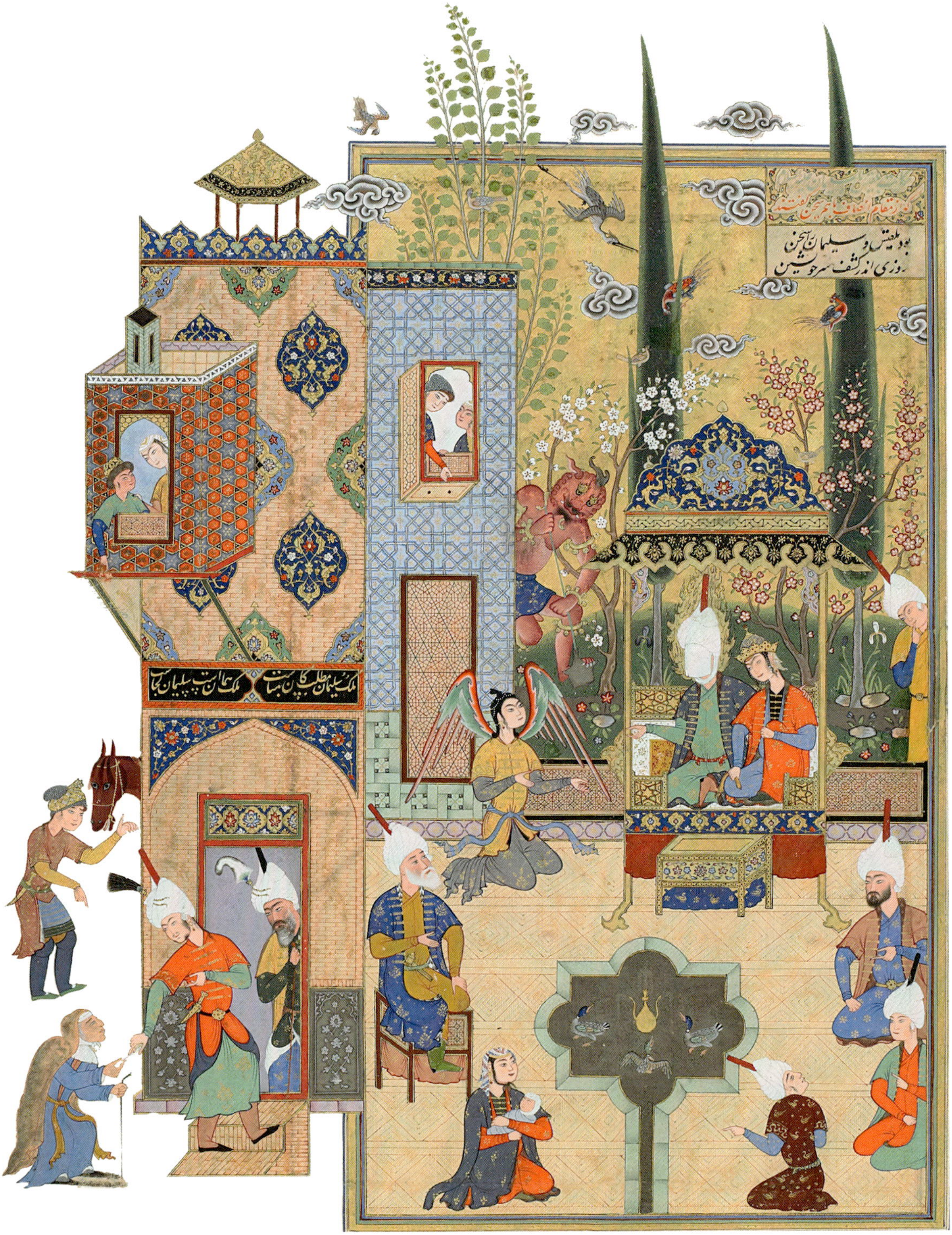

FIGURE 77

Solomon and Bilqis sitting together and conversing about Solomon's findings. From the *Haft Awrang* by Jami, Mashhad, 1556–65.

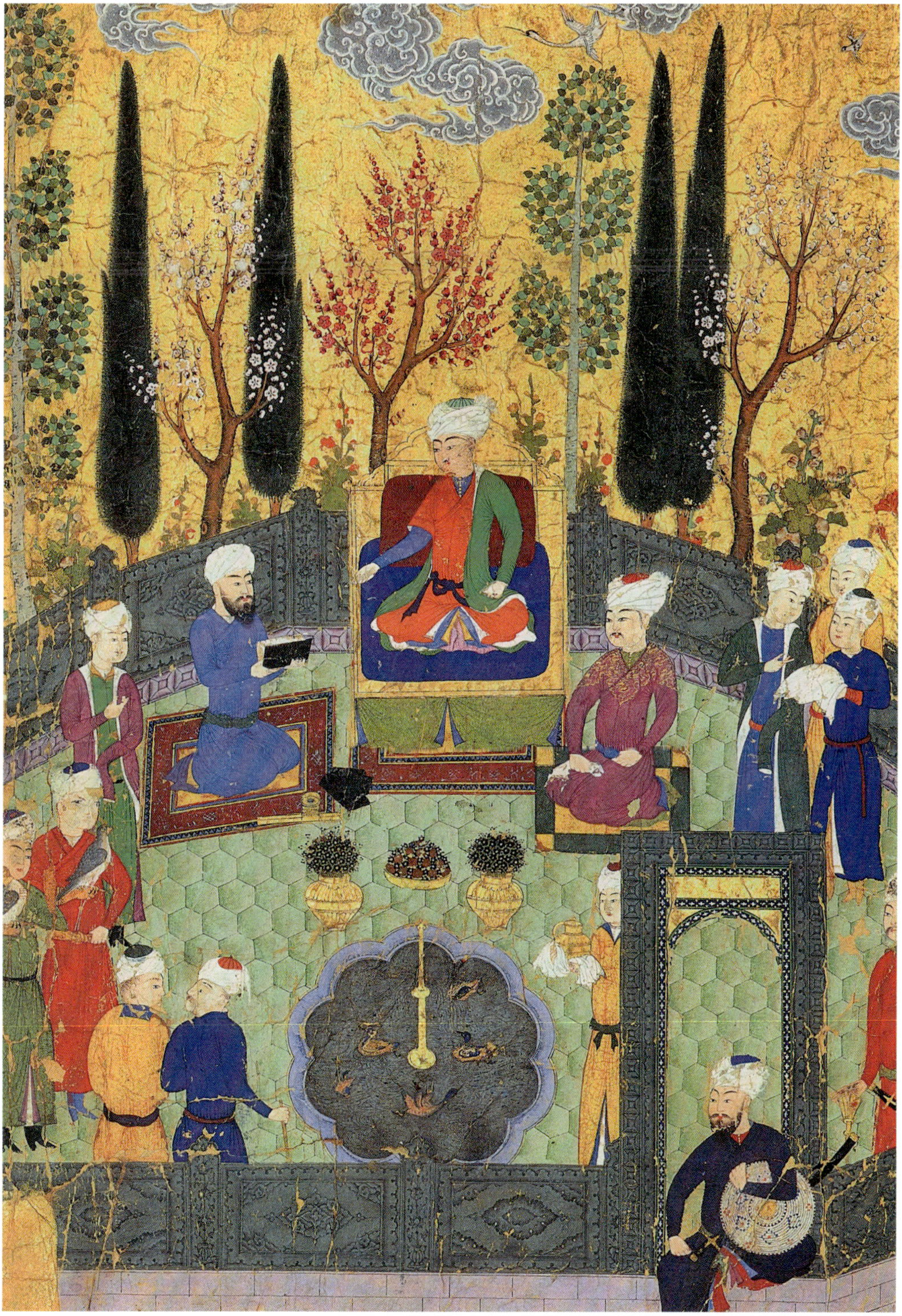

FIGURE 78

Borzuyeh takes the *Kalileh va Damneh* to Anushirvan. From the *Kalileh va Damneh*, 1429.

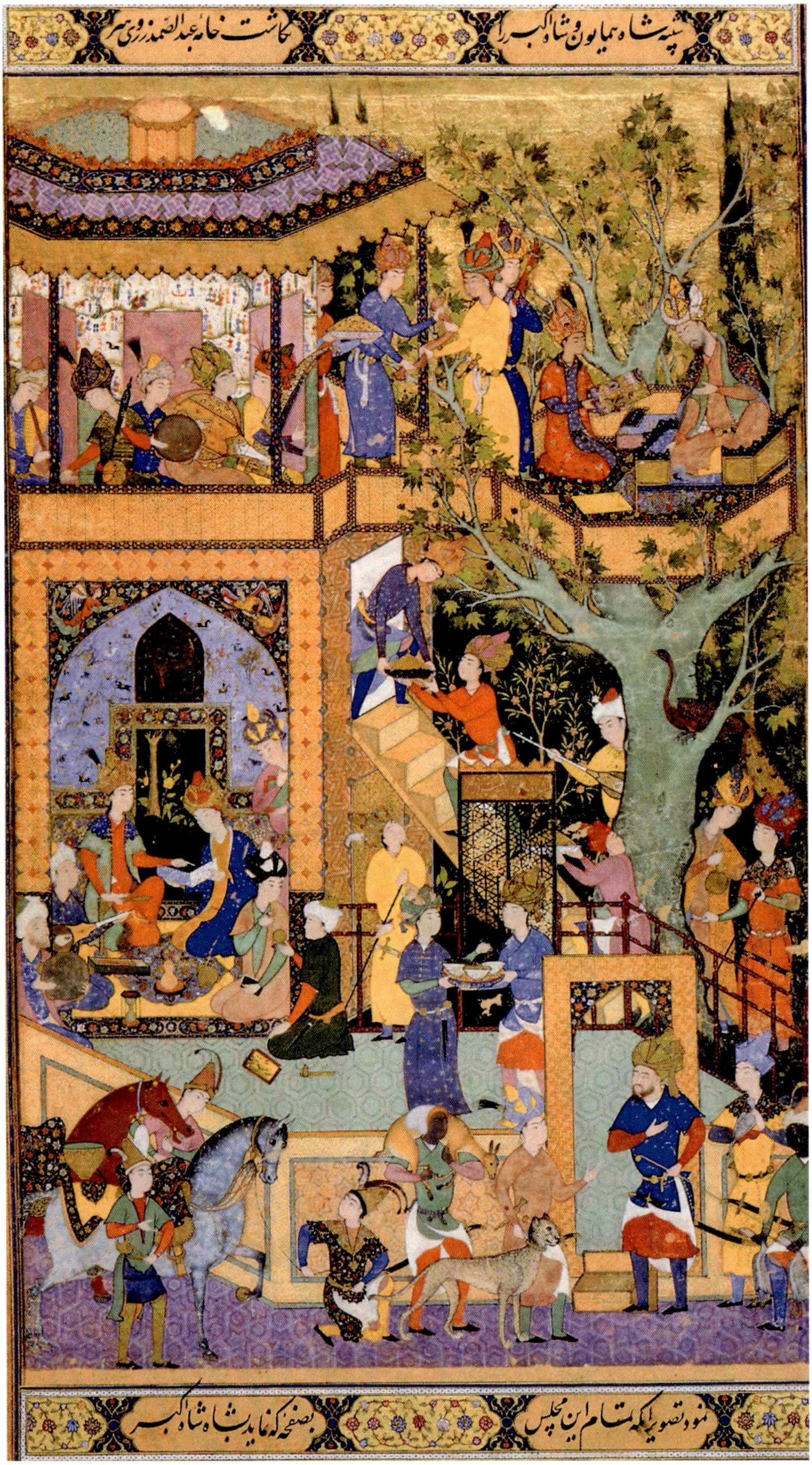

FIGURE 79

Prince Akbar presenting portraits to his father, the emperor Homayun.
Moraqqa' Golshan, attributed to 'Abdol Samad Shirin Qalam, Isfahan, seventeenth century.

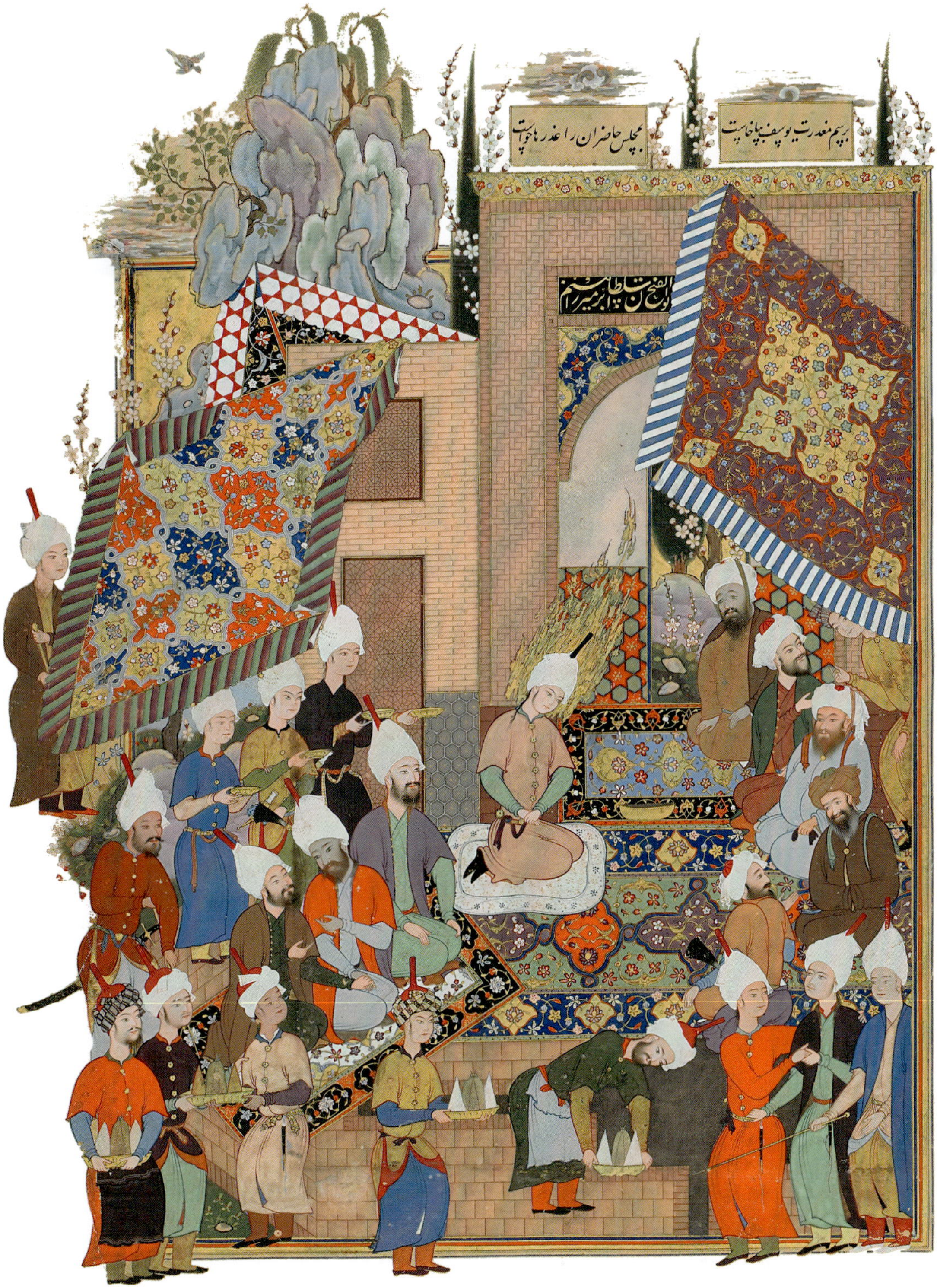

FIGURE 82

Yusof gives a royal banquet in honour of his marriage. From the *Haft Awrang* by Jami, Mashhad, 1556–65.

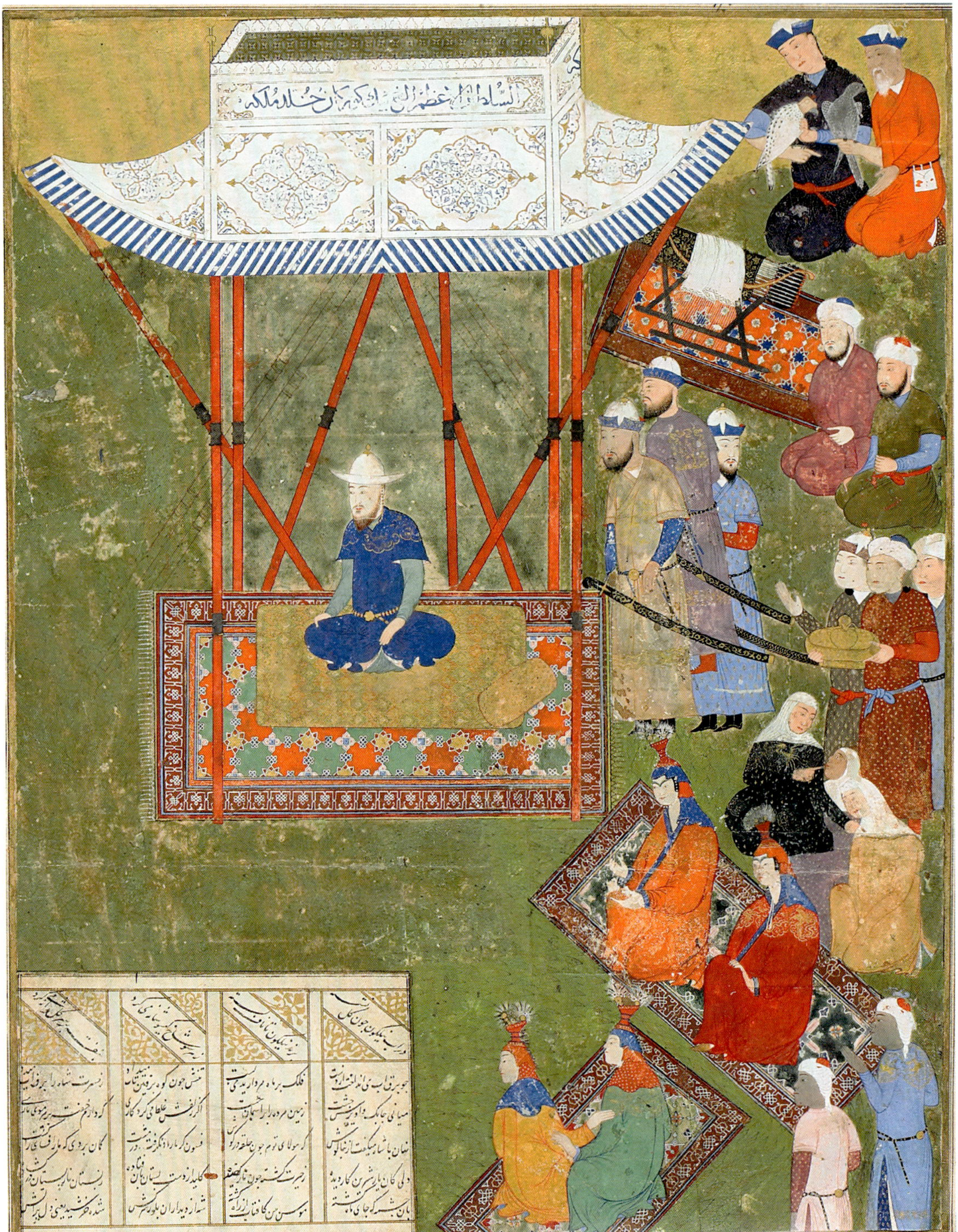

FIGURE 83
The court of Ulugh Beg, 1440.

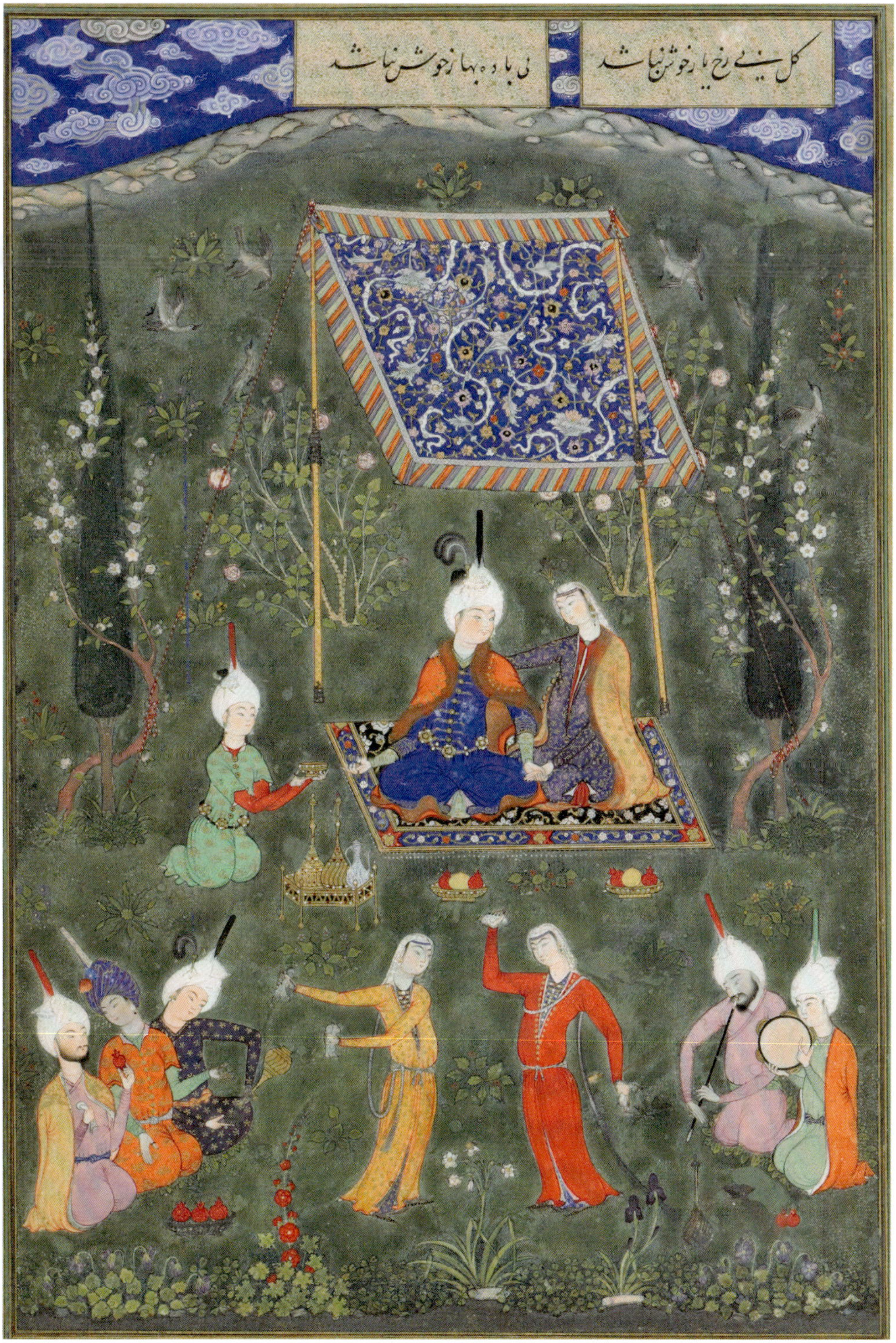

FIGURE 84

A lovers' picnic. From the *Divan* by Hafez, attributed to Soltan Muhammad, Tabriz, 1526–27.

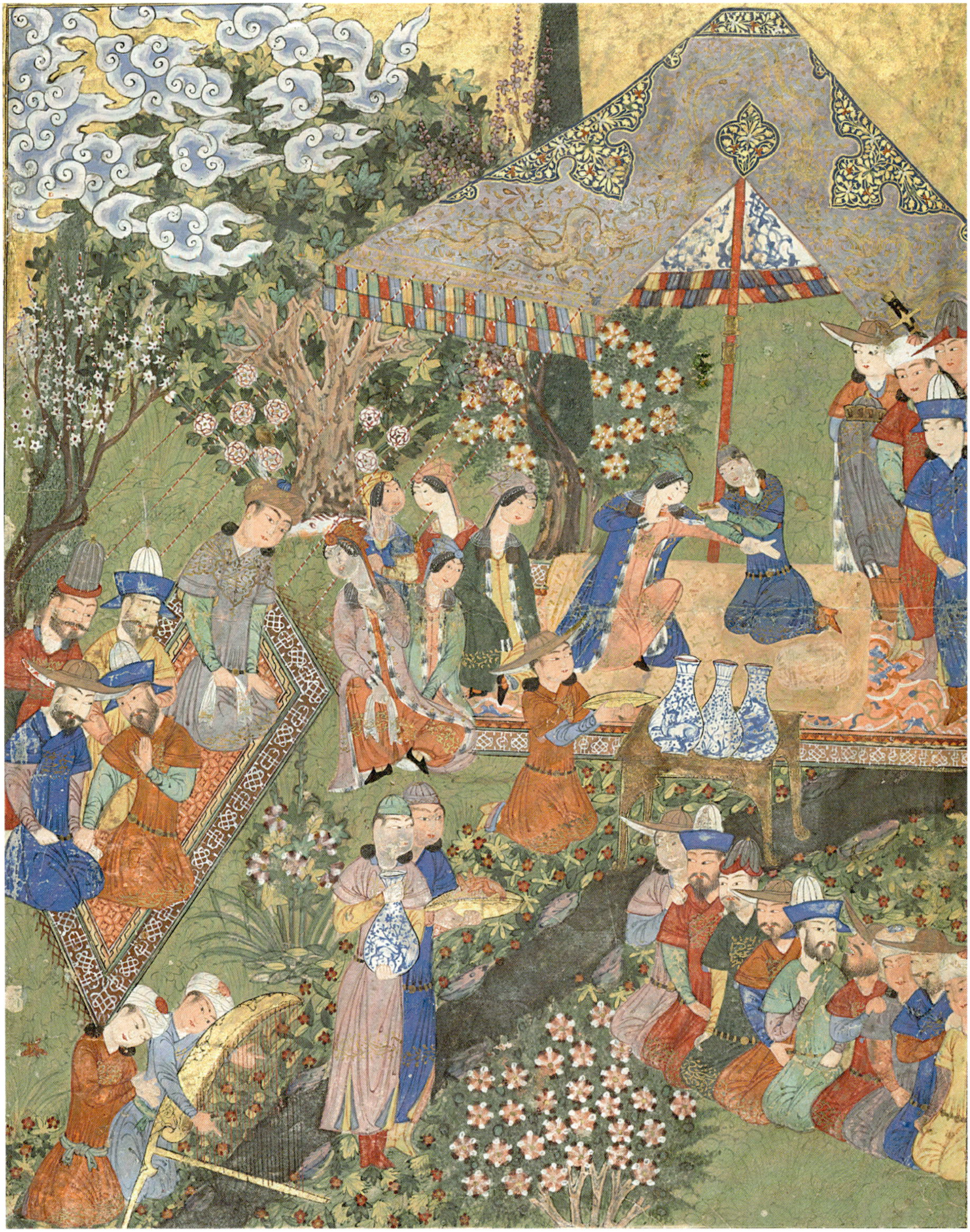

FIGURE 85

A princely banquet in a garden. From the *Shahnameh*, Shiraz, 1444.

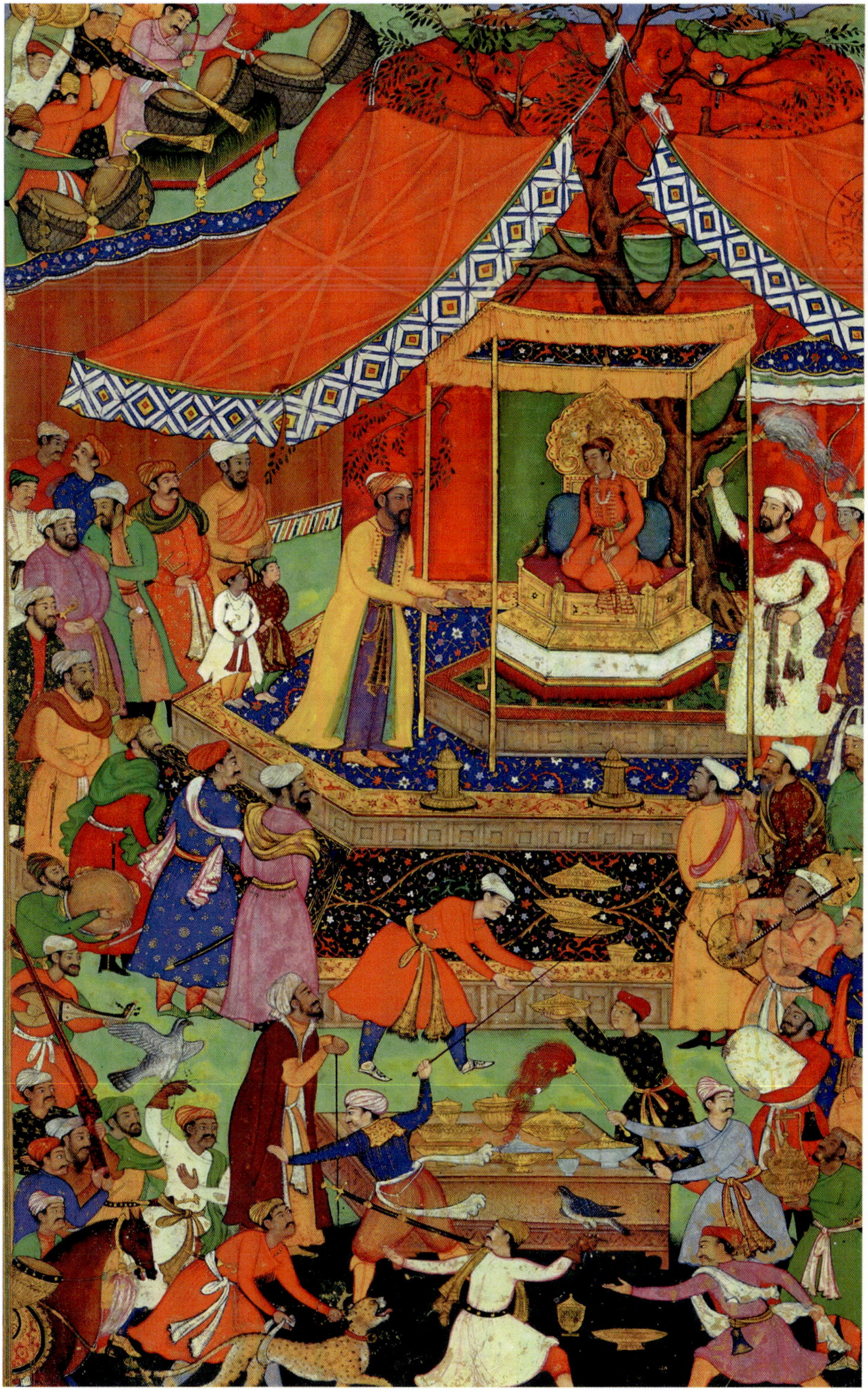

FIGURE 86

The court of Akbar Shah. From the *History of Akbar Shah*, 1822.

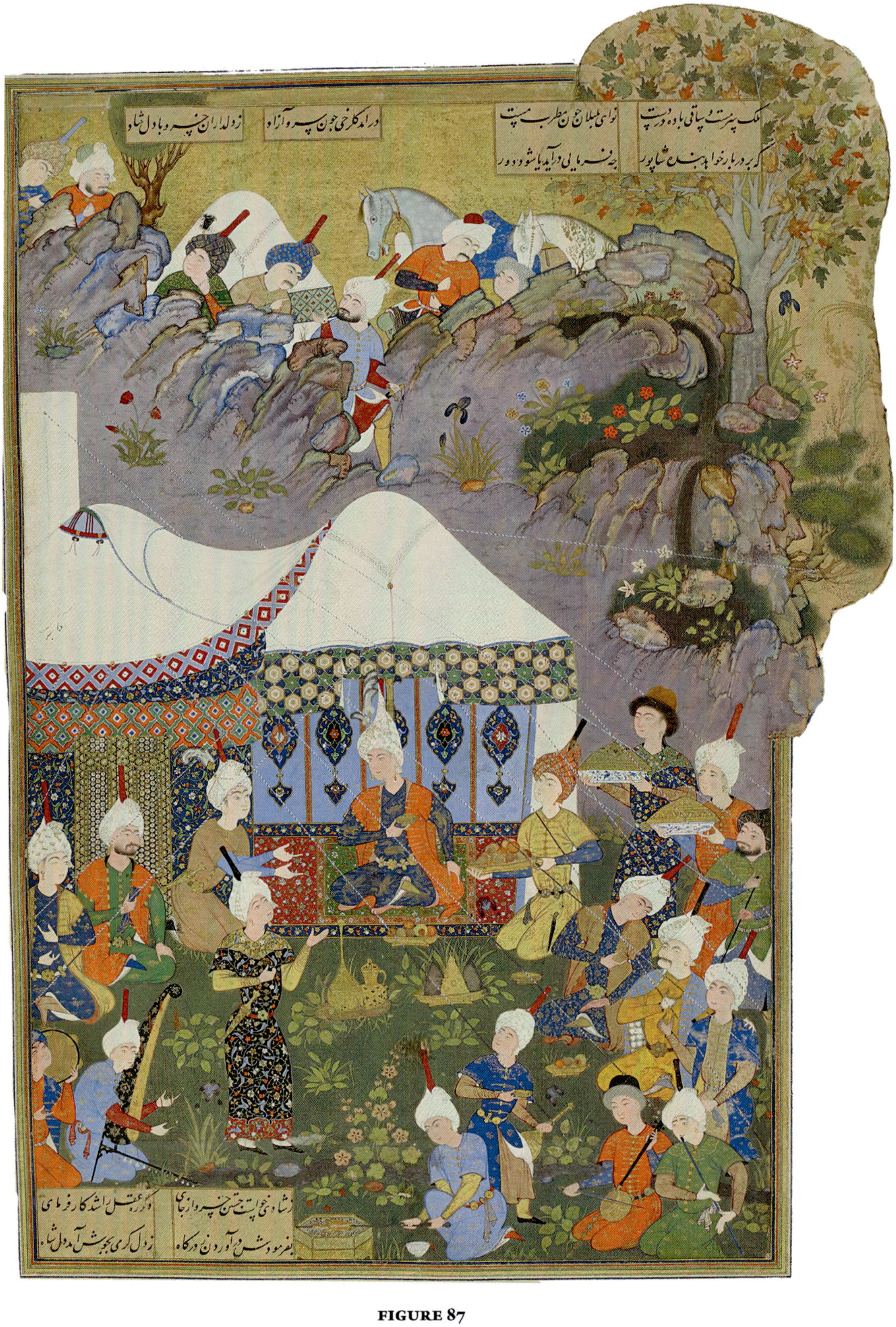

FIGURE 87

The return of Shapur to Khosrow. From *Khosrow va Shirin* by Nezami, 1539–43.

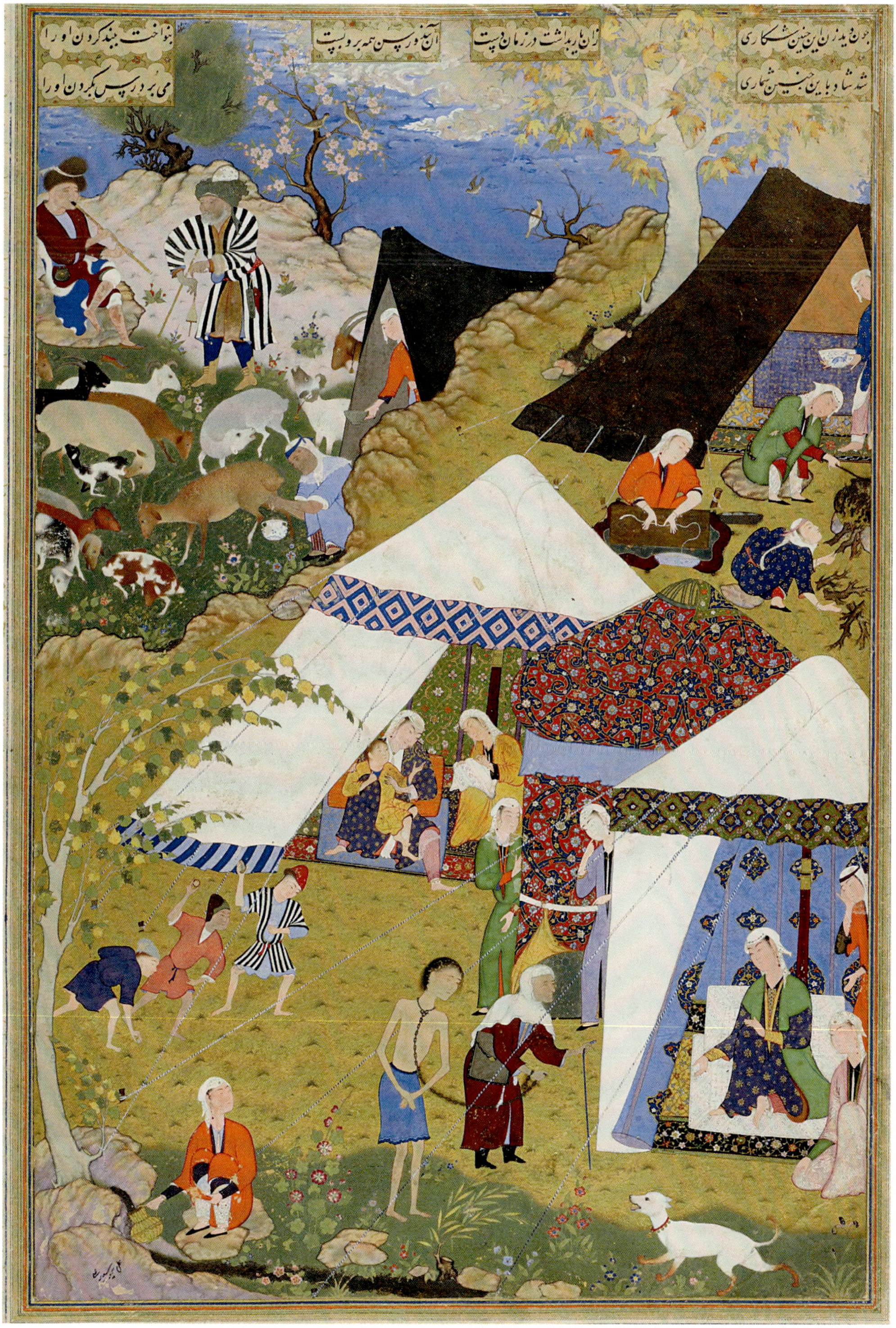

FIGURE 88

Majnun brought in chains by the old woman to Leyla's tent. From the *Khamseh* by Nezami, Tabriz, 1539–43.

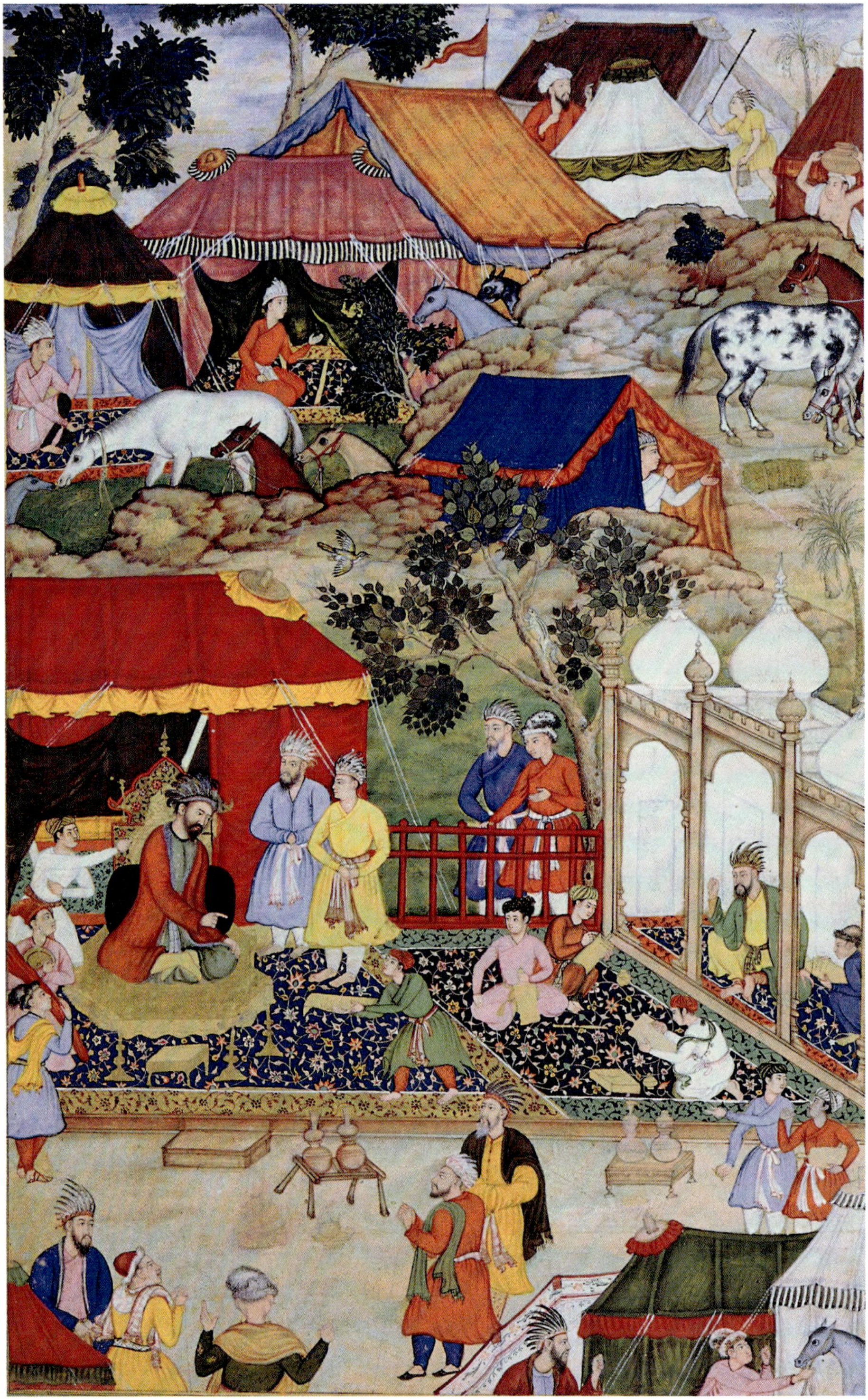

FIGURE 89
Prince Ananda, a grandson of Kublai Khan, and his children having a feast.
From the *Jami' al-Tavarikh,* 1596.

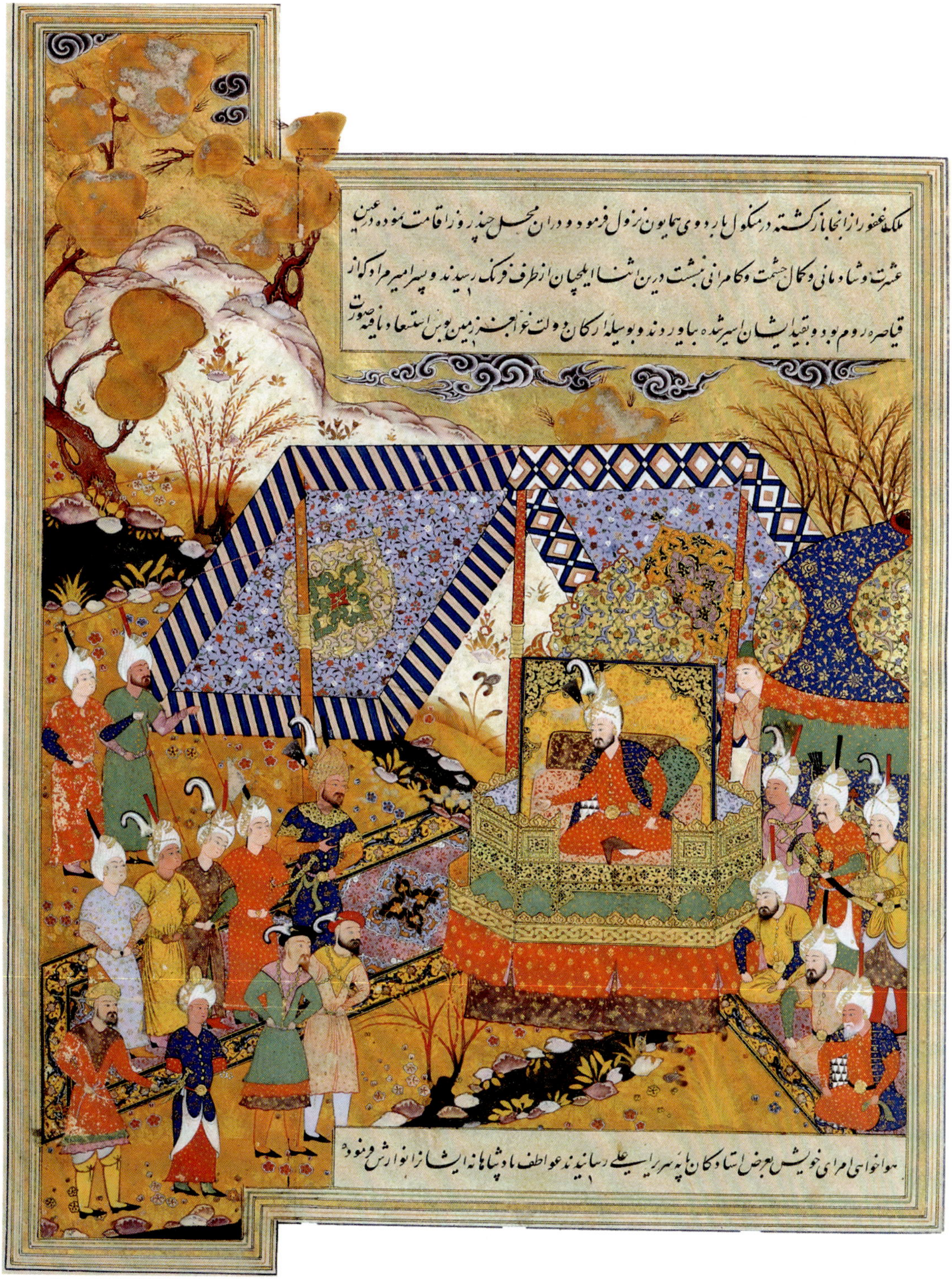

FIGURE 91

The European ambassador brings Ottoman Soltan Morad's son to Timur.
From the *Zafarnameh,* attributed to Kamal-uddin Behzad, 1528.

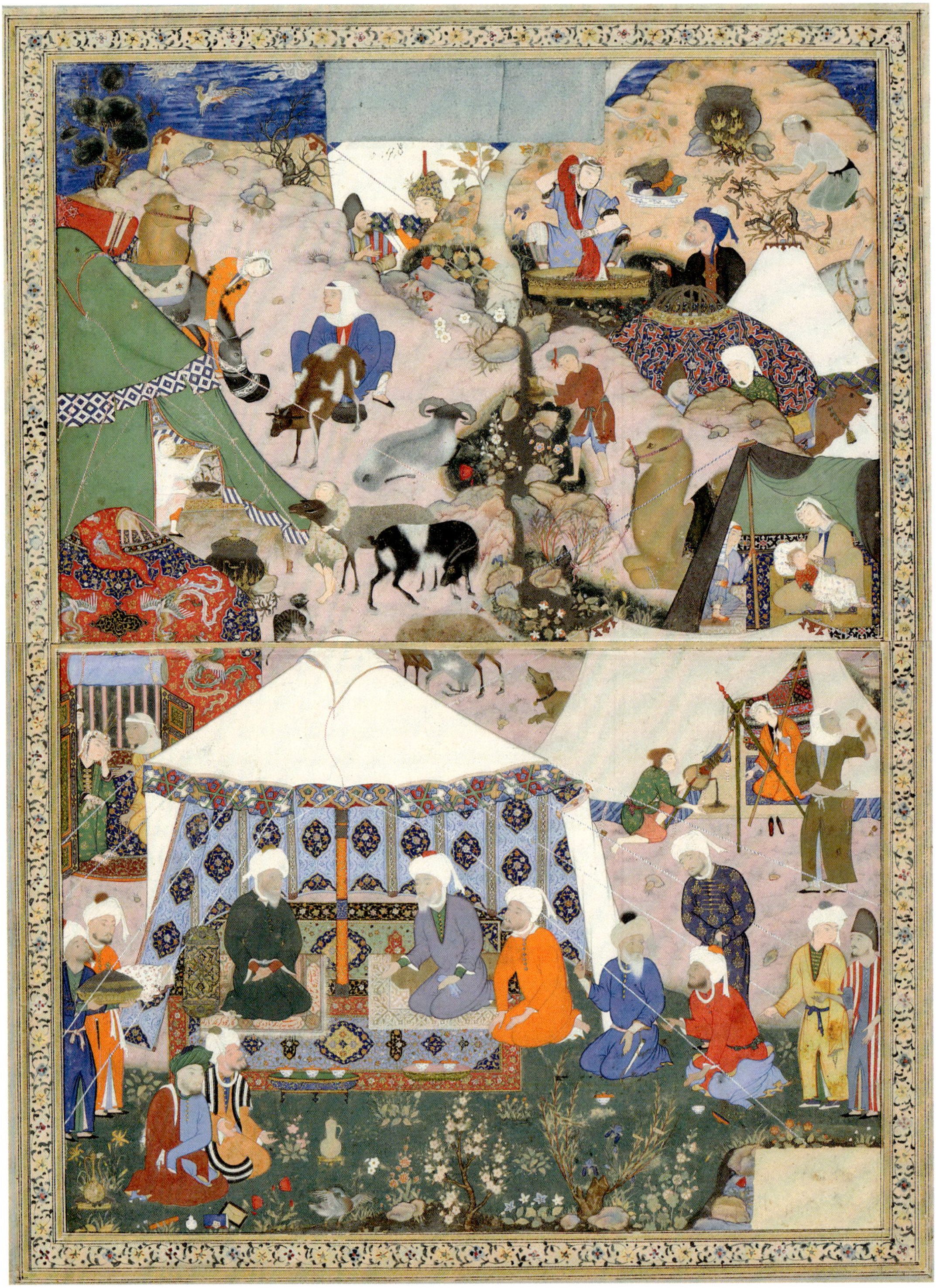

FIGURE 93
A nomadic encampment. From *Leyla and Majnun* by Jami, attributed to Mir Sayyed, Tabriz, 1540.

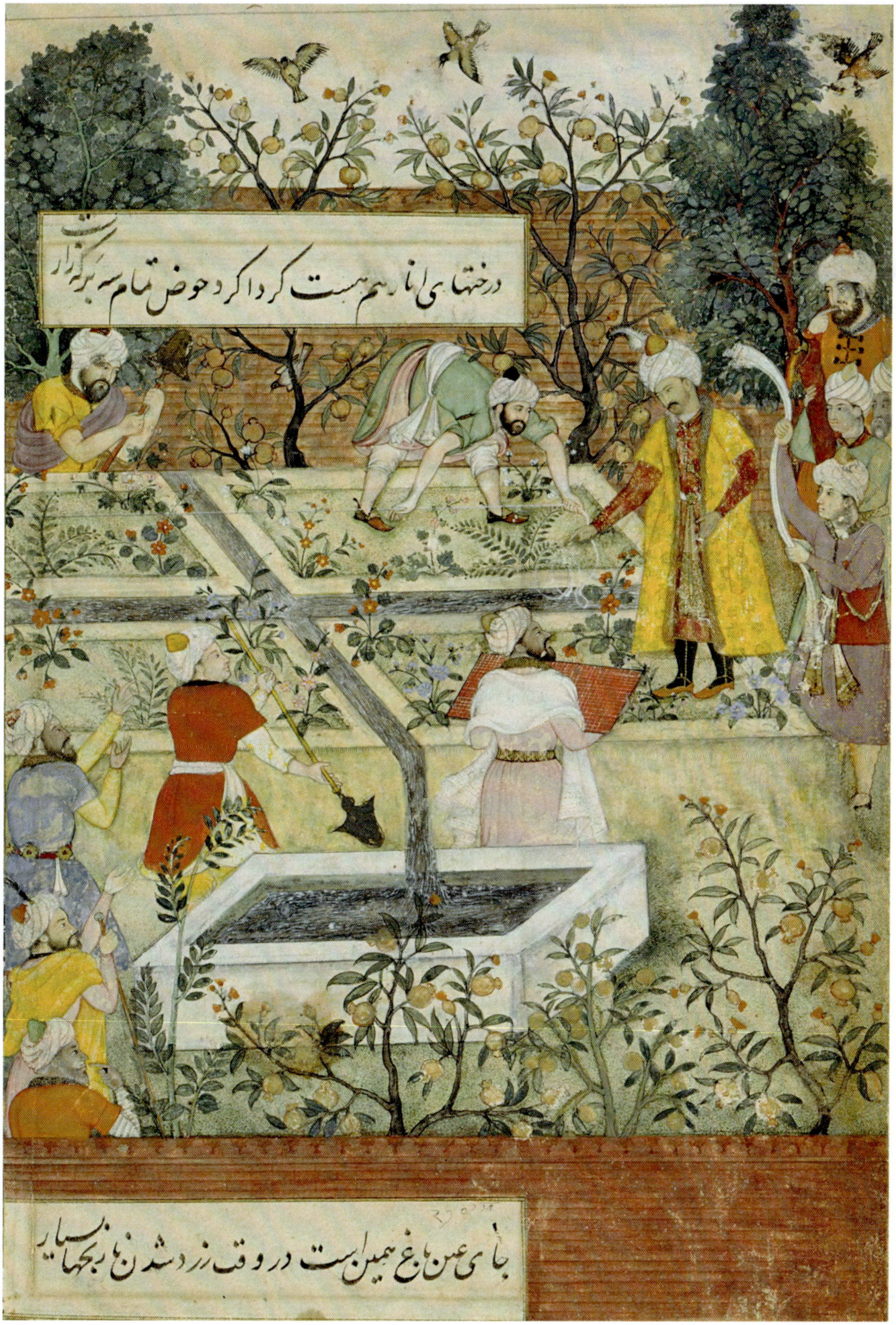

FIGURE 95

Babur supervising the laying out of the Garden of Fidelity (Bagh-e Vafa). From the *Baburnameh,* 1590.

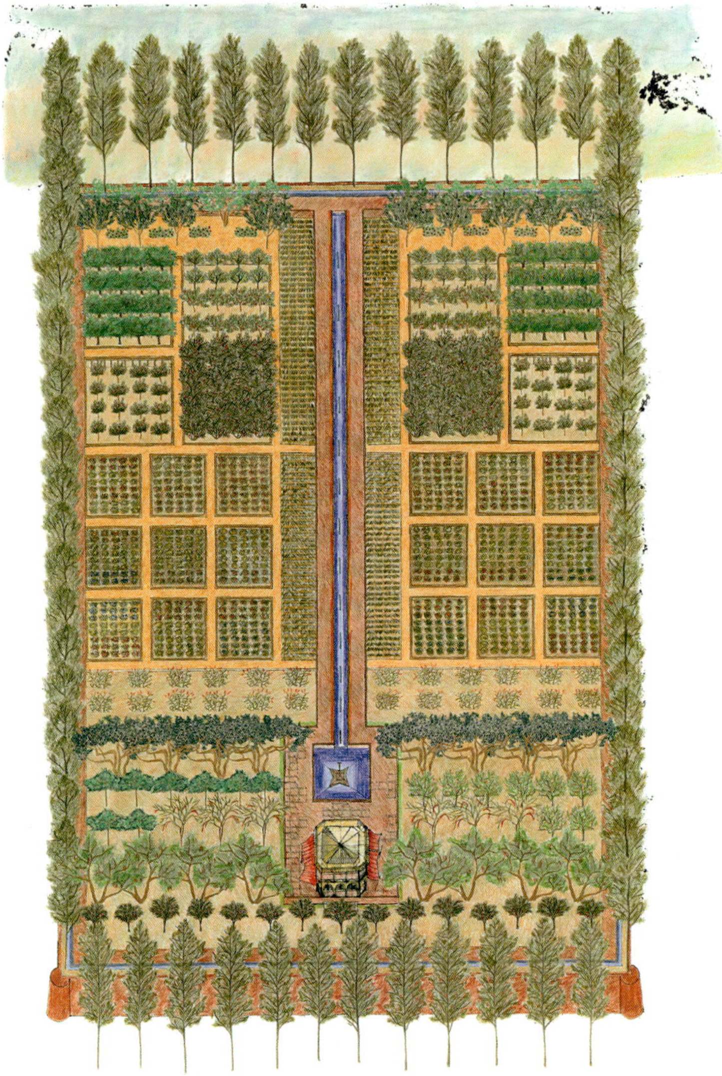

FIGURE 98

A full-colour reconstruction of the garden described in Haravi's *Irshad al-Zira'ah*, including all its prescribed plant species, their colourations and architectural elements in the summer season.

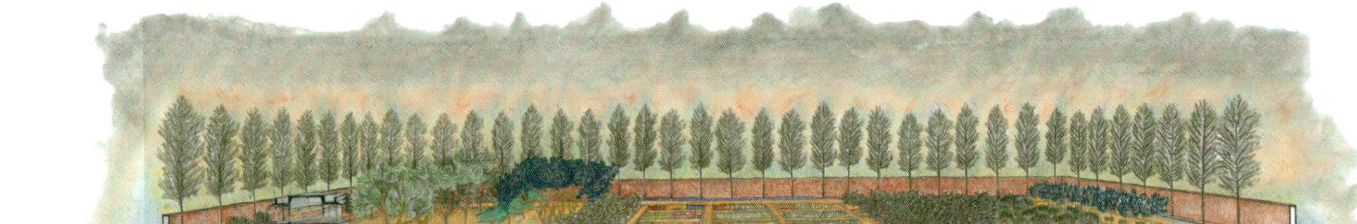

FIGURE 99

The hues seen by the observer walking through the garden environment. A full-colour reconstruction based on Haravi's *Irshad al-Zira'ah*.

Poets, Historians and Travellers

Note: All biographies are drawn from Mohammad Mo'in's *Persian Dictionary* and the *Encyclopedia Iranica*.

POETS

Hakim Awhad-uddin Anvari Abivardi (Abivard, 1126–1189 CE)

A Persian poet in the twelfth century. He was familiar with science, astronomy, and medicine and knew Arabic, Turkish, Hindi and Hebrew. He was a poet at the court of the Seljuk king, Sanjar. A master of poetic panegyrics, most of his poems are in praise of the king and his courtiers. He is an expert in using metaphors and rich vocabulary. His language is close to ordinary speech and is moderately encumbered by rhetoric.

Sheykh Farid-uddin Attar (Nishapur, 1145/46–1221 CE)

A famous Persian poet and Sufi in twelfth-century Khorasan. Despite being an expert in Islamic jurisprudence, Qur'anic exegesis, and Hadith, he originally practised the profession of pharmacy. His interest in Sufism had a huge impact on his poems, which reflect the evolution of the Sufi movement in its experiental, speculative, practical, and educational implications. Attar introduces stories from historical chronicles and collections of anecdotes, while most of his heroes are ascetics and Sufis.

Mowlana Jalal-uddin Muhammad Balkhi (Balkh, 1207–73 CE)

This Persian poet, who lived most of his life in Anatolia (Rum), was a Sufi master and poet whose poems mostly refer to the concept of unity (*tawhid*) between the beloved and lover, and between God and human beings. His major work, the *Masnavi,* uses scenes from everyday life and Qur'anic narratives to explain deep metaphysical concepts. His passion for music, poetry, and dance as a path for reaching God is reflected in his rhythmic poems.

Abu Mansur Muhammad ibn Ahmad Daqiqi Tusi (935/942–76/80 CE)

He lived in the Samanid age. He was probably originally a Zoroastrian and an advocate of Sassanian/Persian cultural trends in the wake of Samanid domination. Daqiqi's main contribution was to create an epic history of Iran which starts with the history of Zoroaster and Gashtasb in order to support the nationalistic tendencies in Persian literature. His book, *Garshaspnameh,* later inspired Ferdowsi to write the *Shahnameh.* A large number of couplets by Daqiqi were included in Ferdowsi's *Shahnameh.*

Amir Khosrow Dehlavi (Patiali, 1253–1325 CE)

A prolific classical poet and musician associated with royal courts of several kings in Mughal India. His poems, which are in Persian, reflect his multicultural identity.

Abul-Hasan 'Ali Farrokhi Sistani (Sistan, 960–1037 CE)

A royal poet who presented his poetry in the Ghaznavid court during the reign of Soltan Mahmud and his brothers and son. Some of his poems have historical value.

Abul Qasem Ferdowsi (Tus, 940–1020 CE)

One of the greatest epic poets of the world and the author of the *Shahnameh,* the national epic of Persia. He started working on the *Shahnameh* after 975, following the death of Daqiqi, another Samanid poet. This book was sponsored by Mansur, the son of Abu Mansur Muhammad, the Samanid king. Although there are no historical accounts regarding his education, his work reflects deep levels of wisdom and understanding in judgement.

'Abbas Forughi Bastami (Karbala, 1798–1857 CE)

A Persian poet in the Qajar period who was introduced to the court of Fath-'Ali Shah when he was in his twenties. He was a close friend of Qa'ani, another famous poet in the Qajar age. Although most his poems followed the style of classical models and are imitations of the metaphors and expressions of Hafez and lyrical mood of Sa'di, they have some original qualities.

Khajeh Shams-uddin Hafez Shirazi (Shiraz, 1315–90 CE)

One of the greatest Persian poets and mystics. His lyrical poems, known as *ghazals*, usually refer to love and mysticism as major themes. Hafez is particularly renowned for his refined and natural use of language and his effective application of rhetorical devices.

Sayyed Ahmad Hatef Esfahani (Isfahan, eighteenth century CE)

An influential poet in the Safavid age. He was one of the first to reject Indian (*Hindi*) style and adopt a poetical idiom based on the principles of early Persian poetry. His lyrics were close to those of Sa'di and Hafez. His poems, despite their simple lyrical structure, reflect his love for the divine.

Nur-uddin 'Abd al-Rahman Jami (Jam, 1414–92 CE)

One of the last great classical Persian poets. As a mystic, he followed the Naqshbani disciple of the Sufi mystical order. His famous epics such as "Salaman and Absal", "Yusof and Zulaykha" and "Leyla and Majnun" reveal his dependence on the Timurid court. Beyond his love stories, there are usually deep and philosophical lessons for Sufis.

Afzal-uddin Khaqani Haqayeqi Shervani (Shirvan, 1100–85 CE)

A Persian poet knowledgeable in the sciences, including philosophy, mathematics and astronomy. His style of writing is quite complex and difficult to comprehend. In addition to the *divan,* he wrote descriptions of his travels to Iraq and *Habsiyeh* after serving a jail term.

Kamal Khojandi (Khojand, fifteenth century CE)

A famous poet in the Jalayirid court. After his immigration from Khojand to Tabriz, he was well received by Soltan Hoseyn Jalayeri, who even built for him a *khanqah* (sufi shrine). He was interested in Hafez and even imitated Sa'di and Hammam Tabrizi.

Muhammad 'Ali Lahiji Esfahani (Gilan, 1692–1766 CE)

A poet and scholar, who was raised at the Safavid court in Isfahan during the reign of Shah Soleyman I. He emigrated to India in 1734 after serving in the Persian army for several years. During this time he made several voyages to the Persian Gulf, Yemen and Arabia. He apparently compiled four *divans*, of which only one remains. Most of his poems were written during his work in the Mughal court of Muhammad Shah in Delhi. His poetic diction is less elaborate than that of his contemporary poets in the Mughal court because he uses simple and direct language.

Abu 'Abdollah Mo'izzi Nishapuri (Nishapur, 1048–1125 CE)

A major poet who worked at the court of four Seljuk kings. His father was also a famous poet at the courts of Alp Arsalan and Malek shah. He dedicated most of his poems to Seljuk kings, viziers and noblemen. His works, which are considered great examples of lyrical poetry, were praised both during and after his life. The principle of his poetry is its clarity. Although he avoided ambiguity or excessive ornamentation, he was capable of invoking a rich imagery in his works.

Muhammad Hoseyn Naziri Nishapuri (Nishapur, 1560–1612 CE)

The first Persian poet to migrate to India, where he joined the court of the great Mughal statesman and literary patron, 'Abd al-Rahim Kan'an, during the reign of Akbar. Compared to other poets of his age, Naziri's poems adhered to earlier standards of poetic diction, and his language is distinguished by a fluent, musical clarity.

Abu Muhammad Elyas Nezami (Ganjeh, 1141–1209 CE)

Probably the greatest romantic epic poet in Persian literature. His famous work is the *Khamseh* (Quintet), a group of five long poems, in which he brought a colloquial and realistic style to the epic.

Abu Mansur Qatran Tabrizi (Tabriz, 1009–72 CE)

A Persian royal poet who presented his poetry to more than thirty patrons in different regional dynasties, making his poems historically valuable. Qatran's poetry is recognized because of a natural use of rhetorical embellishment.

Badr-uddin Qavami Razi (Ray, thirteenth century CE)

A Shi'ite poet who worked in Iraq. While the majority of his poems are in praise of Shi'ite imams and asceticism, his lyrics are considerable in terms of style and quality compared to those of his contemporaries.

Naser ibn Khosrow Qubadiani (Khorasan, 1004–88 CE)

A poet, famous traveller, and the representative of the Fatimid Imams in Khorasan. He had a good knowledge of Arabic, Greek, Turkish and the vernacular languages of India and Sind. His famous book *Safarnameh,* a collection of his travel accounts in the eleventh-century Muslim world, is considered a significant historical document.

'Abdollah Jafar Rudaki (Samarqand, 859–941 CE)

A Persian poet who worked in the Samarqandi court of Nasr ibn Ahmad, the Samanid ruler of Khorasan (not to be mistaken with the present-day state of Khorasan). He was probably the first poet to use the Perso-Arabic alphabet script.

Sheykh Mosleh-uddin Sa'di Shirazi (Shiraz, 1210–91/92 CE)

A famous poet who studied Arabic literature and Islamic sciences at al-Nezamiyyeh of Baghdad (1195–1226 CE). He travelled to Anatolia, Syria, Egypt, Iraq, India and Central Asia during the Mongol invasions. These travels, and his close contacts with ordinary people and Sufi masters, made him very conscious of social issues and helped him have a better understanding of the diversity of cultures in the Muslim world and a profound awareness of the complexities of human existence. Sa'di's best known works are the *Divan, Bustan* (The Orchard), and *Golestan* (The Rose Garden). Most his poems and prose contain aphorisms, advice and humorous reflections. What makes Sa'di different from other Persian poets is his distinction between the spiritual and the practical aspects of life.

Mirza Muhammad 'Ali Sa'eb Tabrizi (Isfahan, 1601–76 CE)

A Persian poet, who presented Persian poetry in the Mughal court in India during the reign of Akbar, Jahangir and Shah Jahan. He is recognized as one of the pioneers of the Indian style in Persian poetry, which is characterized by the deftness of its choice of words, humorous tone, profusion of practical knowledge, supremacy of observation, and its ability to create complex and creative conceits.

Hakim Abul-majd Majdud Ibn Adam Sana'i (Ghazneh, eleventh–twelfth centuries CE)

A Sufi poet acknowledged by Rumi as one of his inspirations. Sana'i's best-known work is *The Walled Garden of Truth*.

Salman Savoji (Saveh, d.1376 CE)

A poet in the Ilkhanid court. While most of his poems are in praise of kings, viziers and courtiers, some poems have historical value because they refer to events in the Ilkhanid age. He is one of the best poets from after the Mongol invasion of Persia. Some of his poems are so similar to those of Hafez that they are even included in the *Divan* of Hafez by mistake.

Nezam-uddin Zakani (Qazvin, fourteenth century CE)

A poet and author who wrote with the financial support of Soltan Oveys Jalayer in Baghdad and Tabriz. He uses scoffing language to criticize aspects of Persian society. His work is noted for its obscene verses. He is probably the most significant satirist in Persian literature.

HISTORIANS

Zahir-uddin Muhammad Jalal-uddin Babur (Farghana, 1483–1531 CE)

Zahir-uddin Muhammad Jalal-uddin Babur, born in the Farghana Valley in Central Asia, was the founder of the Mughal dynasty of India. He claimed direct descent from Genghiz Khan through his mother and from Timur through his father, who gained the throne after several local wars. Although his local language was Chaghatay Turkish, he was deeply under the influence of Persian culture. He was a contemporary of Shah Tahmasp in Persia, who supported Babur's son, Homayun, in regaining power after several years of exile in Persia. The Mughal court was a place for cultural exchange between Persians and Indians in terms of art, architecture and literature. Although the *Baburnameh* is a biography, Babur records some of his observations very cautiously. In that sense, his account is comparable to those of western travellers such as Clavijo, but with a major difference: Babur is not just an ordinary observer, but a decision maker. What makes Babur important in this study is his famous memoirs, the *Baburnameh* (in Chaghatay Turkish), which is not only a precious historical document showing his political progress, but also a highly personalized memoir revealing his special passion for gardens and architecture, an enthusiam he probably inherited from his grandfather, Timur. Unlike most other royal clients who just ordered, Babur participated in designing gardens, supervising the construction process and even complaining about unsuccessful construction details of projects, such as the lack of alignment! Consequently, his memoir, the *Baburnameh*, serves as a valuable historical account which sheds light on the design of gardens and pavilions and their social use, and to some extent clarifies the relationship between the buildings and gardens.[1]

Abul-Fazl Muhammad ibn Hoseyn Beyhaqi (995–1077 CE)

Abul-Fazl Beyhaqi was an officer (clerk) in the courts of Mahmud of Ghazneh (reign 998–1030 CE) and Mas'ud of Ghazneh (reign 1031–41 CE). After studying in Nishapur, he began working in the court of Mahmud under the supervision of Abu Nasr-e Moshkan who was in charge of the office of letters (*divan-e rasa'el*). His famous work is the *Tarikh-e Beyhaqi*, which is written based on his careful observations of contemporary events and happenings, especially those relating to the Ghaznavid court. Beyhaqi was fair-minded in writing history and did not hide his personal interests and emotions about injustice in the Ghaznavid court. He was a companion to Mahmud and Mas'ud of Ghazneh, so the information that he offers is mostly limited to the Ghaznavids' territory, Khorasan, which includes the cities of Ghaznin, Balkh, Herat and Nishapur.

Beyhaqi's book is very sensitive and conscious in terms of cultural behaviour. Although he is not as careful as Khosrow in describing cities and buildings, his book is a good reference for information about the social function of buildings and gardens in the Ghaznavid age, especially in Khorasan. The importance of Beyhaqi's description of gardens is that almost all these gardens were destroyed by the Mughals when they invaded Khorasan, so his is the only extant description dating from before the invasion. There is hardly any historical account in the Persian language that better reflects the complexity of terminology for pavilions than the *Tarikh-e Beyhaqi*. The material discussed in Beyhaqi's text is cross-checked with two of his contemporaries, Farrokhi Sistani and Naser Khosrow.[2]

Qasem Abu Nasr Haravi (Herat, sixteenth century CE)

Qasem Abu Nasr Haravi, also known as Fazil Haravi, was a resident of Herat in the Timurid age. After dreaming about the Sufi Khajeh 'Abdollah Ansari, a famous Sufi, he intended to do something to make God satisfied with him. For divination, he referred to the Qur'an and, since the first verse that he saw was related to horticulture, he determined to write a comprehensive manual and encyclopaedia on herbs, plants and garden products (including fruits, vegetables and even the making of organic food). Haravi's book, which was finished in 1515, became a major reference in horticulture and was widely rewritten and distributed in the Persianate world.[3] This document, unique in the Persian language, illustrates the horticultural significance of gardens. It is also probable that 'Abdi Beyk had access to this manual and used it as a reference in writing his own book.

Jafar ibn-Muhammad ibn Hasan Jafari (Yazd, sixteenth century CE)

Jafar ibn-Muhammad ibn Hasan Jafari was a secretary who worked in the administration in Yazd province in the sixteenth century. There is not much known about Jafari's life but his book, the *Tarikh-e Yazd*, provides information on the governor of Yazd, Amir Chakhmaq, his courtiers, and their achievements such as the construction of gardens, mosques, *madrasas* and other buildings. The city of Yazd was a significant centre in pre-Safavid times and this book is one of the rare documents which clarify the social and political significance of this city. It served as the main reference for several other historical documents, which were written after the Safavids. Despite being a poet and expert in literature, Jafari's writing style seems oversimplified, with a number of technical problems. In the *Tarikh-e Yazd*, Jafari describes several gardens and pavilions in Yazd which no longer exist, and sheds light on their construction and patronage context.[4]

Khajeh Rashid-uddin (thirteenth and fourteenth centuries CE)

Khajeh Rashid-uddin was the vizier of Ghazan Khan (reign 1295–1304 CE), who was the seventh Ilkhanid king. He was a physician, historian and writer who was commissioned to write the history of the Mongols, the *Jami' al-Tavarikh*, or Compendium of Chronicles, which is one of the earliest accounts of world history. This book included the entire history since the time of Adam to the reign of Ghazan Khan, who was also called Muhammad Khodabandeh after his conversion to Islam. His books shed light on the history of the Ilkhanids and to some extent clarify the political role of gardens in the Ilkhanid age.[5]

Hasan Romlu (Qazvin, sixteenth century CE)

Hasan Romlu, born in 1530 or 1531, was the grandson of a Qizilbash chief *amir* in the Safavid army, and the governor of Qazvin and Savoj Bulaq. He trained as a soldier (*qurchi*) and served as a Qizilbash officer in the Safavid court, and even accompanied Shah Tahmasp (1524–76) on most of his expeditions. He wrote a twelve-volume general history of the Timurid and Safavid ages. Because of his military background, he shows a special attention to military and administrative use of gardens, but he does not provide much information on the design of gardens and pavilions.[6]

Adib Shahab-uddin (Shiraz, thirteenth century CE)

Adib Shahab-uddin, also called Sharf-uddin 'Abdollah ibn-Fazl Allah Shirazi (1264–? CE), worked as an officer in the age of Ghazan Khan and Uljaito. Because of his knowledge, he was selected as the secretary and assistant for Rashid-uddin Fazl Allah, a famous Persian vizier in the court of the Ilkhanids. He wrote his book, the *Tarikh-e Vassaf*, in two stages, which were dedicated to Ghazan Khan (1302 CE) and Soltan Uljeito (1312). As the author claims, it is the continuation of another chronicle of Mongol history, the *Tarikh-e Jahangoshay-e Joveyni*. Although this book does not describe gardens in the Ilkhanid age, it explains the military use of gardens and their function for encampments.[7]

'Abdi Beyk Shirazi (Shiraz, 1515–80 CE)

Khajeh Zeyn al-'Abidin 'Ali 'Abdi Beyk Shirazi was probably born in Tabriz and worked as an accountant in the Safavid administration in Ardabil. Although he was a brilliant and creative poet, he was never credited in the history of Persian literature as much as his contemporaries, Mohtasham Kashani and Vahshi Bafqi. His famous book is *Jannat-e 'Adan* (Garden of Eden), commissioned by Shah Tahmasp to celebrate his new palace complex (palace garden) of Sa'adat Abad which was built in the suburb of Ja'far Abad in the east of Qazvin.[8] His work was to some extent neglected by Persian scholars, but it was edited by Abul-Fazl Hashim Awghli Rahimuf and published in Moscow in 1979.[9] Shirazi's book is one of the longest and richest works of descriptive-encomiastic poetry in medieval Persian.

Eskandar Beyk Turkaman (1560–1633 CE)

Eskandar Beyk, known as Monshi, according to himself, began his career as a specialist in rhetoric (*fann-e siyaq va kalam*) but after a while realized that his job did not allow him sufficient opportunities for improvement, so he was hired as a secretary (*monshi*). After some years, he became the Great Secretary (*monshi-ye 'ezam*) and, as the special secretary of Shah 'Abbas, he accompanied him on his trips. His major work, entitled *Tarikh-e 'Alam Aray-e 'Abbasi*, is written in simple language and talks about the emergence of the Safavids and their history until Shah 'Abbas.[10] Iraj Afshar believes the title of Monshi's book is an indirect response to *Tarikh-e 'Alam Aray-e Amini*, which is full of criticism of Shah Isma'il (the founder of the Safavid dynasty) and his cruelty to the Sunnis. The importance of this book is that its author was directly involved in, or at least observed, many of the events he narrates. Although he is usually accurate he is at the same time constrained by his subservience to his patron, the shah. Despite his careful observations and detailed approach, the dates that Monshi provides should be reexamined by researchers and scholars. The value of his work, compared to his predecessors such as Beyhaqi, Joveyni and Rashid-uddin, lies in his attempt to check his sources in order to produce a relatively impartial account and in the considerable amount of information that he includes about personalities outside the narrow circle of the court officials and leading military.[11]

TRAVELLERS

The Anonymous Venetian Merchant (sixteenth century)

Giovan Battista Ramusio, an Italian geographer, compiled an important collection of travel writings, entitled *Navigationi et viaggi* (Navigations and Voyages) between 1550 and 1556 CE. This collection contains his version of Marco Polo's journey and the *Descrittione de l'Africa* (Description of Africa) by the Moor Leo Africanus. Among the narratives he collected is an account of travels by an Italian merchant who was engaged in trading from Damascus and Aleppo to Persia and remained in Persia from 1511–20. Although there have been some attempts to identify this merchant, his name is still unknown. The importance of this account is that it is the only text which provides a brilliant and detailed description of the Hasht Behesht palace complex, built for Uzun Hasan, ruler of the White Sheep Turkman (1466–78), which is located in his new quarter in the immediate outskirts of his capital of Tabriz.[12]

Robert Blair Munro Binning (1814–91)

Robert Blair Munro Binning worked as an administrator in the East India Company Service in Madras. He was familiar with Arabic, Persian and Hindi and collected historic manuscripts. He travelled to Ceylon and Persia in 1847–49, which he described in his book *Journal of Two Years' Travel in Persia, Ceylon, etc.*

Jean-Baptiste Chardin (Lyon, 1643–1713 CE)

Jean Chardin (Sir John Chardin), raised in a French Protestant family, was a jeweller who travelled extensively in Asia and wrote the most detailed foreign account of eighteenth-century Persia. In August 1671, he began his journey to Persia through Smyrna, Constantinople, Caucasia, Mingrelia and Georgia. On reaching the capital of the Safavids, Isfahan, in June 1673, he travelled for four years within Persia, and then visited India before returning to Europe in 1680. As a jeweller, he received the royal patronage of Shah 'Abbas II (d.1666) and his son Safi Mirza. This employment enabled him to become familiar with the Persian court and its affairs, while remaining in close contact with Persian society and culture. After his return to Europe, because of the restrictions for Protestants in France, he moved to London, where he was appointed jeweller to the court of Charles II. He began publishing a memoir of his travel in Iran since 1686, but it was not until 1711 (two years before his death) that the complete work was published.[13]

Although Chardin was not fully conversant with all aspects of Persian life and was more interested in economic and political issues, his information on Safavid Persia outranks all other Western writers in range, depth, accuracy and judiciousness. He provides very specific information regarding the buildings and gardens that he visited and shows a special interest in society and material culture. This can be seen from the way that he estimates the sizes of places through which he passed, usually in terms of the number of houses or the number of people.[14] Moreover, his familiarity with the Persian language helped him meet and interact with ordinary people. Similarly, his direct access to the Safavid court allowed him to describe contemporary politics and administration, albeit with a few mistakes or exaggerations. His notes, especially those on gardens and pavilions, are regarded as reliable witness to the culture, architecture and politics of Safavid Persia.[15] Chardin not only played a significant role in introducing Persia to westerners, but opened new doors to the eastern world. He stood at the opening of a new era, when the West was just beginning to realize its material supremacy over the ancient East, and he had much to say about relations between Europeans and the East that can still be pondered with profit.[16]

Ruy González de Clavijo (Madrid, d.1412 CE)

Ruy González de Clavijo, a nobleman of Madrid, was the chamberlain and ambassador of the Spanish king, Henry III of Castile, to the court of Timur. He travelled from the Black Sea coast of Turkey to Trabazon, from Armenia and Azerbaijan to Samarqand (Central Asia) and then to Ray (Persia). During his trip, he was accompanied by Timur's ambassador, Muhammed al-Kazi, and two of the king's guards. He arrived in Samarqand on 8 September 1404 and spent a couple of months in Timur's court. Despite his lack of success in getting any message from Timur to the Spanish king, he and his companions were forced by Timur's imminent death to leave Samarqand on 21 November 1404.[17]

Clavijo's diary of the journey, which recorded his observations during his trip, was originally published in 1582 and later in English in 1859.[18] His notes on the court and the royal gardens, buildings and tents are not only the most detailed descriptions of Timur's court by a westerner, but also a unique model of this type of writing among travellers' records in the Persianate world. Clavijo provides a detailed account of the cultural behaviour and the social interactions in the Timurid court, but also of the design of pavilions (as tents or buildings) and even their placement in gardens. Moreover, his contact with Timur's army gave him the opportunity to describe the royal encampments in gardens. The information that Clavijo provides is very comprehensive and is almost enough to assemble a visual image of the Timurid garden. In addition to his comprehensive descriptions of gardens, Clavijo talks about different forms of pavilions: raised platforms, tents, palaces or houses inside the gardens.

Pietro Della Valle (Rome, 1586–1652 CE)

Pietro Della Valle, raised in a wealthy noble family in Rome, and one of the most outstanding travellers in the renaissance period, took a long trip in the eastern world during the seventeenth century. After a vow to visit the Holy Land, he left Venice by boat on 8 June 1614 and reached Constantinople, where he stayed for one year, learned Turkish and a little Arabic, and then journeyed on to Alexandria,[19] Cairo and Mount Sinai with nine companions. Eventually he arrived in Jerusalem on 8 March 1616, from where he went on to Persia through Damascus, Aleppo and Baghdad. There he visited Hamadan and reached Shah 'Abbas's camp in his garden in Farah Abad (Mazandaran) in the summer of 1618. Being well received at court and treated as the shah's special guest helped Della Valle to record his unique observations of the court. His marriage in 1616 to Maani, daughter of a Nestorian Catholic father and an Armenian mother, inspired him to meet Shah 'Abbas I, who had a good reputation for his religious tolerance. Moreover, during his stay in Isfahan, which lasted about three years, he tried to strike an alliance with the Cossacks in a renewed war against the Ottomans, who were Europe's main enemy in the seventeenth century.

After visiting Isfahan, Persepolis and Shiraz, he went to India. In South India, he visited the King Vekatappa Nayaka and Vithal Shenoy, the chief administrators of those territories. On his return trip, he went to Muscat in January 1625, and then visited Basra, Aleppo and Cyprus before reaching Rome on 28 March 1626. He sent regular letters to his friend, Mario Schipano, a professor of medicine in Naples, who had been the main source of inspiration for his trip to the East. These letters were slightly edited and published by his four sons only two years before his death. Aside from the immediacy of these letters, Della Valle displayed excellent narrative and descriptive skills and a genuinely scholarly breadth of learning. Despite occasional arrogance and pretentiousness, Valle was an intelligent and high-spirited person. According to Gurney, he showed a gradual appreciation of different aspects of Persian culture, culminating in his deep involvement in the Safavid court and Persian society, worlds that few foreigners ever reached. Unlike other travellers in Persia, Della Valle belonged to a wealthy family and had no need for financial support, so he was not bound by the demands of any particular patron.[20]

Samuel Gottlieb Gmelin (Tübingen, 1744–1774 CE)

Gmelin, who was born at Tübingen in Germany, earned his medical degree in 1763 at the young age of 18 from the University of Leiden. In order to conduct research on the natural history of the Russian empire, he travelled on the Don and the Volga, and to the western and eastern coasts of the Caspian Sea. He carefully described plants and animals and the lands of the northern regions of Iran. He died at the age of 29 while being held hostage in the Caucasus. Gmelin, who travelled to northern Persia, visited and described Safavid palaces in northern regions of Iran decades after their splendour in the Safavid age.[21]

Thomas Herbert (York, 1606–82 CE)

Sir Thomas Herbert was born in York, England, in a minor aristocratic family interested in business affairs. He accompanied the royal embassy of Sir Dodmore Cotton from King Charles I to the court of the Safavid Shah ʿAbbas I in 1626–29. On his return he published the first English account of Persia. His writing is modest rather than profound, has a sense of wonderment, and is lacking in conceit: Herbert believes truth and simplicity are the souls of history. Herbert himself claims that he did not want to publish his notes because he thought they were rude and undigested notions, despite being the simple truth, but that his friends forced him to it.[22] He shows great interest, among other things, in the dangers for the sailors, the changing climatic conditions, the indications of fate reflected in the ruins he saw, especially of Persepolis, and the hardships of travel.[23] He admired Persian entertainers with their feats of strength and agility and was very interested in the pageantry of official occasions, the gorgeous clothing, and the table services of gold plate at banquets.[24] His description of the social culture within the court of Shah ʿAbbas seems deep and reliable. Despite his youth, Herbert was very well educated. Sykes (1867–1945), an expert on travel accounts in Persia, believes Herbert's educational background is reflected in the lengthy and detailed way in which he describes things, cultures and events.[25]

Ibn Battuta (1304–77 CE)

Abu ʿAbdollah Muhammad Ibn Battuta was a Moroccan traveller who visited large parts of the Persianate world in the fourteenth century. He was a jurisprudent in Sunni Islamic law (*fiqh*) and also a judge (*qadi*). In his accounts, which were based on his several travels into Africa and Asia, he provided a great deal of information on elements of architecture, and agricultural and cultural activities. In his trips within Persia, he visited several sufis and religious figures. His writings provide precise information on the geography and history of the medieval Arab world. Although he does not illustrate gardens and pavilions, his descriptions of *ordu* are very original and useful. His account, which was recorded by a scholar named Ibn Juzayy after the approval of the Moroccan king, was referred to as *Rihla* (journey).[26] While some of his comments and observations seem to some extent fictional, there is no other comprehensive historical document from that time that could prove or reject Ibn Battuta's reports or claims.

Michele Membre (Venice, sixteenth century CE)

Michele Membre, a Venetian merchant, was sent to the Safavid court (1539–42 CE) to offer Shah Tahmasp an anti-Ottoman alliance. Although his mission was declined by Shah Tahmasp, he was well received in the court, mainly because of his ability to speak Turkish and a little Persian, which allowed him to make friends. Membre's book is a travel narrative with a great deal of eyewitness detail and mostly devoid of ambassadorial generalities. It provides useful information on the cultural behaviour in Shah Tahmasp's court and the use of gardens and pavilions as mobile structures.

Notes

Chapter 1 Introduction

1. The most famous of these gardens, which was described by the Greek historian and geographer Strabo in 22 CE, are the hanging gardens of Babylon. However, the tendency for orientalists to mythologize these gardens, surrounding them with nonfactual data and turning them into exotic icons of the ancient world, has affected their fair analysis in history.
2. Curl divides pavilions into three categories: outdoor structures (a summer-house or other, often ornamental, building in a park, fair, or garden, used for shelter and entertainment); exhibition tent (a large tent or other temporary structure used for displaying or exhibiting things); and annex (a detached building that forms part of the complex of a hospital or other large public building). J.S. Curl, *Oxford Dictionary of Architecture* (Oxford University Press, 1999), p.486.
3. For example, the *chaharbagh* design is normally thought of as a fourfold garden in the shape of a cross; however, in the Hezarjarib garden in Isfahan, the *chaharbagh* design involved four parallel planted plots located on four different levels. In this garden, the role of the pavilion, which was located at one end, on the highest level, was to work as a visual centre for these four parallel terraces.
4. Arthur Upham Pope and Phyllis Ackerman, 'Garden', in Arthur Upham Pope and Phyllis Ackerman (eds), *A Survey of Persian Art from Prehistoric Times to the Present*, II (London: Oxford University Press, 1939), pp.1427–45.
5. Donald N. Wilber, *Persian Gardens and Garden Pavilions* (Tokyo: Charles E. Tuttle Company, 1962).
6. Richard Ettinghausen, 'Introduction', in Richard Ettinghausen (ed.), *The Islamic Garden* (Washington DC: Dumbarton Oaks, 1976), pp.1–10.

7. David Stronach, 'Parterres and Stone Watercourses at Pasargadae: Notes on the Achaemenid Contribution to the Evolution of Garden Design', *Journal of Garden History*, 14 (1994), pp.3–12.
8. After visiting the Cyrus the Younger's garden at Sardis, Lysander praised the beauty of the trees, the evenness of their planting in straight regular rows, the neat way the corners were made, the prettiness of it all, and, moreover, the many sweet odours. "'All these things, Lysander, I measured out and ordered myself, and there are some of them that I even planted myself,' Cyrus said, and Lysander answered, 'Do I admire; I admire the beauty of the whole, but far more, O Cyrus, do I praise the mind that has designed and ordered it.'" A.J. Arberry, *The Legacy of Persia* (Oxford: Clarendon Press, 1953), p.161.
9. Elizabeth Moynihan, *Paradise as a Garden in Persia and Mughal India* (New York: George Braziller, 1978).
10. James Wescoat Jr, 'The Islamic Garden: Issues for Landscape Research', *Environmental Design: Journal of the Islamic Environmental Design Research Centre*, 1 (1986), pp.10–19.
11. Ibid. p.11.
12. Magdy Tewfik Saad, 'Traditional Urban Gardens in Identified Muslim Environments', *Environmental Design: Journal of the Islamic Environmental Design Research Centre*, 1 (1986), pp.28–31.
13. Bernard O'Kane, 'From Tents to Pavilions: Royal Mobility and Persian Palace Design', *Ars Orientalis*, 23 (1993), pp.249–69.
14. Lisa Golombek, 'The Gardens of Timur: New Perspectives', *Muqarnas*, 12 (1995), pp.137–47.
15. Jonas Benzion Lehrman, *Earthly Paradise: Garden and Courtyard in Islam* (New York: Thames and Hudson, 1980).
16. Hamid Shirvani, 'The Philosophy of Persian Garden Design: The Sufi Tradition', *Landscape Journal*, 4/1 (1981), pp.23–29.
17. Irfan Habib, 'Economic and Social Aspects of Mughal Gardens', in James L. Wescoat and J. Wolschke-Bulmahn (eds.), *Mughal Gardens: Sources, Places, Representations, and Prospects* (Washington DC: Dumbarton Oaks, 1996), p.134.
18. Ibid. p.132.
19. Yotam Tepper, 'The Rose and the Balsam: The Garden as a Source of Perfume and Medicine', in Michel Conan (ed.), *Middle East Garden Traditions: Unity and Diversity* (Washington DC: Dumbarton Oaks, 2007), pp.21–39.
20. Mahvash Alemi, 'Princely Safavid Gardens: Stage for Rituals of Imperial Display and Political Legitimacy', in Michel Conan (ed.), *Middle East Garden Traditions: Unity and Diversity* (Washington DC: Dumbarton Oaks, 2007), pp.113–38.
21. Dede Fairchild Ruggles, *Islamic Gardens and Landscapes* (Philadelphia: University of Pennsylvania Press, 2008), p.106.

Chapter 2 The Garden and Pavilion in Near Eastern Pre-Islamic Texts, the Qur'an and Persian Poetry

1. Bruce Lincoln looks at this topic though a different lens. He stresses the concept of "happiness for mankind" as one of the principles of Zoroastrian Achaemenids. This happiness involves the presence of water, plants and animals, and all species. The Persian paradise, according to him, was a complex of two simultaneous ideas: the memory of the world as a creation of Ahura Mazda and a promise that its perfection will be restored and guaranteed. Bruce Lincoln, 'A La Recherche du Paradis Perdu', *Journal of History of Religions*, 43, no.2, p.153.
2. Allan G. Johnson, *Blackwell Dictionary of Sociology* (Cambridge, MA: Blackwell Publications, 2000).
3. Since some remaining parts of this epic are translations in Old Babylonian and some other fragments from Hittite translation, historians are not sure about its date.
4. Sumer developed in part of the plain laid down by the Euphrates and Tigris Rivers. The earliest settlements in Sumer date from 4500 BCE.
5. The earliest Sumerian versions of the epic date from as early as the third dynasty of Ur (2100–2000 BCE), which is about 400 years after the supposed reign of Gilgamesh, who is now thought to have been a historical figure. James B. Pritchard, *The Ancient Near East* (Princeton: Princeton University Press, 1958), p.40.
6. The goddess of Ishtar, who represents the planet Venus, is also an omnipresent figure in the *Epic of Gilgamesh*. She appears also on the Uruk vase, one of the most famous ancient Mesopotamian artefacts. Pritchard, ibid.
7. "One league city, one league palm gardens, one league lowlands, the open area (?) of the Ishtar Temple, three leagues and the open area (?) of Uruk it (the wall) encloses." Tablet I, *Epic of Gilgamesh*, translated by Maureen Gallery Kovacs, electronic edition by Wolf Carnahan, 1998.
8. Ibid. Tablet V.
9. Ibid. Tablet IX.
10. Pritchard, p.31.
11. The epic names three archaic gods: Apsu, the fresh water, Tiamat, the salt water, and their son Mummu, the mist. The noise of the other created gods provokes Apsu into destroying them. Ea, who is the most powerful god at that time, kills both Apsu and Mummu, and then generates a son, Marduk, who is more powerful than himself. When Tiamat decides to take revenge for the death of her husband, her power grows. She joins with some of the other gods to elevate Kingo, giving him supreme dominion, but Marduk is selected as a champion against Tiamat, and also gains great power. He defeats Tiamat, and forms the world from her dead body. The gods who sided with Tiamat are initially forced to work in the service of the other gods. When Marduk decides to create mankind from his blood, he frees all of them. Babylon is established as the residence of the chief gods. In the end, all gods agree on the kingship of Marduk and hail him with fifty names.
12. *Enuma Elish*, translated by N.K. Sandars, Tablet I. (http://www.angelfire.com/nt/Gilgamesh/enuma.html).

13. Ibid. Tablet I.
14. Ibid. Tablet VII.
15. Pritchard, p.138.
16. Hammurabi, *The Code of Hammurabi,* translated by L.W. King (1910), edited by Richard Hooker, code no.27 (available at http://www.sacred-texts.com/ane/ham/ham05.htm). We can find more examples in the following codes: "If any one buy the field, garden, and house of a chieftain, man, or one subject to quit-rent, his contract tablet of sale shall be broken (declared invalid) and he loses his money. The field, garden, and house return to their owners." Ibid. Code no.37. "If any one fence in the field, garden, and house of a chieftain, man, or one subject to quit-rent, furnishing the palings therefor; if the chieftain, man, or one subject to quit-rent return to field, garden, and house, the palings which were given to him become his property." Ibid. Code no.41.
17. Ibid. Code no.30.
18. Ibid. Code no.165.
19. Ibid. Code no.60.
20. Ibid. Code no.64. There are other similar rules such as this one: "If the gardener has not completed the planting of the field, leaving one part unused, this shall be assigned to him as his." Ibid. Code no.61.
21. Ibid. Code no.62.
22. Ibid. Code no.65.
23. While the explicit reference to four rivers suggests a topology suggestive of a *chaharbagh,* the direct connection remains complex and elusive. The individual books that comprise the Pentateuch, including Genesis, Exodus, Leviticus and Deuteronomy, were not written by one hand at a single time.
24. M. Jack Suggs, Katherine Doob Sakenfeld and James R. Mueller, *The Oxford Study Bible* (New York: Oxford University Press, 1992), p.12 (2:10).
25. Ibid. (2:9).
26. Morgenstern explains the origins of the *Story of Genesis* in the Babylonian creation myth (*Enuma Elish*). Julian Morgenstern, 'The Sources of the Creation Story – Genesis 1:1–2:4', *American Journal of Semitic Languages and Literatures,* 36, no.3 (April 1920), pp.169–212.
27. Suggs, Sakenfeld and Mueller, p.12 (2:1).
28. Ibid. (2:4–6).
29. Ibid. (2:8).
30. The Garden of Eden is called in Genesis the Garden of Yahweh, the God of Israel, and, in Ezekiel, the Garden of God. The term Eden is probably derived from the Akkadian word *edinu,* borrowed from the Sumerian *eden,* meaning 'plain'. *Britannica,* online version, 2008.
31. J.M. Hiesberger (ed.), footnote, Genesis 2:8, p.5, in *Catholic Bible* (New York: Oxford University Press, 1995).
32. Jeremy Black and Anthony Green, *Gods, Demons, and Symbols* (Texas: University of Texas Press, 2003), p.73.
33. Suggs, Sakenfeld and Mueller, pp.12–13 (2:11–14).

34. Until recently scholars found it impossible to agree either about the time or place in which Zoroastrianism flourished. Mary Boyce, *History of Zoroastrianism* (Leiden: E.J. Brill, 1975). A similar challenge occurs when dating early Zoroastrian texts such as *Yasna* and *Vendidad*, though there is less doubt in the dates of the Pahlavid texts compiled during and after the Sassanid period. William W. Malandra, 'Zoroastrianism', *Encyclopedia Iranica*, 2005.
35. Fargard 8 ('Vendidad', *Sacred Books of the East*, translated by James Darmesteter, American Edition, 1898, online version: http://www.avesta.org).
36. Fargard 3:23.
37. *Yasna* 4:21.
38. Fargard 20:4.
39. *Yasna* 17:12.
40. *Yasna* 2:16.
41. *Yasna* 10:4.
42. "Thither thou shalt bring the seeds of every kind of tree, of the highest of size and sweetest of odour on this earth; thither thou shalt bring the seeds of every kind of fruit, the best of savour and sweetest of odour. All those seeds shalt thou bring, two of every kind, to be kept inexhaustible there, so long as those men shall stay in the Vara." Fargard 2:28.
43. "Whereon grow the seeds of my plants of every kind by hundreds, by thousands, by hundreds of thousands." Fargard 5:19.
44. Ibid.
45. Fargard 5:13.
46. *Yasna* 37:1. Another example is: "This I ask Thee, tell me truly, Ahura. Who upholds the earth beneath and the firmament from falling? Who the waters and the plants? Who yoked swiftness to winds and clouds? Who is, O Mazda, creator of Good Thought?" *Yasna* 44:4.
47. Fargard 11:1.
48. Fargard 17:5.
49. *Yasna* 9:71.
50. Fargard 8:3.
51. *Yasna* 16:9.
52. *Yasna* 65:5.
53. *Yasna* 42:1.
54. See Moynihan, p.3.
55. William W. Malandra explains: "The earth was divided into six concentric continents surrounding the central continent, where 'the Iranian expanse' was located. At the centre of the earth was the cosmic mountain, the Alborz, which acted as the axis mundi. At its southern flank was the sacred sea, in the middle of which grew the Tree of Life. Over the earth and expanse of sky arched the stone vault of heaven beyond which was the realm of the Infinite Lights, and the heavenly abode, and the House of Song. Below the earth was the realm of Infinite Darkness. The entire earth rested upon and was

surrounded by the waters of chaos. Fresh water flowed down in the river goddess the Strong Moist, into the Vouru-kaša, and from it the various rivers of the world flowed, accumulating pollutants in their courses, to the salt sea, the Filterer, from which the hydrological cycle repeated itself." Malandra, 'Zoroastrianism'.

56. *The Book of Arda Viraf: The Pahlavi Text*, prepared by Destur Hoshangji Jamaspji, translated by Martin Haug (Bombay: Govt. Central Book Depot, 1872).
57. Mary Boyce, 'Middle Persian Literature', *Iranistik II, Literatur I* (Leiden, 1968), p.48.
58. Her article in Persian is available from: http://www.nimrooz.net/iranistics/amouzgar/ardavirafnameh.htm.
59. *The Book of Arda Viraf*, Part 3 (Heaven), 10:8–15.
60. Pahlavid texts are much more specific in terms of religious instructions, and to some extent political. These texts were compiled by Zoroastrian clerics in the Sassanid age to combat the increasing power of Christian Church, especially in the western borders of Persian territories.
61. Malandra writes: "A significant question, for which there are few definitive answers, is to what extent were Judaism and later Christianity indebted to Zoroastrianism for ideas that surfaced beginning in the fifth century BCE but persisted well into the Parthian period, ideas such as a trans-historical *masiaḥ*, heaven and hell, and a day of judgment." Malandra, 'Zoroastrianism' (online version). In another article, Jal Dastur C. Pavry explains that the development of Manichaeism is to some extent the consequence of the tight rivalry between Zoroastrian and Christian clergies. Jal Dastur Pavry, 'Manichaeism: A Rival of Zoroastrianism and Christianity', *Journal of Religion*, 17, no.2, pp.161–69.
62. Translated by E.W. West, from *Sacred Books of the East*, 18 (Oxford University Press, 1882).
63. Dastur Manushchihr Goshnajaman was a Zoroastrian high priest of Pars and Kerman.
64. Dastur Firoze M. Kotwal and James Boyd, *A Guide to the Zoroastrian Religion* (Harvard University Press, 1982).
65. Dadistan-e Dinik, 6:7 (from http://www.sacred-texts.com).
66. Ibid., 20:3.
67. Similarly, in Islamic texts, heaven is divided into seven levels.
68. Ibid., 24:6.
69. Ibid., 26:2.
70. Ibid., 31:4.
71. *Aban Yasht* (Hymn to the Waters) in Darmesteter, 13:101.
72. Ibid., 13:102.
73. *Frawardin Yasht* (Hymn to the Guardian Angels), in Darmesteter, 13:3.
74. *Ashi Yasht* (Hymn to Ashi), in Darmesteter, 17:60.
75. *The Book of Arda Viraf*, 11:1–4.
76. *Ram Yasht* in Darmesteter, 15:19.
77. 'The Star Track', *The Book of Arda Viraf*, Chapter 7.
78. "When I put forth the third footstep on Huvarsht, there where good deeds are received with hospi-

tality, there I arrived. There is the radiance which they call the highest of the highest; and I saw the pious on thrones and carpets made of gold; and they were the people whose brightness was like unto the brightness of the sun." Ibid., 9:1–4.

79. Ibid., 14:14–18.
80. "And the throne of the righteous in heaven and the supreme heaven is the reward he obtains first, and is his until the resurrection, when even the world becomes pure and undisturbed; he is himself unchangeable thereby, but through the resurrection he obtains what is great and good and perfect, and is eternally glorious." Ibid., 25.
81. Ibid., 15:9–15
82. Ibid., 15:16.
83. *Ram Yasht*, 15:2.
84. The *Bundahishn,* which is in the Middle Persian language, develops ideas which allude to *Avesta.*
85. *Greater Bundahishn,* translated by Behramgore Tehmuras Anklesaria (digital edition by Joseph H. Peterson, 2002), 13–14.
86. *Denkard,* Book Five, edited by Peshotan Dastur Behramjee Sanjana, 1900 (digital edition by Joseph H. Peterson, 1998).
87. C.H. Rempis, 'Die Metrik als sprachwissenschafliches Hilfsmittel im Altiranischen', *ZDMG cv* (1955), pp.64–69.
88. Mary Boyce, *Zoroastrians: Their Religious Beliefs and Practices* (New York: Routledge, 1979), pp.209–11.
89. "And what will explain to thee what *'Illiyun* is? (There is) a Register (fully) inscribed, To which bear witness those Nearest (to Allah)." *The Meaning of the Holy Qur'an,* translated by Abdullah Yusuf Ali (Amana Publications, 2004), 83:19–21.
90. Ibid., 25:15.
91. Ibid., 18:107.
92. Ibid., 30:15.
93. Annemarie Schimmel, in R. Ettinghausen (ed.), 'The Celestial Garden in Islam', in *The Islamic Garden,* edited by R. Ettinghausen (Washington DC: Dumbarton Oaks, 1976), p.19.
94. Qur'an, 41:70.
95. Ibid., 13:23.
96. Ibid., 39:73.
97. "And enclosed Gardens, dense with lofty trees." Ibid., 80:30.
98. Ibid., 44:51.
99. Ibid., 53:14–15.
100. The concept of door keeper of paradise (*ridhvan*) might have origins in the Zoroastrian text, *Vendidad*: "Of Paradise, as Vohu-mano (Good Thought) is the doorkeeper of heaven." Fargard 19:31.
101. "And enclosed Gardens, dense with lofty trees." Qur'an, 80:30.
102. "They will recline on Carpets whose inner linings will be of rich brocade: the Fruit of the Gardens will be Near (and easy of reach)". Ibid., 55:54. "Reclining on green Cushions and rich Carpets of beauty."

Ibid., 55:76

103. "And Cushions set in rows." Ibid., 88:15.

104. Ibid., 18:31. The concept of rivers which are running underneath (*taht*) gardens is mentioned repeatedly in the Qur'an. Here are some other examples: "But those who believe and do deeds of righteousness We shall soon admit to gardens with rivers flowing beneath their eternal home; therein shall they have companions pure and holy; We shall admit them to shades cool and ever deepening." Ibid., 4:57. "But those who believe and work righteousness will be admitted to Gardens beneath which rivers flow to dwell therein for aye with the leave of their Lord: their greeting therein will be: 'Peace!'" Ibid., 14:23.

105. Ibid., 14:23.

106. Ibid., 47:15.

107. Ibid., 15:48.

108. Ibid., 69:22.

109. Ibid., 3:133.

110. "Gardens of Eternity which they will enter: beneath them flow (pleasant) rivers; they will have therein all that they wish: thus doth Allah reward the righteous." Ibid., 16:31.

111. "In the case of those who say 'Our Lord is Allah' and further stand straight and steadfast, the angels descend on them (from time to time); 'Fear ye not!' (they suggest) 'nor grieve! but receive the Glad Tidings of the Garden (of Bliss) the which ye were promised!'" Ibid., 41:30.

112. Ibid., 39:20.

113. The raised thrones from which a good sight is guaranteed are mentioned in several verses. Here are some examples: "And on Thrones (of Dignity) raised high." Ibid., 56:34. "Reclining in the (Garden) on raised thrones they will see there neither the sun's (excessive heat) nor (the moon's) excessive cold." Ibid., 76:13. "On Thrones (of Dignity) will they command a sight (of all things)." Ibid., 83:23. "Therein will be Thrones (of dignity) raised on high." Ibid., 88:13.

114. "Pharaoh said: 'O Chiefs! no god do I know for you but myself; therefore, O Haman! Light me a (kiln to bake bricks) out of clay, and build me a lofty palace, that I may mount up to the god of Moses, but as far as I am concerned, I think (Moses) is a liar!'" Ibid., 28:38.

115. "Pharaoh said: 'O Haman! Build me a lofty palace (*sarh*), that I may attain the ways and means.'" Ibid., 40:36.

116. Ibid., 27:44.

117. Ibid., 26:129.

118. "Companions restrained (as to their glances), in (goodly) pavilions." Ibid., 55:72.

119. "Say, 'The truth is from your Lord'. Let him who will believe, and let him who will, reject (it): for the wrong-doers We have prepared a Fire whose (smoke and flames), like the walls and roof of a tent, will hem them in: if they implore relief they will be granted water like melted brass, that will scald their faces, how dreadful the drink! How uncomfortable a couch to recline on!" Ibid., 18:29.

120. In the Qur'an, the word *bina'* is used for buildings in general, but it does not refer to structures in gardens.

121. "And God sets forth, as an example to those who believe the wife of Pharaoh. Behold she said: 'O my Lord! Build for me, in nearness to Thee, a mansion in the Garden, and save me from Pharaoh and his doings, and save me from those that do wrong'; God has struck a similitude for the believers – the wife of Pharaoh, when she said, 'My Lord, build for me a house in Paradise, in Thy presence, and deliver me from Pharaoh and his work, and do Thou deliver me from the people of the evildoers.'" Ibid., 66:11.
122. Ibid., 9:72.
123. Ibid., 76:13.
124. Ibid., 2:255.
125. Ibid., 9:129.
126. Ibid., 12:100.
127. Ibid., 10:3.
128. Ibid., 11:7.
129. Ibid., 18:31.
130. Ibid., 76:13.
131. Ibid., 83:23.
132. William L. Hanaway, 'Paradise on Earth: The Terrestrial Garden in Persian Literature', in Richard Ettinghausen (ed.), *The Islamic Garden*, (Dumbarton Oaks, 1976), pp.43–67. Hanaway focused on the physical appearance of the garden and the relationship between man and garden.
133. The only exception is 'Abdi Beyk's description of Shah Tahmasp's garden in Qazvin, which is discussed in Chapter 4.
134. 'Ali Akbar Dehkhoda, *Persian Comprehensive Dictionary*, 3 (Tehran: University of Tehran Publications, 1999), p.4176.
135. See Mohammad Gharipour and Douglas Allen, 'The Achaemenid Garden: A Study on Its Contribution to the History of Garden Design and Its Cultural Context', *Journal of Middle Eastern and North African Intellectual and Cultural Studies* (April 2008).
136. The pavilion in Turkish is called *buyukcadir*, in Hindi *papolanaa*, and in Arabic *kheymeh, sardaq* and *jennah*. In Urdu the pavilion as tent is called *kheymeh, tonbu, khargah* and *deyra*, and as a building, is called *jahan-nama* and *qobbeh*.
137. Abolqasem Dehkhoda, *Persian Comprehensive Dictionary*, electronic version (University of Tehran Publications, 2006).
138. *Aban Yasht*, 5:128.
139. See Schimmel, pp.11–39.
140. Mohammad Mo'in, *Farhang-e Farsi* (Persian Dictionary), 5 (Tehran: Amir Kabir Publications, 2005) pp.961–62.

Chapter 3 The Garden and Pavilion in Persian Art

1. Jonas Benzion Lehrman, *Earthly Paradise: Garden and Courtyard in Islam* (Thames & Hudson, 1980).
2. Oleg Grabar, *Mostly Miniatures* (Princeton: Princeton University Press, 2000).
3. Ibid. p.87.
4. Ibid. p.91.
5. Ibid. p.96.
6. Ibid. p.99.
7. Ibid. p.107.
8. Ibid. p.111.
9. Ibid. p.33.
10. For more information, please refer to Sheila Blair, *A Compendium of Chronicles: Rashid-uddin's Illustrated History of the World*, The Nasser D. Khalili Collection of Islamic Art, XXVII (London: Khalili Collection, 1995).
11. Sheila R. Canby, *Persian Painting* (New York: Thames & Hudson, 1993), pp.25–48.
12. For more information, please refer to Yuka Kadoi, *Islamic Chinoiserie: The Art of Mongol Iran* (Edinburgh: Edinburgh University Press, 2009), pp.123–61.
13. Grabar, pp.49–52.
14. Ibid. p.53.
15. Ibid. p.56.
16. Canby, pp.58–59 and Grabar, p.61.
17. Kamal-uddin Behzad Haravi (1450–1535) was the head of royal ateliers in Tabriz and Herat during the late Timurid and early Safavid periods.
18. Grabar, pp.65–67.
19. Ibid. pp.78–81.
20. Even though in some cases patronage explains the origins of the painting and the story of its creation, it is not usually clear enough to justify the design of landscape elements (including garden and pavilion).
21. Jim Wescoat Jr, 'The Islamic Garden: Issues for Landscape Research', *Environmental Design: Journal of the Islamic Environmental Design Research Centre*, 1 (1986), pp.10–19.
22. Using a geometric layout for the garden depends on the artist's aesthetics, the narrative, style and degrees of realism applied in the painting. For instance, Muhammad Zaman, whose drawings are based on his observation of Safavid palaces in Isfahan, uses a more geometric layout, while the Timurid-style artists usually are interested in a naturalistic setting. It also depends on the message of the painting, that is, whether it refers to a poem or narrative. The problem, however, is that the poetry is usually silent about the layout of the garden, and the vocabulary used to describe it is not very specific. In that sense, the *Baburnameh* is one of the rare documents which specifically talk about a certain layout, *chaharbagh*.

23. Donald Wilber, *Persian Gardens and Garden Pavilions* (Tokyo: Charles E. Tuttle Company, 1962), pp.72 and 74.
24. Assadullah Souren Melekian-Chirvani, 'An Anthology of a Sufi Prince from Bukhara', in Robert Hillenbrand (ed.), *Persian Painting* (London: I.B.Tauris, London, 2000), p.164.
25. Gauvin Alexander Bailey, 'The Bernard Berenson Collection of Islamic Painting at Villa I Tatti: Turkman, Uzbek, and Safavid Miniatures', Part II, *Oriental Art*, XLVIII, no.1, 2002, p.13.
26. Pope and Ackerman list four categories of pavilions: kiosk without walls, pergola-type, open-faced room, and true pavilion. According to them, "while tents served as garden shelters, most gardens had permanent kiosk or pavilions in form of a simple or complex structure". Pope and Ackerman, p.1421.
27. This poetry book is about the ethical issues and the objectives and instructions set by Islam.
28. B.W. Robinson, *Persian Drawings from the 14th through the 19th Century* (New York: Shorewood Publishers, 1965), p.104.
29. Adel T. Adamova, 'The Hermitage Manuscript of Nezami's *Khamsa* Dated 835/1431', *Islamic Art V*, p.109.
30. Ibid., p.128.
31. Laurence Binyon, J.V.S. Wilkinson and Basil Gray, *Persian Miniature Painting* (New York: Dover Publications, 1971), p.67.
32. Ebadollah Bahari, *Bihzad, Master of Persian Painting* (London: I.B.Tauris, 1996), fig.93.
33. Ibid. p.60.
34. The hypothesis that such barriers were present in gardens cannot be fully rejected, particularly since the fence was usually made of materials subject to decay, such as wood, or may even be removed from the gardens.
35. Eleanor Sims, Boris Marshak and Ernst J. Grube, *Peerless Images* (New Haven and London: Yale University Press, 2002), p.118.
36. This illustrated book (*Haft Awrang*) was developed under the guidance of Soltan Ibrahim Mirza in Mashhad.
37. Marianna Shreve Simpson, *Persian Poetry, Painting, and Patronage* (Washington DC: Freer Gallery of Art, 1998), p.27.
38. Soltan Muhammad usually treats the building as a two-dimensional layer in his works. In other words, the building in his paintings works as a curtain/wall (not a volume) between two areas in the painting which are involved in the story.
39. Stuart Cary Welch, *Persian Painting, Five Royal Safavid Manuscripts of the Sixteenth Century* (New York: George Braziller, 1976), p.22.
40. Bahari, p.165.
41. The enthronement ceremony is usually depicted in gardens (not inside buildings).
42. See Chapter 4.
43. Welch, *Persian Painting*, p.35.
44. Melikian-Chirvani, p.181.

45. Simpson, p.48.
46. Robinson, p.36.
47. Barrett and Gray, *Indian Painting*, p.76.
48. Lisa Golombek in 'The Gardens of Timur: New Perspectives', speaks about a 'gendered' history behind the creation of Timurid gardens. Based on several Timurid references, she concludes that there is a strong link between the design of gardens and the history of women associated with it. Golombek, pp.137–47.
49. Welch, p.55.
50. Simpson, p.49. Canby suggests that the scene of the conversation between the lover in the street and the beloved on the balcony is a consistent scene in Persian painting.
51. Sims and Marshak, p.123.
52. Amy S. Landau, 'From Poet to Painter: Allegory and Metaphor in a Seventeenth-Century Painting by Muhammad Zaman, Master of Farangi-sazi', *Muqarnas*, 28, pp. 101–31.
53. Canby, p.73.
54. Melekian-Chirvani, p.164.
55. This book should not be confused with Nezami's *Khosrow va Shirin*.
56. Melikian-Chirvani, IA8, p.165.
57. Canby, p.72.
58. Canby suggests that the subject of Khosrow before Shirin's palace was a favourite of Persian painters because it enabled the artists to capture the architecture, landscape and figures together. Canby, p.72.
59. Wilber, p.33.
60. In this painting, the figures are spread out between the roof and ground level. Here the planted area seems a secondary and less significant element.
61. Grabar, p.69.
62. Similar to Binyon, Wilkinson and Gray, p.97.
63. Oleg Grabar, 'Ayvan', *Encyclopaedia Iranica Online*, available at http://www.iranica.com.
64. Sims and Marshak, p.215.
65. Karin Adahl, 'A Copy of the Diwan of Mir Ali Shir Nava'i', in Robert Hillenbrand (ed.), *Persian Painting*, p.13.
66. This semi-octagonal plan of an *iwan* is comparable to semi-octagonal thrones in painting.
67. Titley, p.120.
68. Sims and Marshak, p.187.
69. This painting also sheds light on the frame that most late Safavid artists such as Zaman used to depict the garden and pavilion in their paintings. In other words, it shows that the paved area illustrated in many paintings could be the *iwan*, and not necessarily the courtyard in front of it.
70. For more information, please refer to David Roxburgh, *Micrographia: Toward a Visual Logic of Persianate Painting* (Cambridge: Peabody Museum of Archaeology and Ethnology, 2003).

71. The artist's focus is on colour and formal arrangement of colour areas. Welch believes that this phenomenon under-dramatizes the subject. Welch, *Persian Painting*, p.55.
72. Sims and Marshak, p.123.
73. All components in that part of the painting follow a natural (not man-made) pattern whose elements such as the water channel, rocks, plants and trees might originate in a Chinese garden and not a geometric pattern (e.g., *chaharbagh*). It is not the objective of this book to prove or reject the Chinese origin of the background garden in Persian painting.
74. Welch, *Persian Painting*, p.84.
75. Wilber, p.31.
76. Grabar, fig.31.
77. Bahari, p.85.
78. Dehkhoda, 'Ali Akbar, *Encyclopedia of Persian* (electronic version, available at: http://www.loghatnaameh.org).
79. Simpson, p.9.
80. Simpson believes this painting somehow coincides with the events of the life of the patron, Ibrahim Mirza, who was the governor of Mashhad. This specific scene might be related to the description of the wedding party of his wife, Gowhar Soltan Khanom, and her arrival at Mashhad in 1560. Simpson, p.32.
81. Esin Atil, *Art of the Arab World* (Washington DC: Smithsonian Institute, 1975), p.28.
82. Bahari, p.212.
83. Ibid. p.169.
84. Atil, p.47.
85. Stuart Cary Welch, *Imperial Mughal Painting* (New York: George Braziller, 1978), p.57.
86. This structure is even comparable to the structure of the balcony in Persian painting.
87. Noah M. Titley, *Persian Miniature Painting and Its Influence on the Art of Turkey and India* (Austin: University of Texas Press, 1983), p.139.
88. Bahari, p.115.
89. The elongated bodies and small heads are a signature of Safavid painters.
90. Binyon, Wilkinson and Gray, p.67.
91. Bailey, p.10.
92. Welch, *Imperial Mughal Painting*, p.21.
93. B.W. Robinson, *Persian Miniature Painting from Collections in the British Isles*, p.103.
94. Bailey, p.7.
95. Michael Rogers, 'The Chester Beatty Suleymanname Again', in Robert Hillenbrand (ed.), *Persian Painting*, p.188.
96. Ibid. p.197.
97. 'Abd al-Samad is a Tabriz master who trained artists in Mughal court. Welch, *Imperial Mughal Painting*, p.19.

98. See Bahari, p.152.
99. Welch, *Persian Painting*, p.54. The artist's focus is on colour and formal arrangement of colour areas. There is also a clear separation between the paved and planted areas.
100. Welch, *Imperial Mughal Painting*, p.57.
101. One hypothesis is that the form of the kiosk originates in the throne, but this could be easily rejected especially because there is no clear chronological evolution in the form of kiosks and thrones in Persian paintings.
102. The majority of thrones in Persian painting are not roofed. The roofed throne, which appears only rarely, becomes very similar to the design of the kiosk.
103. *Islamic Art V* (Bruschettini Foundation for Islamic and Asian Art, 2001), plate V.
104. David J. Roxburgh, *The Persian Album, 1400–1600* (New York: Yale University Press, 2005), p.224.
105. Sims and Marshak, p.244.
106. Titley, p.139.
107. Welch, *Persian Painting*, p.53. It shows the story of Barbad and Khosrow Parviz. Barbad was not known in Khosrow's court because of the resistance of Sarkad (the king's leading singer) to auditioning new talent. When Khosrow went out to picnic, Barbad concealed himself behind the trees to play. Sarkad told the king that it was the voice of the wind, but after this, Barbad was appointed court musician in place of Sarkad. Welch, p.53.
108. It was ordered by the Timurid governor of Mashhad, Ibrahim Mirza.
109. Welch, p.116.
110. Welch, p.117.
111. Ibid. p.76.
112. Bahari, p.65.
113. Welch, *Persian Painting*, p.80. Even though this painting is based on the *Khamseh Nezami*, it describes the quirks and foibles of the Safavid courtiers.
114. Soltan Muhammad was a pupil of Aqa Mirak and was Shah Tahmasp's painting instructor.
115. It is believed that this painting was prepared for the Safavid prince, al-Qazi Abul-Muzaffar Sam Mirza, so it is reasonable to suppose that it is a depiction of the Safavid court. Binyon, Wilkinson and Gray, p.128.
116. Wilber, p.48.
117. Ibid. p.49.
118. Bahari, p.63.
119. 'Abd al-Samad was a Tabriz master who trained artists in Mughal court. Welch, p.19.
120. Welch, *Imperial Mughal Painting*, p.15. Welch believes that this is an imitation of Safavid paintings and shows Mughals' desire for "accurate portraiture and anecdotal reportage." It was drawn for Homayun who was in exile in Safavid court Iran for a while and probably had Persian taste. The artist is probably the student of Shah Tahmasp's royal atelier.
121. This painting is an exception because of the overemphasis on the interior even though the pavilion has four windows around it. The throne is in the decorated pavilion.

122. Simpson, p.55.
123. Welch, *Imperial Mughal Painting*, p.65.
124. Titley, p.111.
125. It is in a composite drawing in which there are eight paintings.
126. Roxburgh, p.263.
127. Titley, p.195.
128. Canby, p.8.
129. Wilber, p.47.
130. Bernard O'Kane explores the influence of pastoral nomadism on court life in Iran, especially after Islam, and how it changes the definition of 'place' for Persian kings. He refers to Safavid and Timurid historic accounts to demonstrate imperial encampments (*ordu*) in different periods and explains how they viewed gardens as places for encampments and how this view indirectly changed the stable nature of palace or pavilion for them. (Bernard O'Kane, 'From Tents to Pavilions: Royal Mobility and Persian Palace Design', in Gülru Necipoglu (ed.), *Ars Orientalis*, 23. (Ann Arbor: Department of History, University of Michigan, 1993), pp.249–69.)
131. Wilber, pp.62 and 70.
132. Arthur Upham Pope, 'Tents and Pavilions', *Survey of Persian Art from Prehistoric Times to the Present*, 2 (London: Oxford University Press, 1939), pp.1411–27.
133. Pope believes that the conical tent is the primary form for tents, and the yurt and pyramidal tents are more developed versions of this type. Ibid. p.1413.
134. The pyramidal tent had a straight fall from each of its four sides. Its form reflects the domical structures developed in Persian architecture but it is not known whether this derives from architectural practice.
135. Ruy González de Clavijo, *Narrative of the Embassy of Ruy Gonzalez de Clavijo to the Court of Timour*, translated by Clements Robert Markham (London: Hakluyt Society, 1859), p.131.
136. David J. Roxburgh, 'Ruy Gonzalez de Clavijo's Narrative of Courtly Life and Ceremony in Timur's Samarqand, 1404', in Palmira Brummett (ed.), *The Book of Travels: Genre, Ethnology, and Pilgrimage, 1250–1700* (Leiden: E.J. Brill, 2009), p.139.
137. Robinson, p.50.
138. Welch, *Persian Painting*, p.63.
139. Robinson, *Persian Drawings from the 14th through the 19th Century*, p.119.
140. Binyon, Wilkinson and Gray, p.202.
141. Welch, p.22.
142. Kuyuk (Guyuk) Khan (1206–48) was the third khan of the Mongols and grandson of Genghiz Khan.
143. Canby, p.56.
144. Pope and Ackerman, p.1419.
145. Ibid. p.226.
146. Ibid. p.226.

147. Simpson, p.22.
148. *Islamic Art V* (Bruschettini Foundation for Islamic and Asian Art, 2001), p.106.
149. Marianna Shreve Simpson, *Arab and Persian Painting in the Fogg Art Museum* (Cambridge: Fogg Art Museum, 1980), p.54.
150. Robinson, *Persian Drawings from the 14th through the 19th Century*, p.66.
151. The tent is the last layer of the painting and acts as the least important element.
152. Adahl, p.6.

Chapter 4 The Garden and Pavilion through the Lens of Travellers and Historians

1. J.D. Gurney, 'Pietro della Valle: The Limits of Perception', *Bulletin of the School of Oriental and African Studies*, University of London, 49, no.1 (1986), p.103.
2. Ibid.
3. Paul Losensky, an expert in seventeenth-century literature in Persian, in his paper on 'Abdi Beyk's book, *Jannat al-asmar/Zinat al-awraq/Sahifat al-ikhlas,* refers to the four types of descriptions mentioned by Heinrich Plett. Plett defines *descripto* as the description of things (*descripto rei*), people (*descripto personae*), places (*descripto loci*), and time (*descripto temporis*). Heinrich Plett, 'Descripto', in Thomas O. Sloane (ed.), *Encyclopedia of Rhetoric,* (Oxford University Press, 2001), pp.220–21.
4. For instance, Della Valle's travel notes are drawn from letters to his family members in Italy. Eskandar Monshi's account, on the other hand, was sponsored by Shah 'Abbas to record historical events through a favourable lens for the king.
5. Jafari in the *Tarikh-e Yazd* uses the term *mazra'eh* to name gardens which exclude buildings.
6. Naser E. Khosrow, *Book of Travels,* translated by W.M. Thackston (Costa Meza, CA: Mazda Publishers, 2001), p.129.
7. Ibid. p.128.
8. Ibid. p.9.
9. Eskandar Beyk Turkaman (Monshi) repeatedly names the Naqsh-e Jahan garden a paradise (Eskandar Bayk Turkaman, *Tarikh-e 'Alam Aray-e 'Abbasi,* edited Iraj Afshar (Tehran: Amir Kabir Publications, 2004), p.634). Using paradise as a symbol might be related to the use of *chaharbagh* in the layout of the gardens in Safavid Isfahan.
10. Abul-Fazl Beyhaqi, *Tarikh-e Beyhaqi* (History), edited by Khatib Rahbar (Tehran: Mahtab Publications, 2007).
11. *Kitab Mahasin Isfahan of Mufaddul* by Sa'd al-Husain al-Mafarrukhi al-Isfahani Jalal-uddin al-Husain al-Tihrani.
12. Beyhaqi, 2, p.656.
13. Beyhaqi, 3, p.897.

14. Khajeh Zeyn al-Abedin ʻAli Navidi ʻAbdi Bayk Shirazi, *Jannat al-asmar/Zinat al-awraq/Sahifat al-ikhlas,* edited by Abul-Fazl Hashim Awghili Rahimuf (Moscow: Danesh Publications, 1979), p.9. (Henceforth ʻAbdi Beyk.)
15. ʻAbdi Beyk, p.114.
16. Ibid. p.53.
17. He refers to several buildings in gardens (*ʻemarat*) such as ʻEmarat-e Jahan-nama (p.1111), ʻEmarat-e Sarvestan (p.1111, p.1015), ʻEmarat-e Goldasteh (p.1111), and ʻEmarat-e Negarestan (p.1111).
18. Turkaman, p.405.
19. "*Ravaq-ha va manzare-ha-ye behjatza*" meaning delightful *ravaqs* and landscapes.
20. Beyhaqi, 2, p.401.
21. Beyhaqi, 3, p.884 and p.938.
22. Beyhaqi, 2, p.482.
23. Farrokhi Sistani, Dorj Database for Persian Literature.
24. Khosrow, p.350.
25. Beyhaqi, 3, p.928.
26. Beyhaqi, 2, p.625.
27. Beyhaqi, 1, p.32.
28. Jafar ibn Muhammad ibn Hasan Jafari, *Tarikh-e Yazd,* edited by Iraj Afshar (Tehran: Bongah-e Tarjomeh va Nashr-e Ketab Publishers (BTNK), 1960), pp.140 and 144.
29. Beyhaqi refers to Masʻud's picnics in Bagh-e Piruzi and compares them to his permanent life in his palaces in Ghaznin. Beyhaqi, 2, p.637.
30. Masʻud enjoyed looking at this palace (*kushk*) and the gardens. Beyhaqi, 2, p.722.
31. The word *bagh* is used in plural to name both garden and palace complexes. Moreover, the word *kushk* does not necessarily refer to a palace or pavilions in gardens but may refer to individual palaces inside cities.
32. Beyhaqi, 1, p.198.
33. Jafari, p.143. (He also mentions that there is another garden right in front of this one called Bagh-e Vardanruz, which does not have any building.)
34. Jafari, p.144–45.
35. Ibid. p.146.
36. Masashi Haneda, 'The Pastoral City and the Mausoleum City', in Tsugitaka Satō (ed.), *Islamic Urbanism in Human History* (London: Kegan Paul International, 1997), pp.142–70.
37. Heidi Walcher, 'Between Paradise and Political Capital: The Semiotics of Safavid Iran', in *Yale Forestry and Environmental Studies Bulletin*, 103 (1998) (New Haven: Yale University Press), pp.17–21.
38. Manu Sobti, *Urban Metamorphosis and Change in Central Asian Cities after the Arab Invasions*, PhD dissertation, Georgia Institute of Technology, 2005.
39. The issue of wealth is even related to the location of gardens in Clavijo's and Naser Khosrow's notes. For instance, it can be seen from Clavijo's text that having house gardens within the city is consid-

ered a sign of wealth: "The nobles of the city have their houses amongst these gardens, and they are so extensive that, when a man approaches the city, he sees nothing but a mass of very high trees." Clavijo, p.170. The same observation was made by Naser Khosrow, who writes about gardens which are probably pleasure gardens, and belong to people in higher social classes. Khosrow. p.127. These examples raise a fundamental question regarding the relationship between the social class of owners and the design of gardens and pavilions, which requires further research.

40. Clavijo, p.171.
41. For more information on the definition of public and private realms in Persia, please refer to Ann K.S. Lambton, *Continuity and Change in Medieval Persia* (London: Persian Heritage Foundation, 1988), pp.123–24.
42. Haneda discusses mausoleums as the focal point in the creation of three cities in the Ilkhanid age: Nasriyyeh, Soltaniyyeh and Ghazaniyyeh. Haneda, pp.142–70.
43. This idea was later used in the design of the new neighbourhoods (e.g. Jolfa) in Isfahan, which extended the boundaries of the city.
44. John Dixon Hunt, 'Approaches (New and Old) to Garden History', in Michael Conan (ed.), *Perspectives on Garden Histories* (Washington DC: Dumbarton Oaks, 1999), pp.77–90 (p.79).
45. Mohammad Gharipour, 'The Pavilion in the Persian Garden: Reflections in the Textual and Visual Media', unpublished doctoral thesis, Georgia Institute of Technology (2008), pp.47–64.
46. Jean Baptiste Tavernier, *Tavernier's Travelogue,* translated by Hamid Arbab Shirani (Tehran: Nilufar Publishers, 2005), p.62.
47. Ibid. pp.294–98.
48. Ibid. pp.299–318.
49. Haneda, p.168.
50. 'Abdi Beyk Shirazi, *Jannat-e Adan,* edited by Abul-Fazl Hashim Awghili Rahimuf (Moscow: Danesh Publications, 1979).
51. Adib Shahab-uddin, *Tarikh-e Vassaf,* edited by Abdul-Mohammad Ayati (Tehran: Iran Culture Foundation Publications, 1968), p.115.
52. See Beyhaqi.
53. Ibid., 3, pp.989–90.
54. Nasrollah Falsafi, *Zendegani-e Shah 'Abbas* (Tehran: Elmi Publishers, 1999), p.169.
55. Ibid. p.106.
56. 'Abdi Beyk, *Jannat-e Adan,* p.23.
57. Hasan Beyk Romlu, *Ahsan al-Tavarikh,* edited by 'Abd al-Hoseyn Nava'i (Tehran: Asatir Publications, 2006), p.471.
58. Muhammed Babur, *Memoirs of Zehīr-Ed-Dīn Muhammed Bābur: Emperor of Hindustan,* translated by William Erskine and John Leyden (Oxford: Oxford University Press, 1921), p.370.
59. The names of the majority of royal gardens referred to their characteristics or their role in historical events. For example, Bagh-e 'Adeliyyeh (Garden of Justice), Bagh-e Nasriyyeh (Garden of Victory),

Bagh-e Piruzi (Garden of Victory), Bagh-e Firuzi (Garden of Victory), Bagh-e Zafar (Garden of Victory), Bagh-e Naqsh-e Jahan (Garden of the Image of the World), Bagh-e Khasseh (Garden of the Privileged), Bagh-e Morad (Garden of Desire), Bagh-e Sa'adat (Garden of Prosperity).

60. Beyhaqi, 2, p.507.
61. Ibid. p.506.
62. Ibid., 3, p.870 and 2, p.402.
63. Ibid., 2, p.631.
64. Ibid., 1, p.32.
65. Ibid., 2, p.411.
66. Mirza Mohammad Haidar, *Tarikh-e Rashidi* (*A History of the Mughals of Central Asia*), translated and edited by E. Denison Ross and N. Elias (India: Academica Asiatica, 1973), p.83.
67. See Romlu.
68. Ibid. p.556.
69. Ibid. p.643.
70. Ibid. p.1290.
71. Fadlullah B. Ruzbihan Khunji, *Tarikh'i Alam Aray-e Amini* (Persia in 1478–1490), translated by V. Minorsky (London: Royal Asiatic Society of Great Britain and Ireland, 1957), p.59.
72. Turkaman, p.98.
73. Nasrollah Falsafi, *Zendegani-ye Shah 'Abbas* (Tehran: Elmi Publishers, 1999), p.243.
74. Turkaman, p.249.
75. Ibid. p.116.
76. Falsafi, p.247.
77. Babur, p.137. Babur talks about drinking parties such as at the garden at Alisheng or the Majnun party in Bagh-e Vafa (see p.156). Similarly, Romlu refers to drinking parties in Ilkhanid gardens during peacetime; see Romlu, p.741.
78. For instance in the Malekan garden; Babur, p.146.
79. Ibid. p.316.
80. Ibid. p.358.
81. Michelle Membre, *Mission to the Lord Sophy of Persia (1539–1542)*, translated by A.H. Morton (London: School of Oriental and African Studies, 1993), pp.19–20.
82. Clavijo.
83. Ibid. p.132.
84. Thomas Herbert and William Foster, *A Description of the Persian Monarchy* (London, 1634), p.155.
85. Ibid. p.155.
86. Ibid.
87. Babur, p.358.
88. Haneda, p.161.
89. Clavijo, p.131.

90. Due to the scarcity of archaeological evidence, O'Kane's studies were not followed up by other scholars. There are still ambiguities about the forms of tents, their placement in gardens, and how they affected the design of gardens.
91. O'Kane, p.249.
92. Monika Gronke, 'The Persian Court between Palace and Tent: From Timur to 'Abbas I', in Lisa Golombek and Maria Subtelny (eds), *Timurid Art and Culture: Iran and Central Asia in the Fifteenth Century* (Leiden: E. J. Brill, 1992), pp.18–22.
93. Clavijo, p.107.
94. Fazlullah B. Ruzbihan Khunji, *Tarikh-e Alamara-yi Amini (Persia in* CE *1478–1490)*, translated by Vladimir Minorsky (London: Royal Asiatic Society, 1957), p.20.
95. 'Ala'-uddin 'Ata-Malik Joveyni, *The History of the World-Conqueror,* translated by John Andrew Boyle (Cambridge, MA: Harvard University Press, 1958), p.43. According to Boyle, Emil is the name of a river, south of Chuguchak, and also the name of a town.
96. Romlu, p.232.
97. Ibid. p.553.
98. Ibid. p.610.
99. Beyhaqi, 2, p.637.
100. Kwaja Rashid-uddin, *Tarikh-e Mubarak-e Ghazani,* edited by K. Jahn (London, 1940), p.36.
101. Shahab-uddin, p.318.
102. Ibid. p.92. What he calls house (*khaneh*) may actually refer to a tent because he uses the term "*khaneha bar arfashtand*", which means pitched houses.
103. Romlu, p.465.
104. Ibid. p.741.
105. Ibid. p.1074.
106. Ibid. p.1068.
107. Ibid. p.1140.
108. Ibid. p.555. Choosing gardens based on their location inside or outside cities was a logistic decision. For instance, Soltan Hoseyn who stayed in Bagh-e Jahanaray (outside the city) went to the garden inside the city to protect himself against Uzbeks. Ibid. p.1011.
109. Marco Polo, *The Travels of Marco Polo,* translated by Ronald Latham (Baltimore: Penguin Books, 1958), pp.40–42. Cited in Penelope House, *Gardens of Persia* (Hong Kong: Kale Press, 2004), p.77.
110. Romlu, p.1140.
111. Beyhaqi, 1, p.273.
112. Ibid., 2, p.482.
113. It was even said that when a man lost his horse in the garden near Samarqand, the horse had grazed there for six months before he could find it! Ralph Pinder-Wilson, 'The Persian Garden: *Bagh* and *Chahar Bagh*', *Islamic Garden,* edited by Richard Ettinghausen (Washington DC: Dumbarton Oaks, 1976), p.77.

114. Apparently, Beyhaqi made a mistake in the date of the death of Mahmud, which was 28 April 1030 CE.
115. Beyhaqi, 2, p.406. Despite this, Mas'ud went there again with his son, Amir Mahmud, and once even initiated a drinking competition! Ibid., 3, p.990.
116. Mehrdad Qayyumi Bidhendi, 'Bagh-ha-ye Khorasan dar Tarikh-e Beyhaqi', *Proceedings of the Third Congress on Iranian Architecture and Urbanism* (Tehran, 2007), pp.119–48 (p.127).
117. Romlu, p.339.
118. Battuta, 2, p.318.
119. Haneda believes that the *waqf* played a central role in the survival of these mausoleum cities. He adds, "the city construction by the nomads was not a passing phenomenon but its influence continued through to the building of the new Isfahan by Shah Abbas". Haneda, p.144.
120. Ibid. p.145.
121. Ibid. p.146.
122. Ibid. pp.146–47. Haneda's note seems to contradict *Tarikh-e Vassaf* because apparently Ghazan Khan made this decision after his pilgrimage to Karbala (the mausoleum of Imam Hoseyn) and not Mashhad. Shahab-uddin, p.242.
123. Haneda, p.147.
124. Ibid. p.149.
125. Shahab-uddin described the palace of 'Adeliyyeh and mentions that more than 300 *man* (equal to 1800kg) of lapis lazuli (*lajevard*) was used just for the paintings on the ceiling. He also wrote about several public buildings that were constructed around this garden in order to fund it. Moreover, the taxes (100 *toman* = 1,000,000 dinar) received from other lands (*amval*) and endowments from neighbouring properties (*mowqufat*) were all spent on this new complex, which gradually shaped a new city. Shahab-uddin, p.230.
126. Pinder-Wilson believes that it was a tradition that ambassadors to the Timurid court stopped in Shahr-e Sabz and its gardens before going to Samarqand. Wilber, p.61.
127. *Divan-e Farrokhi Sistani,* Dorj Database, Tehran, 2008.
128. Mafarrukhi is the author of the *Kitab Mahasin Isfahan* (1072 CE and 1092 CE), which is one of the few surviving pre-Mongol accounts of Isfahan. Juergen Paul, 'The Histories of Isfahan: Mafarrukhi's Kitab Mahasin Isfahan', *Iranian Studies,* 33, no.1–2 (2000), pp.117–32.
129. E.G. Browne, 'Account for a Rare Manuscript History of Isfahan', *Journal of the Royal Asiatic Society,* ser.3, 13, pp.411–46.
130. Ralph Pinder-Wilson, 'The Persian Garden: *Bagh* and *Chahar Bagh*' in Richard Ettinghausen (ed.) *Islamic Garden* (Washington, DC: Dumbarton Oaks, 1976), p.76.
131. These gardens in Samarqand are described by Clavijo.
132. Mirza Mohammad Haidar, *Tarikh-e Rashidi* (A History of the Mughals of Central Asia), translated and edited by N. Elias and E. Denison Ross (India: Academica Asiatica, 1973).
133. Turkaman, p.1111. (He also describes the pool which is located in the middle of the garden in 'Emarat-e Delgosha. p.780.)

134. Babur, p.335.
135. Ibid. p.15.
136. Ibid. p.27.
137. John Fryer. *East India and Persia,* edited by William Crooke, II (London: Hakluyt Society, 1915), p.212.
138. Fryer, p.214.
139. Ibid.
140. Fryer, p.195.
141. Beyhaqi, 1, p.46.
142. This is part of the entrance building, which is illustrated in some paintings.
143. Clavijo, p.131.
144. Ibid.
145. Romlu, p.805.
146. Ghazaniyyeh and Soltaniyyeh.
147. Giosofat Barbaro and Ambrogio Contarini, 'Travels of a Merchant in Persia', *Travels to Tana and Persia* (London: Hakluyt Society, 1963), pp.141–207.
148. Ibid. p.174.
149. He writes, "For three yards above the mastabe is all of fine marble. All below is plastered in different colours, and is conspicuous far off like a mirror." Barbaro and Contarini, p.174.
150. "The spout is immensely large, and made in the form of a dragon; they are of bronze, and so large that they would do for a cannon." Ibid. p.175.
151. He is impressed by the huge size of the building: "[it is] made as to be taken for live dragons." Ibid.
152. In his description of this pavilion, he writes that all spaces are located around the audience hall where Uzun Hasan used to give audience.
153. Pinder-Wilson, p.78.
154. According to the Venetian merchant, in the hunting scene, Hasan was accompanied by many lords, all on horseback, with dogs and falcons. There were also many exotic animals to be seen, such as elephants and rhinoceroses, which signified adventures that had happened to him. Barbaro and Contarini, p.175–76.
155. He confirms the realism applied in these paintings: "The figures are so well drawn that they appear like real living human beings." Ibid. p.176.
156. Ibid.
157. To emphasize the huge size of the building, he writes: "harem of one storey, so large that a thousand women might conveniently live there in different rooms." Ibid. pp.173–78.
158. Ibid.
159. Shah 'Abbas moved his capital because Isfahan is located in the centre of Persia and far from his Safavid enemies, the Ottomans and Uzbeks, on the western and eastern boundaries.
160. Safavid achievements in terms of reviving national pride in Iranian society have motivated some scholars

to divide Persian Islamic architecture into two periods: pre-Safavid and post-Safavid. (*Encyclopedia Iranica,* edited by Ehsan Yarshater (New York: Mazda Publications), pp.339–49.)

161. The Safavid square, Naqsh-e Jahan, worked as an imperial centre for cultural, religious, political and economical activities. Naqsh-e Jahan Square (the *meidan*) included two magnificent mosques, Shah and Lotf Allah, and a royal palace, 'Aliqapu, and the portal gate of the main bazaar. Shah 'Abbas also constructed two great bridges in Isfahan, Allah-Verdikhan and Khaju, which were not only connectors between the south and north of the city, but also places for the king and ordinary people to enjoy the natural beauty of the Zayanderud River.
162. Fryer, p.296.
163. Ibid. p.295.
164. Tavernier, p.74. (Such confusion by Tavernier, who is a careful observer, may reveal that even in the Safavid age western ideas did not have much influence on the design of gardens in Iran.)
165. Eskandar Monshi, who described the gardens in the city of Isfahan, mentions that there are chaharbaghs on both sides of the street, and there is a pavilion on the entrance which he calls 'Emarat-e Dargah (p.544). This matches Tavernier's description of Isfahan in which he describes a kiosk at the end of Chaharbagh Street.
166. It is not clear which palace he is talking about, but we can guess that this is Chehelsotun palace, which is located between the square and Chaharbagh Street. Tavernier, p.55.
167. Ibid. p.65.
168. In these times the street becomes a promenade and a connector between the kiosk and Allah-Verdikhan Bridge.
169. He believes that Hasht Behesht is an imitation of Cosroes to make a pleasant pilgrimage. Fryer, p.348–49.
170. Ibid. p.349.
171. Ibid. p.350.
172. Although Binning does not mention the name of this pavilion, his descriptions of the ornamentation and the location of this garden in Chaharbagh Street reveal that he is referring to the Hasht Behesht pavilion.
173. Robert B.M. Binning, *A Journal of Two Years' Travel in Persia, Ceylon, Etc.* (New York: W.H. Allen, 1857), p.143.
174. Ibid. p.144.
175. It seems that Binning has confused the name of the last Safavid king (Shah Soltan Hussein) with Shah Tahmasp, who is the father of Shah 'Abbas. Such a mistake might be because he is confusing this palace with another with the same name in Qazvin, which is described by 'Abdi Beyk.
176. Binning, p.142.
177. There is a pavilion called *namakdan* (literally meaning 'salt-cellar') behind it.
178. Golombeck and Wilber, *The Timurid Architecture of Iran and Turan,* II, map 7.
179. Clavijo, p.130.

180. Ibid. p.136.
181. Ibid. p.129.
182. Heidi Walcher mentions that the life of Shah 'Abbas in Herat during his childhood motivated him to develop a master plan for the city of Isfahan, which was based on the existence of several gardens. Walcher, pp.17–21.
183. Qasem Abu Nasr Haravi, *Irshad al-Zira'ah* (Tehran: University of Tehran Publications, 1968), p.280.
184. Haravi, pp.281–282.
185. Mahvash Alemi, 'Chahar Bagh', *Environmental Design: Journal of the Islamic Environmental Design Research Centre*, no.1, 1986, pp.38–45.
186. Hasan Romlu also talks about ceremony and celebrations in Bagh-e Sa'adat-abad (p.1425) and describes this garden as paradise (*golestan-e eram*). Romlu, p.1520.
187. 'Abdi Beyk, p.23.
188. Ibid. p.9.
189. Ibid. p.120.
190. Ibid. p.114.
191. Ibid. p.53 and p.9.
192. *Moshabbakat az ney.*
193. The residential use of gardens and pavilions inside them required other buildings in gardens, such as bathhouses. It was a common tradition to construct bathhouses in gardens. For instance, Babur talks about pitching a place for a bath on the south-east of the garden (Babur, p.366). This bath, which is located on an elevated platform, is reminiscent of other buildings such as houses and palaces in gardens. Likewise, Ibn Battuta talks about a bathhouse in Halafihan, which is located in the middle of the garden, and is apparently part of a larger public complex in which a sanctuary, *madrasa* and mosque are located. Ibn Battuta, III, p.716.
194. 'Abdi Beyk, p.58. The relationship between the main palace and the bathhouse is not clarified in Beyk's book. However, it could be assumed that, in order to enhance the privacy of users, especially the women in the royal family, the two buildings would have been close together.
195. 'Abdi Bayk, p.114. (The *keryas* is the king's private room in Sarai.)
196. Ibid. p.115.
197. Ibid. p.118.
198. *Zahir* and *batin* are widely discussed in Sufi literature. Based on Islamic instructions, people's faces should be the reflections of their souls.
199. 'Abdi Bayk, p.55.
200. Ibid. p.10.
201. Ibid. p.54.
202. The construction of transparent ceilings and dome chambers was a typical architectural feature developed after the Ilkhanid period in Persia.
203. These illustrations are apparently very similar to those in Chehelsotun palace in Isfahan.

204. Thomas Herbert and William Foster, *Travels in Persia, 1627–1629* (London: G. Routledge & Sons, 2005), p.152.
205. Ibid. p.153.
206. Herbert writes that from this pavilion he had a view of the high mountain Taurus. He has apparently made a mistake and meant Alborz.
207. Herbert and Foster, p.154.
208. R.W. Ferrier, *A Journey to Persia: Jean Chardin's Portrait of a Seventeenth-Century Empire* (London: I.B.Tauris, 1966), p.66.
209. Ferrier, p.67.
210. George Bull, *The Pilgrimage, the Travels of Pietro Della Valle* (London: Hutchinson Publishers, 1989).
211. Ibid. p.152.
212. Ibid. p.153.
213. Samuel Gottlieb Gmelin, *Travels through Northern Persia 1770–1774,* translated and annotated by Willem Floor (Washington, DC: Mage Publishers, 2007), p.247.
214. Ibid. p.247
215. Ibid. p.249.
216. Binning, p.140.
217. Gmelin, p.248.
218. Falsafi, p.1357
219. Ibid. p.1354.
220. Babur, p.858.
221. Leyden and Erskine explain these screens: "during the heats, particularly while the hot winds are blowing it is customary in India to cover the open side doors and windows of apartments with a sweet-smelling species of grass, which is kept moist with water. The air through this, is much softened, and an agreeable coolness produced. These door screens are made of the scented roots of a grass called *khashkhash.*" Babur, footnote, p.358.
222. Babur, p.409.
223. For a complete description of this event, please refer to the *Baburnameh,* p.408.
224. For more information about the sitting style in Babur's court, please refer to Babur, p.358.
225. Ibid. p.360.
226. Barbaro and Contarini, pp.173–78.
227. The gate in is made of brick and arched.
228. Clavijo, p.130.
229. Jafari, p.140.
230. Ibid. p.142.
231. Babur, p.319.
232. Haneda, p.150.
233. Membre, p.24.

234. Ibid. p.32.
235. Ibid. p.21.
236. Ibid. p.19.
237. Although the *ordu* (royal encampments outside cities) is discussed in contemporary literature, other aspects of tents, such as their structure, construction and ornamentation, are not discussed.
238. Rashid-uddin Fazl Allah Abil-Khair, *Tarikh-e Mubarak-e Ghazani,* translated by Karl Jahn (London: Mouton and Co., 1941), p.78.
239. Pinder-Wilson p.77.
240. Haneda, p.151.
241. Rashid-uddin, p.94.
242. Haneda, p.154.
243. Pinder-Wilson, p.77.
244. Beyhaqi, 2, p.402.
245. Beyhaqi, 3, p.888
246. Anthony Jenkinson, *Early Voyages and Travels to Russia and Persia,* edited by Edward Delmar Morgan and Charles Henry Coote (London: Hakluyt Society, 1886), p.55.
247. Membre, pp.17–18.
248. Turkaman, p.115.
249. "After three or four days, twenty thousand men were assembled round the tents of the lord, and a day did not pass without many arriving from all parts." Clavijo, p.140.
250. They are also called *sarapardeh* in the Persian language.
251. Clavijo, p.145.
252. Ibn Battuta, II, p.343.
253. Ibid. p.342.
254. Babur, p.137.
255. This separation was even reflected in Monshi's terminology. Considering the simple language that Monshi uses in his history, the wide range of terminology that he uses to name tents shows the categorization of tents based on the level and gender of their inhabitants. Turkaman, p.405.
256. Clavijo, p.141.
257. Ibn Battuta, II, p.342.
258. Clavijo, p.144.
259. Ibid.
260. Ibid. p.142.
261. Ibid. p.140.
262. Ibid.
263. John Andrew Boyle, 'The Seasonal Residences of the Great Khan Ogedei', *Central Asiatic Journal,* 16 (1972), p.127.
264. 'Ala'-uddin 'Ata-Malik Juvaini, *The History of the World-Conqueror,* translated by John Andrew Boyle

(Manchester, 1958), p.239.

265. Rashid ad-Din, *The Successors of Genghis Khan*, translated by J.A. Boyle (London, 1971), p.63.
266. William Rubruck, *The Journey of William of Rubruck to the Eastern Parts of the World, 1253–55*, translated and edited by William Woodville (London: Rockhill, 1900), pp.192–24.
267. Ibid. pp.21–22
268. Boyle, p.128.
269. Likewise, Marco Polo, who visits the tent of Kubilai Khan, calls it the largest palace that he has seen. Marco Polo, *The Travels of Marco Polo*, translated by Ronald Latham (Baltimore: Penguin Books, 1958), pp.115–16.
270. Clavijo, p.143.
271. Membre, p.19.
272. Clavijo, p.144.
273. A man on horseback was a standard scale for the height of tents. For instance, Ibn Battuta writes that they entered tents while riding horses. This shows the huge height of the tent.
274. Clavijo, p.144.
275. Ibid., p.145.

Poets, Historians and Travellers

1. F. Lehman, 'Babor, Zahir-al-Din Mohammad', *Encyclopaedia Iranica Online*, available at http://www.iranica.com.
2. Khalil Khatib Rahbar, 'Beyhaqi va Tarikh-e Mas'udi', *Tarikh-e Beyhaqi* (Tehran: Mahtab Publications, 2007), pp.11–37.
3. Iraj Afshar, 'Introduction', *Irshad az-Zara'ah* (Guide for Horticultures) (Tehran: University of Tehran Publications, 1966).
4. Iraj Afshar, 'Introduction', *Tarikh-e Yazd* (Tehran: Bongah-e Tarjomeh va Nashr-e Ketab Publishers (BTNK), 1960).
5. Reuven Amitai, *The Mongols in the Islamic Lands: Studies in the History of the Ilkhanate* (Ashgate/Variorum, 2007), p.34.
6. R.M. Savory, 'Hasan Rumlu', *International Encyclopaedia of Islamic Dynasties: A Continuing Series*, edited by Nagendra Kr. Singh (Anmol Publications PVT, 2000), p.408.
7. Abd'ul-Mohammad Ayati, 'Introduction', in 'Abdul Mohammad Ayati (ed.), *Tarikh-e Vassaf* (Iran Culture Foundation Publications, 1968), pp.1–2.
8. It took 'Abdi Beyk two and a half years (1557–60) to compose more than 4100 verses.
9. Abul-Fazl Hashim Awghli Rahimuf, 'Introduction', *Jannat al-asmar/Zinat al-awraq/Sahifat al-ikhlas* (Moscow: Danesh Publications, 1979).
10. Iraj Afshar, 'Introduction', *Tarikh-e 'Alam Aray-e 'Abbasi* (Tehran: Amir Kabir Publications, 2004), p.16.

11. J.D. Gurney, 'Review: *History of Shah Abbas the Great* by Iskandar Munshi; Roger Savory,' *International Journal of Middle East Studies*, 17, no.2 (May 1985), pp. 276–27.
12. Giosofat Barbaro and Ambrogio Contarini, 'Travels of a Merchant in Persia', *Travels to Tana and Persia* (London: Hakluyt Society, 1963), pp.141–207.
13. His notes were published under the title *The Travels of Sir John Chardin in Persia and the Orient.*
14. John Emerson, 'Chardin, John', *Encyclopaedia Iranica Online*, available at http://www.iranica.com.
15. John Emerson writes: "Together with the books of general description, then, the encyclopedic nature of his work thus easily takes precedence over its aspect as a travel account. Most of what is known about his methods, sources, and attitude toward his subject must be deduced from his own words, as few sources of independent information on him and his experience have so far emerged." (Emerson, 'Chardin, John'.)
16. H.A.R. Gibb, 'Review: *Sir John Chardin's Travels in Persia* by Percy Sykes', *Geographical Journal*, 71, no.4 (April 1928), p.396.
17. Clements R. Markham, 'Preface', in Clavijo, pp.i–x.
18. The English version was published under the title of *Narrative of the Embassy of Ruy Gonzalez de Clavijo to the Court of Timour at Samarcand, A.D. 1403–6.*
19. He travelled to Alexandria on 25 September 1615.
20. John D. Gurney, 'Pietro Della Valle: The Limits of Perception', *Bulletin of the School of Oriental and African Studies*, 49, no.1 (1986), p.103.
21. Samuel Gottlieb Gmelin, *Travels through Northern Persia 1770–1774*, translated and annotated by Willem Floor (Washington, DC: Mage Publishers, 2007).
22. Thomas Herbert and William Foster, *A Description of the Persian Monarchy* (London, 1634), p.1.
23. R.W. Ferrier, 'Herbert, Sir Thomas', *Encyclopaedia Iranica Online*, available at http://www.iranica.com.
24. Thomas Herbert, p.61. (For more information please refer to R.W. Ferrier, 'Herbert, Sir Thomas'.)
25. P.M. Sykes, 'Review: *Travels in Persia, 1627–1629* by Thomas Herbert; William Foster', *Geographical Journal*, 73, no.6 (June 1929), pp. 559–60.
26. Ross E. Dunn, *The Adventures of Ibn Battuta – A Muslim Traveler of the Fourteenth Century* (Berkeley, CA: University of California, 2004).

Bibliography

'Abdi Beyk Shirazi, Khajeh Zeyn al-Abedin 'Ali Navidi. *Jannat al-asmar/Zinat al-awraq/Sahifat al-ikhlas,* edited by Abul-Fazl Hashim Awghili Rahimuf, Moscow: Danesh Publications, 1979.

Abolqasemi, Latif. 'Iranian Garden in the History', *History of Iranian Architecture and Urbanism,* Bam: Iranian Cultural Heritage Organization, 1994.

Adahl, Karin. 'A Copy of the Diwan of Mir Ali Shir Nava'i', *Persian Painting,* edited by Robert Hillenbrand, London: I.B.Tauris, 2000, pp.3–18.

Adamova, Adel T. 'The Hermitage Manuscript of Nezami's Khamsa Dated 835/1431', *Islamic Art V,* Genoa: Bruschettini Foundation for Islamic and Asian Art, 2001, pp.53–133.

Ad-Din, Rashid. *The Successors of Genghis Khan,* translated by J.A. Boyle, London, 1971.

— *Tarikh-e Mubarak-e Ghazani,* edited by K. Jahn, London, 1940.

Afshar, Iraj. 'Introduction', *Irshad al-Zara'ah* (Guide for Horticulture), Tehran: University of Tehran Publications, 1966.

Alemi, Mahvash. 'Princely Safavid Gardens: Stage for Rituals of Imperial Display and Political Legitimacy', in Michel Conan (ed.), *Middle East Garden Traditions: Unity and Diversity,* Washington DC: Dumbarton Oaks, 2007, pp.113–38.

— 'Persian Gardens and Courtyards: An Approach to Designing Contemporary Architecture', in *Understanding Islamic Architecture,* edited by Attilio P. Petruccioli, New York: Routledge Curzon, 2003, pp.75–84.

— 'The Royal Gardens of the Safavid Period: Types and Models', *Gardens in the Time of the Great Muslim Empires: Theory and Design*, edited by Attilio Petruccioli, Leiden: E.J. Brill, 1997, pp.72–96.

— 'Chahar Bagh', *Environmental Design: Journal of the Islamic Environmental Design Research Centre*, 1, 1986, pp.38–45.

Ali, Abdullah Yusuf, *The Holy Qu'ran: Text, Translation and Commentary*, Lahore, Sh. Muhammad Ashraf Publishers, 1934; available online at http://www.al-quran.info.

Amitai, Reuven. *The Mongols in the Islamic Lands: Studies in the History of the Ilkhanate*, Ashgate/Variorum, 2007.

Ardalan, Nader and Bakhtiar, Laleh. *The Sense of Unity*, Chicago: University of Chicago Press, 1973.

Atil, Esin. *Art of the Arab World*, Washington DC: Smithsonian Institute, 1975.

Aubin, Jean. 'Eléments pour l'étude des agglomérations urbaines dans l'Iran médiéval', in *The Islamic City*, edited by S.M. Stern and A. Hourani, Oxford: Bruno Cassirer and University of Pennsylvania Press, 1970, pp.69–71.

Babaie, Sussan. 'Paradise Contained: Nature and Culture in Persian Gardens', *The Studio Potter*, 25, no.2, 1997, pp.10–13.

Babur, Muhammed. *Memoirs of Zehīr-Ed-Dīn Muhammed Bābur: Emperor of Hindustan*, translated by William Erskine and John Leyden, Oxford: Oxford University Press, 1921.

Bahari, Ebadollah. *Bihzad, Master of Persian Painting*, London: I.B.Tauris, 1996.

Bailey, Gauvin Alexander. 'The Bernard Berenson Collection of Islamic Painting at Villa I Tatti: Turkman, Uzbek, and Safavid Miniatures', Part II, *Oriental Art*, XLVIII, no.1, 2002, pp.2–16.

— 'The Bernard Berenson Collection of Islamic Painting at Villa I Tatti: Mamluk, Ilkhanid, and Early Timurid Miniatures', Part I, *Oriental Art*, XLVII, no.4, 2001, pp. 53–62.

Barbaro, Giosofat and Contarini, Ambrogio. 'Travels of a Merchant in Persia', *Travels to Tana and Persia*, London: Hakluyt Society, 1963.

Barrett, Douglas. *Persian Painting of the 14th Century*, Faber Gallery of Oriental Art, London: Faber and Faber, 1962.

Barrett, Douglas and Gray, Basil. *Indian Painting*, New York: Rizzoli, 1978.

Beyhaqi, Abul-Fazl. *Tarikh-e Beyhaqi*, edited by Khatib Rahbar, Tehran: Mahtab Publications, 2007.

Bidhendi, Mehrdad Qayyumi. 'Bagh-ha-ye Khorasan dar Tarikh-e Beyhaqi', *Proceedings of the Third Congress on Iranian Architecture and Urbanism*, 2007, Tehran, pp.119–48.

Binning, Robert B.M. *A Journal of Two Years' Travel in Persia, Ceylon, Etc.*, New York: W.H. Allen, 1857.

Binyon, Laurence, Wilkinson, J.V.S. and Gray, Basil. *Persian Miniature Painting*, New York: Dover Publications, 1971.

Black, Jeremy and Green, Anthony. *Gods, Demons, and Symbols*, Texas: University of Texas Press, 2003.

Blair, Sheila. *Illustrated History of the World*, The Nasser D. Khalili Collection of Islamic Art, XXVII, London: Khalili Collection, 1995.

Blair, Sheila and Bloom, Jonathan. *The Art and Architecture of Islam 1250–1800*, New York: Yale University Press/Pelican History of Art, 1996.

— *Images of Paradise in Islamic Art*, Hood Museum of Art, Hanover, 1991.

The Book of Arda Viraf: The Pahlavi Text, prepared by Destur Hoshangji Jamaspji and translated by Martin Haug, Bombay: Govt. Central Book Depot, 1872.

Boyce, Mary. *Zoroastrians: Their Religious Beliefs and Practices*, New York: Routledge, 2001.

— *History of Zoroastrianism*, Leiden: Brill Publishers, 1975.

— 'Anahid', in *Encyclopedia Iranica*, edited by Ehsan Yarshater, New York: Mazda Publications, pp.1003–6.

— 'Middle Persian Literature', *Iranistik II, Literatur I*, Leiden: E.J. Brill, 1968, pp.31–66.

Boyle, John Andrew. 'The Seasonal Residences of the Great Khan Ogedei', *Central Asiatic Journal*, 16, 1972, p.125–31.

Brend, Barbara. 'A 14th Century Khamseh of Nezami from Western Iran with Early Ottoman Illustrations', *Islamic Art V*, Genoa: Bruschettini Foundation for Islamic and Asian Art, 2001, pp.133–83.

— 'Beyond the Pale: Meaning in the Margin', in *Persian Painting*, edited by Robert Hillenbrand, London: I.B.Tauris, 2000, pp.39–55.

Bronstein, Leo. *Space in Persian Painting*, New Brunswick: Transaction Publishers, 1994.

Brookshaw, Dominic. 'Palaces, Pavilions and Pleasure-Gardens: the Context and Setting of the Medieval Majlis', *Middle Eastern Literatures*, 6, no.2, 2003, pp.199–223.

Browne, E.G. 'Account for a Rare Manuscript History of Isfahan', *Journal of the Royal Asiatic Society*, Ser. 3, no.13, pp.411–46.

Browne, Edward G. *Literary History of Persia*, Bethesda: Iranbooks, 1998.

Bull, George. *The Pilgrimage, The Travels of Pietro Della Valle*, London: Hutchinson, 1989.

Canby, Sheila R. *Persian Painting*, New York: Thames & Hudson, 1993.

Clark, Ebba. *The Art of the Islamic Garden*, Marlborough: Crowood Press, 2004.

Clark, Kenneth. *Masterpieces of Fifty Centuries*, New York: E.P. Dutton, 1970.

Clavijo, Ruy González de. *Narrative of the Embassy of Ruy Gonzalez de Clavijo to the Court of Timour*, translated by Clements Robert Markham, London: Hakluyt Society, 1859.

Conan, Michel (ed.). *Middle East Garden Traditions: Unity and Diversity*, Washington DC: Dumbarton Oaks, 2007.

Curl, James Stevens (ed.). *Oxford Dictionary of Architecture*, Oxford: Oxford University Press, 1999.

De Bruijn, J.T.P. 'Hafez's Poetic Art', *Encyclopedia Iranica*, edited by Ehsan Yarshater, XI, New York: Mazda Publications, 2003, pp.469–74.

Dehkhoda, 'Ali Akbar. *Persian Comprehensive Dictionary*, 15 vols, Tehran: University of Tehran Publications, 1999 (digital version available at: http://www.loghatnaameh.org/).

Denkard, Book Five, edited by Peshotan Dastur Behramjee Sanjana, 1900 (digital edition by Joseph H. Peterson, 1998, available at: http://www.avesta.org/denkard/dk5s.html).

Dickie, James. 'The Mughal Garden: Gateway to Paradise', in *Muqarnas: An Annual on Islamic Art and Architecture*, 3, edited by Oleg Grabar, Leiden: E.J. Brill, 1985, pp.128–37.

— 'The Hispano-Arab Garden: Its Philosophy and Function', *Bulletin of the School of Oriental and African Studies*, University of London, 31, no.2 (1968), pp.237–48.

Dunn, Ross E. *The Adventures of Ibn Battuta: A Muslim Traveler of the 14th Century*, Berkeley, CA: University of California, 2004.

Emerson, John. 'Chardin, John', *Encyclopedia Iranica*, edited by Ehsan Yarshater, V, New York: Mazda Publications, 1991, pp.369–77.

Ettinghausen, Richard. 'Introduction', *The Islamic Garden*, edited by Richard Ettinghausen, Washington DC: Dumbarton Oaks, 1976, pp.1–10.

Ettinghausen, Richard and Grabar, Oleg. *The Art and Architecture of Islam, 650–1250*. Middlesex and New York: Puffin, 1988.

Fakour, Mehdi. 'Garden in the Achaemenid Period', *Encyclopedia Iranica*, edited by Ehsan Yarshater, X, New York: Mazda Publications, 2001, pp.297–98.

Falsafi, Nasrollah. *Zendegani-ye Shah 'Abbas*, Tehran: Elmi Publishers, 1999.

Ferrier, R.W. *A Journey To Persia: Jean Chardin's Portrait of a Seventeenth-Century Empire*, London: I.B.Tauris, 1966.

Fryer, John. *East India and Persia*, edited by William Crooke, London: Hakluyt Society, 1915.

Gharipour, Mohammad and Allen, Douglas C. 'The Achaemenid Garden: A Study on Its Contribution to the History of Garden Design and Its Cultural Context', *Journal of Middle Eastern and North African Intellectual and Cultural Studies*, 4, issue 2 (November 2008), pp.1–35.

Gharipour, Mohammad. 'Achaemenid Architecture and Gardens' with a sidebar on 'Persepolis', *Encyclopedia of World History*, edited by Josef Castaneda-Liles, 3, ABC-Clio Publishers, 2011, pp.197–98.

— 'Persian Architecture and Hunting Gardens during the Sassanian Dynasty', *Encyclopedia of World History*, edited by Wilfred Bisson, 4, ABC-Clio Publishers, 2011, pp.160–62.

— 'Persian Architecture', *Oxford Companion to Architecture*, 1, edited by Patrick Goode, Oxford: Oxford University Press, 2009, pp.465–71.

— 'Transferring and Transforming the Boundaries of Pleasure: Multi-functionality of Gardens in Medieval Persia', *Journal of Garden History*, 39, no.3 (November 2011), pp.249–62.

— 'The Genesis in Thought and Ideas behind the Design of the Mughal Gardens in India', *Virginia Review of Asian Studies* (Spring 2009), pp.97–113.

— 'Pavilion Structure in Persianate Gardens: Reflections in the Visual and Textual Media', PhD dissertation, Georgia Institute of Technology, May 2009.

Gibb, Hamilton Alexander Rosskeen. 'Review: *Sir John Chardin's Travels in Persia* by Percy Sykes', *The Geographical Journal*, 71, no.4 (April 1928), pp.395–96.

Gmelin, Samuel Gottlieb. *Travels through Northern Persia 1770–1774*, translated and annotated by Willem Floor, Washington DC: Mage Publishers, 2007.

Golombek, Lisa 'The Gardens of Timur: New Perspectives', *Muqarnas: An Annual on Islamic Art and Architecture*, 12, Leiden: E.J. Brill, 1995, pp.137–47.

— '[Persian] Garden in Islamic.' *Encyclopaedia Iranica Online*, 1993, available at http://www.iranica.com.

Golombek, Lisa and Wilber, Donald. *The Timurid Architecture of Iran and Turan*, Princeton: Princeton University Press, 1998.

Gordon, Marshall. *Oxford Dictionary of Sociology*, New York: Oxford University Press, 1998.

Grabar, Oleg. *Mostly Miniatures*, Princeton: Princeton University Press, 2000.

Gray, Basil. *Persian Painting*, Geneva: Editions d'Art Albert Skira, 1961.

— *Persian Painting from Miniatures of the XIII–XVI Centuries*, New York: Iris Books, 1940.

— *Persian Painting*, London: Ernest Benn, 1930.

Greater Bundahishn, translated by Behramgore Tehmuras Anklesaria (digital edition by Joseph H. Peterson, 2002, available at: http://www.avesta.org/mp/grb.htm).

Gronke, Munika. 'The Persian Court between Palace and Tent: From Timur to 'Abbas I', in *Timurid Art and Culture: Iran and Central Asia in the Fifteenth Century*, edited by Lisa Golombek and Maria Subtelny, Leiden: E.J. Brill, 1992, pp.18–22.

Gurney, J.D. 'Pietro della Valle: The Limits of Perception', *Bulletin of the School of Oriental and African Studies, University of London*, 49, no.1, 1986, pp.103–16.

Habib, Irfan. 'Economic and Social Aspects of Mughal Gardens', *Mughal Gardens*, edited by Jim Wescoat and J. Wolschke-Bulmahn, Washington DC: Dumbarton Oaks, 1996, pp.134–43.

Haidar, Mirza Mohammad. *Tarikh-e Rashidi (A History of the Mughals of Central Asia)*, edited by N. Elias and translated by E. Denison Ross, India: Academica Asiatica, 1973.

Hanaway, William L. 'Paradise on Earth: The Terrestrial Garden in Persian Literature', *The Islamic Garden*, edited by Richard Ettinghausen, Washington DC: Dumbarton Oaks, 1976.

Haneda, Masashi. 'The Pastoral City and the Mausoleum City', *Islamic Urbanism in Human History*, edited by Tsugitaka Satō, London: Kegan Paul International, 1997, pp.142–70.

Haravi, Qasem Abu Nasr. *Irshad al-Zira'ah*, Tehran: University of Tehran Publications, 1968.

— *Irshad al-Zara'ah* (Guide for Horticulture), edited by Iraj Afshar, Tehran: Farhang-e Iran Zamin, 1966.

Herbert, Thomas. *Travels in Persia, 1627–1629*, edited by G. William Foster, London: Routledge, 2005.

Hillenbrand, Robert (ed.). *Persian Painting*, London: I.B.Tauris, 2000.

— 'Safavid to Qajar architecture', *Encyclopedia Iranica*, edited by Ehsan Yarshater, New York: Mazda Publications, 1993, pp.345–49.

Hirschfeld, Yizhar. 'The Rose and the Balsam: The Garden as a Source of Perfume and Medicine', in *Middle East Garden Traditions: Unity and Diversity*, edited by Michel Conan, Washington DC: Dumbarton Oaks, 2007, pp.21–39.

Hobhouse, Penelope. *Gardens of Persia*, San Fransisco: Kales Press, 2004.

Ibn Battuta, *The Travels of Ibn Battuta*, translated by H.A.R. Gibb, New York: Cambridge University Press, 1962.

Jafari, Jafar ibn-Muhammad ibn Hasan. *Tarikh-e Yazd*, edited by Iraj Afshar, Tehran: Bongah-e Tarjomeh va Nashr-e Ketab Publishers (BTNK), 1960.

Jenkinson, Anthony. *Early Voyages and Travels to Russia and Persia*, edited by Edward Delmar Morgan and Charles Henry Coote, London: Hakluyt Society, 1886.

Johnson, Allan G. *Blackwell Dictionary of Sociology*, Cambridge, MA: Blackwell Publications, 2000.

Juvaini, 'Ala al-Din 'Ata-Malik. *The History of the World Conqueror*, translated by John Andrew Boyle, Manchester: Harvard University Press, 1958.

Kadoi, Yuka. *Islamic Chinoiserie: The Art of Mongol Iran*, Edinburgh: Edinburgh University Press, 2009, pp.123–61.

Katouzian, Shahab. 'The Sense of Place in Persian Gardens', *Environmental Design: Journal of the Islamic Environmental Design Research Centre*, 2, 1986, pp.42–47.

Khansari, Mehdi. Moghtader, Mohammad Reza. Yavari M. *The Persian Garden, Echoes of Paradise*, Washington DC: Mage Publishers, 2004.

Khorramshahi, Baha' al-Din. 'Hafez'z Life and Times.' *Encyclopedia Iranica*, edited by Ehsan Yarshater, XI, New York: Mazda Publications, 2003, pp.465–69.

Khosrow, Naser. *Book of Travels*, translated by W.M. Thackston, Costa Mesa, CA: Mazda Publishers, 2001.

Khunji, Fadlullah B. Ruzbihan. *Tarikh'i Alam Aray-e Amini (Persia in 1478–1490 A.D.)*, translated by V. Minorsky, London: Royal Asiatic Society of Great Britain and Ireland, 1957.

Khajeh Zeyn al-Abedin 'Ali Navidi 'Abdi Beyk Shirazi, *Jannat al-asmar/Zinat al-awraq/ Sahifat al-ikhlas*, edited by Abul-Fazl Hashim Awghili Rahimuf, Moscow: Danesh Publications, 1979.

Koch, Ebba. 'The Architectural Forms', *Fatehpur Sikri*, edited by M. Brand and G.D. Lowry, Bombay: Marg Publications, 1987, pp.29–56.

— *Mughal Architecture*, New Delhi: Oxford University Press, 2002.

— 'Mughal Palace Gardens from Babur to Shah Jahan, 1526–1648', in *Muqarnas: An Annual on the Visual Culture of the Islamic World*, edited by Gülru Necipoglu, 14, Leiden: E.J. Brill, 1997, pp.143–65.

Lambton, Ann K.S. *Continuity and Change in Medieval Persia*, London: Persian Heritage Foundation, 1988.

Landau, Amy S. 'From Poet to Painter: Allegory and Metaphor in a Seventeenth-Century Painting by Muhammad Zaman, Master of Farangi-sazi', *Muqarnas: An Annual on the Visual Culture of the Islamic World*, edited by Gülru Necipoglu, 28, Leiden: E.J. Brill, 2011, pp.101–131.

Lehman, F. 'Babor, Zahir al-Din Mohammad', *Encyclopaedia Iranica Online*, available at http://www.iranica.com.

Lehrman, Jonas Benzion. *Earthly Paradise: Garden and Courtyard in Islam*, New York: Thames & Hudson, 1980.

Lillys, William. *Persian Miniatures, The Story of Rustam*, Tokyo: Charles E. Tuttle Company, 1958.

Lillys, William, Reiff, Robert and Esin, Emel. *Oriental Miniatures*, Tokyo: Charles E. Tuttle Company, 1965.

Lincoln, Bruce. 'A La Recherche du Paradis Perdu', *Journal of History of Religions*, 43, no.2, pp.139–54.

Losensky, Paul E. 'The Palace of Praise and the Melons of Time: Descriptive Patterns in 'Abdi Bayk Shirazi's Garden of Eden', *Eurasian Studies*, 2, no.1, 2003, pp.1–29.

Losensky, Paul. 'Naziri of Nishapur', *Encyclopaedia Iranica Online*, available at http://www.iranica.com.

Malandra, William W. 'Zoroastrianism', *Encyclopaedia Iranica Online*, available at http://www.iranica.com.

Markham, Clements R. 'Preface', *Narrative of the Embassy of Ruy Gonzalez de Clavijo to the Court of Timour*, London: Hakluyt Society, 1859, pp.i–x.

Melikian-Chirvani, Assadulah Souren. 'An Anthology of a Sufi Prince from Bukhara', *Persian Painting*, edited by Robert Hillenbrand, London: I.B.Tauris, 2000, pp.151–85.

Membre, Michele. *Mission to the Lord Sophy of Persia (1539–1542)*, translated by A.H. Morton, London: School of Oriental and African Studies, 1993.

Mo'in, Mohammad. *Farhang-e Farsi* (Persian Dictionary), Tehran: Amir Kabir Publications, 2005.

Morgenstern, Julian. 'The Sources of the Creation Story: Genesis 1:1–2:4', *American Journal of Semitic Languages and Literatures*, 36, no.3 (April 1920), pp.169–212.

Moynihan, Elizabeth. *Paradise as a Garden in Persia and Mughul India*, New York: George Braziller, 1979.

O'Kane, Bernard. 'From Tents to Pavilions: Royal Mobility and Persian Palace Design', *Ars Orientalis*, 23, edited by Gülru Necipoglu, Ann Arbor: Department of History, University of Michigan, 1993.

Paul, Juergen. 'The Histories of Isfahan: Mafarrukhi's Kitab Mahasin Isfahan', *Iranian Studies*, 33, no.1–2, 2000, pp.117–32.

Pavry, Jal Dastur. 'Manichaeism: A Rival of Zoroastrianism and Christianity', *Journal of Religion*, 17, no.2, pp.161–69.

Petruccioli, Attolio. *Gardens in the Time of the Great Muslim Empires: Theory and Design*, Leiden: Brill Academic Publications, 1997.

Pinder-Wilson, R. 'The Persian Garden', *The Islamic Garden*, edited by Richard Ettinghausen, Washington DC: Dumbarton Oaks and Trustees for Harvard University, 1976, pp.71–85.

Plett, Heinrich. 'Descripto', *Encyclopedia of Rhetoric*, edited by Thomas O. Sloane, Oxford: Oxford University Press, 2001, pp.220–21.

Polo, Marco. *The Travels of Marco Polo*, translated by Ronald Latham, Baltimore: Penguin Books, 1958.

Pope, Arthur Upham. *Persian Architecture*, New York: George Braziller Publications, 1965.

— 'Tents and Pavilions', *Survey of Persian Art from Prehistoric Times to the Present*, II, edited by Arthur Pope and Phyllis Ackerman, London: Oxford University Press, 1939, pp.1411–26.

Pope, Arthur Upham and Ackerman, Phyllis. 'Garden', *Survey of Persian Art from Prehistoric Times to the Present*, II, edited by Arthur Upham Pope and Phyllis Ackerman, London: Oxford University Press, 1939, pp.1427–445.

Pritchard, James B. *The Ancient Near East*, Princeton: Princeton University Press, 1958.

Rahbar, Khalil Khatib. 'Beyhaqi va Tarikh-e Mas'udi', *Tarikh-e Beyhaqi*, Tehran: Mahtab Publications, 2007.

Rashid-uddin, Fazl Allah Abil-Khair, *Tarikh-e Mubarak-e Ghazani*, translated by Karl Jahn, London: Mouton and Co., 1941, p.78.

Robinson, B.W. 'A Magnificent MS: The British Library Shahnama of 1486', *Islamic Art* V, Genoa: Bruschettini Foundation for Islamic and Asian Art, 2001, pp.167–83.

— *Fifteenth Century Persian Painting: Problems and Issues*, New York: University Press, 1991.

— *Persian Miniature Painting from Collections in the British Isles*, London: Crown Publishers, 1967.

— *Persian Drawings from the 14th through the 19th Century*, New York: Shorewood Publishers, 1965.

Rogers, Michael. 'The Chester Beatty Suleymanname Again', *Persian Painting*, edited by Robert Hillenbrand, London: I.B.Tauris, 2000, pp.187–200.

Romlu, Hasan Beyk. *Ahsan al-Tavarikh*, edited by 'Abd al-Hoseyn Nava'i, Tehran: Asatir Publications, 2006.

Roxburgh, David J. 'Ruy Gonzalez de Clavijo's Narrative of Courtly Life and Ceremony in Timur's Samarqand, 1404', in *The Book of Travels: Genre, Ethnology, and Pilgrimage, 1250–1700*, edited by Palmira Brummett, Leiden: E.J. Brill, 2009, pp.113–58.

— *The Persian Album, 1400–1600*, New York: Yale University Press, 2005.

— *Micrographia: Toward a Visual Logic of Persianate Painting*, Cambridge: Peabody Museum of Archaeology and Ethnology, 2003.

Rubruck, William. *The Journey of William of Rubruck to the Eastern Parts of the World, 1253–55*, translated and edited by William Woodville Rockhill, London: Hakluyt Society, 1900.

Ruggles, Dede Fairchild. *Islamic Gardens and Landscapes*, Philadelphia, PA: University of Pennsylvania Press, 2008.

— *Landscape and Vision in the Palaces of Islamic Spain*, University Park, PA: Penn State University Press, 2003.

Rypka, Jan and Jahn, Karl. *History of Iranian Literature*, Dordrecht: D. Reidel, 1968.

Saad, Magdy Tewfik. 'Traditional Urban Gardens in Identified Muslim Environments', *Environmental Design: Journal of the Islamic Environmental Design Research Centre*, 1, 1986, pp.28–31.

Schimmel, Annemarie. 'The Celestial Garden in Islam', *The Islamic Garden*, edited by E.B. Macdougall and Richard Ettinghausen, Washington DC: Dumbarton Oaks, 1976, pp.11–40.

Shahab-uddin, Adib. *Tarikh-e Vassaf*, edited by 'Abd al-Mohammad Ayati, Tehran: Iran Culture Foundation Publications, 1968.

Shirvani, Hamid. 'The Philosophy of Persian Garden Design: The Sufi Tradition', *Landscape Journal*, 4, no.1, 1981, pp.23–29.

Simpson, Marianna Shreve. *Persian Poetry, Painting, and Patronage*, Washington DC: Freer Gallery of Art, 1998.

— *Arab and Persian Painting in the Fogg Art Museum*, Cambridge: Fogg Art Museum, 1980.

Sims, Eleanor, Marshak, Boris and Grube, Ernst J. *Peerless Images*, New Haven and London: Yale University Press, 2002.

Skyes, P.M. 'Review: *Travels in Persia, 1627–1629* by Thomas Herbert; William Foster', *Geographical Journal*, 73, no.6 (June 1929), pp.559–60.

Sloane, Thomas O. (ed.), 'Decripto', *Encyclopedia of Rhetoric*, Oxford: Oxford University Press, 2001, pp.220–21.

Sobti, Manu. *Urban Metamorphosis and Change in Central Asian Cities after the Arab Invasions*, PhD dissertation, Georgia Institute of Technology, 2005.

Sobti, Manu and Gharipour, Mohammad. 'Hues of Paradise: Color in Persian Gardens', *Color in Islamic Art*, edited by Sheila Blair and Jonathan Bloom, Yale University Press, 2011, pp.306–25.

Soucek, Priscilla. 'The Ann Arbor Shahnama and Its Importance', *Persian Painting*, edited by Robert Hillenbrand, London: I.B.Tauris, 2000, pp.267–81.

Stirlin, Henry. *Islamic Architecture from Isfahan to the Taj Mahal*, New York: Thames & Hudson Publications, 2002.

Strika, V. 'The Umayyad Garden: Its Origin and Development', *Environmental Design: Journal of the Islamic Environmental Design Research Centre*, no.1, 1986, pp.72–75.

Stronach, David. 'Parterres and Stone Watercourses at Pasargadae: Notes on the Achaemenid Contribution to the Evolution of Garden Design', *Journal of Garden History*, 14, 1994, pp.3–12.

— 'Chaharbagh', *Encyclopedia Iranica*, edited by Ehsan Yarshater, New York: Mazda Publications, 1993, p.624.

Swietochowski, Marie Lukens and Carboni, Stefano. *Illustrated Poetry and Epic Images*, New York: Metropolitan Museum of Art, 1994.

Tavernier, Jean Baptiste. *Tavernier's Travelogue*, translated by Hamid Arbab Shirani, Tehran: Nilufar Publishers, 2005.

Titley, Norah M. *Persian Miniature Painting and Its Influence on the Art of Turkey and India*, Austin: University of Texas Press, 1983.

Turkaman, Eskandar Beyk. *Tarikh-e 'Alam Aray-e 'Abbasi*, edited by Iraj Afshar, Tehran: Amir Kabir Publications, 2004.

Walcher, Heidi. 'Between Paradise and Political Capital: The Semiotics of Safavid Iran', *Yale Forestry and Environmental Studies Bulletin*, 103, 1998. New Haven: Yale University Press, pp.17–21.

Welch, A. 'Gardens that Babur Didn't Like', in *Mughal Gardens*, edited by Jim Wescoat and J. Wolschke-Bulmahn, Washington DC: Dumbarton Oaks, 1996, pp.59–93.

Welch, Stuart Cary. *Imperial Mughal Painting*, New York: George Braziller, 1978.

— *Persian Painting, Five Royal Safavid Manuscripts of the Sixteenth Century*, New York: George Braziller, 1976.

Wescoat, James L. Jr. 'Mughal Gardens and Geographic Sciences, Then and Now', in *Gardens in the Time of the Great Muslim Empires: Theory and Design*, edited by Attilio Petruccioli, Leiden and New York: E.J. Brill, 1997, pp.187–202.

Wescoat, James L. and Wolschke-Bulmahn, J. *Mughal Gardens: Sources, Places, Representations and Prospects*, Washington DC: Dumbarton Oaks, 1996.

Wescoat, Jim Jr .'The Islamic Garden: Issues for Landscape Research', *Environmental Design: Journal of the Islamic Environmental Design Research Centre*, 1, 1986, pp.10–19.

Wilber, Donald N. *Persian Gardens and Garden Pavilions*, Tokyo: Charles E. Tuttle Company, 1962.

Index

Entries in bold denote illustrations' numbers

Aban Yasht, (*see also* Zoroastrian texts), 20, 29
'Abbas, Shah, 2, 5, 53, 108, 112, 113, 123, 129, 131, 133, 139
Abraham (patriarch), 46
Abu Sa'id, Soltan, 112
Achaemenids, 1–5, 11, 16, 23, 28, 109
Ackerman, Phyllis, 3
Adam, 15, 23, 28, 37
Administration, 108, 112, 115, 116, 128, 136
Administrative meeting, 111–3
Administrative offices (*Davit-khaneh*), 137
Afrasyab, **45 and 52**, 69, 73, 77
Africanus, Leo, 176
Agra, **61**, 77, 112, 113
Agriculture, 1, 6, 32
Agricultural fields, 14, 15, 110
Agricultural and fruit gardens, 110
Agricultural use of gardens, 32
Agriculturalist, 21
Ahsan al-Tavarikh, 110, 116
Ahura Mazda (*see also* Ohrmazd), 16–8, 21–2
Akbar, Prince, **79**, 91
Akbar, Shah, **86**, 95
Akkadian, 15
'Ala'-uddin, 116
Albares, 114
Alemi, Mahvash, 5, 125
Aleppo, 174, 178
Alexander the Great, **43 and 76**, 69, 90
'Ali, Imam, 129
'Ali, Mir Sayyed, **65**, 95, 96
'Ali, Qasem, 48, 50, 66, 67–8, 70
'Ali Shah, Taj-uddin, 114
Alighieri, Dante, 18
Allah (*see also* God), 25, 26, 52, 93
Alp Arsalan, 119, 168
Amir Chakhmaq, 108, 111
Amir Mahmud, 111, 115, 117, 137
Amir Mas'ud, 111, 115, 117, 137
Amir Mo'ezzi, 27, 30
Amir Mortaza, 107

Amirzadeh Eskandar, 107
Amol, 33
Amorite dynasty, 14
Amusements in gardens (*see* Games)
Anahita, 18, 29
Angels, 18–9, 20–3, 57, 66
Animals, **49**, 30, 40–2, 53, 78, 136
  Bird, 17, 53, 78
  Camel, 30, 71, 72, 135, 137
  Cattle, 21
  Eagle, 142
  Horse, 20, 29, 63, 71, 115, 129, 135
Anonymous Venetian merchant, the, 119, 121, 133–4, 174
Anteroom, 122
Anushirvan, **78**, 90
Anvari Abivardi, Hakim Awhad-uddin, 29, 30, 32, 35, 165
Apple (*see* Fruit)
Apricot (*see* Fruit)
Apsu, 13
Aqqoyunlu, Soltan Yaqub, 114
Archaeological evidence, 1, 6, 9, 27, 50, 125, 133, 150
Architecture
  Architectural elements of gardens, **98**, 25, 40, 44, 46, 57, 77, 93
  Architectural elements of pavilions, 20, 44, 66, 73
  Persian architecture, 9, 28, 43, 123
Ardashir, **29**, 59
Ardaviraf, 18–9, 21
  Ardavirafnameh, 18, 21
Arghun Khan, 136
Army (*see also* Military), 111, 116
  Army leaders, 107, 112, 114
Aromatic plants (*see* Plants)
Arzan, 105
Ashi Yasht (*see Yasht*)
Ashraf, 129–32
  Ashraf pavilion, 119, 121
Ashta-kaozhdaka ("golden crown with 100 stars"), 29
Asshur River, 15
Astarabad, 115
Asar al-Baqiyah ("Remain of the Past"), 42
Attar, Sheykh Farid-uddin (or Attar Nishapuri), 34–6, 41, 165
Automata (*see* al-Jazari)
Avenue, 134–8
Awning (*Sayeban*), 95, 96, 101, 135, 163

Babur, Zahir-uddin Muhammad Jalal-uddin, **61 and 95**, 44–5, 77, 111–5, 120, 133–5, 170
  Baburnama (or *Baburnameh*), **61 and 95**, 44–5, 77, 111–5, 120, 134, 135, 138, 170
Babylon, 12–5
Backgammon (*see* Games)
Bagh, 28, 195n31
Baghcheh ("small garden"), 105, 159
Baghdad, 33, 42, 110–1
Bagh-e
  'Adeliyyeh, 118, 136
  'Adnan, 120
  'Adnani, 106
  Amir Shahi, 107
  Bakr, 119
  Bulbul, **97**
  Buldi, 119
  Chenar, 116
  Delgosha, 114
  Dilkushai, 119
  Falasan, 119

Firuzi, 110
Hasht Behesht, 112
Jahanara, 120
Jennat ("paradise garden"), 35
Karan, 119
Khan, 119
Khass, 106
Khasseh, 107, 117
Khorram, 115
Layestan, 108
Mahmud, 108
Mehtar 'Alishah-e Farrash, 135
Mokhtar, 115
Morad, 117
No, 124
Piruzi, 115–9, 137
Sa'adat Abad, 112
Sabat, 135
Sad-Hezareh, 111
Sarafraz, 116
Sefid, 111, 115–20
Shadyakh, 105, 106, 111
Shahi ("royal garden"), 31
Shahr, 119
Taghanshahi, 107
Vafa ("Garden of Fidelity"), **4 and 95**
Zaghan, 110, 111, 115, 116
Baharestan, **66**
Bahmannameh, 42
Bahram Gur, **34**, 61
Bala-khaneh ("second floor"), 105
Balconies, 57–63, 70, 84
Balkh, 106, 111, 115, 119, 166
Balkhi, Mowlana Jalal-uddin Muhammad, 166
Banquet, **3, 82 and 85**, 44, 93
Banqueting-houses, 120, 129
al-Baqara, Sura, 26
Barbad, 70
Barriers (*see* Fences)
Basreh, 33
Bath, **33**, 136, 138
Bathhouse, 128, 135, 149
Batin ("inside"), 128
Baysonghor, Shahzadeh, 112
Bayzid, 78
Bazaars (*see* Markets)
Beams, 21, 22
Beauty, 35, 37
Behesht ("paradise"), 28
Behzad, Kamal-uddin, **81**, 43, 48, 73, 93
Beyhaqi, Abu'l-Fazl Muhammad ibn Hoseyn, 105–8, 111, 114–7, 133, 137, 171
Beyk Soltan, 116
Beylaqani, Mojir-uddin, 30, 34
Beyt ("house"), 26
Binning, Robert Blair Munro, 123–4, 132, 174
Birds (*see* Animals)
Blossom, 33, 48, 85
Blue Pavilion, **35**, 62, 84
Boat, **50 and 53**, 73–4, 84, 123
Borundo Meerza, 113
Borzuyeh, **78**, 90
Bostan (or *Bustan*; "Fruit garden"/"Orchard"), 23, 28, 30, 36, 41–6, 50, 54, 105, 110
Boulevard, 123
Boundaries, 98, 103
Boyce, Mary, 18, 22
Brocade, 24
Bukhara, 32
Burial (*see also* Gardens as pilgrimage sites, Mausoleum garden), 117
Buzarjumehr, 46
Byzantine Empire, 1, 5, 6

Calligraphy, 122
Camel (*see* Animals)
Canopy, (*see also* Kiosk; Umbrella), 93–5, 101
Capital cities, 108, 114, 115
Caravanserais (*see Ribat*)
Carpet, 21, 36, 61, 63, 77, 125, 129, 135, 144, 148, 149
  Garden, **37**, 39, 63
  Woollen, Plate 46
Carpini, John de Plano, 140–1
Carriage (*see also* Horses), 29
Cart, 137, 141
Caspian Sea, 129, 136
Castle (*see Qasr*)
Cattle (*see* Animals)
Cedar (*see* Plants)
Celebration, **55**, 32, 74
Central Asia, 29, 42, 93, 95, 96
Ceremonies, 53, 109, 111
Chaghatay Turkish, **40**, 59
Chaharbagh ("Fourfold garden"), 1, 4, 28, 44, 46, 62, 63, 90, 108, 109, 125
Chaharbagh Street, **96**, 123–4
Chamber (*see Ghurfa*)
Chaos, 139
Chardin, Jean-Baptiste, 123, 129, 131, 174–5
Chehelsotun palace, 124, 128, 129
Cherries (*see* Fruit)
Chess (*see* Games)
Chestnut (*see* Plants)
China, 23, 42, 111, 116
Chinwad Bridge, 18–9
Christianity, 22
Chronology of Persian Painting, 40
Circulation, 6, 23, 131, 150
Cistern, 124, 129, 136
Clavijo, Ruy Gonzáles de, 111–2, 114, 124–5, 137–43
Code of Hammurabi, 11, 12, 13, 14–5
Comfort and pleasure, 19, 20
Communal prayers (*terawih*), 50, 112, 118, 134
Cords, 142
Cosmology, 22
Cosmos, 18
Couch, 24, 30, 106
Court, 39–43, 61–3, 86, 96, 112–3
Courtiers, **18**, 44–7, 52–61
Creativity, 27, 93
Cush, 15
Cushions, 21, 24
Cypress tree *see* plants
Cyprus, 174
Cyrus the Great (also known as Cyrus II), 2, 16

Dadestan-e Denig ("Religious Decisions"), 19
Dai Ming Khan, 111
Damascus, 110, 174
Dance, **22**, 53, 164
Daqiqi Tusi, Abu Mansur Muhammad ibn Ahmad, 166
Dargah, 107–8, 120
Decoration (*see also* Ornamentation), 53, 54, 70, 95, 96, 101, 122, 124, 145
Decorative patterns, 58, 77, 128
Dehkhoda, 'Ali Akbar, 28, 106
Dehlavi, Amir Khosrow, **35, 51 and 73**, 30, 34, 62, 73, 84, 86, 166
Dehliz ("Corridor"), 106, 122
Delhi, 2, 168
Della Valle, Pietro, 104, 119, 131, 176
Denkard, 22

Dervishes, **5, 22 and 42**, 46, 54, 66
Desert, 101
Deylami, 'Abdol Rashid, **28**, 58
Dhulpur, 120
Divan ("Offices"), 42, 43, 52, 54, 58, 66, 71, 95, 105, 106, 107, 111
Divan-e rasa'el, 160
Divan-khaneh, 107, 131, 133
Doctor (*see also* Physician), **7**, 47
Dokkan (*see* Couch)
Dome, 72, 77, 78, 95, 96, 122, 136
Dream journey (*see also Ardaviraf-nameh*), 18
Drinking parties (*see also* Drunkard), 32, 34, 44, 50
Drunkard, **39**, 66

Eagle (*see* Animals)
Earth, 15–8, 20–1, 25, 26, 37
Edinu, 15
Egypt, **48**, 72
'emarat ("building"), 28–9, 105–7, 120, 135
'Emarat-e Dargah (or 'Emarat-i Dargah), 123, 144
Emil, 114
Encampments (*see also Ordu*), 2, 4–5, 48, 53, 77, 109, 114–5, 117, 118, 136–9, 143–4, 148, 149
Enclosure, 23, 54, 62, 66, 86, 136, 143, 148
Enki, 18, 37
Entertainment (*see also* Game), 34, 78
Enthronement, **19**, 52, 53, 71, 74, 84, 95, 111, 141
Entrance (*see also Dargah*), 30, 48, 53, 57, 70, 86, 107–8, 112, 120–1, 122, 124, 125, 131, 135, 140–3
Enuma Elish, 11, 12, 13–4, 15, 18, 37
Envoy, **61 and 69**, 46, 77, 113, 116
Epic (*see also Shahnameh*), 13, 40, 41, 42, 44
Epic of Gilgamesh, The, 11, 12, 13, 14, 37
Ettinghausen, Richard, 3, 84
Eunuch, 57
Euphrates, 15
European influence, 69, 100
Eve, 15–6, 23, 28, 37
Excursion, **12**, 50, 95
Execution, 111

Fairies, **80**, 91
Faithful, 22, 23, 24, 25, 26, 44
Farah Abad, 132, 174
Farahani, Adib al-Mamalek, 29, 32
Farangi-sazi, 61
Fargard, 16
Farhad va Shirin, **20**, 53
Farm, 105, 132
Farrokhi Sistani, Abu'l-Hasan 'Ali, 12, 32, 33, 35, 106, 119, 166
Feast of Sadeh, **2**
Feasts (*bazm*) (*see also* Ceremonies; Parties), **57**, 46, 53, 111, 128, 140
Fences, 50, 52, 58, 59, 62, 66, 71, 77, 86
Ferdows, 23, 25, 37
Ferdowsi, Abul Qasem, 30–1, 32, 34–6, 41, 43, 166
Feyz Kashani, Molla Hoseyn, 31
Fig (*see* Fruit)
Firdevsi Burusevi, 78
Flexibility, 74, 107, 110, 117
Flood, 17
Flower (*see* Plants)
Food, 1, 14, 15, 32, 93, 110, 135

Foreground, 47, 53, 69, 70, 86
Formal garden, 6, 44, 46, 100
Foroughi Bastami, 'Abbas, 33
Fountain (*see also* Fountain room; *Hoz-khaneh*), 46, 69, 71, 74, 86, 90, 101, 106, 107, 112, 122, 132, 134, 144
Fountain room (*see also Hoz-khaneh*), 105, 107, 108, 120
Freedom, 32, 41
Friday, 135, 137
Fruit
  Apple, 85
  Apricot, 120
  Cherry, 120
  Fig, 120
  Fruit garden see *Bustan*
  Hazelnut, 120
  Lime, 120, 134
  Nectarine, 120
  Orange, 120
  Peach, 120
  Pistachio, 120
  Pomegranate, 85
  Quince, 120
  Wall-fruit, 120
Fryer, John, 120, 123
Function, 2, 3–4, 5, 7, 28, 32, 53–4, 57, 91, 100, 101, 105, 109, 111, 120, 144–50
Functional flexibility, 110

Gallery, 122, 134
Games
  Amusements in gardens, 111
  Backgammon, **44**, 69
  Chess, **6 and 44**, 46, 52
Ganjvar Ardavan and Golnaz, **29**, 59
Garden
  as pilgrimage sites (*see also* Burial; Mausoleum), 117–8
  as living cells, 107–8
  of Abode, 24
  of Ahmad Siah, 119
  of Eden, 15–6, 19, 22–3, 31, 37
  of Eternity, 24
  of Nowruzi, 110
Gardener, 14–5, 32, 34, 52, 59
Gardesh (*see* Walking)
Garment, 21, 24
Garshaspnameh, 42, 166
Gate (or Gateway), **26**, 23–4, 71, 78, 85, 89, 91, 121–2, 143
Gender, 134, 142, 143, 149
  Gender segregation, 58–9, 96, 101, 138, 144
Genesis, story of, 11, 12, 15–6, 23, 37
Geometric, 44, 46, 47, 70, 78, 90, 96
Gesture, 54, 61, 74, 85, 123
Ghazan Khan, 42, 118, 136, 172, 173
Ghaznavids, 29, 105, 110, 111, 115, 117, 119, 137, 150, 166, 171
Ghaznin, 105, 107, 108, 115, 117, 119, 133, 171
Ghorfeh (*see Ghurfa; see also* Room)
Ghurfa ("chamber"), 25, 122, 124, 125, 129
Gifts, **67**, 85, 95, 111, 134
Gihon, 15
Gmelin, Samuel Gottlieb, 104, 131–3, 177
God (*see also* Allah), 15, 26, 28, 31, 105, 128
Gohar Shad Beygom Madrasa, 118
Gold, **67**, 15, 21, 24, 29, 35, 53, 54, 78, 84, 121, 122, 123, 124, 125, 128, 129, 136, 140–2
Golden-*orda*, 141
Golden pavilion (*khargah-e zarrin*), 136
Golestan (*see also Bustan*), 28, 34, 105

Golombek, Lisa, 4–5
Golshan, 28, 105
Golzar, 28
Gorgani, Fakhr-uddin As'ad, 30, 32, 34, 36
Goshnajaman, Dastur Manushchihr, 19
Governors, 112, 113
Grabar, Oleg, 40, 69
Grain, 14, 18
Grass (*see Khas*)
Gronke, Monika, 114–5
Guilds (*Senf*), 42
Gurney, John D., 103, 174
Guy va Chowgan, **92**, 96

Hafez Shirazi, Khajeh Shams-uddin, **18, 22, 39 and 84**, 29, 41, 43, 52, 54, 58, 66, 71, 95, 167
Haft Awrang, **17, 25, 48, 70, 77 and 82**, 43, 52, 57, 58, 59, 72, 85, 90, 93, 95
Haft Dast, 124
Hamedani, Adib al-Mamalek, 31, 36
Hammurabi, 11, 12, 13, 14–5, 31, 37
Hamzenameh, **30**, 59
Haneda, Masashi, 108, 110, 114, 118, 121, 136
Happiness, 20, 31
Haravi, Qasem Abu Nasr, **98 and 99**, 104, 125, 171–2
Herbert, Thomas, 104, 111–3, 119, 123, 129, 131, 177
Harem, 4, 29, 57, 58, 69, 122, 134, 137
Hasan, Uzun, 108, 121, 122
Hasht Behesht, **97 and 100**, 112, 119, 121, 123–4
Hatef Esfahani, Sayyed Ahmad, 12, 35, 167
Havilah, 15
Hayat al-Abrar, **13**, 50
Hazelnut (*see* Fruit)
Hazin Lahiji, Muhammad Ali ibn Abi Taleb, 33
Healing, 16
Heaven (*see also* Garden of Eden; Paradise), 15–6, 17, 18–21, 22–3, 31, 37
Hell, 16, 18–9, 26
Herat, 42, 43, 50, 70, 93, 96, 110, 111–2, 115, 116, 119, 125
Herzfeld, Ernst, 3
Hexagonal, 50, 63, 71, 72, 77, 78, 82, 85, 86, 89, 90, 91, 96
Hezar Jarib Garden, 108
Hierarchical order, 61, 74, 91, 112, 113
Hijab, 59
Hills, 42, 46, 85, 124, 131
Hindi, 33, 165
History of Akbar Shah, The, **79**, 77, 91, 95
History of the World Conqueror, The, 115, 141
Holy creatures, 16–8
Homay, **26**, 57, 58, 71
Homayun, **79**, 57, 58, 71, 91
  Homayun's tomb, 2
Horse (*see* Animals)
Hospital, 108, 121
Hoseyn, Shah, 132
Hoseyn Mirza, Soltan, **81**, 115
Houris, 26
Hoz-khaneh (*see also* Fountain room), 105–6, 107, 120
Hulagu, 42, 116
Hunt, John Dixon, 109

Ibn Battuta, Abu 'Abdollah, 110, 118, 120, 138–9, 177–8
Ibrahim Mirza, Soltan, 52

Iconography, 40, 61
'Id, **18**, 52
Ilkhanids, 39, 40–1, 42, 44, 96, 100, 108, 110, 114, 115, 118, 121, 137, 141, 144, 148
'Illiyun, 23
Imagination, 7, 12, 27, 41, 48, 63, 91, 93
Immortality, 17, 18
Imperial encampments (*see also Ordu*), 4, 114
Inana, Goddess (or Ishtar), 13, 15, 32
Incense burner, **49**, 72
Income, 110–1
India, **34**, 2, 4, 5, 29, 43, 46, 61, 95, 111
Interior, **23 and 100**, 32, 44, 47–8, 54, 57, 63, 69, 70, 74, 85, 95, 123, 125, 128–9, 139–43
Irrigation, 1, 6, 46
Irshad al-Zira'ah, **98 and 99**, 125, 133
Isfahan, **96 and 100**, 2, 108, 112, 117, 119, 121, 123–4, 129, 133
Isfandyar, **58**, 77
Isma'il, Shah, 41, 43, 173
Italian style, 132
Iwan (*see also* Terrace; Verandah), 28, 29, 30, 31, 34, 35–6, 47, 48, 52, 53, 54, 57, 58, 61, 66, 68, 69, 71, 74, 77, 85, 86, 100, 106, 111, 122, 123, 125, 128

Jafar Abad, 128
Jafari, Jafar ibn-Muhammad ibn Hasan, 104, 105–6, 107, 119, 120, 135, 172
Jahangir, Shah, 134, 170
Jami, Nur-uddin 'Abd al-Rahman, **7, 9, 17, 25, 48, 66, 70, 77, 82, 89 and 93**, 32, 33, 35, 36, 43, 85
Jami' al-Tavarikh ("Compendium of Chronicles"), 40, 42, 95, 135, 172
Jamshid, **56**, 74
Jannat al-khalid, 23
Jarib, 119
al-Jazari, Badi' al-Zaman, **53**, 73
Automata, **53**, 73
Jenkinson, Anthony, 137
Jinn, 78
Joveyni, 'Ata Malek Ibn Muhammad, **67**, 84, 95, 114, 173

Kabul, 44
Kaempfer, Engelbert, 123
Kakh, 28–30, 105, 115
Kakh-e Piruzi, 119
Kalileh va Damneh, **78**, 41, 42, 90
Keif Palace (*Iwan-e Keif*), 106
Kerman, 114
Kermani, Khaju, 35, 42, 43
Keryas, 128
Kesh, 119, 124, 125
Khajeh 'Abdollah Ansari, **13**, 50, 171
Khajeh Amir Shah, 107
Khajeh Nezam al-Molk, 116
Khajeh Rashid-uddin, 104, 115, 118, 135, 136, 172
Khal'at, 111
Khamseh, **10, 15, 19, 24, 27, 33, 34, 35, 43, 47, 54, 61, 71, 72, 76 and 88**, 43, 48, 50, 53, 54, 58, 59, 62, 69, 70, 71, 74, 77, 84, 86, 90, 91, 95, 96, 100
Khan Maleki Bazaar, 110
Khan, Ghazan 42, 118, 136, 172, 173
Khan, Genghiz, 42, 84, 118, 140, 141
Khan, Mohsin, 25
Khaneh, 28–9, 105, 107, 120, 137
Khanqah, 120
Khaqani Haqayeqi Shervani, Afzal-uddin, 28, 167

Khargah, 28–9, 30
Khas ("grass"), 133
Khazra', 105
Kheymeh (*see also Sardaq*; Tent), 26, 28, 29, 30
al-Khiyam, 26
Khojandi, Sheykh Kamal, 33, 165
Khorasan, 111, 114, 115, 117
Khormastan ("Palm grove"), 105
Khorshid, **56**, 74
Khosrow, Key, **19, 27, 52, 57, 59, 60, 62 and 87**, 50, 52, 57–8, 63, 70, 73, 74, 77, 95, 96, 105, 128
  Assassination of, **10**, 48
  Khosrow va Shirin, **15, 32, 36, 62, 87 and 90**, 59, 62, 63, 70, 95, 96
Khosrow, Naser, 29, 31, 35, 110
Khunji, Fazl Allah, 112
Khwarazm, 112, 114
Kingship, 52, 86
Kiosk, (*see also* Canopy; Umbrella), **62, 63, 64, 65 and 66**, 87, 9, 29, 39, 40, 46, 70–4, 81–4
Kitayans, 140
Kuk Sarai, 119
Kushk, 28–30, 105, 107–8, 115
Kushk-e Mahmudi, 105
Kushk-e No-ye Mas'udi, 107
Kuyuk Khan, **67**, 84–5, 95

Lahiji, Muhammad Asiri, 33
Lahiji Esfahani, Muhammad 'Ali, 168
Landau, Amy, 61
Landscape, 4, 23, 41–4, 48, 58, 70, 71, 77, 84, 98, 147
al-Latif, 'Abd, 73
Legal terms, 14
Lehrman, Jonas Benzion, 5
Leyla and Majnun, **24, 40, 54 and 93**, 54, 66, 74, 95, 128
Lifestyle, 4, 8, 39
Lime (*see* Fruit)
Loggia, 131
Love, **17**, 47, 57, 61, 129
Lover, **25**, 57, 58, 59
Luck, 32
Lysander, 4

Madrasa, 50, 54, 121
Mafarrukhi, Mufazzal ibn sa'd, 119
Magi, **63**, 22, 78, 91
Mahalleh, 138
Mahmud of Ghazneh, 117, 171
Maid, **29**, 59
Majmu' al-Tavarikh, 40, 41, 42, 95, 110, 116, 135
Male, 57, 59, 86, 96, 101, 138, 144, 147
Malek Shah, Soltan, 27, 119
Manafi al-Hayawan, 42
Mansion, 25, 26, 105
Mantiq al-Teyr, 43
Manuchehri Damghani, 35
Maqsud, **12**, 50
Marble, 118, 122, 123, 124, 129, 132, 134
Marco Polo, 116, 174
Marduk, 13
Marghzar, 105, 136
Markets, 110, 121, 123, 138, 144, 147, 157
Marriage, **21, 28 and 82**, 54, 93, 140
Marv, **14**, 50
Masakin, 26
Mashhad, 118
Masnavi-ye Jamshid va Khorshid, **56**, 33, 74
Material, 3, 4, 6, 15, 20, 22, 29, 31, 84, 129

Mausoleum, 6, 118, 121, 148
gardens (*see also* Burial; Garden as pilgrimage sites), 4, 117–21, 135, 150
of Imam Reza, 118
Mazandaran, 174
Mazra'eh (*see also* Farm), 105
Me'rajnameh, 41, 42
Meadows (*see also Riyad*), 119, 137
Medieval Age, 109, 114
Meerzas (*see also* Courtiers; Nobles), 112, 113
Mehrdokht, **30**, 59
Meidan ("courtyard" or "city square"), 119, 122, 135
Membre, Michele, 104, 112, 135–7, 142, 178
Mesopotamia, 1, 11, 12–16, 18, 37, 109
Metaphorical (*see also* Symbolic), 7, 23, 27, 31
Middle-ground, 53
Military (*see also* Army), 104, 109, 114, 115–7, 137, 138, 144, 145, 148, 149
Mir Mosavvar, 71
Mirak, Sayyed Aqa Jalal-uddin (or Aqa Mirak), 43, 48, 86
Mirror, 33, 124
Mirza 'Ali, **50–1,** 70, 73, 86
Mirza Baysonghor, 118
Mirza Muhammad Heydar, 111, 119
Mirza Shah Mahmud, 115
Mo'izzi Nishapuri, Abu 'Abdollah (or Amir Mo'izzi), 35, 168
Mobility (*see also* Portable), 6, 72, 73, 93, 100, 114, 145–9
Module, 122
Muhammad Khodabandeh, Soltan, 172
Mojtaba, Amir 'Emad-uddin, 107
Molla, 31, 113
Mongols, 93, 114, 115, 118, 137, 139
Moon, 16, 17, 26, 35, 52
Moses, 25
Moshkuy, 29
Mosque, 46, 50, 69, 107, 108, 114, 121, 138, 145
Moynihan, Elizabeth, 4
Mozaffar, Shahzadeh, 111
Mu'azzens, 138
Mughal Gardens: Sources, Places, Representations, and Prospects, 5
Mughals, 4, 5, 8, 29, 33, 40, 43, 59, 62, 69, 77, 84, 95, 111, 119
Muhammad, Prophet, 41, 42–3, 93
Muhammad, Soltan, **2, 18, 63 and 84**, 47, 48, 52, 66, 86, 95
Muhammad Mirza, Soltan, 112
Munis al-Ahrar ("Free Men's Companion"), 42
Murder (*see also* Execution), 47, 116
Muzahheb, Sheykh Zadeh Mahmud, 53
Myrtle (*see* Plants)

Narratives, 11, 12, 22, 41, 44, 48, 54, 59, 100, 148
Nasriyyeh, 108, 118, 121–2, 134
Natural elements (*see also* Plants; Trees; Water), 3, 11–13, 16, 23, 24–5, 27, 62, 78, 101, 147
Natural garden (*see also* Natural landscape; Naturalistic garden), 44, 61
Natural landscape, 23, 43, 44, 70, 71
Naturalistic garden, 44
Nava'i, Mir 'Ali Shir, **13, 20 and 31**, 43, 53
Naziri Nishapuri, Muhammad Hoseyn, 34, 168
Nezami, Abu Muhammad Elyas (Ganjeh), 32, 33, 34, 41, 43, 48, 49, 54, 64, 70, 74, 75, 79, 86, 90, 95, 96, 97, 168

Nezami, Yusof, 95
al-Nezamiyyeh, 169
Night banquet, **1**, 44
Nishapur, 105, 106, 111, 119
Noah, 74
Nobles, **67**, 95, 111, 112, 113, 137
Nowruz, **59**, 77, 95
Nushabeh, Queen, **43 and 76**, 69, 86, 90
Nushirvan, Shah (*see also* Anushirvan), **6, 41 and 78,** 46, 66, 90

O'Kane, Bernard, 4, 114, 115
Objects, 8, 9, 41–2, 44, 109
Octagonal, 52, 63, 69, 90, 113, 122, 134, 135
Offerings, 21–2
Ogetei, 114
Oghuz, 95–6
Ohrmazd (*see also* Ahura Mazda), 19, 21, 22
Old Testament, 15
Olearius, Adam, 103
'Onsori, 29
Orange (*see* Fruit)
Orchard, **70**, 28, 120
Order, 6, 40, 47
Ordu (*see also* Encampments; Military), 4, 96, 114, 115, 135–45
Oriental drawings, 44
Ornamentation, 31, 34–5, 53, 54, 70, 72, 77, 90, 91, 95, 96, 101, 119, 124, 128, 133, 141, 142, 145
Oshtorgan, 110
Otaq ("room"), 136
Ottomans, **91**, 1, 43, 78, 95, 122
Owners, 5, 31, 33, 144, 148
Ownership, 7, 14

Pahlavi, 19, 22
  Language, 28
  Script, 19
Palace (*see Qasr*)
Palun ("packsaddle"), 30, 72
Panj Ganj, **9, 12**, 48, 50, 70
Panjikants, 42
Paradise, 1, 2, 4, 7, 12, 22–4, 25–6, 28, 29, 30–1, 34–6, 37, 89, 105, 109, 116, 125, 128, 147, 150, 151
  Ridhwan (the Doorkeeper), 24
Parthians, 1, 11
Parties (*see also* Ceremonies), 2, 32, 34, 44, 46, 50, 53, 70, 96, 109, 112
Pasargadae, 2, 3, 4
Pastoral cities, 118
Pathway, 36, 44, 52, 73, 82, 89, 93, 101, 131, 149
Patronage, 7, 9, 27, 39, 42–3, 54, 74, 104
Paved area, 44, 47, 50, 52, 53, 58, 62, 66, 70, 71, 74, 78, 82, 85, 86, 89, 90, 96
Peace, **69**, 24, 32, 85
Peach (*see* Fruit)
Perspective drawing, 69
Pharaoh, 25, 26
Physician, **14 and 71**, 50
Piazza, 108, 112, 135
Pilgrimage (*see also* Masoleum), 2, 109, 117, 118, 143, 148
Pinder-Wilson, Ralph, 105, 136
Pine tree (*see* Plants)
Pishgah, 134
Pistachios (*see* Fruit)
Plan, 2, 7, 63, 66, 71, 84, 86, 90, 91, 100, 123, 125, 131, 137, 141, 145, 150
Plants,
  Aromatic plants, 17, 119
  Pine tree, 119

Cedar, 13
Chestnut, 120
Cypress tree, 32, 34, 36, 120
Flowers, 33–7, 71
Myrtle, 119
Raz, 105
Plasterwork, 78, 134
Platform, 7, 36, 73, 74, 78, 90–1, 95, 101, 106, 110, 111, 125, 133, 134, 135, 144, 149, 150
Pleasure, 1, 3, 19–20, 26, 32, 105, 110–1, 117, 118, 120, 132
Pleasure gardens (*basatin*), 1, 105, 109, 110–1
Poetry, 7–8, 12, 23, 27–31, 32, 33, 34, 37, 38, 39, 41, 47, 48, 57, 89, 96, 100
Pole, 93, 95, 125
Political meetings, 2, 109
Polygonal, 124
Pomegranate (*see* Fruit)
Ponds (*see also* Fountain; Pool), 44, 78, 120, 123
Pool (*see also* Fountain; Ponds), 44, 46, 47, 48, 52, 59, 62, 70, 71, 77, 78, 90, 96, 107, 118, 119, 125, 133, 135
Pope, Arthur, 3, 150
Portable, 21, 71, 85, 93, 100, 136
Portico, 52, 66, 69, 77, 106
Posture (*see* Gesture)
Power, 1, 22, 38, 57–8, 61, 116, 142, 144, 148
Princess of the Blue Pavilion, **35**, 62
Privacy, 2–3, 36, 42, 47, 48, 50, 53, 57, 58–9, 71, 73, 86, 90, 100, 101, 105, 108, 109, 110, 118, 121, 134, 135, 135, 145
Promised garden (*see also* Paradise), 25
Prose, 31, 35, 39, 41, 48
Prosperity (*see also* Wealth), 33, 86
Psychological, 33–5
Public, 2–3, 47, 53, 71, 73, 86, 100, 101, 105, 108, 109, 110, 118, 120, 122, 133, 135, 139
Punishment, 19

Qaboq, 114
Qadi, 175
Qajars, 124, 166
Qanat, 1
Qasr, 25, 28, 29, 30, 35, 105, 108, 112, 119, 128, 135
Qasr-e jenan ("Paradise palace"), 35
Qasr-e shahi ("Royal palace"), 31
Qatran Tabrizi, Abu Mansur, 35, 168
Qavami Razi, Badr-uddin, 34, 169
Qaydafa, Queen, **8**, 7
Qawarir ("crystal"), 25
Qazvin, 53, 110, 111, 112, 119, 123, 128, 170, 170
Qazvini, Va'ez, 36
Qibla, 111
Qizilbash, 113, 172
Quince (*see* Fruit)
Qur'an, 7, 12, 22–6, 113
Qurchis ("cavalrymen"), 112

Railing, 50, 52, 66, 69, 73, 85
Rajan, 119
Rajput, **61**, 77
Ram Yasht, 21, 22
Ramadan, 52, 112, 135
Rashid-uddin, Khajeh, 40, 42, 104, 115, 118, 135, 136, 141, 172
Ravaq (*see also* Portico; Verandah), 106, 125
Rawdha, 23, 25, 125
Raz ("grapevine"/"vineyard") (*see* Plants)

Realism, 9, 12, 40, 41, 69
Rebellion, 111, 139
Rectangular, 2, 63, 69, 71, 78, 86, 90, 95, 113, 133, 144
Regulations (*see also* Rules), 14, 22
Relaxation, 2, 29, 33, 34
Residential use, 34, 63
Residents, 2, 26, 33, 36, 53, 101, 139, 141, 142, 144
Restoration, 23, 24, 33, 104, 109, 124
Reward, 17, 21, 33, 37
Ribat ("caravanserais"), 110, 115, 117
Righteous, 17, 19–20, 21, 23–5, 26, 37
Rivalry, 22, 54
Rivers, 11, 15–6, 18, 23, 24, 25, 26, 37
Road, 122
Robe, 20, 111, 140
Rocks, 42, 44
Romanticism, 40, 42
Romlu, Hasan, 104, 111, 115, 116, 117, 118, 121, 172
Roof, 52, 57, 58, 59, 66, 69, 85, 90, 91, 95, 96, 100, 101, 124, 128, 129, 133, 134, 135, 144
Room (*see also Otaq*), 25, 47, 48, 113, 129, 131, 136
Royal administration, 128
Royal family, 58, 110, 111, 138, 144
Royal gardens, 5, 53, 86, 107, 110, 111, 113, 115, 116, 118, 143, 148
Royal hunting parks, 109
Royal palace, 31, 86, 115, 122
Royal tent (*Sarapardeh*), 136, 137, 142, 143
Rudabeh, **28, 68 and 75**, 57, 58, 85
Rudaki Samarqandi, 'Abdollah Jafar, 36, 169
Rug (*see* Carpet)
Ruggles, D. Fairchild, 5, 6
Rulers (*see also* Courtiers; Viziers), 4, 46, 96, 110, 114, 115
Rules (*see also* Regulations), 14, 15, 32, 46
Rumi, 29, 32–6, 169
Rustam, **57–8**, 77

Sa'adat Abad Garden and Palace, 53, 110, 111, 112, 119, 121, 123, 128, 137, 139, 144
Sa'd, Atabak, 116
Saad, Magdy Tewfik, 4
Sabat, 106, 107, 108
Sacred, 5, 7, 11, 12, 17, 19–20, 23, 37
Sacrifice, 17, 18, 21, 22
Safarnameh, 105, 167
Safavids, 4, 5, 8, 39, 40, 43, 44, 53–4, 61, 62, 66, 69, 77, 85, 86, 91–2, 100, 103, 106, 113, 114, 119, 120, 121, 128, 132, 137, 145, 148
  Capital, 108, 121, 123–4
  Court, 110, 115, 131
  Kings, 5, 41, 43, 96, 110, 112, 123–4, 129
Sama', 54
al-Samad, 'Abd, 82, 89
Samarqand, **11, 55**, 2, 48, 74, 108, 110, 114, 116, 119, 121, 124–7
Sarai (*see also Khaneh*; *Qasr*), 29, 34, 105, 121, 138
Sarai-e 'Adnani, 120
Sarai-e Shahi, 105, 128
Sardaq (*see also* Tent), 26, 28, 29, 30
Sarh, 25, 119
Sari, 33
Sassanids, 1, 11, 16, 18, 19, 22–3, 37
Savoji, Salman, 34, 35, 36, 170
Sayyed Majd-uddin, 120
Scale, 8, 46, 62, 63, 100, 145, 151
School (see also *Madrasa*), **24, 54 and 73**, 54, 74

Scroll, **94**, 96
Sculpture, 8, 39, 72
Security, 24, 91, 145
Semi-open space (*see also Iwan*; Portico), 47, 105, 106
Semi-public, 53, 139
Separator, 89, 143
Servants, 4, 36, 50, 52, 53, 58, 84, 89, 118, 135, 136
Sex, 47
Seyda-ye Nasafi, 32, 34
Shabestan, 29
Shade (*see also* Shadow), 13, 24, 26, 78, 90, 95, 111, 128, 134, 143
Shadow (*see also* Shade), 34, 95, 128
Shadyakh Garden, 105, 106
Shahab-uddin, Adib, 104, 110, 115–6, 173
Shahnameh (*see also* Ferdowsi), **2, 6, 8, 21, 28–9, 38, 45, 50, 52, 57, 58, 59, 60, 63, 64, 68, 69, 75, 85 and 94,** 30, 32, 39, 41, 42, 43, 44, 46, 47, 53, 58, 69, 73, 77, 78, 85, 91, 95, 100
  Shahnameh of Baysonghor, 58–9
  Shahnameh of Shah Tahmasp, **2, 21, 38, 50, 63 and 94,** 53, 63, 66, 73, 78, 85, 96
Shahrokh, King (*see also* Timur; Timurids), 43, 115, 118
Sham, 136
Shapur, **32 and 87**, 95
Sharuyaz, 114
Sheba, the Queen of, 78
Shervani, Khaqan, 32, 35, 52
Sheykh of San'an, 59
Shi'ism, 73, 118, 129
Shida, **60**, 77
Ships (*see* Boats)
Shira-Ordu (or Sira-Orda), 141
Shiraz, 42, 84, 110, 115–6, 117, 118, 120
Shirazi, 'Abdi Beyk, 104, 173
Shirin, **15, 20, 32, 36, 62, 72 and 90**, 50, 53, 57, 58, 59, 62, 63, 70, 77, 95, 96
Shirinkar, 'Abdol-Samad, 91
Shrubs (*see also* Plants; Trees), 71
Sight, 26, 123
Sightseeing (*see Tamasha*)
Sikri, 135
Silk, 24, 125, 131, 137, 140, 141, 142, 143
Siyavash, **45 and 69**, 69
Sky, 30, 36
Slaves (*Gholams*), 137
Sobhat al-Abrar, **7**, 47
Sobti, Manu, 108
Social class (*see also* Hierarchical order), 31, 33
Social organization, 112, 138
Soffeh, 106, 107, 111, 135
Soffeh-ye no, 106
Soleymannameh, 78
Solid, 2, 36, 47, 52, 53
Solomon, **64 and 77**, 25, 90
Soltaniyyeh, 114, 118
Space (*see also* Spatial qualities), 2, 3, 6, 23, 30, 40, 47, 48, 2, 57, 58, 59, 69, 91, 96, 104, 105, 106, 108, 128, 129, 133, 137, 138, 140, 142, 148, 150
Spain, 5, 23
  Spanish ambassador, 133
Spatial qualities, 57–71
Spectators, 57, 112
Sphinx, 78
Spiritual, 1, 11, 18, 20, 27, 31, 38, 44, 54, 109, 147, 148
Square, 2, 63, 69, 71, 72, 78, 90, 100, 119, 123, 129, 131, 132, 136, 141, 142, 144
Staircase, 91

Stars, 16, 17, 21, 29
Stone, 122, 132
Stream, 46, 77, 122, 124, 131, 136
Stronach, David, 3–4
Style, 8, 40, 100
Sufi, 12, 120, 128
Summer-houses (*see also Soffeh*), 120, 123
Sun, 16, 17, 22, 30, 78, 86, 112
Survey of Persian Art, A, 3
Susani-khaneh, 120
Symbolic, 3, 5, 26, 30, 31, 36, 37, 38, 57, 58, 77
Symmetric plan, 131
Syria, 46, 73

Tabriz, 42, 43, 110, 112, 118, 119, 121, 135, 137, 142
Tabrizi, Mirza Muhammad 'Ali Sa'eb, 29, 33, 34, 169
Taghanshah, Atabak, 107
Tahmasp, Shah, 52, 53, 63, 66, 78, 80, 85, 96, 99, 111, 112, 113, 124, 128
Takht, 30, 36
Takya-namad, 135
Talar ("Halls"), 5, 28, 29
Tamasha ("Sightseeing"), 33, 117
Talicia Garden, 124, 134
Taq (*see also Iwan*), 29
Tarab-khaneh, 120
Tarikh-e 'Alam Aray-e 'Abbasi, 106, 114, 120
Tarikh-e 'Alam Aray-e Amini, 112
Tarikh-e Beyhaqi, 107, 136
Tarikh-e Ghazani, 115, 136
Tarikh-e Jahan Goshay, **67**, 84, 95
Tarikh-e Jahangoshay-e Joveyni, 173
Tarikh-e Rashidi, 119
Tarikh-e Vassaf, 115, 173
Tarikh-e Yazd, 105, 107, 120, 134, 172
Tarkhani courtiers, 116
Tassels, 125
Tavernier, Jean Baptiste, 103, 110, 123
Tent (*see also Khargah*), **88**, 2, 8, 9, 26, 30, 34–5, 40, 46, 77, 85, 93–101, 109, 114, 136–50
  Conical, 95–9
  Yurt, 95–9, 114
  Pyramidal, 93
Tepper, Yotam, 5
Terminology, 6, 7–8, 27, 28–31, 33, 100, 104–6, 110, 143, 147, 151
Terrace (*see also Iwan*), 3, 25, 122, 125, 132
Three-dimensionality (*see also* Spatial qualities), 43, 100
Throne (*Arika*), **5, 56 and 64**, 3, 9, 21–2, 26, 30–1, 32, 36, 46, 5, 58, 61, 66, 69, 71, 73, 74–8, 84–93, 95, 96, 100–1, 106, 112, 113, 129, 132, 135, 126
Tiamat, 13
Tigris, 15
Tiles, 44, 121, 124, 125, 128
Timur, **11, 55, 65 and 91**, 89, 95, 112, 113, 114, 115, 124, 125
Timurids, 3, 4, 8, 29, 39, 40, 43, 59, 62, 84, 91, 93, 96, 100, 110, 111, 114, 116, 117, 118, 119, 121, 124–7
Tonob, 106, 107
Trade, 12
Transparency, 3, 25, 101, 128, 144
Travel, 12, 115, 136
Travellers, 7, 8–9, 40, 50, 93, 103–46
Treasury (*Khazaneh*), 137
Turkaman, Eskandar Beyk (or Eskandar Monshi), 53, 104, 112, 115, 119, 120, 173
Turkaman, Qara Yusof, 111

Turkaman-style painting, 85
Turks, 93, 136
Turktazi, King, **34**, 61
Turret, 123
Typology, 3, 6, 8, 9, 62, 128, 150

Ulugh Beg Mirza, 120
Umbrella (*see also* Canopy; Kiosk), 2, 4, 90, 95, 144
Urban development, 108, 118, 122
Urban quarters (*see also Mahalleh*; *Mohol*; Residential quarters), 109, 118
Uruk, 13, 15
Uzbek, **61**, 41, 77, 113, 114, 116

Vahishto, 19–20, 37
Valley of the Assassins, 116
Vaqi'at-e Baburi, **4**
Vassals, 112
Vegetables (*see also* Fruits), 2, 28, 110
Vegetation, 48
Vendidad, 12, 16
Verandah (*see also Iwan*), 30, 36, 106
Victory, 32, 42
View, 23, 26, 33, 36, 37, 47, 48, 50, 53, 57–8, 66, 69, 70, 71, 77, 78, 86, 89, 90–1, 93, 101, 106, 110, 111, 119, 129, 132, 133, 134, 147
  Panoramic view, 57, 62, 74, 100, 144, 148, 149
Village, 21, 101, 125
Vis va Ramin, 30
Visibility, 70, 74, 85, 101, 144
Viziers (*see also* Rulers), 4, 42, 114, 138
Void, 36, 52

Walcher, Heidi, 108
Walking (*see also Gardesh*), 33, 59
Wall, 2, 54, 59, 62, 66, 71, 86, 95, 113, 122, 124, 132, 134, 136, 138, 140, 142
Wall-fruit (*see* Fruit)
Waqf, 4, 128
War (*Razm*), 12, 77, 111, 115, 117, 123, 128
Water, 1, 13–14, 15, 16–19, 21–6, 30, 34, 37, 70, 78, 86, 95, 101, 112, 114, 122, 124, 128–48
  Channels, **85**, 44–6, 70, 71, 78, 86, 95, 96, 101, 105, 107, 120, 123
  Irrigation, 1, 6
  Qanat, 1
  Springs of, 16, 17, 18
Wealth (*see also* Prosperity), 31, 33, 36, 38, 42, 118
Welfare, 20
Wescoat, James, 4
Wilber, Donald, 3, 124
Wind, 16, 17, 30, 32, 35, 106
Wind-catcher (*Badgir*), 108
Windows, 20, 48, 53, 57, 59, 66, 69, 70, 122, 123, 128, 131, 140
Wine, 24, 32, 34, 35, 52, 86, 90, 112, 129
Wood, 69, 71, 82, 84, 136, 141

Yahya, Shah, 107, 108, 135
Yaqub, Soltan, 114, 119
Yashts ("Hymns"), 20–2, 29
  Ashi Yasht, 21
Yasna, 17–18
Yazd, 105–6, 107, 120, 135
Yurt (*see* Tent)
Yusof, **9 and 82**, 48, 70, 71, 72, 90, 93, 128

Zafarnameh, **11, 55 and 91**, 41, 42, 43, 96
Zahhak, **38**, 63
Zahir ("Outside"), 128

Zakani, Nezam-uddin, 35, 170
Zal, **28, 63, 68 and 75**, 57, 78, 85, 91
Zaman, Muhammad, **34**, 69
Zarah, Lake, **52**, 73
Zayanderud River, 119, 123
Zoroaster, 12, 16–18, 20
Zoroastrian texts, 11, 12, 16–22, 23, 29, 37
Zulaykha, **48**, 48, 72, 90